Ancient Burial Practices in the American Southwest

Ancient Burial Practices in the American Southwest:
Archaeology, Physical Anthropology, and Native American Perspectives

EDITED BY
DOUGLAS R. MITCHELL
JUDY L. BRUNSON-HADLEY

FOREWORD BY
DOROTHY LIPPERT

UNIVERSITY OF NEW MEXICO PRESS
ALBUQUERQUE

Library of Congress Cataloging-in-Publication Data

Ancient burial practices in the American Southwest : archaeology, physical anthropology, and
Native American perspectives / edited by Douglas R. Mitchell, Judy L. Brunson-Hadley.—1st ed.
    p.   cm.
  Includes bibliographical references and index.
  ISBN 0-8263-3461-x (pbk : alk. paper)
1. Indians of North America—Southwest, New—Funeral customs and rites. 2. Indians of
North America—Anthropometry—Southwest, New. 3. Indians of North America—
Material culture—Southwest, New.   4. Human remains (Archaeology)—Southwest,
New—Repatriation. 5. Cultural property—Southwest, New—Repatriation. 6. Grave
goods—Government policy—Southwest, New. 7. Archaeologists—Southwest, New—
Attitudes. 8. United States. Native American Graves Protection and Repatriation Act.
9. Southwest, New—Antiquities—Collection and preservation.   I. Mitchell, Douglas R.
II. Brunson-Hadley, Judy L., 1952–
E78.S7 A62 2001
393'.1'08997079—dc21

                        2001001179

Contents

List of Figures

List of Tables

Foreword

Speak my name and I will live again. The ancient Egyptians carved this prayer and many others on walls, stelae, and other funerary equipment. As a people, they loved life so much that at their deaths, they hoped to renew their ways of existence through magic and spells. A common request was that the name of the dead person must be remembered and spoken aloud. If this did not happen, and the person was forgotten, then it was believed that a true death would occur.

Archaeology is a way of honoring this request, not just for the Egyptians, but for all peoples being studied. Through scientific analyses, we believe that we can resurrect the lives and cultures of people from the distant past. The analyses in this book are an attempt to examine many aspects of ancient Southwestern culture through study of the material remains of activities surrounding the disposition of the dead. This process goes beyond basic skeletal analysis and can include a variety of techniques and questions. The social systems that structured these people's lives may be revealed through their treatment at death. Theories about relations between social strata, distant communities, and the cosmological world can all be stimulated by analyses of burial data.

The American Southwest provides an intersection for many different means of data recovery. It has a very long history of occupation by human beings. It has a useful set of records from the period of early European contact through the present day. Many of the Native peoples in the area continue to hold traditions linking them to the earliest occupants. Some are genetically and culturally linked to these people. All of these factors mean that research in the area can be profitably undertaken and a variety of approaches can be utilized.

The chapters in this book also highlight some of the problems inherent in archaeological analysis. Careful, meticulous data recovery is important, and the early excavations in the area often failed to meet the requirements of modern analyses. The importance of careful excavation, collection, and record keeping is shown throughout the studies. Many early sites could have been useful but for the study methods of the time. It brings to mind the concern that future archaeologists may chastise us for not collecting a certain type of data that we do not yet know to be important. These studies also rebut the common image of archaeology as skeletally focused. Although they are studies of burial practices, most do not focus solely on the human skeleton. Many other factors are considered, some of which might be surprising to the nonarchaeologist. Things such as the construction of the grave and the placement of the body can be revealed through careful excavation but not through studying only the skeleton.

As archaeologists, we are careful to differentiate between groups of people; in fact many of the chapters in this volume show how this can be done with burials. The ancient Egyptians were very clear about what they wished for after their deaths. Museums are full of ancient objects that illustrate how much they loved life and how much they wanted to go on living after their deaths. It would be dangerous, however, to generalize this desire to all human cultures. It is important that in our enthusiasm for revealing the lives of the ancient Southwestern people, we not ignore that we are aware of their beliefs.

One way of theorizing about ancient religions is to turn to contemporary Native peoples. It is quite fascinating to read that Hopi informants were able to describe items that should be found with a person that were then later excavated. Although not all tribes in the area today are culturally or genetically linked to the early inhabitants, many are presently empowered to direct the treatment of the material remains of the ancients.

The chapter by Ferguson, Dongoske, and Kuwanwisiwma provides a much-needed perspective on skeletal analyses. I have often perceived that some archaeologists view the Native American Graves Protection and Repatriation Act (NAGPRA) as a means for Native Americans to exercise political power through crusades against a relatively helpless discipline. Often ignored or discounted are the deeply held religious beliefs of Native peoples. These beliefs are sometimes treated as "tradition," "myth," or an outmoded way of thinking about the cosmos. The idea given sometimes seems to be "surely no one really believes this sort of thing anymore."

While there are differing degrees of adherence to traditional religion among all human groups, this should never be seen as a factor that would allow an attack on physical evidence of these beliefs. For example, many Catholic people deny some of the basic tenets of their faith, but few outsiders would say that parts of St. Peter's Cathedral should be torn down in order to analyze the architectural methods of the Renaissance more completely. This sort of action would never be undertaken without consultation with the affected parties.

By including Hopi perspectives, it becomes evident that not all people might wish to be brought back to life in the way that archaeologists are able to accomplish. According to the Tribe's belief, once people have made their journey, it is callous and dangerous to call them back. Disturbance of burials, however, appears to have occurred throughout the history of the Southwest, and the present situation is now addressed through legal routes. NAGPRA has and will continue to change the nature of archaeology. Although it is certain that future studies will be impacted, limited, or placed beyond the reach of archaeologists, due to reburial or restrictions placed on testing, it may also be that new areas of study will be opened due to the creation of working relationships with tribes.

It has long been my personal belief that a major objection to studies involving human burials is that the ancient human beings are treated more as data sets or specimens than as people who were once alive. It is vitally important that archaeologists address this concern. We strive to recreate ancient human lives, only to deny their humanity in the telling of it. We reconstruct society and ways of human interaction only to speak of these using clinical jargon. If our work is to be of importance and interest outside our discipline, we must try not to hide from the humanity of the ancient people whose essential fabric we hold in our hands when we disturb what they believed to be their final resting place.

I have noticed that the study of burials and human skeletons often makes people uneasy. Confronting another person's decayed remains inevitably brings to mind the picture of one's own body, hundreds of years in the future. For some, this is a disturbing thought that can only be dispelled by looking past the humanity of the contents of the grave. A couple of the chapters in this book do this very well. One author chooses to use descriptions like "mating pair" to describe a possible husband and wife buried together. Other authors manage to address both the needs of science and the call of compassion by the simple use of masculine and feminine pronouns. This allows a human body to become more than a "burial." It allows the person to retain their essential humanity while still providing information accurately and clearly.

The chapter by Ferguson, Dongoske, and Kuwanwisiwma illustrates the modern situation in archaeology with respect to burial studies. It is interesting that even with "Native American Perspectives" as one part of the triad of study types purportedly presented in this book, this chapter is the only one that completely focuses on this idea. I appreciate it for showing the two sides to consultation. Archaeology has much that can be learned through cultivating relationships with indigenous groups. This approach is underutilized in most of these chapters, but the inclusion of this piece perhaps points the way to the future of mortuary analyses in the Southwest.

The chapters in this work all reveal the devotion that modern archaeologists have toward the process of unraveling the ancient Native American past. In reading through them, I am struck by the meticulous care that so many people take to try and understand the lives of the ancient Indian people. Ferguson, Dongoske, and Kuwanwisiwma quite rightly point out that archaeology is practiced in a social context whether or not we choose to recognize this. In noting that archaeology has affected public opinion with regard to Native Americans, they reveal a possible path toward reconciling the harm done by burial excavation with concerns for contemporary people.

There are many major stereotypes that face Indian people today. Many of these derive from early European theories about the evolution of human societies. For many, the early peoples in the Americas were somehow not quite human and incapable of creating monumental architecture, elaborate literature, or complex social structures. Over the last hundred years, archaeology has been instrumental in addressing this misinformation. Studies have shown the ability of the Mississippian peoples to organize labor, control trade, and create monumental earthworks. As a Choctaw, reading studies of Southeastern archaeology brings a sense of pride and satisfaction to me. I am always struck by the thought that I derive my heritage from people who were fully human and thus capable and intelligent beings.

I believe that this is one of the more important contributions archaeology can make to modern Native peoples. In revealing the accomplishments of our ancestors, archaeology rejects the opinions of the early explorers and binds us completely to the human family. The chapters in this volume, although perhaps not with this as a stated goal, all do their part to humanize the ancient people of the Southwest. It would be impossible to read this work and cling to an idea that these were not true, complex, human creatures, just like ourselves.

DOROTHY LIPPERT
HALL OF THE AMERICAS,
HOUSTON MUSEUM OF NATURAL SCIENCES

ACKNOWLEDGMENTS

This book began in the mid-1990s following studies that we had both done on mortuary assemblages in the Phoenix area. The idea was to gather information from archaeologists who had conducted studies in the Southwest and present a collection of papers from a variety of contexts. Our interests are in the Phoenix area so that was the initial focus of the book. As we talked with different archaeologists and specialists, the current configuration of the book began to emerge. Along the way, people who were most helpful with their time and wise advice included Patty Crown, of the University of New Mexico, and L. Durwood Ball, formerly of UNM Press. Durwood was enthusiastic and supportive throughout the process. An anonymous reviewer provided comments that allowed us to sharpen our focus, and members of UNM Press helped with the editing and production aspects of the monograph. T. J. Ferguson was instrumental and diplomatic in providing assistance and perspective for the Hopi chapter, introduction, and epilogue. Brent Kober, and Stephanie Sherwood of Compass Rose Technical Services, provided the illustrations in chapters 1 and 4. Others who, in less tangible ways, inspired us and served as advisors throughout the long process include Chris Carr, Mike Foster, Alfred E. Dittert, Jr., and Charles Merbs. And, of course, we would like to thank our families, who were supportive throughout.

CHAPTER ONE
Introduction

Douglas R. Mitchell and Judy L. Brunson-Hadley

THE SOUTHWESTERN UNITED STATES HAS BEEN referred to as a natural laboratory for studying the past. Many ruins are still intact and well-preserved, and archaeologists and explorers have actively investigated this area for well over a century. The Southwest includes Arizona, New Mexico, and parts of the bordering states as well as northern Sonora and Chihuahua, Mexico. Here, the great ancient cultures of the Hohokam, Mogollon, Anasazi, Sinagua, Salado, Trincheras, and others began and ended. These pottery-producing groups were dynamic, constantly adapting societies that included extensive trade networks, shifting alliances, and great centers (for example, Chaco Canyon). With a few notable exceptions, many of these cultures did not survive as distinct recognizable cultural entities to the present day.

The range of ethnic and social complexity across the Southwest is enormous. The papers in this book seek to explore these issues through an examination of burial practices in the Southwest. The purpose of this book is twofold. First, the authors seek to continue the exploration of past social complexity through several specific studies of ancient cemeteries. Many of the studies include an evaluation of old and new theories and methods used to address the issue of complexity. The second goal is to place these studies into the current context of changes brought about by recent laws and new dialogues between archae-

ologists and Native Americans. Today, few modern studies of prehistoric Native American burial populations can avoid the issue of reburial and the concerns of present-day Native Americans, and a discussion of these issues from the perspective of one tribe is presented. New federal laws have changed the face of archaeological mortuary studies, and as can be seen in a few of the chapters of this book, have affected the studies to be completed. Before focusing on the use of mortuary analysis to study social complexity, we believe that some brief comments on the changing laws, and more importantly changes in relationships between Native Americans and archaeologists, are needed.

In 1990, the Native American Graves Protection and Repatriation Act (NAGPRA) was passed, greatly changing how archaeologists and physical anthropologists may work with human remains and how museums and federal agencies may act on projects and with collections. Much has been written on the effects of NAGPRA on projects. Rose et al. (1996) provide an overview of NAGPRA in their review of the effect of NAGPRA on osteological studies, and Swidler et al. (1997) provide an interesting array of articles discussing some of the positive results of NAGPRA related activities (see also King 1998 for a discussion of NAGPRA issues). In this volume, Ferguson, Dongoske, and Kuwanwisiwma's chapter presents one tribe's perspectives on how NAGPRA has changed their involvement in archaeological projects, and the tribe's view of archaeological studies. While the chapter represents only one tribe's view, the authors produce an eloquent overall discussion of the effects of NAGPRA, and the reader is encouraged to read their chapter for a more in-depth discussion of NAGPRA effects and of the struggles of one Native American group to deal with mortuary analyses.

Briefly, the passage of NAGPRA came about due to the historical use and treatment of human remains by some federal agencies, archaeologists, and museums in ways that many tribes found offensive. Details of some of the offenses can be found in the testimonies before Congress (U.S. Government Printing Office 1990). Some of the complaints involved historical archaeological practices; for instance, many early excavations were aimed at recovering the burial goods for museum collections, and the skeletons were actually discarded as they were perceived to have no value. In other cases, skeletal studies were done in order to study "racial" differences with respect to superiority issues, and often times the skeletons were carelessly stored in a less than dignified manner, usually disarticulated with various parts stored in different locations. It should be made clear that not all archaeologists had the attitude described above, and many scientific studies were directed toward the archaeological goal of better understanding the people who lived before. Even with the best intentions, anthropologists and some Native American groups have divergent opinions on the subject; but certainly enough examples of insensitivity were present to encourage tribes to push for the passage of NAGPRA. Many archaeologists also supported the passage of NAGPRA as it was discussed and described during the hearings, and the national professional archaeological organization, the Society for American Archaeology, testified on behalf of the bill. Despite this auspicious new start, many aspects of NAGPRA and the subsequent regulations and federal actions remain controversial as many argue that the resultant implementation has not always reflected the discussions that had been put forth before Congress as to how NAGPRA was to be interpreted (see U.S. Government Printing Office 1990). Issues regarding criteria necessary for determining tribal affiliations to identifiable earlier groups, the level of scientific studies, or even if scientific studies may be done, and what scientific information may be published have all become major issues of contention. "Who does the past belong to?" has become an issue to be confronted by everyone.

One can easily argue that there have been both positive and negative effects on scientists' abilities to learn about "our" past ("our" being the entire human population), but clearly NAGPRA has opened the door to many positive interfaces, which have been neglected and ignored in the past, between archaeologists and tribes. The history of archaeology, itself, reflects a changing attitude toward the value of Native American input on projects. Early Southwest studies, both archaeological and ethnographical, often involved acquiring oral histories from living tribes to better understand the ancient population; but rarely were tribal views on how to study and analyze the burials, solicited. In some cases, tribal personnel were hired to work as excavators, and they provided important interpretations of the findings, but it does not appear that they had a role in any decision-making capacity (see Smith et al. 1966). Later, the archaeological theory of the time argued that historical tribes would not necessarily understand manifestations of the earlier archaeological sites due to changes through time. Rigorous scientific hypothesis testing was advocated, and while it did not advocate eliminating oral interviews, such interviews became rarer, and tribes were involved even to a lesser degree in studies. This is not to argue that archaeologists and tribes had no communication. Especially in the Southwest, there continued to be occasions where archaeological studies and tribal oral histories were utilized to argue on behalf of the tribe during federal land claim cases (see Ferguson and Hart 1985; Hart 1995), and tribal input was solicited for interpretation of sites (Dittert and Brunson-Hadley 1999). It is clear, though, that from about the 1930s to the 1970s most archaeological studies did not routinely include input from tribes, or any other ethnic group, which may have been associated with an archaeological site being investigated. As a result of NAGPRA and other legal changes in federal guidance and laws, including the National Register's Bulletin 38 guidance on "traditional cultural properties (Parker and King 1990) and the inclusion of traditional cultural properties in the 1992 amendments to the National Historic Preservation Act with the resultant revised regulations, a much more productive interface between Native Americans and anthropologists is emerging (see Department of Interior [DOI] 1993; Swidler et al. 1997).

Clearly the current editors' biases are of the belief that mortuary studies can provide important additional insight into learning about ancient populations. We believe an understanding of the past is important for all people, and it is hoped that many of the dialogues that are growing between archaeologists and Native Americans continue to be positive for all involved. We understand that the anthropologists' desire to study the past and learn about our heritage sometimes collides with the spiritual beliefs of others, and it is a difficult and sensitive matter for many tribes to deal with. Archaeologists tend to look at human remains in terms of their potential to understand and learn about the past. Many Native Americans deal with the human remains as an issue of the present with the human remains needing special care and attention. Hopefully, many of these issues will be resolved for the benefit for all as time goes on. Certainly, the studies in our book were done with a full respect for the people who once lived before us and a desire to learn more about them. It was with these thoughts in mind, that people associated with the Hopi Cultural Preservation Office were asked to contribute their chapter, and it with great appreciation that we acknowledge their contribution.

The central theme of our book deals with the concept that the desire to understand the evolutionary history of a culture is common to archaeological studies. The ranking schemes of Service and Fried and others sought to provide a framework for describing past cultural systems. Southwestern groups, and probably most groups worldwide, tend to slip in and out of these categories through time and according to the observer's perspective. Mortuary studies in particular have been narrowly focused on attempts to elicit ranking within individual villages. Only recently, have broader, explicitly regional studies become more commonplace (e.g., Beck 1995, O'Shea 1996). How do we measure complexity? Can we directly compare the complexity of one culture or system to another (for example, Crown and Judge 1991)? As we continue to distance ourselves from the decades-old stigma of earlier deterministic monolithic causal theories, such as migration, disease, warfare, and environmental degradation, we seem to return to some of them in a more cautious manner.

Southwestern cultures were clearly affected by their surroundings. The Hohokam, for example, were able to use technology (irrigation canals) to turn an arid desert into a bread basket. They almost certainly had excess agricultural produce that was traded to other groups. The Mogollon however, lived in the mountainous areas of Arizona and New Mexico where the agricultural opportunities were far more limited. It is these contrasts that make an assessment of complexity in the Southwest a challenge. Were there chiefdoms, petty-states, middle-

range societies? Were Puebloan societies egalitarian or led by warrior cults? The diversity of answers presented by the researchers in this study reflects the nature of their data.

Mortuary studies presuppose that the manner in which people are buried, the locations of their graves, evidence of skeletal biology, and the types of artifacts buried with them are a reflection of that person's role in life. Cross-cultural studies tend to support this pattern, although many factors affect this relationship (see Binford 1971; Carr 1995; Goldstein 1976; Saxe 1970; Tainter 1978). These data can be effectively used to address issues of social complexity and the manner in which societies changed through time. Perhaps one of archaeology's fundamental strengths, the study of change over time, can be effectively used to monitor the change in life statuses and relationships within and between communities. This temporal component allows comparisons to be made within single societies or between regions regarding the adaptations and changes that occurred in the past. Perhaps some of the most effective mortuary studies include those that are the most holistic. This can include grave location, grave furniture, skeletal biology, demography, and nonburial attributes such as settlement hierarchies. A recent study by O'Shea (1996) of an bronze age culture in Hungary provides a good example. Using settlement pattern data, demography, and traditional mortuary attributes, he reconstructs the nature of this society through time.

This volume presents a Native American perspective on archaeologists' study of human remains and grave artifacts and the results of eight studies including six archaeological analyses of prehistoric burial practices and two physical anthropological analyses of populations. Concentrating on the American Southwest, the major culture groups that are reported on include the Hohokam, Anasazi, Salado, Sinagua, Zuni, and Mogollon (figure 1.1). Not all areas of the Southwest or all time periods are represented in our book. To do so, would require a series of volumes. It is difficult to extrapolate social organization from only small fragments of a village. In most cases, emphasis was placed on projects where large databases were present in order to study the larger village population. The data sets themselves came from a variety of sources. Some projects involved recent excavations, and others included data from excavations completed over 100 years ago. Because of the large database from recent projects in the Hohokam area, as well as the large database from the Hemenway excavations in the 1880s in the Hohokam area, the book has several

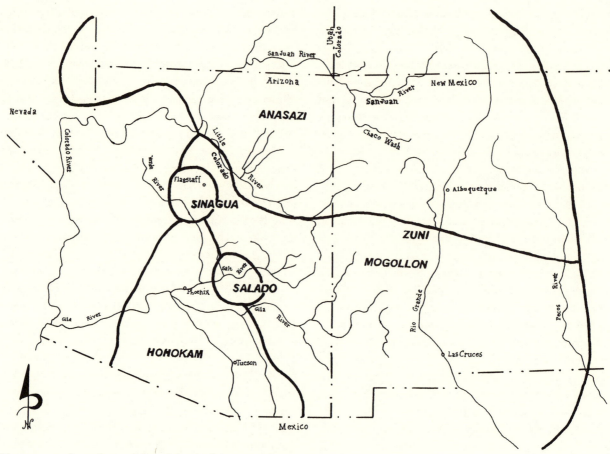

FIGURE 1.1   Locations of the Major Prehistoric Culture Areas

chapters discussing Hohokam society. The common theme throughout the book is the use of mortuary data to describe and understand a particular prehistoric society. The archaeological studies use traditional mortuary patterns, such as grave accompaniments, location, body position, as well as demographic attributes, and site typologies, to reconstruct the societies' organizational characteristics through time. Physical anthropological studies also are included that utilize the study of skeletal remains to add another dimension of understanding to the lifestyles of the Hohokam and Anasazi. The final paper in the volume is a review of the papers by an archaeologist who initiated much of the current direction in mortuary studies.

The book began with the editors' interest and involvement in mortuary studies in southern Arizona. There is a bias toward this region because of our familiarity with it, as well as an abundance of data. The book did not

begin with a conference but rather as an attempt to assemble large-scale and diverse studies by archaeologists on the prehistory of the Southwest, as told through the investigation of mortuary studies.

The book begins with the chapter by scholars associated with the Hopi Cultural Preservation Office discussing the status and implications of American archaeological mortuary studies from the perspective of one Native American tribe. The Hopi believe that many archaeological sites in Arizona are related to their ancient migrations, and therefore, related ancient burials are the remains of their ancestors. With passage of NAGPRA in 1990, Hopi and other Native American tribes are obliged to consider the effects of archaeological mortuary studies. Ferguson, Dongoske, and Kuwanwisiwma point out in chapter 2 that it is not possible to view such research outside the limits of the Hopi belief system. Accordingly, they discuss Hopi views on death and how these views conflict with archaeological mortuary practices, the pressures forced on Hopi by NAGPRA, and future potential resolutions to these issues.

The archaeological and physical anthropological studies for the remainder of the book begin with two studies of Hohokam burial practices.

Chapter 3, by Randall McGuire, presents the results of his analyses of cremation burials from the pre-Classic Hohokam village of La Ciudad. McGuire's study is important for two reasons. First, his introduction of the Grave Lot Value (GLV) in 1987 was a significant innovation in the analysis of burial artifacts and their relation to inequality. Using artifact context, he assigned values to individual artifacts in order to score the value of individual burials. This methodological technique offers much potential when used in a critical manner, and McGuire discusses some of the issues in the current paper. In addition, McGuire views the burial ceremony and the inclusion of widely differing amounts of grave artifacts as a way in which the Hohokam expressed their power relations within the society. During the time that this village was occupied, the later Hohokam pre-Classic of about A.D. 700–1100, McGuire believes that the social organization was one of lineage or extended family groups who expressed power relationships through their burial ceremonies.

Using a specific theoretical framework, McGuire then examines the burial data through various multivariate techniques. One of the primary attributes in these analyses include the GLV. He found evidence for house group leaders through their artifact associations within the cemeteries. His study explores the traditional evaluations of pre-Classic Hohokam social organization while at the same time providing alternative ways of discussing our views of social relationships and the manner in which they are expressed through burial practices.

Chapter 4 is a study of Hohokam burial practices in the Classic period, from about A.D. 1100–1400. Mitchell and Brunson-Hadley examine analyzed burial data from hundreds of burials recovered from a half dozen villages in the Hohokam core area in the lower Salt River Valley. These villages include some of the largest ever occupied by the Hohokam. Inhumation was the dominant burial method by the Hohokam during the Classic period, and the artifact assemblages associated with the burials are examined for evidence of ranking. This study examines the presence and absence of artifacts rather than using multivariate techniques. Burial location data also

are examined, in particular, the locations of burials on top and adjacent to platform mounds. The nature and abundance of grave goods are used to argue for some combination of religious-secular leadership during the Classic period. Leaders existed within the communities, but their power and authority were intricately intertwined with both lineage segment relationships and religious responsibilities.

Chapter 5 by Whittlesey and Reid explores the social organization of the Grasshopper Mogollon. Grasshopper Pueblo contained 500 rooms that were occupied during Pueblo IV times, between A.D. 1300–1400. Their study includes information on 674 burials. Previous models of social reconstruction are reviewed in the course of evaluating differing analytical methods. The Grasshopper mortuary profile is described with regard to normative burial practices and variation within these practices. These data are used to discuss two aspects of the village's social organization: coresidence and ethnic variation, and the presence of sodalities. Cranial deformation and trace element analysis are used to suggest the presence of a small Anasazi population within the predominantly Mogollon village. Whittlesey and Reid suggest that sodalities, ceremonial associations that crosscut kinship groups, were one of the structural bases of Grasshopper social organization and the foundation of political leadership. The presence of sodalities is inferred based on the occurrence and distribution of specific artifacts as grave accompaniments. The artifacts included bone hairpins, shell ornaments, and quivers of arrows. Their limited distribution (among adult males) suggests the existence of sodalities.

Whittlesey and Reid also point out the similarities in burial practices among the post-twelfth century cultures in central Arizona. They view this as evidence for migrations of Mogollon and Salado groups to the southern deserts, a view that has gone in and out of favor over the last few decades. They further explore the variations in social organization, in particular a katsina based ritual versus one organized around irrigation based labor. They use this model to explain the absence of kivas, with the implied presence of the katsina cult, in the Salado heartland of the Tonto Basin. Finally, they point out the potential of mortuary data for reconstructing individual site-specific organizational characteristics, as well as regional organizations, as they changed through time.

Chapter 6 considers the burial practices and social organization for the Sinagua culture of northern Arizona. The study focuses on the change in organization between the late Pueblo II period, including the Angell Winona phase (A.D. 1050–1100), and the Pueblo III period, the Elden phase (A.D. 1125–1200). Following earlier researchers methods, Hohmann seeks to identify quantitative and qualitative differences in the mortuary program. The qualitative distinctions are used in hope of identifying particular symbols associated with ranking and leadership. Traditional attributes, such as grave furniture and body positioning, are examined by univariate and multivariate methods. Monitoring Sinaguan social change over the course of only a couple of generations, Hohmann describes a significant change. In the earlier period, the Sinagua are characterized by a simple form of organization, an achieved status system, where elder males commonly were associated with a greater number of artifacts. He found that the later groups displayed evidence for ascribed status, with different levels. These levels included leaders associated with secular and religious activities and individuals associated with regional trade networks.

Chris Loendorf discusses Salado burial practices in chapter 7. This study is based on the recent analysis of nearly 500 burials associated with a reservoir project in east-central Arizona. This area, known as the Salado heartland, contains a variety of settlement hierarchies including platform mound sites, compound-walled villages, and smaller hamlets. The nature of Salado social organization is examined through the distribution of burials and their associated grave goods. The sites were occupied during the Salado Classic period, from about A.D. 1150–1450, with the majority of the sites dating to the Roosevelt phase, A.D. 1280–1320.

Loendorf describes the burial methods and discusses the frequent phenomenon of multiple burials. This burial type appears to have been related to a restricted group of communities. These burials were only found at the more elaborate sites and generally had large numbers of artifacts associated with them. Quantitative analyses of artifacts from all burials found that adult males tended to have a greater number and diversity of artifacts. They also contained particular artifacts that may have been symbols of authority, such as painted wooden sticks, pigment staining, and animal effigies. These patterns may have changed through time with a greater variation in the earlier period replaced by more standardized burial practices in the later period. The quantitative and qualitative analyses lead Loendorf to suggest that the Salado organization during this time was based on a system of ascriptive social hierarchies.

Chapter 8 considers the social organization at the ancestral Zuni village of Hawikku through an analysis of artifact and skeletal data from burials. The mortuary assemblage includes over 900 burials that were excavated in the early 1900s. The 800-room village of Hawikku was occupied from about A.D. 1325–1680. Todd Howell uses the data to examine the role of leadership in pueblo life. He points out that current models of authority include one of egalitarian-based, consensual decision making for the pueblos while a contrasting model views the existence of ascriptively selected leaders where intervillage power and authority was centralized.

Howell analyzes funerary objects and skeletal indicators of health to identify potential leaders and then to assess the degree to which these leaders controlled economic processes. He assumes that the greater number of roles that a leader would have had would be manifest in the burial, through grave furniture, body position, and so on. To quantify this, a diversity measure was used. Those burials with the highest diversity scores were considered to be preeminent leaders, of which there were four. Multivariate techniques were used to examine the remainder of the burial population for additional leaders. In addition, individuals identified as leaders were then examined for health indicators using age at death, incidence of iron-deficiency anemia, and stature. Based upon his analyses of leaders, their health, and grave furniture, Howell speculates that this prehistoric society was egalitarian based but that leaders were ascriptively selected and their power and authority was manifest through ideological manipulation. This manipulation included military power and, to a much lesser extent, economic power.

In chapter 9, Nancy Akins tackles the thorny issue of Chaco Canyon complexity in her analysis of mortuary practices from that Anasazi community. Her data consisted of 179 burials from small sites and larger sites dating between about A.D. 900–1300. Akins describes the characteristics of many of the burials, in itself a contribution due to the nature of this disparate data set. Akins purports that status can be identified through mortuary analysis because the status of the deceased is manifest through the qualitative content of grave furniture, skeletal indicators of health, and demographic variables. Hereditary ascribed status should not be restricted to adult males but should include a greater number of females and children. Using a Puebloan ethnographic analogy, Chaco is viewed as a complex system with an elite group of individuals at the apex of the system.

Complexity is supported by differential evidence for health, burial artifacts, and a settlement hierarchy. Akins proposes that hereditary leaders, concentrated at Pueblo Bonito, ruled with power and authority through their controlled access to ritual knowledge, paraphernalia, and ceremonies that also were important for the distribution of material goods and information about natural (agricultural) cycles.

Chapters 10 and 11 provide reconstructions based on skeletal data from the Hohokam and Anasazi culture areas. In chapter 10, Sheridan evaluates the demography and health of the inhabitants of the Hohokam Classic period village of Pueblo Grande. Several hundred burials excavated at this site allow for a detailed bioarchaeological reconstruction of the diet, demography, and health of this population. Analytical studies include: (1) a detailed demographic reconstruction, (2) trace element analysis, (3) investigation of enamel hypoplasias, porotic hyperostosis and diploic thickening of the cranium, and (4) a study of age-related bone loss (osteopenia).

Summarizing the results of a variety of studies, Sheridan paints a picture of a population that was on the decline. Infant mortality was high, and the frequency of enamel hypoplasias, bands of depressed enamel, on adult teeth indicate that subadult nutritional stress was common. Hypoplastic activity reflects a syndrome of early childhood stress, combining chronic nutritional difficulty with repeated bouts of infectious disease. Another study found evidence for iron-deficiency anemia. This was monitored by the presence of porous lesions of the cranial vault associated with childhood, porotic hyperostosis, and a thickening of the cranial vault, diploic thickening. For women, anemia was chronic, exacerbated during the child bearing years, while male anemia tended to increase with time. Analysis of nine trace elements found that there was a tendency for females to have a greater frequency of elements associated with a non-meat diet. Osteopenia was also measured and found to have increased significantly through time at Pueblo Grande. This study used a comprehensive approach to a single population to arrive at a biological reconstruction of the health of these ancient villagers.

Chapter 11 examines the health of some Anasazi populations. The study area is at the border of New Mexico and Colorado in the La Plata River Valley. Martin and Akins note that this fertile area was between the political centers of Mesa Verde to the north and Chaco Canyon to the south. Their data include between 50 and 100 burials dating to the period from A.D. 1000–1300. Burial location and grave goods are reviewed as a backdrop for the osteological exploration of the burials. The location, treatment, and skeletal health of individuals is quite variable throughout this region. Trauma is disproportionately identified on the adult female skeletal remains, and particular attributes were found indicative of intensive labor. Combined with burial location and condition, these attributes are used to tell a story of increasing social hardship and stress as the regional population increased.

Chapter 12 is an overview of the papers from an archaeologist outside the American Southwest. Lynne Goldstein provides encouragement and a critique of the methods and perspectives of archaeologists working in the Southwest on mortuary studies. She provides some cautionary statements about relying too heavily on material culture studies, instead suggesting that Southwest burial studies could perhaps be more productive by considering the larger, spatial relationships of burials and cemeteries.

References Cited

Beck, Lane A. (editor)
1995   *Regional Approaches to Mortuary Analysis.* Plenum Press, New York.
Binford, Lewis R.
1971   Mortuary Practices: Their Study and Their Potential. In *Approaches to the Social Dimensions of Mortuary Practices*, organized and edited by J. A. Brown, pp. 6–29. Memoirs of the Society for American Archaeology, no. 25. Society for American Archaeology, Washington, D.C. (Issued as *American Antiquity* 36(3) Pt. 2, July 1971.)
Carr, Christopher
1995   Mortuary Practices: Their Social, Philosophical-Religious, Circumstantial, and Physical Determinants. *Journal of Archaeological Method and Theory* 2:105–200.
Crown, Patricia L., and W. James Judge (editors)
1991   *Chaco and Hohokam: Prehistoric Regional Systems in the American Southwest.* School of American Research Press, Santa Fe.
Department of Interior (DOI)
1993   *Traditional Cultural Properties: Cultural Resource Management*, vol. 16. National Park Service, Washington, D.C.

Dittert, Alfred E., Jr., and Judy L. Brunson-Hadley
1999   Identifying Acoma's Past: A Multidisciplinary
        Approach. In *La Frontera: Papers in Honor of
        Patrick H. Beckett*, edited by M. S. Duran and
        D. T. Kirkpatrick, pp. 59–69. Archaeological
        Society of New Mexico, Albuquerque.
Ferguson, T. J., and E. Richard Hart
1985   *A Zuni Atlas*. University of Oklahoma Press,
        Norman.
Goldstein, Lynn G.
1976   *Spatial Structure and Social Organization:
        Regional Manifestations of Mississippian
        Society*. Unpublished Ph.D. dissertation,
        Department of Anthropology, Northwestern
        University, Evanston.
Hart, E. Richard (editor)
1995   *Zuni and the Courts, A Struggle for Sovereign
        Land Rights*. University Press of Kansas,
        Lawrence.
King, Thomas F.
1998   *Cultural Resource Laws and Practice*. AltaMira
        Press, Walnut Creek, California.
O'Shea, John M.
1996   *Villagers of the Maros: A Portrait of an Early
        Bronze Age Society*. Plenum Press, New York.
Parker, Patricia L., and Thomas F. King
1990   *Guidelines for Evaluating and Documenting
        Traditional Cultural Properties*. National
        Register Bulletin 38. National Register of
        Historic Places, National Park Service,
        Washington, D.C.
Rose, Jerome C., Thomas J. Green, and Victoria D. Green
1996   NAGPRA is Forever: Osteology and the
        Repatriation of Skeletons. *Annual Review of
        Anthropology* 25:81–103.

Saxe, Arthur A.
1970   *Social Dimensions of Mortuary Practices in a
        Mesolithic Population from Wadi Halfa,
        Sudan*. Ph.D. dissertation, Department of
        Anthropology, University of Michigan, Ann
        Arbor.
Smith, Watson, Richard B. Woodbury,
    and Nathalie F. S. Woodbury
1966   *The Excavation of Hawikuh By Frederick Webb
        Hodge, Report of the Hendricks-Hodge
        Expedition 1917–1923*. Museum of the
        American Indian, Heye Foundation, New
        York.
Swidler, Nina, Kurt E. Dongoske, Roger Anyon,
    and Alan S. Downer (editors)
1997   *Native Americans and Archaeologists: Stepping
        Stones to Common Ground*. AltaMira Press,
        Walnut Creek, California.
Tainter, Joseph A.
1978   Mortuary Practices and the Study of
        Prehistoric Social Systems. In *Advances in
        Archaeological Method and Theory*, vol. 1,
        edited by M. B. Schiffer, pp. 106–43.
        Academic Press, New York.
U.S. Government Printing Office
1990   Native American Grave and Burial Protection
        Act (Repatriation); Native American
        Repatriation of Cultural Patrimony Act; and
        Heard Museum Report. Hearing Before the
        Select Committee on Indian Affairs, United
        States Senate. U.S. Government Printing
        Office, May 14, Washington, D.C.

CHAPTER TWO

Hopi Perspectives on Southwestern Mortuary Studies

T. J. Ferguson, Kurt E. Dongoske, and Leigh J. Kuwanwisiwma

INTRODUCTION

THE HOPI INDIAN RESERVATION IS LOCATED IN northeastern Arizona where the Hopi people occupy twelve villages situated on three mesas known as First, Second, and Third Mesas. The Hopi people have resided in villages on these same mesas for at least 800 years. Prior to fulfilling their destiny by establishing villages at *Tuuwanasavi* (the earth center), the Hopi clans migrated extensively throughout and beyond the southwestern United States. These migrations resulted from a spiritual pact the Hopi made with *Ma'saw*, guardian of the Fourth World, wherein the Hopi agreed to act as stewards of the earth and place their footprints throughout the land as they migrated on a spiritual quest to find the earth center (Dongoske et al. 1993:271).

During their migrations, the *Motisinom* and *Hisatsinom* (the ancestors of the Hopi people) established villages where they resided until it was time to continue their journeys. Eventually, Hopi priests received omens and spiritual signs through supernatural phenomena or natural events, like pestilence or earthquakes, that signaled it was time for the Hopi ancestors to continue their migrations. When the *Motisinom* and *Hisatsinom* moved on to new areas, they left behind the graves of their ancestors along with ruins, potsherds, shrines, petroglyphs, and other physical evidence

that they had vested the area with their spiritual stewardship and fulfilled their pact with *Ma'saw*. From the Hopi perspective, archaeological sites in the Southwest provide physical evidence verifying the clan histories and religious beliefs that are part of the migrations ordained by *Ma'saw* (Dongoske et al. 1993:27; Ferguson and Dongoske 1994).

The Hopi people believe the villages of their ancestors were never abandoned because they retain a strong emotional and spiritual tie to these places, and in many cases, they continue physical use of these sites. Hopis know their ancestors were laid to rest at these sites to maintain a spiritual guardianship over them, and these ancestors continue to play an important role in Hopi rituals and ceremonies. Some of these villages are still referred to by name during the recounting of clan histories by Hopi elders within the ceremonial context of kiva rituals (Dongoske et al. 1993:27). Even though the names of other villages may not be remembered, these places are still important to Hopis. All of these villages and the Hopi ancestors buried in them continue to play a vital role in Hopi culture. Hopi ancestors are as much alive in the present as they were in past.

Given the ritual and familial obligations the Hopi people have to care for their ancestors, it should not be surprising that Hopis are more concerned about the proper treatment of the dead than they are about scholarly studies intended to reconstruct past history or better understand the people who lived before us. This is not to say that the Hopis have no interest in scholarly studies of mortuary behavior because there are some tribal members who think this information can assist the Hopi in a better understanding of their past. But Hopi interest in mortuary studies is secondary to making sure their ancestors are accorded the proper respect. Archaeologists interested in what Hopis think about mortuary studies should strive to understand the *deep reverence* the Hopi people have for their ancestors. It is this reverence that governs the types of studies the Hopi people think are acceptable and how they want to formally interact with scholars.

SOUTHWESTERN MORTUARY STUDIES IN A SOCIAL CONTEXT

All scholarly research occurs in a social context, and the practice of archaeology consequently has political implications whether or not archaeologists choose to recognize this (Devine 1994:14–17; Ferguson 1996:64–66; McGuire 1992; Trigger 1984; Zimmerman 1994:211). While some archaeologists would like to divorce what they think of as "scholarly research" from programmatic tribal policies that they think are essentially "political," this is simply not possible. The passage of the Native American Graves Protection and Repatriation Act (NAGPRA) has forever changed how archaeology will be practiced in the United States (Rose et al. 1996). Implementation of NAGPRA has placed a tremendous administrative, intellectual, and spiritual burden on tribes. It is therefore not surprising that the Hopi Tribe is currently preoccupied with the proper treatment by archaeologists of the remains of their ancestors and the implications scholarly research has for issues related to NAGPRA.

For more than a century, Southwestern explorers, antiquarians, and archaeologists excavated archaeological sites, recovered human remains and associated funerary objects, and curated these materials in museums and private collections. Most of these activities were conducted with little or no regard for the concerns of the Hopi people and other Native Americans. By neglecting to consult with Native Americans, non-Indian archaeologists alienated living people from their ancestors and their history. The Hopi Tribe is today working to redress this historical situation and prevent similar alienation of their ancestors from continuing in the future.

Archaeologists have often constructed interpretations of the archaeological record with little input from Native Americans. As they did so, these archaeologists influenced governmental policy and public attitudes about social and economic issues that have had a profound impact on contemporary tribes. The United States government and the American public have political uses for archaeology, even if archaeologists themselves naively refuse to recognize this aspect of their work. The taking of a vast amount of Hopi land by the United States without payment in the nineteenth century and the claims that were eventually adjudicated by the Indian Claims Commission to quiet Indian title to these lands, provide two examples of how archaeological science has affected the Hopi people. In the first instance, the archaeological notion of "abandonment" helped to facilitate the taking of land—if the land was not being used, it was free for the taking, and the myriad of "abandoned ruins" throughout the Southwest was perceived as "evidence" that the land had indeed been "deserted." In the second instance, archaeological evidence about the historical ties between ancient and contemporary populations, including data derived from mortuary studies, was marshaled to both support and refute Hopi land claims (Colton 1974; Ellis 1974).

Until 1990, archaeologists were free to excavate the graves of Hopi ancestors virtually at will and then to control the curation of these human remains and grave goods in museums. These activities constituted a political statement about the power of the dominant culture in relation to the Hopi Tribe. It also had very real spiritual and social implications for the well-being of the Hopi people, and the political message it communicated will not be soon forgotten. With the passage of NAGPRA in 1990, the Hopi Tribe gained a legally defined role in the regulation of exhumation, analysis, and final disposition of ancestral human remains and associated funerary objects on federal lands. Since then, the Hopi Tribe has actively participated in the consultation process to ensure that the remains of their ancestors are treated with respect and dignity.

For the Hopi, the presence of ancestors buried in archaeological sites entails a real and continuing use of ancient villages even in the absence of physical visitation. These ancestors are important to the spiritual and physical well-being of the Hopi people. Archaeological notions of abandonment and assertions that the people buried in Puebloan and other archaeological sites are not Hopi ancestors are incomprehensible to the Hopi people. The failure of archaeologists to recognize Hopi ancestors has political implications for the ability of the Hopi Tribe to exercise its legal rights to protect its ancestors in a culturally appropriate manner. Archaeologists must therefore recognize that all mortuary studies have a political dimension, even if this is incidental to the scholarly research that archaeologists consider to be their primary interest.

From the Hopi perspective, the complete avoidance of disturbance of ancestral graves is always the best course of action, and this is what the Hopi Tribe always recommends. Given the political and economic realities of development in the Southwest, however, complete avoidance is not always possible, and agencies other than the Hopi Tribe continue to make decisions to disturb ancestral graves. To articulate Hopi views about this situation, in the remainder of this chapter we examine (1) traditional Hopi concepts of death and dying, (2) how these Hopi eschatological concepts conflict with the excavation and curation of human remains and associated grave goods, (3) the burden NAGPRA has placed on the Hopi Tribe to assume responsibility for ancestral human remains that have been and continue to be excavated on federal lands, and (4) the ways that the Hopi Cultural Preservation Office expects to work with archaeologists when mortuary studies must be conducted. We assume that all responsible archaeologists working in the Southwest are now familiar with NAGPRA, so we don't recapitulate the specific language or provisions of the law. Our goal in explaining Hopi perspectives on the issues addressed in this chapter is to increase the understanding archaeologists have about Hopi concerns for their ancestors and to sensitize archaeologists to a more humanistic treatment of human remains.

HOPI BELIEFS AND CUSTOMS RELATED TO DEATH AND THE AFTERWORLD

The afterlife is a fundamental concept in Hopi religion and ceremonies (Bradfield 1973:41–42; Geertz 1984:228; Hieb 1979:577; Loftin 1982:30; O'Kane 1953:169; Parsons 1939:216; Quinn 1983:41; Titiev 1944:197, 1958:535; Voth 1912a:99). Most of the anthropological writing about the Hopi afterlife derives from research conducted at Oraibi and Hotevilla, and the anthropological literature thus provides what is primarily a Third Mesa perspective on this topic. The *Sipapuni* (Place of Emergence) in *Öngtupqa* (the Grand Canyon) is integral in the Hopi beliefs about death. As a man from Walpi observed, "you go west when you die to the Grand Canyon, over where the Hopis go for their salt" (Courlander 1982:101). *The Sipapuni* is the passage to the underworld for people after death, so *Öngtupqa* is viewed as the ultimate destiny for many Hopis when they die. Death and the *Sipapuni* are inextricably linked in the Hopi worldview. Regarding this, Loftin wrote,

After the first Two Heart emerged from the *Sipapuni* he brought death to the Hopi. Death upset the Hopi, who then decided to send the witch back down the *Sipapuni* from which he came. However, the witch told the father of the deceased child to look down into the underworld and there the father saw his child alive and playing a game. The witch said death is not final and is indeed necessary to transform humans into purely spiritual beings, from which comes more life. Thus, the Hopi decided to let the witch remain for they felt his evil was a necessary component in the maintenance of the world. In other words, though the Hopi seek rain, fertility, long life, and good health in this life, they recognize also that life springs from death and thus they accept ultimately the presence of death in the world. (Loftin 1982:197)

Many scholars have discussed how the Hopi believe that after death the souls of the departed travel west to *Maski,* literally "home of the dead people" or the "Skeleton House" but more accurately translated as "home of our ancestors' spirits." *Maski* is often described as being located at the bottom of the Grand Canyon (Carle 1941:55–59; Dorsey 1903:128; Eggan 1994:10; Fewkes 1907:566; Lockett 1933:76; Schwartz 1966:476–77). *Maski* in its true context, however, is *everywhere*. The term "underworld" is greatly influenced by the physical and tangible geographic location of the *Sipapuni* in the Little Colorado River Gorge near the Grand Canyon but this term also signifies other spiritual concepts. What is essential, as Colton (1946:3–4) explained, is that *Maski is* "the abode of spirits of the dead. Here the unseen spirits are believed to live in invisible pueblos and carry on their life like living Hopis in the world above."

Anthropologists have commented on the fact that data on Hopi death customs are difficult to collect because the Hopi are reticent to discuss death (Beaglehole and Beaglehole 1935:14–15; Murdock 1934:345). Kennard observed this reticence stems from the fact that,

A man who thinks of the dead or of the future life instead of being concerned with worldly activities is thereby bringing about his own death. In folklore are tales of people who wonder about what happens to the dead and are given the opportunity to visit the underworld by magical means, and return to life to tell the people about it. In such tales the living are urged not to be lonesome and not to long for the deceased. (Kennard 1937:492–93).

Bradfield (1973:41–42) and Geertz (1984:228) described some aspects of Hopi burial customs that relate to the afterlife. The *hiqwsi* (spirit breath) of a person is immortal and at death leaves the body through the mouth. The *kya'a* (eldest paternal aunt) washes a deceased man's hair and dresses it, washes the dead body, and gives the corpse a new name. The deceased man's father or other male relatives prepare prayer feathers and a *pötavi* (spiritual path prayer feather) consisting of a cotton string about a meter long with a feather at one end. The father blackens the chin and places a "white-cloud mask" of raw cotton over the face. Bradfield (1973:42) remarks, "The underlying idea behind each of these ritual elements is the same: namely, that the 'breath body' may be light, not 'heavy' . . . and so be enabled to go on its way to the land of the dead." The people who place offerings of food and vessels of water in the grave say or imply "You are no longer a Hopi, you are changed [grown into] a katçina, you are Cloud [*O'mauwû*]. You are to eat once of this food, i.e., accept this food offering, and when you get yonder, you are to tell the chiefs [i.e., of the six directions] to hasten to bring the rain clouds here." In the process of leaving the corpse, the "breath body" undergoes a metamorphosis into Katsina or Cloud.

For three days after the interment, bowls of food are placed at the grave. In some villages, the father or uncle of the deceased makes prayer-offerings and takes these to the grave. A *pötavi* is laid on the ground pointing to the west of the grave. Four parallel lines are drawn across the trail to the village to make certain that the spirit does not return there. Upon returning home, all the members of the household wash their hair and ritually purify themselves in the smoke of a fire. The hair washing and naming rituals that accompany burials signify a change in status comparable to birth or initiation (Bradfield 1973:44–45; Whiteley 1992:211).

On the fourth day, the deceased Hopi makes the journey to *Maski* (Stephen 1894:7–9). On this day, as Bradfield described,

Early in the next morning, according to Hopi belief, the

'breath body' . . . of the dead person rises from the grave, partakes of the 'breath' of the food, mounts the 'breath' of the single black prayer-stick, and then travels westward along the 'road' to the house of the dead, taking the 'breath' of the double green *pa'ho* with it as an offering to the *Masau'u*. (Bradfield 1973:44)

Titiev (1944:177) noted that the complete cycle of death applies only to those who "travel the full course of life on earth according to the Hopi pattern." Thus, the spirit of a child who dies before Katsina initiation must remain on earth until it is reborn in its mother's next child or to accompany her to the afterworld when she dies. Some Hopis believe that girls who are unwed cannot fulfill their functions as rain bringers since they lack the requisite wedding garments. According to Titiev, men who have never passed through the *Wuwtsim* (ritual initiation into one of four priesthoods) must return to the general afterworld in contrast to the spirits of the initiates who have special homes. The journey to *Maski* is painfully slow for witches and mean people, some of whom are consumed in ovens from which they emerge as beetles.

Some anthropologists have suggested the Hopi beliefs about the journey after death to *Maski* entail the concept of punishment (Parsons 1939:216). Hopi scholar Hartman Lomawaima, however, disputes this idea, pointing out how the Hopi concept of *Maski* has been misunderstood by some scholars. He explained,

It is difficult to know precisely what foreign concepts entered Hopi life as a result of contact with other native populations or missionization. The Hopi concept of *Maski*, or Land of the Dead, has been misinterpreted as a kind of purgatory or hell (Courlander 1982:xxi), but *Maski* has no punitive connotation for Hopis: It refers to the destination of souls when they leave the present world. If *Maski* was derived from an introduced concept it has certainly been imbued with Hopi values so that its origin is difficult to ascertain. Making the correct interpretation is all the more difficult for the outsider because of the secretive nature of Hopi religious institutions, which to this day are treated as the private property of individuals and collectives. (Lomawaima 1989:97)

The integration of death into other aspects of the Hopi life cycle is evident in the fact that garments received during the Hopi wedding ceremony are needed in order to journey to the underworld after death and provide clothing for future life (Geertz and Lomatuway'ma 1987:181–189; Kennard 1937:491–92; Page and Page 1982:111). Concerning this, Geertz and Lomatuway'ma wrote,

> It seems that, somewhere along the path which the dead travel, there is a large house which is occupied by the Kookopngyam, who are phratry brothers to the Maasaw Clan. Here is where all wedding garments end up. The house is filled with robes, gowns, shoes, and belts hanging all over the place. The unfortunate woman who does not own such garments is forced to grind corn all over again in this house. . . . Other sources stress that the robe carries the deceased swiftly to her destination and helps her float down to the bottom of the Grand Canyon where the entrance to the Underworld lies. It should be noted that the above mentioned wicker plaque, which is made for the groom as repayment, has similar functions. This plaque, which is called *hahawpi*, "instrument of descending," is specially designed and assures his swift and safe journey down to *Sipapuni* and below. Thus, the accouterments of the marriage ceremony have direct influence on the individual eschatology of the man as well as of the woman. (Geertz and Lomatuway'ma 1987:187)

The Hopi do not consider the death of an individual to be a loss. Instead, they regard death as an important change in status in which the person is reborn into the Afterworld. Once admitted to the Afterworld, the spirits engage in similar pursuits to what they did on earth. The deceased Hopis who are deserving acquire supernatural power to bring rain. Titiev (1944:172) observed that in all ceremonies the deceased ancestors play an important role and that each ceremony has a means for making the desire for rain known to the spirits in the Afterworld. Prayer-offerings in the form of prayer sticks and prayer feathers are the most common way to establish a spiritual connection with deceased ancestors. Titiev (1944:171) explained, "Each day the spirits are said to rise from the original *sipapu*, which is the entrance to the realm of the dead, and to look east toward the Hopi mesas. They select the best ones . . . and go to visit them." It should be stressed that the Hopis do not summon the dead; they petition the clouds who represent the ancestors. As Loftin explained,

> The spiritual source of all life and forms issues from . . . the underworld, where it appears as life-giving water. Indeed, the Hopi petition their own departed ancestors to

visit their villages in the form of clouds to bless them with the sacred gift of rain. Thus, death is understood by the Hopi as a return to the spiritual realm from which comes more life. (Loftin 1991:11–12)

Several aspects of Hopi burial customs relate to deceased adults becoming clouds (Beaglehole and Beaglehole 1935:14–15; Kennard 1937:491; Murdock 1934:345–46; Stephen 1894:5–8). After death the face of the corpse is covered with raw cotton, which signifies its future existence as a cloud. After the deceased person is buried, prayer feathers and a pottery bowl of corn meal is taken to the grave. The meal is to feed the spirit of the dead man, the prayer feathers to help it on its journey to become a cloud.

In 1912, Joshua He-mi-yesi-va, a Hopi from Shungopavi attending the Carlisle Indian School, described how the deceased Hopis who become Cloud People bring rain. He said,

> Those of the dead who were good people while on earth become Cloud People after death. They have a round, nearly flat tray made of cotton . . . in which they carry water; another in which lightening is carried; and a third in which thunder, is kept. . . . They lift them up to the wind, and water sprinkled from them causes rain. They . . . take water out of these trays with their hands, and sprinkle it out into the air, but never throw out all of it. (Wallis and Titiev 1945:545)

Maski thus plays a vital role in the reciprocity between living Hopis and their ancestors that is essential to Hopi religion (Hieb 1979:580; Loftin 1986:185–91; Thompson 1945:541). As described by Hieb (1994:19–27) the elementary structure of Hopi religion includes four basic concepts: (1) a universe divided between an Upper World of the living and a Lower World of the spirits or deceased ancestors; (2) the *sipapu*, a channel of communication and exchange between the Upper and Lower Worlds; (3) the concept of reciprocity wherein prayers and prayer offerings are made to the spirits of the Lower World who respond with gifts, the most important of which is moisture; and (4) religious specialists or priests who mediate between the occupants of the Upper and Lower Worlds. In explicating the spiritual relationship between these elements, Hieb (1994:20) wrote, "This world and the world of the spirits are transformations of each other and yet are of the same essential substance." According to Hieb (1994:24), "As 'messengers of the gods,' the katsinas come

. . . to receive prayers and prayer offerings and to recip-rocate with assurance and gifts of food."

In discussing Hopi culture, Titiev (1944:177) concluded that the Hopi believe that life after death is merely a stage in the continuous cycle of events, and this means that Hopis do not regard their deceased ancestors as outsiders but as powerful members of society whose sphere of activity has been changed from the physical to the spiri-tual realm. Titiev (1944:178) astutely observed that the Hopi have nothing to fear if an essential religious cere-mony is about to lapse because in the afterlife the different religious modalities will continue to perform these rites.

Eggan (1994:10) added that, "The equation of the dead with clouds and rain, by means of the concept of katsi-nas, provides a system in which the dead maintain their interest in the living and continue to help their relatives by sending rain." Thus, as Kennard (1937:491) observed, "In every ceremony, the spirits of the dead are involved, whether as katcina, clouds, or those living in the under-world."

HOPI BELIEFS ABOUT DEATH RELATED TO THE ARCHAEOLOGICAL INVESTIGATION OF BURIALS AND ASSOCIATED GRAVE GOODS

Some archaeologists may wonder why the Hopi people are concerned about the remains of their ancestors after the journey of the breath body to *Maski*. In this regard, the Hopi people have continuing spiritual concerns about the physical remains of deceased people and their associated grave offerings, and these religious beliefs entail a prohi-bition against the archaeological excavation of burials.

When deceased Hopis are buried, they are laid to rest in a cemetery that constitutes its *kiiat* (final home), a *tip-kya* (womb) that is physically and spiritually integral to the lifeblood of their community. It is important for the physical remains of people to return back into the earth from which they came through the natural processes. It is through this means that the spiritual goodness inher-ent in the corporeal remains of people returns to earth to bless the world for the betterment of future genera-tions. At the same time, any negative elements associated with the individual are contained by the earth and thus kept from adversely affecting the living people in the vil-lage and the world.

The physical remains of people thus play an important

role in Hopi culture that is complementary to the spiri-tual essences that journey to *Maski* to become cloud peo-ple. Both the physical and spiritual remains provide the fertility and good things that are essential to the contin-uance of life.

The archaeological excavation of graves to recover human remains or grave goods interrupts the natural process of returning to the earth that is essential to the metamorphosis of human remains into the fertile, life sus-taining *tipkya* associated with each Hopi village. Similarly, destructive analysis of human remains prevents their return into the earth where the deceased Hopis were laid to rest. Consequently, the archaeological excavation of human remains and osteological analyses are emotionally charged issues of great consequence to Hopi people.

The funerary offerings that are deposited in graves belong to the deceased, placed there to assist them on their journey to *Maski*. From a Hopi perspective, there can be no legitimate recovery of or use of these associ-ated grave goods. Removal and curation of grave goods is perceived as grave robbing and is thus abhorrent to Hopi people. Not surprisingly, many Hopi people do not understand why archaeologists want to excavate or study grave goods, and this too is an emotionally charged issue.

The knowledge archaeologists gain from the investiga-tion of human remains and associated grave goods does not offset the spiritual danger and consequences involved in the endeavor. The Hopi people believe that the distur-bance of their ancestors by archaeologists has immediate and long-term spiritual and physical consequences for the deceased people, their descendants, archaeologists, and the world in general. From the Hopi perspective, it is important for deceased ancestors and their associated grave goods to remain exactly where they were interred, or as a difficult alternative, to be reburied as close as pos-sible to their original location.

In the best of all possible worlds, these ancestors would never be disturbed. In the contemporary world, where graves are destroyed by construction and other develop-ment, the conventional way to mitigate impacts is by archaeological excavation, followed by osteological analy-sis. The Hopi Tribe maintains this archaeological work is in itself another impact. As a result, choosing between the destruction of ancestral graves by construction or the disturbance through archaeological excavation places the Hopi people into the difficult situation of having to make a tragic choice. A "tragic choice" (Calabresi and Bobbit 1978) occurs when the members of a society are forced to make a decision that affirms one fundamental cultural value while simultaneously conflicting with another, equally significant value. In dealing with this type of tragic choice, the Hopi Tribe has formulated ways in which the adverse impacts of scientific investigation need to be mitigated. These are: (1) nondestructive osteological analyses for the limited purpose of establishing cultural affiliation, (2) documentation oriented toward assisting Hopi elders with the performance of reburial ceremonies, and (3) the timely reburial of the human remains and associated grave goods as close as possible to where they originated.

THE BURDEN OF NAGPRA

Since the passage of NAGPRA, the Hopi Cultural Preservation Office has responded to numerous requests for consultation concerning the inadvertent discovery or intentional excavation of human remains on federal lands throughout the Southwest. In this effort the Cultural Preservation Office has performed more than 300 reburial ceremonies in an area that extends from Utah and southwestern Colorado to southern Arizona, and from Aztec National Monument to the Kaibab National Forest in the west.

Until recently, the reburial of human remains was an unknown concept to the Hopi people. Once people are buried in accordance with Hopi ceremonies their remains are never intended to be unearthed. The development of a reburial ceremony was debated by the Hopi Cultural Resources Advisory Task Team in 1989, which reluctantly decided that such a ceremony should be performed to give final respect to the deceased. The development of this ceremony by Hopi religious leaders was in direct response to the escalating demand for consultation by federal and state agencies concerning the final disposition of excavated human remains and associated funerary objects. Hopi elders that perform reburials do so because they are committed to respecting and honoring their ancestors' spiritual and physical remains by providing these deceased people with a brief ceremony congruent with traditional Hopi burial rituals. These Hopi elders perform reburial ceremonies with the knowledge that these rituals may entail serious spiritual and physical repercussions for them. Archaeologists and cultural resource managers need to know that NAGPRA places a solemn burden on these Hopi men and the Cultural Preservation Office.

Reburial is an emotionally trying and spiritually perilous endeavor—necessary because of developments in the modern world beyond the control of the Hopi Tribe.

RECONCILING HOPI CONCERNS WITH MORTUARY STUDIES

In reconciling the political and intellectual impacts of NAGPRA, archaeologists should realize that Hopi concerns about ancestral graves can sometimes result in more mortuary studies than would otherwise be done. The archaeological investigation of human remains in a coal strip mine on Black Mesa provides an example of this. The original archaeological investigations for this project were undertaken under the auspices of the Black Mesa Archaeological Project between 1967 and 1983 (Powell et al. 1983). Archaeological survey of the mine lease documented a total of 2,600 archaeological sites, but compliance with Section 106 of the National Historic Preservation Act only required the partial or full excavation of 220 archaeological sites (Spurr 1993:3). The Black Mesa Archaeological Project thus entailed an archaeological sampling of 11.8% of the total number of archaeological and historical sites. While this sample may have been sufficient for scientific purposes associated with federal compliance with historic preservation legislation, Hopis had serious concerns about the remains of their ancestors in archaeological sites that were not included in the Black Mesa archaeological research program. The knowledge that the remains of these ancestors were being destroyed by strip mining was troublesome. When the Hopi Cultural Preservation Office was established in 1989, one of its first tasks was to analyze how many Hopi graves may exist in unexcavated archaeological sites on Black Mesa. This was done by preparing a chart that quantified the number of archaeological sites in the mine area that had not been archaeologically investigated, which of these sites had a high probability for human remains, and the archaeological contexts these human remains would likely be associated with (e.g., middens, kivas, structure interiors). This information was then used in litigation to force the Office of Surface Mining to comply with NAGPRA by placing a stipulation on the Peabody Western Coal Company's mining permit to implement a project for the purposes of recovering and reburying human remains before they were impacted by mining.

As a result of administrative complaints by the Hopi

Tribe, a salvage archaeological project was mounted to locate, disinter, and reinter human remains from ancient Puebloan sites that would be adversely impacted by mining operations in the Peabody leasehold on Black Mesa. This work, undertaken by the Navajo Nation Archaeology Department—Northern Arizona University Branch Office, resulted in the excavation of an additional 32 archaeological sites (Spurr 1993). Thirty-two Hopi ancestors from 31 burials were located, moved out of harm's way, and reburied with a ritual performed by Hopi elders. In summarizing this project, Spurr (1993:188) concluded that "The reburial of the human remains recovered during the NNAD Black Mesa project was a satisfying end to the project. Throughout the project the remains were treated with respect, and they have now been returned to the ground with proper ceremony." Although many Hopis would disagree that the disturbance of their ancestors followed by reburial was "satisfying" in any respect, most would agree that this was a better alternative than having these remains destroyed by mining activities.

What is pertinent to the interests of archaeologists is that the monograph reporting the findings of this project includes archaeological data, osteological analyses, and a study of the mortuary ceramics (Hays-Gilpin 1993; Spurr 1993). This information would not have been collected had it not been for the Hopi Tribe's insistence that the remains of its ancestors be treated with respect and dignity rather than be subjected to destruction by strip mining.

There is a tacit negotiation that goes on in the management of human remains in projects like that conducted on Black Mesa. The Hopi Tribe recognizes that the remains of Hopi ancestors are better treated by having archaeologists do the exhumation than they would be by other potential groups that might do this work, e.g., professional morticians. Archaeologists are not interested in doing this work, however, unless some level of scientific study can be conducted. How much and what kinds of scientific study are acceptable need to be negotiated in order to reach what is essentially an "uneasy" accord where the legitimate concerns of both groups are met to some degree. At the present time, and for the foreseeable future, the fit between the concerns of the Hopi Tribe and the desire of archaeologists to extend their knowledge base has to be determined through project specific consultation. This is a difficult process, but it affords all parties the opportunity to make the best of a difficult situation. In these negotiations, the main concern of the Hopi Tribe is

to protect its ancestors and the balance of nature; reburial thus has a higher profile than the mortuary studies that are a part of this process.

The Hopi Tribe is not intractable in negotiations to reconcile its concerns with those of archaeologists interested in mortuary studies (Dongoske 1996:290–93). For instance, in 1991 the Hopi Cultural Preservation Office received a request from the Office of Contract Archeology at the University of New Mexico to conduct more detailed, nondestructive analyses of excavated skeletal remains than had previously been negotiated for the Transwestern Pipeline Expansion Project (Ogilvie and Hilton 1993). This request was based on the unanticipated finding of an assemblage of human remains comprised of the disarticulated skeletons of 14 individuals scattered on the floor and bench of a Pueblo II kiva. The assemblage was characterized by fragmented skeletal remains with perimortem modification consisting of green bone fractures, impact marks, cut marks, and burning. Given the complex nature of this assemblage, it was not possible to adequately study it in the field, and this prompted the request for laboratory analysis of the remains in Albuquerque.

The Hopi Tribe agreed to a laboratory analysis, provided the human remains were reburied within a four month time period. This length of time was determined as appropriate because the number four is sacred in Hopi culture, and Hopi cultural advisors thought if the spirits represented in the assemblage became aware of the number four in the allowed time period, they would recognize the Hopi involvement and find the analysis nonthreatening (Dongoske 1996:292). The Hopi Tribe agreed to the laboratory analysis of the assemblage in part to establish whether the individuals represented by these disarticulated remains were ancestors of the Hopi or if they may have been enemies of the Hopi. The cultural affiliation of these individuals is important because this information is needed to determine the necessary level and nature of Hopi involvement in reburial ceremonies.

The Transwestern Pipeline Expansion Project provides a good example of how the Hopi Tribe is willing to engage in negotiations to reconcile its concerns with those of archaeologists. This project demonstrates that the research interests of archaeologists can sometimes be accommodated at the same time that the remains of Hopi ancestors are protected. The reconciliation of these different interests is contingent upon all parties effectively communicating what they want and why.

Scholarly Issues Pertaining to Mortuary Studies

Ethics and Research

The Hopi Cultural Preservation Office affirms the contemporary archaeological ethics which mandate that all analysis of ancestral Hopi human remains and associated grave goods be conducted in consultation with the Hopi Tribe (Watkins et al. 1995; World Archaeological Congress 1991). Some scholars apparently still do not understand these ethics, and research about Hopi human remains continues to be published without Hopi collaboration or the opportunity for tribal review and comment (e.g., Kohn et al. 1994; Kohn et al. 1995). This is unfortunate, because it is through consultation with the Hopi Tribe that scholars have an opportunity to have their work intellectually critiqued by the people who are most affected by their work. The staff of the Hopi Cultural Preservation Office think that tribal collaboration in research and review of scholarly work has benefits for both scholars and the Hopi Tribe. Scholars gain because they have access to tribal knowledge to which they would otherwise not be exposed. This knowledge can be useful in correcting misrepresentations of Hopi culture in published works and in adding new information pertinent to the research being conducted. The Hopi Tribe benefits because it can engage in a dialog with scholars about Hopi views about the past, as well as the need to protect the sanctity of certain types of esoteric information by managing its dissemination to the public.

Mortuary Analyses to Investigate Social Organization

It has long been known that the Hopi people have much to offer archaeologists in interpreting the social significance of mortuary offerings. The classic example of this is the so-called Magicians Burial excavated by the Museum of Northern Arizona at Ridge Ruin, a Pueblo III masonry pueblo about 20 miles east of Flagstaff. In this burial, a man was interred with more than 600 associated grave goods, including ceramics, painted baskets, lithics, pigments, crystals, jewelry, exotic trade items, and wooden ceremonial objects (McGregor 1943). The archaeologists who excavated this burial consulted with Hopi men to help interpret this burial assemblage. McGregor described this consultation, noting that,

Hopi informants were shown portions of the material recovered from this burial soon after it was taken from the ground, and before any particular interpretation was undertaken, to see what reaction they would have toward it. All of them agreed without hesitation that many of the objects were definitely ceremonial. After some discussion, each in turn further decided that they could definitely identify the ceremony represented by the objects. Questioned individually, they all agreed that it was the same ceremony, although they often called it by different names. This latter fact is not necessarily conflicting, for each mesa, and often each village, has a slightly different name, even a different formula, for the same ceremony. (McGregor 1943:295)

Most impressive was the fact that when an informant was shown only part of the objects, he often described, sometimes quite accurately, other things that should have been found with them. This was the case of a Shungopavi man who indicated there should have been a clublike object with serrated edges, a double-horn-like object, and a cap with a point on the top, when certain of the sticks were shown to him. These were later produced, much to his gratification.

The Hopis McGregor consulted determined the ceremony represented in this burial assemblage was the *Moochiwimi* or *Nasot wimi*, a ritual that includes sword swallowing. The man himself was a *Ka-leh-ta-ka* (war leader).

McGregor (1943:296) found it notable that one of the Hopi consultants asked if the burial was located somewhere near Diablo Canyon because the ceremony represented by the grave goods belongs to clans that have proprietary rights to gather eagles in this area. In fact, Diablo Canyon is located near Ridge Ruin. McGregor concluded that the occupants of Ridge Ruin were ancestral to the Hopi culture and that it is "therefore, more gratifying than surprising that this ceremony could have been identified so completely by living Hopi Indians." As McGregor found, the Hopi ceremony represented in the Ridge Ruin burial has a history in Hopi culture extending at least 800 years. This historical continuity is not unique, and the Hopi people know that much of their culture can be traced in the archaeological record. Given the historical relationship between the Hopi people and their ancestors, it seems logical that the interpretation of the archaeological record should give consideration to the material correlates of Hopi mortuary behavior as documented ethnographically. To some degree, this can be done using published information, but in serious research this information should be reviewed by Hopi cultural advisors to provide a contemporary and project specific basis for archaeological interpretation. To date, consultation with Hopis like that undertaken by McGregor has not been common. Most consultation has focused on disposition, with little or no research effort on cultural affiliation or interpretation of the mortuary context.

In the future, the Hopi Tribe invites archaeologists undertaking mortuary studies involving Hopi ancestors to consult with the Hopi Cultural Preservation Office. It should be anticipated, of course that there are some Hopi beliefs and information about mortuary behavior that the Hopi people do not want used in scholarly research. Consultation with Hopi advisors will identify such information, and, at the same time, provide other data that archaeologists may find useful.

Disarticulated and Commingled Human Remains

In recent years, archaeologists have documented an increasing number of archaeological sites associated with disarticulated and commingled human remains. Many of the skeletal elements in the assemblages of human bones at these sites have been subjected to cutting, breaking, burning, and other perimortem modification. One of these sites on Polacca Wash near the Hopi Mesas is attributed directly to the Hopi people (Olson 1966; Turner and Morris 1970), and many of the other sites appear to be affiliated with ancestors of the Hopi people. The Hopi people thus have an interest in how archaeologists interpret these sites.

While some archaeologists think these assemblages of human bone can be attributed to warfare, corpse mutilation, battering, witchcraft, or secondary mortuary practices (Bullock 1992:205; Darling 1998; Larralde 1998; Ogilvie and Hilton 1993:128), other archaeologists infer they represent cannibalism (Turner and Turner 1992a, 1992b, 1995, 1999; Turner et al. 1993; White 1992). Before discussing the more general claims of cannibalism, we would like to examine the specific assertion that the site on Polacca Wash (NA8502) is associated with the destruction of Awatovi in 1700 (Turner and Morris 1970).

An assemblage of human bone excavated by Olson (1966) along Polacca Wash contains the highly fragmented remains of at least thirty men, women, and children. In their reanalysis of this site, Turner and Morris (1970:331) assert this "massacre was the work of Hopi warriors who also destroyed Awatobi village about A.D. 1700."

This inference appears to be based largely on a single uncalibrated radiocarbon date of 370 ± 95 B.P. (I-3658), obtained from one of the human bones in this assemblage. Whether or not NA8502 is associated with the destruction of Awatovi is an important question for the Hopi people.

The correlation of archaeological sites with specific historical events is a difficult archaeological endeavor, especially when using radiocarbon dates obtained from bone. Advances in radiocarbon dating since Turner and Morris's work in 1970 now make it possible to calibrate single radiocarbon dates and thereby increase their interpretive strength (Stuiver and Becker 1986; Stuiver and Reimer 1987, 1993). Calibration of sample I-3658 yields a direct calibration of A.D. 1492, 1604, or 1610. One of the two methods of calibration yields a 1 sigma range of calibration of A.D. 1438–1649. The second method yields 1 sigma date ranges of A.D. 1448–1532 (48% probability) and A.D. 1546–1635 (52% probability), and a 2 sigma date range of A.D. 1404–1635 (94% probability). We think the calibrated dates, with the accompanying date ranges, indicate the correlation of NA8502 with the destruction of Awatovi is tenuous. It is likely that the human remains at NA8502 actually date earlier than 1700. In our opinion, in the absence of more secure dating, the assertion that NA8502 is associated with events at Awatovi in 1700 remains an unconfirmed hypothesis and should be treated as such, and not be considered a fact. The centuries before and after A.D. 1700 were characterized by raids on Hopi villages by Navajo, Apache, Ute, Spanish, Mohave, Chemeuvi, and other groups (Brew 1979:519–22; James 1974:33–76; McNitt 1972:16, 60–61), and this raises the possibility that whatever happened to produce the bone assemblage at NA8502 may have been the result of confrontation between Hopis and other people rather than internecine violence.

Assemblages of disarticulated and commingled human remains in the northern Southwest are phenomena that span at least 800 years and tens of thousands of square kilometers of space (White 1992:348). These assemblages occur in a variety of archaeological contexts, including rock shelters, crypts, open sites, pit structures, kivas, and pueblo rooms. Patterns of perimortem modification of the human remains in these assemblages vary, and there are many different possible explanations to account for their presence in archaeological sites. Several archaeologists make the inference that some (but not all) of these assemblages are the result of cannibalism (e.g., Flinn et al. 1976; Nickens 1975; Turner 1989; Turner and Turner 1992a, 1992b, 1995, 1999; White 1992). Other archaeologists discount the inference of cannibalism (e.g., Bullock 1992, 1998; Darling 1998).

Turner and Turner (1992a, 1995) and other archaeologists who identify cannibalism do so using a set of attributes of perimortem modification to bone including breakage, cutting, anvil-hammer stone abrasions, burning, missing vertebrae, and fragment end polishing. These attributes are held to be a taphonomic signature of cannibalism, which is defined as the conspecific consumption of human tissue (White 1992:9). Typologies of cannibalism are still largely theoretical and include consumption for purposes of funerary ritual, revenge, gastronomic preferences, and survival (Flinn et al. 1976; White 1992:13).

To date, the identification of cannibalism is *inferred* on the basis of similarities between the processing and deposition of human bones and the processing and deposition of faunal bones known to be used for subsistence (White 1992). If human bones were processed and deposited in the archaeological record in a manner similar to the bones of game animals, then the inference is made that human flesh was consumed. As Nickens (1975:290–91) and White (1992:337–40) admit, however, there is as yet no concrete *evidence* of cannibalism (Arens 1979, 1998). Some archaeologists hold that the only form of such evidence would be the presence of human bones or flesh in demonstrably human coprolites, which to date has not been found in the Southwest (White 1992:340). The alleged presence of human myoglobin in a coprolite at Cowboy Wash has recently been proposed as constituting proof of cannibalism (Billman et al. 1999), but potential problems with the reliability and replicability of the blood analysis preclude the acceptance of this "evidence" without further research (Dongoske et al. 2000). Nonetheless, conclusions drawn from inferences are fundamental to archaeology, and an increasing number of archaeologists are concluding that cannibalism occurred in the northern Southwest. Turner and Turner (1995, 1999), for instance, think this was the case at 40 archaeological sites in Arizona, Utah, Colorado, and New Mexico.

The identification of perimortem modification or processing of human remains through careful analytical procedures is obviously a matter of great interest to archaeologists. We caution, however, that the public is more interested in the inferences drawn from patterns of disarticulated and commingled human remains than

they are about archaeological techniques and methodology. Archaeologists attempting to explain assemblages of disarticulated human remains need to think carefully about their work and how it is being appropriated by the popular press (e.g., Dold 1998; Florio 1996; Rushton 1996).

As White (1992:346, 348) observes, "The difficulty of explaining *why* cannibalism occurred . . . is orders of magnitude greater than the difficulty of warranting the inference that it *did* occur" [emphases in original]. A number of different explanations for cannibalism have been proposed. Turner and Turner (1992a, 1992b) originally suggested that the assemblages they attributed to cannibalism were the result of "social pathology," defined as the behavior of a socially pathological individual that was transmitted to others, leading them to acquire the same or similar behavior (Turner and Turner 1990:188). In other words, social pathology is a form of "mob behavior." The explanation of social pathology was advanced in part to avoid the suggestion that cannibalism and physical mutilation of humans was a strongly institutionalized or regularly occurring behavior. Nonetheless, Turner and Turner (1992b:679) suggested these behaviors need to be considered in assessing the "chaotic contribution interpersonal conflict and social pathology had on the collapse of prehistoric population and cultural systems in the Southwest." More recently, Turner (1993:430–36, Turner and Turner 1995, 1999) has proposed that cannibalism was part of an institutionalized violent social control that accompanied the rapid development of the Chacoan regional system after A.D. 900, perhaps as a result of Mesoamerican influences. Other explanations for cannibalism include warfare, conflict, ritual, witchcraft, starvation, and food stress (White 1992:13, 355–56).

Given the relative rarity of sites with assemblages of disarticulated and commingled human remains, and the long time span they date to, we think it is probable that there are multiple explanations for their occurrence. As White (1992:355–56) concludes, "It is premature to offer comprehensive regional explanations for the assemblages . . . and there is no reason to conclude that the reasons behind them will not be multiple and independent."

The broad-brushed characterization of ancient Puebloan people as "cannibals" is premature, yet this is how the popular press appropriates scholarly research on the subject. If the consumption of human tissues did in fact occur, it may have been due to exigencies of survival, much like that of the Donner Party in 1846 (Grayson 1990,

1993:277–96) or the airline crash in the Peruvian Andes in 1972 (Flinn et al. 1976:316). And, as White (1992:xix) cautions, "Just as no person characterizes all American pioneers of the last century as cannibals on the basis on cannibalism among the Donner party . . . no person should characterize all Anasazi as cannibals." Furthermore, *if* such cannibalism did occur it may have been due to violent interactions with non-Puebloan peoples rather than violence between Puebloan groups.

The issue for the Hopi Tribe is not so much the topic that archaeologists choose to study but the lack of consultation with the people who are most affected by that work. As Bullock (1992:205) observes, among scientists work is evaluated and reviewed through the use of published sources. At Hopi, however, this form of published discourse is an ineffective method for obtaining a meaningful review of work. It is far more effective for scholars truly interested in obtaining a Hopi perspective to ask for time on the agenda of one of the monthly meetings of the Hopi Cultural Resources Advisory Task Team, and all scholars have an open invitation to do this. With respect to disarticulated and commingled human remains, the scholarly questions are so complex that a single meeting with the Cultural Resources Advisory Task Team may not be sufficient to explore all the issues, and more intensive consultation may be needed.

We think such formal consultation with Hopi cultural advisors is necessary because scholars glean tidbits of information from the ethnographic literature and use these to construct arguments that sometimes appear to be out of context from a Hopi perspective. For instance, Turner (1989:151) cites a note by A. M. Stephen (Stephen 1936:99) describing how bits of flesh scraped from scalps were fed to Hopi male children to make them bravehearted. Turner and Morris (1970:325) cite Titiev's (1944:135) statement that Hopi Kwan Society members were obligated to dismember witches if they were apprehended in the village during tribal initiation, and they also cite Fewkes's (1893, 1895) assertion that captives from Awatovi were severely mutilated and dismembered. Bullock (1991:10) cites Parsons (1933:617) to document that Hopis took human heads as war trophies. Responsible scholars should discuss these and other uses of Hopi ethnographic data to make sure valid Hopi perspectives are adequately considered.

Archaeologists writing about cannibalism may see themselves as "academics coming up with theories in a distant ivory tower" (Rushton 1996) but when their work is appropriated in a sensationalistic manner by the popular press, it has a negative impact on Hopi people and other Native Americans. This is a seemingly intractable problem but one that we think can be mitigated if scholars interested in cannibalism consult Hopi cultural advisors and incorporate Hopi interpretations and caveats into their findings, thus affording Hopis the same consideration scholars give one another.

Cultural and Biological Affiliation

Under NAGPRA, cultural affiliation is key to Hopi control of ancestral human remains and associated grave goods. The Hopi Tribe thus has a vested interest in how archaeologists attempt to develop and implement an operational definition of this concept. For purposes of NAGPRA, cultural affiliation is "a relationship of shared group identity which can be reasonably traced historically or prehistorically between a present day Indian tribe . . . and an identifiable earlier group" (Public Law 101–601).

The Hopi Tribe's cultural affiliation with their ancestors (*Motisinom* and *Hisatsinom*) is founded on the migration histories of the clans that comprise Hopi society and culture. During migrations to Hopi, each clan followed its own unique route and established its own history. The Hopi people think that the area occupied by the *Motisinom* and *Hisatsinom* transcends the traditional culture areas defined by archaeologists, e.g., Anasazi, Mogollon, Hohokam (Ferguson et al. 1993, 1995a, 1995b).

Archaeological constructs of prehistory and Hopi traditional history have some congruence since they both describe the same past with narratives that often focus on the same archaeological sites. However, archaeologists and Hopis view history in fundamentally different ways for different purposes, and as a result, the fit between the two types of knowledge is not always consistent. This is most evident when the concept of archaeological cultures is compared to how Hopi view their relationship to the ancient past. The Hopi view their ancient past in terms of their ancestors, the living people who resided in the sites now studied by archaeologists (Dongoske et al. 1997:603–4). Archaeologists in the Southwest have traditionally viewed the past in terms of archaeological cultures, abstract units of analysis defined by comparative sets of material traits, which are conceived in essentially ethnographic terms.

Some archaeologists consider these archaeologically delineated groups to have been "tribes" or ethnically distinct groups of people (Colton 1943). For instance, in interpreting ceramic distributions Haury commented,

I am well aware that pottery cannot always be used as a central identifier of a people, but one need look only at the pottery produced today by Southwestern Indians to realize that there is a one-to-one correlation between type and tribe for most of the vessels produced. I believe this situation obtained in antiquity as well, and that the inference that Anasazi-Mogollon ceramic differences denote "tribal" differences is sound. (Haury 1985:xvii)

Many archaeologists still think this way, rarely, if ever, considering the underlying epistemological issues. Archaeological cultures represent static configurations of architecture, pottery, and forms of material culture. At best, change in these archaeological cultures is punctuated into phases, and it is thus hard to deal with continuous variation. Hopi traditional histories offer dynamic views of the past that do not always fit well with the essentially static view of the past represented by archaeological cultures (Dongoske et al. 1997:603–4).

Hopi traditional histories are long and incorporate many individual groups of people (i.e., clans), each with a unique history. Thus, there is not one tribal history but multiple tribal histories that operate on numerous levels. Each Hopi clan and religious group has a unique tradition that specifically accounts for how it came to be at Hopi. In many respects, the very concept of "Hopi" as a distinct ethno-political unit does not really have an archaeological reality until the "gathering of the clans" on the Hopi Mesas, ca. A.D. 1050–1100. Prior to this, the ancestors of the Hopi were organized not as a single tribe but as many distinct clans (Ferguson and Dongoske 1994:24). Although these Hopi clans had a philosophical concept of "Hopi" entailing living a humble life as farmers and a cognized destiny of becoming *Hopisinom* (Hopi people), the fully realized ethnic identity of the Hopi people as currently constituted in the Hopi Tribe was not attained until the completion of all of the clan migrations.

The Hopi view of their past is more dynamic than the past portrayed by archaeologists. At any point in time until their arrival at *Tuuwanasavi,* the spiritual center of the earth, the ancestors of the Hopi may have belonged to any number of archaeological cultures. It is for this specific reason that the Hopi Tribal Council passed Resolution H-70–94, which officially declares the Hopi Tribe's cultural affiliation to the Paleo-Indian, Archaic, Basketmaker, Anasazi, Hohokam, Mogollon, Mimbres, Sinagua, Salado, Cohonina, and Fremont archaeological cultures of the Southwest.

The determination of cultural affiliation is a difficult intellectual and political endeavor (Rose et al. 1996:91). Osteology and mortuary studies can potentially play an important role in this regard but to date the lack of a well-developed method and theory for determining cultural affiliation for the purposes of NAGPRA has severely limited the usefulness of these sources of information. Many archaeological research designs that consider cultural affiliation still do so primarily in the context of trying to assign human remains to archaeological cultures rather than trying to relate those remains to contemporary tribes who share a group identity with them (e.g., Van West and Huber 1995).

It is important to note that cultural affiliation as defined in NAGPRA is not the same as biological affinity. Thus, osteological studies that indicate a close biological relationship between an ancient and modern population may or may not be evidence for cultural affiliation. For instance, the offspring of two people who come from different tribes may have a close *genetic* relationship to both of the tribes of their parents but only be enculturated into one of the tribes. These individuals would thus have a *cultural* affiliation to only one set of ancestors. Other progeny of intertribal marriages may be multicultural and thus have cultural affiliation to all of their ancestors. The point is that data about biological affinity can play an important role in determining cultural affiliation but these data need to be interpreted using other contextual information about historical and cultural relationships. Using a preponderance of the evidence, archaeologists need to consider geographical relationships, kinship, human biology and genetics, linguistics, folklore, tribal knowledge, and historical information in addition to archaeological data.

The current taxonomy of archaeological cultures does not adequately incorporate the clan-based migrational history of Hopi ancestors. It is probable that through time many Hopi clans historically participated in more than one of the archaeological cultures that archaeologists label Anasazi, Mogollon, Hohokam, and so forth. The differences in scale between archaeological cultures and the small clan-based populations that historically contributed to Hopi culture mean that assigning human remains to archaeological cultures is virtually meaningless for the current interests of the Hopi Tribe, driven as they are by the necessity of participating in the implementation of NAGPRA. Given this situation, the Hopi Tribe calls for Southwestern archaeologists to develop the methods and theory of mortuary analysis needed to construct an operational definition of cultural affiliation using archaeological data. We think the development of this method and theory should be done in consultation with the Hopi people and the other Native Americans whose ancestors are the subject of archaeological investigations.

CONCLUSION

As Rose and his colleagues (1996:100) point out, in the post-NAGPRA era, which will last forever, bioarchaeological analyses will become more ethical and fair to the deceased than they have been in the past. This is because NAGPRA requires the same consultation process for the exhumation and analysis of ancient human remains as it does for the relocation of historic cemeteries. We think there is still a long way to go in creating equity between the legitimate interests of the Hopi Tribe and the scholarly interests of archaeologists. NAGPRA creates new opportunities for intellectual interaction between archaeologists and Native Americans, and the Hopi Tribe looks forward to the consultation and collaboration that is needed to fully realize the potential that exists for simultaneously advancing tribal interests and scholarly knowledge.

One thing archaeologists should keep in mind is that the disturbance of human remains is agonizing for Hopi people. The Hopis who do reburial rituals testify to the personal grief they experience when they have to deal with the broken bones, headless infants, and other skeletal trauma that is sometimes inadvertently associated with archaeological data recovery, especially that conducted using mechanized equipment. In presenting results of mortuary studies, archaeologists need to understand that for the Hopis, the heartfelt spiritual concerns about the disruption of graves far outweighs any mitigation of impacts by scientific studies. What archaeologists find to be interesting results and findings are colored by the desecration of the graves that led to those results. This is not to say that archaeologists should not try to share their findings with the Hopis; they should. However, archaeologists should understand why many Hopis exhibit a lack of enthusiasm for the scientific findings.

For archaeologists, the goal is to reconstruct the history of the past and thereby gain a better understanding of the people who lived before us. The paradigm used to achieve this lofty scholarly objective, however, sometimes alienates contemporary Native Americans by objectifying their ancestral human remains and associated grave goods that exist in the present. In the Hopi worldview, the ancestors the Hopis still care for cannot be separated from the "things" that archaeologists seek in the archaeological record. These are vitally tied to one another. The Hopis are committed first and foremost to caring for their ancestors. The scholarly work that can be done in the context of caring for their ancestors is important but secondary. Archaeologists have to accept this.

REFERENCES CITED

Arens, William
1979   *The Man-Eating Myth*. Oxford University Press, New York.
1998   Rethinking Anthropophagy. In *Cannibalism and the Colonial World*, edited by Francis Barker, Peter Hulme, and Margaret Iverson, pp. 39–62. Cambridge University Press, Cambridge.

Beaglehole, Ernest, and Pearl Beaglehole
1935   Hopi Death Customs. In *Hopi of the Second Mesa*, by Ernest and Pearl Beaglehole, pp. 11–14. Memoirs of the American Anthropological Association 44. Menasha, Wisconsin.

Billman, Brian R., Patricia M. Lambert, and Banks L. Leonard
1999   Cannibalism, Warfare, and Drought in the Mesa Verde Region during the Twelfth Century A.D. *American Antiquity* 65:145–78.

Bradfield, Richard M.
1973   *A Natural History of Associations, A Study in the Meaning of Community*. Duckworth, London.

Brew, J. O.
1979   Hopi Prehistory and History to 1850. In *Southwest*, edited by A. Ortiz, pp. 514–23. Handbook of North American Indians, vol. 9, W. C. Sturtevant, general editor Smithsonian Institution, Washington, D.C.

Bullock, Peter Y.
1991   A Reappraisal of Anasazi Cannibalism. *Kiva* 57:5–16.
1992   A Return to the Question of Cannibalism. *Kiva* 58:203–5.

1998   *Deciphering Anasazi Violence.* HRM Press, Santa Fe.

Calabresi, Guido, and Philip Bobbit
1978   *Tragic Choices.* W. W. Norton, New York.

Carle, Peggy
1941   *Burial Customs of the Indians of the Southwest.* Master's thesis, Department of Anthropology, Texas Technological College.

Colton, Harold S.
1943   Reconstruction of Anasazi History. *Proceedings of the American Philosophical Society* 86:264–69.
1946   Fools Names Like Fools Faces-. *Plateau* 19:1–8.
1974   History of the Hopi Indians from Archaeological Evidence [written ca. 1954]. Published as "Hopi History and Ethnobotany" in *Hopi Indians,* pp. 279–86. Garland Press, New York.

Courlander, Harold
1982   *Hopi Voices, Recollections, Traditions, and Narratives of the Hopi Indians.* University of New Mexico, Albuquerque.

Darling, Andrew
1998   Mass Inhumation and the Execution of Witches in the American Southwest. *American Anthropologist* 100:732–52.

Devine, Heather
1991   The Role of Archaeology in Teaching the Native Past: Ideology or Pedagogy? *Canadian Journal of Native Education* 18(1):11–22.
1994   Archaeology, Prehistory, and the Native Learning Resources Project: Alberta, Canada. In *The Presented Past: Heritage, Museums, and Education,* edited by P. G. Stone and B. L. Molyneaux, pp. 478–94. Routledge, New York.

Dold, Catherine
1998   American Cannibal. *Discover* 19(2):64.

Dongoske, Kurt E.
1996   The Native American Graves Protection and Repatriation Act: A New Beginning, Not the End, for Osteological Analysis—A Hopi Perspective. *American Indian Quarterly* 20:287–96.

Dongoske, Kurt E., Leigh Jenkins, and T. J. Ferguson
1993   Understanding the Past Through Hopi Oral History. *Native Peoples* 6(2):24–31.

Dongoske, Kurt E., Debra Martin, and T. J. Ferguson
2000   Critique of the Claim of Cannibalism at Cowboy Wash. *American Antiquity* 65:179–90.

Dongoske, Kurt E., Michael Yeatts, Roger Anyon, and T. J. Ferguson
1997   Archaeological Cultures and Cultural Affiliation: Hopi and Zuni Perspectives in the American Southwest. *American Antiquity* 62:600–608.

Dorsey, George A.
1903   *Indians of the Southwest.* Passenger Department, Atchison, Topeka & Santa Fe Railroad.

Eggan, Fred
1994   The Hopi Indians, with Special Reference to Their Cosmology or World View. In *Kachinas in the Pueblo World,* edited by P. Schaafsma, pp. 7–21. University of New Mexico Press, Albuquerque.

Ellis, Florence Hawley
1974   The Hopi: Their History and Use of Lands. In *Hopi Indians,* compiled and edited by David A. Horr, pp. 25–278. Garland Press, New York.

Ferguson, T. J.
1996   Native Americans and the Practice of Archaeology. *Annual Reviews* 25:63–79.

Ferguson, T. J., and Kurt Dongoske
1994   *Hopi Ethnographic Overview, Navajo Transmission Project Environmental Impact Statement.* Prepared for Dames & Moore by the Hopi Cultural Preservation Office and Institute of the North American West. Ms. on file, Hopi Cultural Preservation Office, Kykotsmovi, Arizona.

Ferguson, T. J., Kurt Dongoske, Leigh Jenkins, Mike Yeatts, and Eric Polingyouma
1993   Working Together: The Roles of Archaeology and Ethnohistory in Hopi Cultural Preservation. *CRM,* Vol. 16, Special Issue, pp. 27–37.

Ferguson, T. J., Kurt Dongoske, Mike Yeatts, and Leigh Jenkins
1995a   Hopi Oral History and Archaeology, Part I: The Consultation Process. *Society for American Archaeology Bulletin* 13(2):12–15.
1995b   Hopi Oral History and Archaeology, Part II: The Consultation Process. *Society for American Archaeology Bulletin* 13(3):12–15.

Fewkes, J. Walter

1893   A-Wa'-tobi: An Archaeological Verification of a Tusayan Legend. *American Anthropologist* 6:363–75.

1895   Archaeological Expedition to Arizona in 1895. In *Seventeenth Annual Report of the Bureau of American Ethnology*, Part 2. Government Printing Office, Washington, D.C.

1907   Hopi. In *Handbook of American Indians North of Mexico*, Part 1, edited by F. W. Hodge, pp. 560–67. Bureau of American Ethnology, Bulletin 30. Smithsonian Institution, Washington, D.C.

Flinn, Lynn, Christy G. Turner II, and Alan Brew

1976   Additional Evidence for Cannibalism in the Southwest: The Case of LA 4528. *American Antiquity* 41:308–18.

Florio, Gwen

1996   Experts Debate: Did Anasazi Eat Their Own? *The Salt Lake Tribune*, Monday, August 12, 1996. [Internet, http://www.sltrib./96/AUG/12/twr/00010226.htm].

Geertz, Armin W.

1984   A Reed Pierced the Sky: Hopi Indian Cosmography on Third Mesa, Arizona. *Numen* 31:216–41.

Geertz, Armin W., and Michael Lomatuway'ma

1987   *Children of Cottonwood, Piety and Ceremonialism in Hopi Indian Puppetry.* University of Nebraska Press, Lincoln.

Grayson, Donald

1990   Donner Party Deaths: A Demographic Assessment. *Journal of Anthropological Research* 46:223–42.

1993   *The Desert's Past, A Natural History of the Great Basin.* Smithsonian Institution, Washington, D.C.

Haury, Emil W.

1985   *Mogollon Culture in the Forestdale Valley, East-Central Arizona.* The University of Arizona Press, Tucson.

Hays-Gilpin, Kelly

1993   Mortuary Ceramics. In *NAGPRA and Archaeology on Black Mesa, Arizona*, by Kimberly Spurr, pp. 161–70. Navajo Nation Papers in Anthropology Number 30. Navajo Nation Archaeology Department, Window Rock, Arizona.

Hieb, Louis A.

1979   Hopi World View. In *Southwest,* edited by A. Ortiz, pp. 577–80. Handbook of North American Indians, vol. 9, W. G. Sturtevant, general editor. Smithsonian Institution, Washington, D.C.

1994   Hopi Thought and Archaeological Theory: The Sipapu Reconsidered. *American Indian Religions* 1(1):17–36.

James, Harry C.

1974   *Pages from Hopi History.* University of Arizona Press, Tucson.

Kennard, Edward. A.

1937   Hopi Reactions to Death. *American Anthropologist* 39:491–96.

Kohn, Luci Ann P., Steven R. Leigh, and James M. Cheverud

1995   Asymmetric Vault Modification in Hopi Crania. *American Journal of Physical Anthropology* 98:173–95.

Kohn, Luci Ann P., Michael W. Vannier, and James M. Cheverud

1994   Effect of Premature Sagittal Suture Closure on Craniofacial Morphology in a Prehistoric Male Hopi. *The Cleft Palate-Craniofacial Journal* 31:385–96.

Larralde, Signa

1998   The Context of Early Puebloan Violence. In *Deciphering Anasazi Violence*, edited by P. Y. Bullock, pp. 11–33. HRM Books, Santa Fe.

Lockett, Hattie Greene

1933   *The Unwritten Literature of the Hopi.* University of Arizona, Tucson.

Loftin, John D.

1982   *Emergence and Ecology: A Religio-Ecological Interpretation of the Hopi Way.* Ph.D. dissertation, Department of Religion, Duke University.

1986   Supplication and Participation: The Distance and Relation of the Sacred in Hopi Prayer Rites. *Anthropos* 81:177–201.

1991   *Religion and Hopi Life in the Twentieth Century.* Indiana University Press, Bloomington.

Lomawaima, Hartman

1989   Hopification, a Strategy for Cultural Preservation. In *Archaeological and Historical Perspectives on the Spanish Borderlands West, Columbian Consequences*, vol. I, edited by

D. H. Thomas, pp. 93–99. Smithsonian Institution, Washington, D.C.

McGregor, John C.
1943   Burial of an Early American Magician. *Proceedings of the American Philosophical Society* 86:270–98.

McGuire, Randall H.
1992   Archaeology and the First Americans. *American Anthropologist* 94:816–36.

McNitt, Frank
1972   *Navajo Wars, Military Campaigns, Slave Raids, and Reprisals.* University of New Mexico, Albuquerque.

Murdock, George Peter
1934   *Our Primitive Contemporaries.* Macmillan Company, New York.

Nickens, Paul R.
1975   Prehistoric Cannibalism in the Mancos Canyon, Southwestern Colorado. *The Kiva* 40:283–93.

Ogilvie, Marsha D., and Charles E. Hilton
1993   Analysis of Selected Human Skeletal Material from Sites 423–124 and –131. In Human Remains and Burial Goods. In *Across the Colorado Plateau: Anthropological Studies for the Transwestern Pipeline Expansion Project.* Vol. XVIII by Nicholas Hermann, Marsha D. Ogilvie, Charles E. Hilton, and Kenneth L. Brown, pp. 97–128. Office of Contract Archeology, University of New Mexico, Albuquerque.

O'Kane, Walter C.
1953   *The Hopis, Portrait of a Desert People.* University of Oklahoma Press, Norman.

Olson, Alan P.
1966   A Mass Secondary Burial from Northern Arizona. *American Antiquity* 31:822–26.

Page, Susanne, and Jake Page
1982   *Hopi.* Harry N. Abrams, New York.

Parsons, Elsie Clews
1933   Some Aztec and Hopi Parallels. *American Anthropologist* 35:611–13.
1939   *Pueblo Indian Religion,* 2 vols. University of Chicago Press, Chicago.

Powell, Shirley, Peter P. Andrews, Deborah L. Nichols, and F. E. Smiley
1983   Fifteen Years on the Rock: Archaeological Research, Administration, and Compliance on Black Mesa, Arizona. *American Antiquity* 48:228–52.

Quinn, William W.
1983   Something Old, Something True: A Hopi Example of the Need for Cosmology. *South Dakota Review* 21(2):20–55.

Rose, Jerome C., Thomas J. Green, and Victoria D. Green
1996   NAGPRA is Forever: Osteology and the Repatriation of Skeletons. *Annual Review of Anthropology* 25:81–103.

Rushton, Ted
1996   The Anasazi—Were They Cannibals? *Gallup Independent,* May 6, 1996. [Internet, http://www.cia-g.com/~gallpind/cannibal.html].

Schwartz, Douglas W.
1966   A Historical Analysis and Synthesis of Grand Canyon Archaeology. *American Antiquity* 31:469–84.

Spurr, Kimberly
1993   *NAGPRA and Archaeology on Black Mesa, Arizona.* Navajo Nation Papers in Anthropology Number 30. Navajo Nation Archaeology Department, Window Rock, Arizona.

Stephen, A. M.
1894   Letter to Jesse Walter Fewkes dated January 11, 1894. Ms. No. 4408, 2–5, Folder 1894, Fewkes Collection, National Anthropological Archives, Smithsonian Institution, Washington, D.C.
1936   *Hopi Journal,* edited by Elsie Clews Parsons. Columbia Contributions to Anthropology Vol. 23. Columbia University Press, New York.

Stuiver, Minze, and B. Becker
1986   High-precision Decadal Calibration of the Radiocarbon Time Scale, A.D. 1950–2500 B.C., *Radiocarbon* 28:863–910.

Stuiver, Minze, and Paula J. Reimer
1987   *User's Guide to the Programs CALIB & DISPLAY 2.0.* Quaternary Isotope Lab, University of Washington, Seattle.
1993   Extended ^{14}C Data Base and Revised Calib 3.0 ^{14}C Age Calibration Program. *Radiocarbon* 35:215–30.

Thompson, Laura
1945   Logico-Aesthetic Integration in Hopi Culture. *American Anthropologist* 47:540–53.

Titiev, Mischa

1944   *Old Oraibi, A Study of the Hopi Indians of Third Mesa.* Papers of the Peabody Museum of American Archaeology and Ethnology, 22(l), Harvard University, Cambridge.

1958   The Religion of the Hopi Indians. In *Reader in Comparative Religion,* edited by W. A. Lessa and E. Z. Vogt, pp. 532–39. Row, Peterson and Company, Evanston, Illinois. [Originally published 1950 in *Ancient Religions*, edited by V. Ferm. Philosophical Library.]

Trigger, Bruce

1984   Alternative Archaeologies: Nationalist, Colonialist, and Imperialist. *Man* 19:335–70.

Turner, Christy G., II

1989   Teec Nos Pos: More Possible Cannibalism in Northeastern Arizona. *Kiva* 54:147–52.

1993   Cannibalism in Chaco Canyon: The Charnel Pit Excavated in 1926 at Small House Ruin by Frank H. H. Roberts, Jr. *American Journal of Physical Anthropology* 91:421–39.

Turner, Christy G., II, and Nancy T. Morris

1970   A Massacre at Hopi. *American Antiquity* 35:320–31.

Turner, Christy G., II and Jacqueline A. Turner

1990   Perimortem Damage to Human Skeletal Remains from Wupatki National Monument. *Kiva* 55:187–212.

1992a   On Peter Y. Bullock's "A Reappraisal of Anasazi Cannibalism." *Kiva* 58:189–201.

1992b   The First Claim for Cannibalism in the Southwest: Walter Hough's 1901 Discovery at Canyon Butte Ruin 3, Northeastern Arizona. *American Antiquity* 57:661–82.

1995   Cannibalism in the Prehistoric American Southwest: Occurrence, Taphonomy, Explanation, and Suggestions for Standardized World Definition. *Anthropological Science* 103(1):1–22.

1999   *Man Corn, Cannibalism and Violence in the Prehistoric American Southwest.* University of Utah Press, Salt Lake City.

Turner, Christy G., II, Jacqueline A. Turner, and Roger C. Green

1993   Taphonomic Analysis of Anasazi Skeletal Remains from Largo-Gallina Sites in Northwestern New Mexico. *Journal of Anthropological Research* 49:83–110.

Van West, Carla, and Edgar K. Huber

1995   *Data Recovery Plan for Archeological Investigations in the Fence Lake Transportation Corridor—Arizona.* Statistical Research Technical Series 56, vol. 1. Tucson.

Voth, Henry R.

1912   Notes on Modern Burial Customs of the Hopi of Arizona. In *Brief Miscellaneous Hopi Papers II,* Anthropological Series No. 11, Publication 157, pp. 99–103. Field Museum of Natural History, Chicago.

Wallis, Wilson D., and Mischa Titiev

1945   Hopi Notes from Chimopavy. *Papers of the Michigan Academy of Science, Arts, and Letters* 30:523–55.

Watkins, Joe, Lynne Goldstein, Karen Vitelli, and Leigh Jenkins

1995   Accountability: Responsibilities of Archaeologists to Other Interest Groups. In *Ethics in American Archaeology: Challenges for the 1990s,* edited by M. J. Lynott and A. Wylie, pp. 33–37. Society for American Archaeology, Washington, D.C.

White, Tim D.

1992   *Prehistoric Cannibalism at Mancos 5MTUMR-2346.* Princeton University Press, Princeton.

Whiteley, Peter M.

1992   Hopitutungwni: "Hopi Names" as Literature. In *On the Translation of Native American Literatures,* edited by Brian Swann, pp. 208–27. Smithsonian Institution, Washington, D.C.

World Archaeological Congress

1991   World Archaeological Congress First Code of Ethics (Members' Obligations to Indigenous Peoples). *World Archaeological Congress Bulletin* 5:22–23.

Zimmerman, Larry J.

1994   Human Bones as Symbols of Power: Aboriginal American Belief Systems toward Bones and "Grave-robbing Archaeologists." In *Conflict in the Archaeology of Living Traditions*, edited by Robert Layton, pp. 211–16. Routledge, New York.

CHAPTER THREE

Ideologies of Death and Power
in the Hohokam Community of La Ciudad

Randall H. McGuire

THE NATURE OF HOHOKAM SOCIAL ORGANIZATION has always been at the core of debates surrounding the prehistory of southern Arizona. Changing theoretical perspectives have shifted the directions and foci of controversy, but the differences in these orientations can largely be described in terms of the assumptions made about social organization. A continuing thread in the arguments has been disagreement over the nature of power relationships in Hohokam society and the importance of such relationships to our understanding of prehistory. At various times, social organization in the Colonial and Sedentary periods (A.D. 800–1150) has been characterized as egalitarian (Haury 1976), big men (McGuire 1983; Upham and Rice 1980; Wilcox and Shenk 1977), and ranked (Doyel 1980; Wood and McAllister 1980). Even more disagreement surrounds the Classic period (A.D. 1150–1450), as researchers claim social organization was egalitarian (Haury 1976), big men (Doyel 1980), ranked (McGuire 1983; Teague 1984; Wilcox and Shenk 1977) or stratified (McAllister 1976). These studies have based their inferences primarily on examinations of architecture, settlement patterns, and artifacts. Only in the last decade and a half have mortuary analyses figured prominently in such debates (Antieau 1981; Nelson 1981; Teague 1984).

Recent studies of Hohokam society have tended to characterize social organization in terms of an evolutionary category or a single underlying dimension of complexity. In doing so, they reduce an immense amount of both inter- and intrasocietal variability to an imposed unilinear order. Some studies assumed that culture is a functionally integrated system and that the different parts of culture are interconnected. Other studies determined that the nature of one part, for example mortuary ritual, necessarily implied the existence of specific organizations, practices, and relations in other parts, for example social organization, economy, and inequality.

On a methodological level, the studies share a set of assumptions about the relationship of material culture and social organization that allows them to draw inferences from the archaeology of southern Arizona. They assume that the material culture record will provide a direct, but not unambiguous, reflection of the cultural system, as long as the formation processes of the archaeological record are controlled for adequately. Thus, a certain mortuary assemblage corresponds to a given evolutionary stage or level of complexity and should be accompanied by a given range of architectural variability. Because culture is a system, each material cultural category should reflect the evolutionary stage or level of cultural complexity of its culture. This means that architecture, mortuary assemblages, or other material categories can be studied independently, without

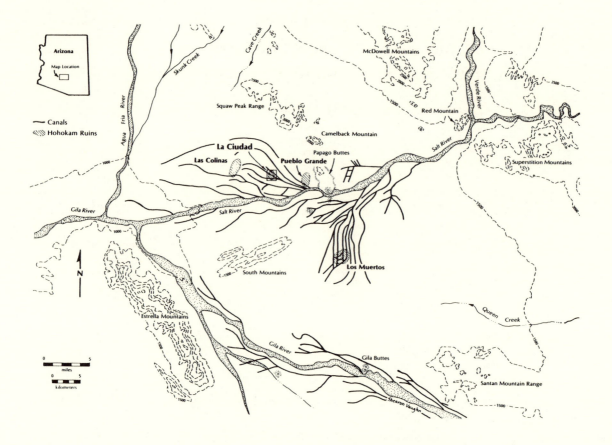

FIGURE 3.1   Map of the Salt River Valley Showing the Location of La Ciudad

reference to their larger context, because each reflects an evolutionary stage or level of complexity.

This general approach to the study of Hohokam social organization has resulted in a welter of competing estimations of evolutionary stages and levels of complexity. Researchers have arrived at these varied opinions not only because they interpret the data differently but also because they have focused on different material categories, and these different categories appear to reflect different stages and levels. For example, during Colonial and Sedentary periods, Hohokam domestic architecture was relatively ephemeral, and there are no clear examples of elite structures that would indicate high levels of inequality (Wilcox and Shenk 1977). Cremations, however, vary greatly in the richness of their grave goods, from burials with hundreds of exotic items to burials with none, suggesting real inequalities (Nelson 1981). The current theoretical and methodological assumptions in

Hohokam archaeology cannot resolve the dilemma caused by these seeming contradictions in the data.

La Ciudad (the city) analyses sought to arrive at a substantive interpretation of the historical processes embodied in the archaeological record of death, society, and ideology in the Hohokam community. I have not attempted to force the data into predetermined evolutionary stages or reduced the richness of Hohokam social relations to a single dimension of complexity. The analyses treat the relationship between social organization and mortuary ritual as an empirical question. The key underlying assumptions are that burial ritual was a manifestation of Hohokam ideology and that it played an active role in the negotiation of power relations in Hohokam society.

This contextual approach requires that the mortuary remains be examined in the larger contexts in which they were embedded to determine how such ritual was active in the negotiation, reproduction, and legitimization of the social order. The key to this methodology is a search for contradictions between different artifact classes, such as burials and architecture and different social contexts such as mundane and ritual. In the processualist analysis, such contradictions are anomalies. In a contextual analysis, they become the keys for understanding prehistoric ideology and social structure.

The conclusions of the Ciudad analyses suggest Hohokam social organization was too intricate to yield to characterizations of evolutionary stages, levels of complexity or simple oppositions between egalitarian and ranked, or achieved and ascribed status. The village of La Ciudad was composed of lineage or extended family groups that occupied discrete clusters of houses with shared courtyards and cemeteries. These groups maintained and enlarged their power and position by recruiting a larger group of kin, followers, and dependents. Only the most powerful of such groups could reproduce the social group beyond the life of a founding couple. The inequalities that existed between groups and between individuals were masked by an egalitarian ideology expressed in day-to-day life. The mortuary rituals within Hohokam society mediated tensions between the egalitarian ideology and the existing inequalities of the social order by revealing and then destroying the material symbols of these inequalities. The analyses leading to these conclusions begin with a consideration of the ethnographic data on cremation and then look at the patterns of burials and houses at the site.

THE SITE OF LA CIUDAD

La Ciudad is one of over 15 major Hohokam sites in the lower Salt River basin (figure 3.1). Observations made before the expansion of Phoenix concealed the site suggest that the site covered an area of approximately a square mile (Turney 1929). The core area, of Classic period age, included a major platform mound, several compounds, numerous trash mounds, a ballcourt, and a series of canals (Wilcox 1987). Agricultural fields, and later urban expansion, obliterated all surface indications of these and other features. Beneath the ground surface, however, remains a record of Hohokam prehistory from the Pioneer period (A.D. 150–1150) to the Classic period.

In 1982 and 1983, Arizona State University conducted excavations in the periphery of La Ciudad. The excavators (Rice 1987) called this particular area the Northern

Resource Zone and divided it into five smaller loci named Brill, Belleview, Moreland, 21st Street and 22nd Street (figure 3.2). The Arizona Department of Transportation and the Federal Highway Administration funded these investigations to mitigate the adverse impacts associated with the construction of the proposed Papago Freeway—Inner Loop of Interstate 10.

The Northern Resource Zone sat along a major prehistoric canal that cut diagonally from the southeast to the northwest across the project area and through each locus. Excavators found very little prehistoric material and no burials to the north of the canal. The prehistoric occupation of the area (constrained by project boundaries) was concentrated in a strip of 100–125 m in width, along the southern bank of the canal. This occupation extended from the Pioneer period to the Sedentary period. There was little or no evidence of Classic period occupation in the project area.

Pithouses, burials, and other features were concentrated within this linear strip in clearly definable village segments with associated cemeteries that corresponded to the loci defined in this analysis (figure 3.3). Two of the loci included entire village segments. The Belleview Locus contained almost all of the largest village segment that included a Gila Butte Phase ballcourt and the largest of the four cemeteries at the site. The Moreland Locus contained an entire village segment and its cemetery. The other three loci contained only portions of village segments. The Ciudad project recorded a total of 2,933 features and subfeatures. These included 205 pithouses, 26 activity surfaces, 17 ovens, 189 trash-filled pits, 1 ballcourt, 2 canal gradients, and 254 burials (McGuire 1992; Rice 1987).

The excavations exposed both cremation and inhumation burials. As is usually the case in Colonial and Sedentary period sites, the vast majority of the burials (229) were cremations. The 25 inhumations accounted for less than 10% of the burial sample.

Six of the cremations were primary cremations where the body had been burned and interred in the same pit. In each of these cases the cremation contained the remains of a single individual.

Secondary cremations made up 88% (226) of the total burial sample. We encountered all three of the general types of secondary cremations identified by Haury (1976:164) for the site of Snaketown: (1) pit depositories of varying sizes and shapes that contained burned bone and offerings, (2) urn cremations where the Hohokam placed the burned bone and occasionally offerings in a

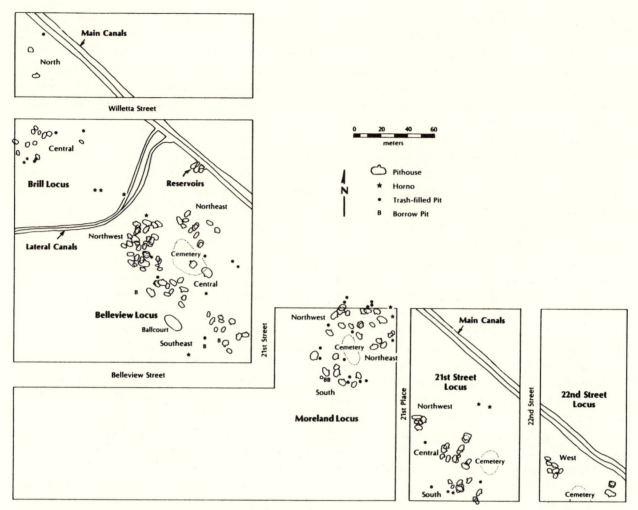

FIGURE 3.2   Map of La Ciudad Showing the Distribution of Features

ceramic vessel and then interred the vessel in a pit, and (3) trench depositories where the Hohokam dug a long trench shaped pit and then placed burned bone and offerings into the trench.

The 25 inhumations exhibited very little regularity, with bodies positioned and oriented in a number of ways. Both male and female remains were recovered: they ranged in age from infants to old adults. None of the inhumations occurred in cremation cemeteries. Excavators found them intermixed in the courtyards and in the fill of the ballcourt. All do appear to date to the occupation of the Northern Resource Zone and are not later Classic period intrusions.

Despite the presence of Pioneer period pithouses in the Northern Resource Zone, all of the datable burials came from the Gila Butte, Santa Cruz, and Sacaton phases. None of the burials contained Pioneer period pottery or other objects distinctively Pioneer in age.

The sample of burials from the Northern Resource Zone of La Ciudad has advantages and disadvantages for making inferences about the nature of Hohokam social organization. The sample of burials is relatively large and complete. The extensive excavations in the Northern Resource Zone exposed a high percentage of the burials that were present at the site. In the case of the Moreland Locus, we have very close to a 100% excavation of a Hohokam village segment. The discussions in this paper will focus on this very well excavated locus. The village segments in the Northern Resource Zone appear very typical of Hohokam village segments elsewhere in the Phoenix

Basin. The Northern Resource Zone, however, lacks rare burial features such as the cremation mounds found at the largest Hohokam sites of Grewe and Snaketown. Our artifact assemblage also lacks the rarest Hohokam mortuary goods such as iron pyrite mirrors and etched shell that show up in the aforementioned large Hohokam towns. My interpretations for the Northern Resource Zone may reflect the general experience of most of the Phoenix Basin Hohokam population, who lived in village segments like Moreland, and communities like the Northern Resource Zone. They do not, however, adequately deal with the most elaborated burial practices found only in the largest towns, nor with the variety of burial practices found throughout the whole geographical range of the Hohokam.

Ethnographic Analogy

Cremation burial occurred commonly among Native American groups in California and western Arizona. In all the ethnographic cases of cremation from western North America, the grave goods destroyed at the cremation rite appeared to reflect the relative status of the deceased (McGuire 1987;1992).[1] From this fact, the formal analogy could be drawn that in cremation burial, a reasonably direct correspondence exists between the status of the dead person and property destroyed in the funeral. To accept such an assumption would be to commit the fallacy of "perfect analogy" (Wylie 1985:94). Just because the funerary practice was similar does not necessarily mean that the relation of the practice to social organization is also similar in each case. The relations that create this association in the ethnographic case should be examined to see if evidence of them can be found in the prehistoric situation.

In both the California and Yuman cremation rites, the funeral is not a simple statement expressing the "social persona" of the individual. It is, instead, intimately involved in the establishment and maintenance of relations between social groups. These groupings tend to correspond to extended families or lineages, and they, not the individual, establish the primary relations of social organization. These groups usually had at their core a married couple and their children but would also include other individuals, usually relatives. In rare cases the groups would be built around a polygynous household. Individuals have no

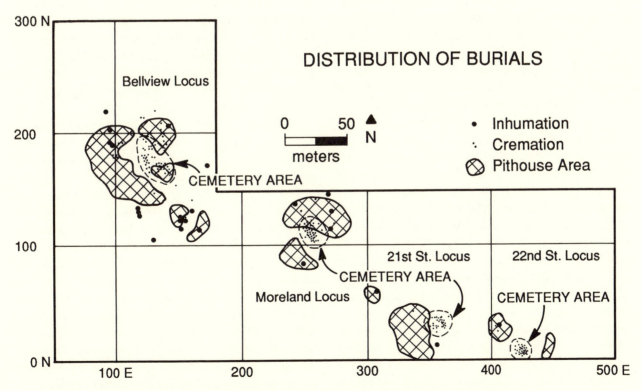

Figure 3.3   Map of La Ciudad Showing the Relationship of Village Segments and Burials

status or social position independent of membership in these groups. The cremation rite is a complex statement about the status of the group, of the individual within that group, and of the relationship of the group with other groups.

The goods that were destroyed in the funerary ritual originated not just from the bereaved household but also from other comparable social groups. Behind the public display, an elaborate accounting was kept of debts being made and debts being paid. Through the presentation and receipt of grave goods, relations between the groups were negotiated. The ritual affirmed the unity and existence of the bereaved social group; at the same time, it recreated the relations of dependency and power that linked the different social groups into a larger social whole.

Yuman extended family groups depended upon a complementary mix of male and female labor to survive. Agricultural activities were shared with men doing most of the field preparation, men and women doing the planting, and women doing the cultivating and harvesting. Other activities were more strongly gender specific. Women wove baskets, made pottery, gathered wild foods, cooked vegetal food, ground grains, and spun thread. Men hunted, fished, cooked animal foods, built structures, and wove cloth. In war, men were primarily responsible for fighting and protecting the village, but women would form a rear rank in battle and use their staves to kill wounded enemies and drive cowardly men back into the line. As long as vacant arable land was available, any couple could put it under cultivation. Labor was the limiting productive resource in Yuman society, and successful extended families were those who could recruit and hold the most productive individuals. Since labor power remained the property of the individual, persons could change residence easily (their labor power being in demand), and marriages were often of short duration with frequent divorce.[2] Young adults enjoyed a special status in these relations because they had adult labor power and could move between the households of a number of kin. A household would try and entice these individuals to stay with the household as long as possible. Once the young adults married and had children, they would seek to establish their own households.

Maintaining an extended family group involved considerable social effort. A family head, usually male, drew followers through a combination of spiritual power and charisma. The woman was expected to bear children, enlist the help of unmarried sisters, and established reciprocal relations of food sharing with other like groups. A woman could become the family head if her husband died, none of her sons were of an adult age, and if she could maintain the family's following. A couple founded a new extended family by building a winter house and attracting kin and others to provide a labor pool to advance the interest of the group. Followers benefited from the leader's ability to negotiate relations with other groups, his control of necessary resources such as the winter house, and his ability to acquire and distribute valued goods. They gained from the woman's ability to organize and direct household work, establish networks of reciprocity that buffered against famine, and from her skill as a basket maker and potter.

Couples advanced their own position only through their ability to form and manipulate a large household; other couples in the household could seek to break off and form their own groups, especially once they had children old enough to make meaningful labor contributions. The reproduction of such groupings was a generational process linked to the life of the founding couple. All couples could seek to establish their own households, but not all achieved it.

Among some California tribes, such as the Pomo, the extended family groups appear to have been ranked, some remaining more powerful across numerous generations (Kroeber 1925). In these situations, the funerary ritual became important in maintaining dominant and subordinate relations within the villages. The presentation of goods for destruction at the ritual reaffirmed the relations of power between groups and guaranteed their continuance.

Among the Yumans, a variety of other adult statuses existed in addition to the family head. Higher level tribal leaders could call upon the family heads to act as a tribal unit in times of war. War leaders in each village could organize raiding parties based on their reputations and charisma. There were some specialists, principally of a ritual nature, such as doctors and funerary specialists. The family/household provided the basic identity and source of power and position for all members of the society.

To evaluate the appropriateness of the Yuman analogy for the Hohokam data, we need to examine the cremation data in its larger context to look for material patterns that correspond to the types of relations we see in the analogy. The fact that there exists considerable diversity and inequality in the grave lots is consistent with the analogy, but not sufficient to accept it.

THE MORELAND LOCUS

Based on the Wilcox et al. (1981) reanalysis of Snaketown, archaeologists have come to recognize that Colonial and Sedentary period Hohokam villages are made up of groups of houses facing a common activity area or residential yard (Henderson 1987). Rice (1987:148–49) has identified an internal structure to these yards with the smallest yard being a single core house and larger yards having a core house and several support houses. He equates these yards with extended family households. These residential yards often are clustered into larger village segments, called cemetery groups, containing several residential yards, hornos, trash areas, and a cemetery (figure 3.3)(Henderson 1987; Howard 1985). Anderson (1986) maintains that the cemeteries contain the dead of the village segment who were probably a lineage group. Rice (1987:147) argues that the early Hohokam village was organized as a nested hierarchy of households, cemetery groups, and ballcourt complexes. This interpretation of Hohokam village organization allows for two to three levels of leadership: residential yard head, village segment head, and village head. No striking domestic architectural distinctions appear to identify these levels of leadership.

At least four village segments, each with its own cemetery, existed at La Ciudad. Of these, the Moreland Locus was the best preserved and most fully excavated. The sample of houses and cremations for this locus is as close to 100% as is possible given currently available excavation techniques (figure 3.4). It therefore provides an excellent location to examine the relationship between cemeteries and architecture at the site.

Henderson (1987) has reconstructed the sequence of residential yards in the Moreland Locus. This discussion summarizes her results; the full report should be consulted for more details and discussions of methods and assumptions.

The Moreland cemetery group was founded by the construction of a single large core house, Feature 1660, at about A.D. 880. This house eventually burned, and the area over it became the location of the crematoria for the Moreland cemetery. The placement of the crematoria over the original house in the village segment and the location of the cemetery near to it may not be coincidental.

In the Middle Colonial period (A.D. 880–960), the Hohokam established the cemetery and two contemporary residential yards, one to the northeast of the cemetery and the other to the south. The early northeast yard

lasted about 50 years and included six houses. The southern yard lasted about 40 years and grew to include four houses, then declined to a single house (Feature 169).

Toward the end of the Middle Colonial period, a single house, Feature 160, was built in the northwest portion of the cemetery group. Feature 160 was the "founding" house for a new yard that developed in the succeeding Late Colonial period (A.D. 960–1000), lasting into the early Sedentary period (A.D. 1000–1100). This yard contained seven houses, not all of which were occupied at the same time.

In the Early Sedentary period, Feature 1056 was built at a right angle to the northwest yard to establish a late northeast yard. This residential yard was occupied until about A.D. 1060 and included up to five houses.

Two contrasting models have been advanced to account for the growth and decline of Hohokam residential yards. Wilcox et al. (1981:166) and Howard (1985:314) argue that yards develop as part of the growth cycle of a domestic group. Doelle et al. (1987) contend that the development of a yard results from the ability of a family head to accumulate wealth and power, both to maintain the cohesion of the group and to attract new members. As Henderson (1987:125–35) demonstrates in her analysis of La Ciudad community patterns, these processes are not incompatible since one necessarily entails the other, and she argues that both appear to have taken place at La Ciudad.

The existing interpretations of Hohokam residential yards suffer from three major limitations. The first of these is a strong androcentric bias such as is seen in many archaeological studies, especially at a household scale of analysis (Brumfiel 1991; Conkey and Gero 1991; Tringham 1991). They tend to interpret courtyard development in terms of the actions of male courtyard heads who found and develop the courtyards to advance their own position and power. Women are not mentioned in these discussions, or their labor is only seen as serving male interests. Change occurs due to the actions of men while women remain passive and unchanging in their activities. My initial attempt at interpreting La Ciudad data made this same mistake (McGuire 1987). Second, this male-centered view interprets prehistory in terms of a modern Capitalist sense of individualism and individual striving for gain. Such individualism is a relatively recent product of the Enlightenment (Foucault 1974; Marx 1906:92). In all ethnographically known Southwestern aboriginal cultures, an individual exists only as a member of a social group, and this membership provided the basic identity and source of position

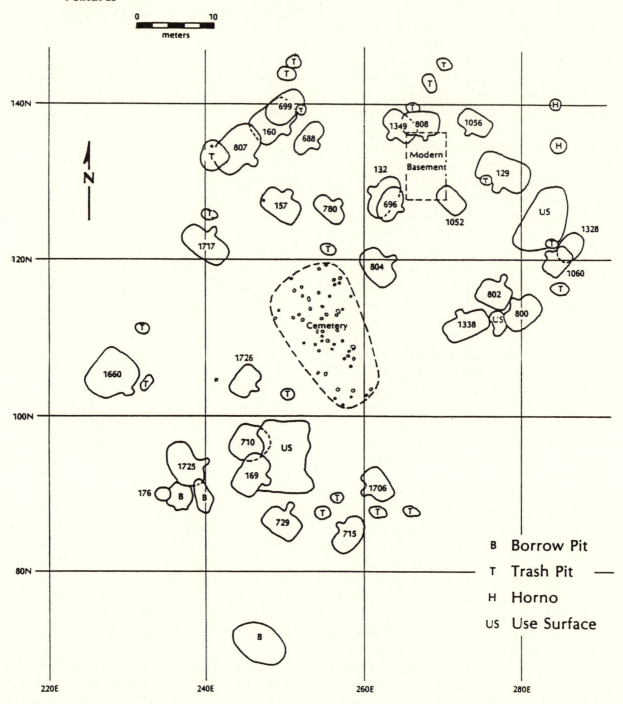

FIGURE 3.4   Map of the Moreland Locus at La Ciudad

for all members of society (Eggan 1983). Finally, they treat household organization as a consequence of changes in material conditions such as population growth, irrigation technology, or exchange, rather than seeing this organization as a dynamic aspect of change affecting other levels of organization.

The full developmental cycle of residential yards at La Ciudad ranges from 30 to 100 years. It seems that some yards lasted for only a generation, while others last several generations. In addition, individual core houses were present at La Ciudad that were not part of yards (six in Moreland). Henderson (1987:135) suggests that the members of these households might not have been able to "garner the support of additional families necessary for further development."

In the ethnographic case of the Yumans, the process by which individuals attempt to establish new extended family households begins with the establishment of a new separate winter house. The growth and success of this new household depends on the fecundity of the founding couple and their ability to attract new members. This process is not always equally successful. Some founding couples are more fertile, effective, and persuasive than others and attract a larger group of kin, followers, and dependents. The increased labor provided by these individuals is both a source and a result of the household's power. Once established, these powerful households could try and maintain the household across generations and reproduce the social group beyond the life of the founders (Forde 1931). The process of residential yard development at La Ciudad fits well with the type of dynamic process of extended family reproduction seen in the Yuman example.

Evidence for productive activities at the site also support the Yuman analogy. Kisselburg's (1987) analysis of such activities at La Ciudad revealed very little evidence for household specialization in production. Each residential cluster produced its own pottery, weaving, lithic tools, and food. Long-distance procurement of items appears to have occurred at the level of the village segment or cemetery group. Some specialization did exist for ceremonial objects with some houses making slate palettes that were used in the cremation ritual and others making the stone or pottery censors that were used with these palettes. The level of household self-sufficiency that Kisselburg infers for La Ciudad would mean that the only effective way for a household to increase its access to goods would be to secure more labor.

The mortuary evidence from La Ciudad is also consistent with the Yuman analogy. In Yuman villages, as at La Ciudad, the people built crematoria and cemeteries associated with distinct social groups. We might also expect that the special statuses of young adults and household heads would be marked in Hohokam cremations.

THE MORTUARY ANALYSES

Of the 254 burials recovered from the Northern Resource Zone, 116 contained associated artifacts. The artifacts in these assemblages appear typical for Colonial and Sedentary period cremations. Archaeologists have noted that during these periods the Hohokam produced a group of ornate goods that appear to have been primarily intended for the burial ritual. Our collection included the most common of these, palettes, censers, and serrated projectile points. The burials also contained common, ordinary, or utilitarian goods such as plainware pottery, stone axes, schist knives, hammer stones, manos, red-on-buff pottery, metates, and polishing stones. The analyses of mortuary goods at La Ciudad used several different statistical techniques and several different organizations of the data to look for relationships between the contents of graves and the gender, age, phase, and location of those individuals buried there (see McGuire 1992 for a detailed presentation of the analyses).

Oblique principal components analysis was used to arrive at a scheme for grouping categories of burial goods in La Ciudad cremations. Only those cremations containing artifacts were used in the analysis. The VARCLUS procedure in the SAS statistical package was employed to perform the analysis. Both Anderberg (1973) and Harman (1976) discuss the technique in detail. The nature of the underlying data distribution is important in these analyses primarily when inferences are drawn from a sample to a population. Even then most data distributions are appropriate for this test as long as they are not excessively skewed, multimodel, or truncated (Harman 1976:25).

The best solution produced by the oblique principal components analysis was a six cluster solution. The six cluster solution accounts for 54% of the variance in the sample. As is consistent with other problems caused by the great variance in the sample, a relatively large proportion of the variance is left unaccounted for (46%) in the six cluster solution.

These clusters occurred in markedly different frequencies. The obvious differences in the distribution of clusters raises the possibility that some of the clusters might covary with other characteristics of the cremations. I used contingency tables and chi-square tests to search for associations between clusters and other characteristics of the cremations (gender, age, phase, and location of the burial). The analysis found no association between gender or locus. It did reveal that cremations in cemeteries had artifacts from significantly more clusters in them than cremations from outside of cemeteries. I also found that Sacaton phase cremations consistently contained artifacts from more clusters than cremations from the earlier two phases.

The only cluster that could have been emblematic of a specific social role or position was Cluster 1. This cluster includes hairpins, turtle shells, and turquoise and occurs principally in adult cremations, in cemeteries, during the Sacaton phase. Only 17% of all the cremations and 26% of the adult cremations were associated with this cluster, so that its distribution is restricted even within these parameters. If the proposition that the cemeteries relate to social groupings is accepted, then it can be assumed that Cluster 1 may have been an important marker of a distinct or limited adult status within the social grouping.

A second analytical exercise looked for inequality in the grave goods between cremations. This required that a value, weight, or rank be assigned to each burial artifact so that the relative position of that cremation vis-à-vis others could be assessed. Using such a ranking, dummy variable regression analyses were performed to assess if differences existed in the mean value of goods per cremation between the groups of cremations defined by previous analyses. Finally, Gini indices were used to identify any differences in the inequality between these groupings.

Analyses that rank artifacts along a single dimension often are seemingly the most successful in finding patterns and relationships in archaeological mortuary studies (O'Shea 1984; Tainter 1978). The ease with which these analyses find patterns results from how the analysis simplifies the data. The weight, rank, or value assigned to burial goods or treatments imposes a uniformity or order on the data. In the past, the scheme used to rank the goods has been primarily derived from theoretical premises, such as the ecological emphasis on energy expenditure in artifacts and the treatment of burials. In evaluating such analyses, we must keep in mind that the simplification inherent in them has obscured more complex relations and that the method used to order the data can determine the outcome.

The ranking used in the Ciudad analysis attempts to link theoretical concerns with empirical clues to assign values to the grave goods. The major theoretical assumption invoked is that those artifacts that were the most easily controlled would be the most valuable. The assumption is not that any characteristics of artifacts make them inherently more valuable but that some characteristics of artifacts make obtaining them more difficult and, therefore, make those artifacts easier to control. The two characteristics chosen were: (1) the origin of the artifact, as determined by either where it was made or the material it was made from and (2) the relative labor investment in producing the artifact. These criteria are based on the assumptions that Hohokam individuals could restrict access to objects coming from outside the Phoenix Basin more easily than objects from inside the basin and that artifacts incorporating more labor in manufacture would be more easily restricted than those incorporating less labor.

Not all artifacts of foreign origin and/or requiring a lot of labor are necessarily of high value. These characteristics only make a high value more likely. A complex set of ideological, social, and historical conditions determine which artifacts will become of high value. For this reason, the context of the artifact also was considered in the ranking. The three social contexts are (1) ordinary, (2) ritual-burial, and (3) ornamental. Each artifact type was assigned to a social context on the basis of its function and distribution in the site. Items of utilitarian function that primarily occurred in secondary refuse deposits on the site were classified as ordinary. Artifacts that occurred primarily in burials were classified as ritual-burial (none of these artifacts turned out to be utilitarian in function). Finally, artifacts that lacked obvious utilitarian functions and are normally classified as jewelry by Hohokam archaeologists were classified as ornamental. Ritual-burial artifacts received the highest value in the ranking, followed by ornamental and then ordinary artifacts.

Each cremation was assigned a Grave Lot Value (GLV) by totaling the ranking of all of the artifacts in the grave lot (McGuire 1992:126–27). The GLV, and the statistics generated from it, are not meant to be interpreted as absolute measures of wealth or inequality in La Ciudad cremations. The values and statistics only have meaning as heuristics for making comparisons between groupings of burials within the site of La Ciudad. The numbers generated can be used in intersite comparisons only if the same ranking scheme is used and if similar contexts exist in the other sites. Rankings based on the frequency of items or energy investment would result in orderings of the burial items that could differ in important ways from that presented here.

The analyses suffer from several limitations. The Hohokam cremated their dead very thoroughly and may even have ground up the cremated bone before burying it. For this reason age and sex characteristics of the bodies were difficult to determine with only 181 bodies assigned to age categories and only 44 to sex categories. Furthermore, only four of the sexed burials were female; therefore, no conclusions could be drawn about relations of grave goods to sex. The Hohokam practice of secondary cremation also means that not all artifacts involved in the burial ritual may have been gleaned from the cremation fires and placed with the bodies. Finally, the types of artifacts placed with the burials were highly diverse.

The age category with the highest GLV and the most diverse collection of artifacts consisted of subadults, aged 10 to 20 years. These cremations were particularly rich in shell ornaments, bracelets, and beads. Subadults were 15 times more likely to be buried with shell beads than adults and five times more likely to be buried with shell bracelets. This age category was clearly marked as having a special status in La Ciudad cemeteries.

What evidence existed in La Ciudad cemeteries for the leaders of extended family or lineage groups? If the leader's status was marked, then the number of cremations so marked should at least roughly correspond with the number of residence yard heads that would have lived in the village segment. Such leaders would presumably be adults and, given their centrality to the social group, buried in the cemetery. A plausible estimate of the number of residence yard heads that should be in the Moreland cemetery can be generated by examining the occupational spans of the yards (table 3.1). If each of the courtyards gained a new leader with each generation, then the number of leaders who should have been buried can be estimated by dividing the occupation span of each yard by 25 years. The sum of the products of this division for each of the four courtyards suggests that 8–10 courtyard heads should lie in the cemetery.

In his discussion of architectural variability at La Ciudad, Rice (1987) defined two types of domestic structures: core houses and support houses. The Hohokam constructed both houses using basically the same materials, techniques, and forms. Core houses were slightly larger and usually had a floor assemblage including evidence of manufacturing activities and a variety of special artifacts such as palettes and censers. Rice (1987) suggests that the core houses were the homes of residence yard leaders and their wives, and support houses were the homes of their dependents. The Moreland Locus contained eight definite and three possible core houses suggesting the number of residence yard heads in the locus should have been between 8 and 11.

Nine cremations in the Moreland Locus held Cluster 1 artifacts (bone hairpins, turquoise, turtle shell). Cluster 1 is not the only cluster to occur in the cemetery at about the right frequency for the number of residence yard heads. Cluster 1 was, however, the only cluster to show associations with adult age and cremations in cemeteries. None of the other clusters were associated with adult age or cremations in cemeteries and therefore appear to be poor candidates for artifacts marking a status as household head.

The key artifact in Cluster 1 was bone hairpins; burials with hairpins tend to be richer than burials without them. A dummy variable analysis on all cremations with grave goods from the site was done to compare the mean GLV for cremations with hairpins to those without. The graves

TABLE 3.1. Occupation Spans of Moreland Courtyards

Courtyard	Dates (A.D.)	Occupation Span (years)	No. of Generations
South	920–969	49	1–2
Early Northeast	910–960	50	2
Northwest	950–1040	90	3–4
Late Northwest	1010–1060	50	2
		TOTAL	8–10

with hairpins had a mean GLV of 46.26, and those without, 17.77 (R^2 = .12, p = .0001, n = 125).[3] This mean also exceeds the mean for the previously discussed subadult cremation category (35.58).

Bone hairpins would have been a very good symbol of residence yard head status. Hairdos would have been highly visible icons of certain meanings, and the hairpins would have reiterated such meanings. The special status of these individuals would have been apparent at a glance to all in the village.

The occurrence of a hairpin with a single female cremation also is consistent with the Yuman analogy, because Yuman women could become household heads upon the death of a husband. At La Ciudad, courtyard heads appear to have been predominantly male but not to the exclusion of females.

Wilcox and Sternberg (1983) have postulated that the Hohokam cremation rite, like the Yuman, was the central religious ritual of the society. Evidence at La Ciudad suggests that the cremation ceremony was a public rite requiring the interaction of different residence yards or clusters for performance. The spatial identification of the ritual with the cemetery group village segment defined a group identity, while the execution of the rite linked different clusters.

The cremation rite itself must have been a public event at La Ciudad, and at other contemporary Hohokam sites (Hood 1985). None of the cemetery groups were walled, and none of the houses blocked the view of the crematorium or cemeteries from all possible sides. The gathering of people for the funeral, the destruction of property, and the secondary burial of the remains would have been visible to individuals not within the spatial boundaries of the cemetery group. The funerary pyre itself would have required a large amount of wood (in order to totally consume the body) and would have put up a plume of smoke during the day or a glow at night visible across the entire community and in nearby communities.

The specialized artifact set that appears in all of the cemeteries at La Ciudad, and in other contemporary Hohokam sites, was not produced in each of the residence yards or cemetery groups (loci). Kisselburg's (1987) analysis of special artifacts from La Ciudad suggests that, at each point in time, residents of only a few yards manufactured projectile points, censers, and palettes. The Moreland cemetery was rich with censers and palettes, but there is little evidence that the residents of this locus ever manufactured these items. The social groups that

occupied the residence yards probably could not have assembled the necessary special items for funerals without getting many or most of them from other comparable groups.

These discussions suggest that a similar set of relations structured the Hohokam and the Yuman funerary rituals. Based on this conclusion, the grave lots in La Ciudad cemeteries did not help to mystify the social order through a process of denial. The statements made by the cremation ritual reflect both on the social group and on the individual's position in that group.

IDEOLOGY

If burial ceremonialism did not mystify the nature of social inequalities among the Hohokam through a denial of those inequalities, it remains to be determined how the funerary ritual was an active force in the reproduction, negotiation, and legitimization of the Hohokam social order. Answering this question requires returning to an examination of the cremations in their social context, and a consideration of how the material culture from the site would have been used in meaningful action in that context.

In the past, it has been assumed that both architecture and burials have the same meaning for the interpretation of inequality in prehistoric contexts (McGuire 1983:124). This assumption is not necessarily valid, and in the case of the Hohokam, it is exceedingly misleading.

Architecture is part of an overall cultural landscape. This landscape includes other human-produced features like canals and hornos, and the human modifications of the environment. The cultural landscape forms the stage for all human action. In the context of daily life, it is part of the mundane and taken for granted. In Giddens's (1984:281) terminology, it is nondiscursive, that is, rarely subject to explicit consideration. As a nondiscursive phenomenon, architecture is crucial to the reproduction of social practice because it provides part of the mundane, everyday, reality that verifies the ideology by fulfilling the expectations of the ideology.

Mortuary ritual is not, except under exceptional circumstances, a mundane, everyday occurrence. As discussed by Huntington and Metcalf (1979:23), death has the potential of having an immense emotional impact on the survivors. The reasons for this are numerous, including the shock of separation from a loved one, the fear of one's own death, anger at the powers that control death, fear of the dead person, and finally, reactions to the corpse itself. Death is the final transition in life's passage, a transition that stresses not only individuals but also the social linkages that create social groups. The position of individuals in these sets of relations determines how intensely and widely the impact of their deaths will be felt, both emotionally and structurally. The diversity of cultural reactions, rituals, and funerary rites in the ethnographic record is immense, but regardless of how frequently it occurs, death is rarely mundane (Huntington and Metcalf 1979).

The funeral and burial of a Hohokam person was not the stuff of everyday experience but a single, limited, culturally meaningful statement. Once the ceremony was complete and the grave goods had been deposited in the ground, they were no longer visible and could not be used in a meaningful way in the society, except through the memory of people. Hohokam cemeteries may have been marked, but the types of markers (large sherds, small mounds of earth, and inverted ceramic vessels) suggest but do not reveal the magnitude or nature of the grave goods contained in the grave.

The funeral ritual would have linked the living and the dead in a purposeful, discursive way. We can speculate from the data available, and the Yuman analogy, that the richest funerals would have been great spectacles, with a large pyre, flames and smoke, and the display of wealth to be destroyed in the ceremony. Songs and oratory would have filled the air. The ceremony would have explicitly called upon the participants to examine the social relations that brought them together and were being recreated in the process.

The architecture of Colonial and Sedentary Hohokam sites does not overtly pronounce the inequality within and between the households that composed the society. All of the houses were constructed of similar materials, had similar functions, were relatively impermanent, and varied primarily in size. The Hohokam village resembles what Wilk (1983) has called a closed village economy, in which inequality finds expression through portable objects, not architecture.

Wilcox and Sternberg (1983) have identified some possible specialized storage houses that they think were associated with more powerful courtyard groups at Snaketown. These houses, however, differed from other houses primarily in their internal structure and would not have been ostentatious statements of wealth and power. No such structures were identified at La Ciudad.

Wilcox et al. (1981) identified a set of Sacaton houses at

Snaketown inside the circle of mounds as special residences. In a large village, with a major ceremonial precinct, the positioning of houses could well indicate status differences. In the Snaketown example, the household clusters in the inner ring included the possible specialized storage structures but again in outward appearance would not have been greatly different than other houses in the community.

The distinction between core and support houses certainly would have been obvious to the site's inhabitants (Rice 1987). However, each of the loci at La Ciudad had both house types, and no conspicuous architectural distinctions would have existed between courtyard groups.

The inequality apparent in the grave lots greatly exceeds the same among the pithouses. A Gini index calculated for the variation in floor area among all the pithouses in the site (data from Henderson 1987: figure 3.4) has a value of .10.[4] This value is substantially less than the Gini index for the GLVs from all cremations on the site (.74).

The public architecture on Hohokam sites, such as the ballcourt at La Ciudad, is quite impressive when compared to the pithouses. These public structures, mounds and ballcourts, were not associated with specific courtyard groups. Some courtyards would be closer to or farther from the public structures, but none were situated in such a way as to indicate a proprietary control of these edifices. Most Hohokam archaeologists interpret these structures as stages for ritual performances and/or games (Wilcox and Sternberg 1983).

The day-to-day message conveyed by architecture on Colonial and Sedentary period Hohokam sites denied the existence of inequalities in the social order. The architecture reinforced an image of variance by degree that was linked to generational development. The lasting public architecture of the site was spatially associated with no particular social group, producing an impression of institutions shared by, and for the benefit of, all people.

The mundane, day-to-day world of the Colonial and Sedentary period Hohokam reinforced an ideology that denied inequality in the social order. I agree with Wilcox and Sternberg (1983) that an egalitarian ethos governed the everyday lives of the Hohokam in these periods. Their position acknowledges that this egalitarian ideology masked the existing inequalities in the social order.

I would suggest that the egalitarian ideology of everyday life was reproduced and legitimated in a seemingly contradictory mortuary ritual. In the mortuary display at La Ciudad, the inequalities within courtyard groups were expressed, possibly even exaggerated. On average, the richest burials were those of residence yard heads who appeared to have achieved their status in their lifetime. The richest burials, however, included subadults too young to have achieved much status; subadults, on average, had richer grave lots than juveniles or adults. The mortuary data suggest that forces archaeologists would traditionally assign to both achieved and ascribed status determined the distribution and inequality of grave lots.

The cremation ritual would have resolved the crises to the social order caused by death. The more important or extensive the dead individual's relationship to the household and the household's relationships with other households, the greater the social crises caused by the individual's death. The death of an infant would have stressed the social structure less than the death of a prominent resident yard head, and the death of an elderly person less than a subadult. In the cremation rite, the property that the deceased could call upon within his/her group or through obligations and relations with other groups would be assembled and then destroyed. The inequalities in the social order were ritually revealed in the assemblage of items. Then the destruction of the items would deny the permanence of such inequalities and seemingly limit accumulation across generations.

If the analogy to the Yuman and California cremation complexes is appropriate, this also was a process of social negotiation within and between social groups. The giving of goods for the funeral was involved in a complex system of accounting, debts being paid, and debts being made. When the head of a residence yard died, both succession to the leadership role and the relative standing of different yards would be in question. The bereaved social group could be reduced in position, or possibly even destroyed, by the imposition of debts it could not hope to repay, or internal conflicts it could not resolve.

In the end, the Hohokam gathered up the few remaining fragments of bone and the broken artifacts, placing them in the ground. Even if a surface marker were left, the wealth of the funeral was confined to memory and the possible memorial ceremony. In the mortuary ritual, tensions between the egalitarian ideology of the Hohokam and the existing inequalities in the social order would be revealed and then mediated. The egalitarian ideology is affirmed, and the social order is reproduced and legitimated.

POSTSCRIPT

I originally completed the analyses of La Ciudad burials in 1987 (McGuire 1987), and I subsequently revised the interpretations while preparing *Death, Society, and Ideology in a Hohokam Community* (McGuire 1992). Since 1992, at least four reviews have appeared of *Death, Society, and Ideology in a Hohokam Community* (Doyel 1993; Fish 1994; Powell 1993; Riley 1993). The study has also been cited and used in a number of subsequent analyses of Hohokam mortuary assemblages (e.g., Marmaduke and Schroeder 1993; Mitchell 1994). The various reviews and comments on the study have not led me to substantially alter my original interpretations, but this summary of the study seems like an appropriate place to reflect upon my own reservations about the study and upon the various commentaries on it.

In many ways, this analysis was the most difficult and frustrating that I have ever done. I had never before had to work so hard to find patterning in an archaeological data set. The lack of information due to the practice of cremation and the striking diversity of objects in the burials greatly hampered my attempts to find patterning in the data. This led me to an exhaustive statistical analysis that as Powell (1993) aptly points out produced lots of tables and numbers, and not a lot of results.

My use of the GLV measure stemmed, in large part, from my frustration with my other attempts to find patterns in the data. The immense variation in number and types of grave goods resisted my attempts to categorize and organize them. But, when I reduced this variation to a single quantity, the GLV, the data fell neatly into order; an order that I could regress, address, and explain. In the simplicity of this order lies a potential methodological delusion. Simply stated, if we reduce a complex phenomena to a single quantity, we will always succeed in our analysis, we will always be able to order burials. We may well delude ourselves by assuming that the ordering reflects a reality, rather than merely being a product of the method that we used to reduce the phenomena to a quantity.

To my mind, the GLV is the weakest aspect of the Ciudad mortuary study. I have, therefore, been somewhat surprised that, with the notable exception of Doyel (1993), the reviewers have not commented on the limits of the method or the particulars of my measure. A number of researchers in southern Arizona have used the GLV as a model for their own analyses. I am sure that they have done so out of the same type of frustration that motivated me to use it. I would, however, hope that future research will be more critical of this approach and methodologically more creative.

At least two commentators (Fish 1994; Marmaduke and Schroeder 1993) have faulted the Ciudad study for failing to consider alternative interpretations to the one that is presented. This comment presumes that the study has positivist goals, that is, to arrive at an interpretation that is the truest, most correct, or most objective. This is not a positivist study. I would make no claim that the conclusions that I have reached are the best, truest, or most correct. I do believe that the interpretation presented here still fits the data we have on Phoenix Basin Hohokam cremation, but there certainly must be a large number of other, alternative, interpretations that would fit this data.

My goal was to incorporate all of the disparate archaeological evidence into a comprehensive interpretive framework. Like all archaeological interpretations, this framework is a complex construction from the data, a set of methods, a theoretical perspective, and my own experience. It will cease to be a productive framework as the limitations in all these things are realized both by my critics and myself. This framework will be productive as long as it allow us to ask interesting questions about Hohokam prehistory and as long as it sparks empirical, methodological, and theoretical debate that will further our knowledge of that prehistory.

NOTES

1. The ethnographic sources from which this summary is constructed are Forde (1931), Spier (1933), Castetter and Bell (1951), Kroeber (1925), and Kelley (1977). These sources are extensively discussed in McGuire (1987, 1992). Readers interested in a more detailed consideration of the sources should consult one of these monographs.

2. Some readers may object to my use of a Yuman analogy because they feel that the O'odham are the descendants of the Hohokam. The gender and family relations described in this paragraph were, however, similar among the O'odham, and indeed among most lower Southwestern cultural groups (McGuire 1991; Russell 1975; Underhill 1939). Furthermore, I would argue that the Hohokam of the Phoenix Basin (but not necessarily the Hohokam of other areas in southern Arizona) were Yumans, but that is another paper.

3. Executing a dummy variable analysis on the presence or absence of Cluster 1 is problematical because individ-

ual cremations could include more than one cluster, violating the assumption of independence of cases. The mean value for cremations containing Cluster 1 artifacts was 43.62.

4. In an earlier article (McGuire 1983), I report Gini indices for the Colonial and Sedentary periods considerably higher than .10. The higher indices result from the inclusion of public architecture in the earlier calculations. This lumping of domestic and ritual architecture obscures the processes and relationships which the present study seeks to discover.

REFERENCES CITED

Anderberg, M. R.
1973   *Cluster Analysis for Applications.* Academic Press, New York.
Anderson, Keith M.
1986   Hohokam Cemeteries as Elements of Settlement Structure and Change. In *Anthropology of the Desert West*, edited by C. J. Condie and D. D. Fowler, pp. 180–201. University of Utah Anthropological Papers 110. Provo.
Antieau, John M.
1981   *The Palo Verde Archaeological Investigations Hohokam Settlement at the Confluence: Excavations along the Palo Verde Pipeline.* Museum of Northern Arizona Research Paper 20. Museum of Northern Arizona, Flagstaff.
Brumfiel, Elizabeth M.
1991   Weaving and Cooking: Women's Production in Aztec Mexico. In *Engendering Archaeology*, edited by J. Gero and M. Conkey, pp. 224–54. Basil Blackwell, Oxford.
Castetter, Edward F., and Willis H. Bell
1951   *Yuman Indian Agriculture: Primitive Subsistence on the Lower Colorado and Gila Rivers.* University of New Mexico Press, Albuquerque.
Conkey, Margaret, and Joan Gero
1991   Tensions, Pluralities, and Engendering Archaeology: An Introduction to Women and Prehistory. In *Engendering Archaeology*, edited by J. Gero and M. Conkey, pp. 3–30. Basil Blackwell, Oxford.
Doelle, William H., Frederick W. Huntington, and Henry D. Wallace
1987   Rincon Phase Reorganization in the Tucson Basin. In *The Hohokam Village: Site Structure*

and Organization, edited by D. E. Doyel, pp. 71–96. Southwestern and Rocky Mountain Division of the American Association for the Advancement of Sciences, Glenwood Springs, Colorado.

Doyel, David E.
1980   Hohokam Social Organization and the Sedentary to Classic Transition. In *Current Issues in Hohokam Prehistory*, edited by D. E. Doyel and F. Plog, pp. 23–40, Anthropological Research Papers 23. Arizona State University, Tempe.
1993   Review of Death, Society, and Ideology in a Hohokam Community. *American Anthropologist* 95:1016–17.

Eggan, Fred
1983   Comparative Social Organization. In *Southwest*, edited by A. Ortiz, pp. 723–42. Handbook of North American Indians, vol. 10, W. G. Sturtevant, general editor. Smithsonian Institution, Washington, D.C.

Fish, Suzanne K.
1994   Review of Death, Society, and Ideology in a Hohokam Community. *American Antiquity* 59:787–88.

Forde, C. Daryll
1931   *Ethnography of the Yuma Indians.* Publications in American Archaeology and Ethnology 28. University of California, Berkeley.

Foucault, Michel
1974   *The Order of Things.* Tavistock, London.

Giddens, Anthony
1984   *The Constitution of Society.* Polity Press, Cambridge.

Harman, H. H.
1976   *Modern Factor Analysis.* University of Chicago Press, Chicago.

Haury, Emil W.
1976   *The Hohokam: Desert Farmers and Craftsmen: Excavations at Snaketown 1964–1965.* University of Arizona Press, Tucson.

Henderson, T. Kathleen
1987   *Structure and Organization at La Ciudad.* Anthropological Field Studies No.18. Arizona State University, Tempe.

Hood, J. Edward
1985   *Hohokam Burial Practices: A Contextual Approach.* B.A. honors thesis, Department of Anthropology, State University of New York at Binghamton.

Howard, Jerry B.
1985   Courtyard Groups and Domestic Cycling: A Hypothetical Model of Growth. In *Proceedings of the 1983 Hohokam Symposium Part 1*, edited by A. E. Dittert Jr. and D. E. Dove, pp. 311–26. Occasional Paper 2. Arizona Archaeological Society, Phoenix.

Huntington, Richard, and Peter Metcalf
1979   *Celebrations of Death: The Anthropology of Mortuary Ritual.* Cambridge University Press, Cambridge.

Kelley, William H.
1977   *Cocopa Ethnography.* Anthropological Papers of the University of Arizona 29. Tucson.

Kisselburg, Jo Ann
1987   The Economy of Community Systems at La Ciudad. In *The Hohokam Community of La Ciudad*, edited by G. E. Rice, pp. 173–84. Office of Cultural Resource Management Report 67. Arizona State University, Tempe.

Kroeber, Alfred L.
1925   *Handbook of the Indians of California.* Bureau of American Ethnology Bulletin 78. Washington, D.C.

Marmaduke, William S., and K. J. Schroeder
1993   Mortuary Practices at Shelltown and the Hind Site. In *Shelltown and the Hind Site*, edited by W. S. Marmaduke, and R. J. Martynec, pp. 144–170. Northland Research Inc., Flagstaff.

Marx, Karl
1906   *Capital: A Critique of Political Economy.* The Modern Library, New York.

McAllister, Martin
1976   *Hohokam Social Organization: A Reconstruction.* Master's thesis, Department of Anthropology, San Diego State University, San Diego.

McGuire, Randall H.
1983   Breaking Down Cultural Complexity: Inequality and Heterogeneity. *Advances in Archaeological Method and Theory*, vol. 6, edited by M. B. Schiffer, pp. 91–142. Academic Press, New York.
1987   *Death, Society, and Ideology in a Hohokam Community: Colonial and Sedentary Period Burials from La Ciudad.* Office of Cultural Resource Management Report 67. Arizona State University, Tempe.
1991   From the Outside Looking In: The Concept of Periphery in Hohokam Archaeology. In *Exploring the Hohokam: Prehistoric Desert*

Peoples of the American Southwest, edited by G. J. Gumerman, pp. 347–82. University of New Mexico Press, Albuquerque.

1992 *Death, Society, and Ideology in a Hohokam Community.* Westview Press, Boulder.

Mitchell, Douglas R. (editor)
1994 *The Pueblo Grande Project, Volume 7: An Analysis of Classic Period Mortuary Patterns.* Soil Systems Publications in Archaeology No. 20. Soil Systems, Phoenix.

Nelson, Richard S.
1981 *The Role of a Puchteca System in Hohokam Exchange.* Ph.D. dissertation, Department of Anthropology, New York University, New York.

O'Shea, John M.
1984 *Mortuary Variability: An Archaeological Investigation.* Academic Press, Orlando.

Powell, Shirley
1993 Review of *Death, Society, and Ideology in a Hohokam Community. American Indian Culture and Research Journal* 17(3):202–5.

Rice, Glen E.
1987 *A Spatial Analysis of the Hohokam Community of La Ciudad,* with contributions by T. K. Henderson. Anthropological Field Studies 16. Arizona State University, Tempe.

Riley, Carroll L.
1993 Review of *Death, Society, and Ideology in a Hohokam Community. American Indian Quarterly* 17:211.

Russell, Frank
1975 *The Pima Indians.* The University of Arizona Press, Tucson. (Originally published 1908 in *Twenty-sixth Annual Report of the Bureau of American Ethnology, 1904–1905,* pp.3–389. Smithsonian Institution, Washington, D.C.)

Spier, Leslie
1933 *The Yuman Tribes of the Gila River.* University of Chicago Press, Chicago.

Tainter, Joseph A.
1978 Mortuary Practices and the Study of Prehistoric Social Systems. In *Advances in Archaeological Method and Theory,* vol. 1, edited by M. B. Schiffer, pp. 105–41. Academic Press, New York.

Teague, Lynn S.
1984 Role and Ritual in Hohokam Society. In *Hohokam Archaeology along the Salt Gila Aqueduct, Central Arizona Project,* vol. IX:

Synthesis and Conclusions, edited by L. S. Teague and P. L. Crown, pp. 155–85. Arizona State Museum Archaeological Series No. 150. Tucson.

Tringham, Ruth E.
1991 Households with Faces: The Challenge of Gender in Prehistoric Architectural Remains. In *Engendering Archaeology,* edited by J. Gero and M. Conkey, pp. 93–131. Basil Blackwell, Oxford.

Turney, Omar A.
1929 Prehistoric Irrigation. *Arizona Historical Review* 2(2):11–52. Phoenix.

Underhill, Ruth
1939 *Social Organization of the Papago Indians.* Columbia University Contributions to Anthropology 30. Columbia University, New York.

Upham, Steadman, and Glen Rice
1980 Up the Canal without a Pattern: Modelling Hohokam Interaction and Exchange. In *Current Issues in Hohokam Prehistory,* edited by D. E. Doyel and F. Plog, pp. 78–105. Anthropological Research Papers 23. Arizona State University, Tempe.

Wilcox, David R.
1987 *Frank Midvale's Investigation of the Site of La Ciudad.* Anthropological Field Studies 19. Arizona State University, Tempe.

Wilcox, David R., Thomas R. McGuire, and Charles Sternberg
1981 *Snaketown Revisited.* Arizona State Museum Archaeological Series 155. Arizona State Museum, Tucson.

Wilcox, David R., and Lynette O. Shenk
1977 *The Architecture of the Casa Grande and Its Interpretation.* Arizona State Museum Archaeological Series 115. Arizona State Museum, Tucson.

Wilcox, David R., and Charles Sternberg
1983 *Hohokam Ballcourts and Their Interpretation.* Arizona State Museum Archaeological Series 160. Arizona State Museum, Tucson.

Wilk, Richard R.
1983 Little House in the Jungle: The Causes of Variation in House Size Among the Modern Kekchi Maya. *Journal of Anthropological Archaeology* 2:99–116.

Wood, J. Scott, and Martin E. McAllister

1980   Foundation and Empire: The Colonization of the Northeastern Hohokam Periphery. In *Current Issues in Hohokam Prehistory*, edited by D. E. Doyel and F. Plog, pp. 180–200. Anthropological Research Papers 23. Arizona State University, Tempe.

Wylie, Allison

1985   The Reaction Against Analogy. In *Advances in Archaeological Method and Theory*, vol. 8, edited by M. B. Schiffer, pp. 63–112. Academic Press, New York.

CHAPTER FOUR

An Evaluation of Classic Period Hohokam Burials and Society: Chiefs, Priests, or Acephalous Complexity?

Douglas R. Mitchell and Judy L. Brunson-Hadley

INTRODUCTION

THE HOHOKAM OF SOUTHERN ARIZONA ARE WELL known for their extensive irrigation canal systems that allowed them to tame the desert for centuries. Archaeologists have speculated at length on the type of social hierarchy that was present in order for the Hohokam to control these complex irrigation systems and to maintain their far-flung trade networks. Recent excavations at a number of prehistoric village cemeteries in the Phoenix metropolitan area in southern Arizona, together with archival materials from the 1880s Hemenway expedition, provide important data for reconstructing the social structure of Classic period Hohokam society. Data from hundreds of burials recovered from the sites of Pueblo Grande, Los Muertos, Grand Canal Ruins, Casa Buena, and Pueblo Salado are considered in this chapter to provide insight into the lifestyles and social organization of the Hohokam (figure 4.1).

In this chapter, we evaluate Hohokam mortuary data in relation to two models of social development that can be used to explain the level of complexity attained by the Hohokam during the Classic period. One model considers a regional Hohokam system based on kinship and lineage systems where a few lineages held more power and economic control than others. A second model consid-

ers a Hohokam society that was based on a group of leaders who held important religious positions. Analysis of the existing mortuary data leads us to conclude that aspects of both models were probably operative within the Classic period Hohokam culture.

HOHOKAM CULTURE, SOCIAL ORGANIZATION, AND SOCIETY

Hohokam society was a powerful force in the American Southwest, and it was intimately involved in the movement of a variety of goods and agricultural produce among many of the different ethnic groups of the Southwest. Different trade networks for select pottery types (Abbott 1994), shells, foods, and cotton textiles helped sustain local alliances and regional networks (Doyel 1979). In one of their primary population centers, the lower Salt River Valley in southern Arizona, the Hohokam constructed an intricate network of irrigation canals that allowed them to produce vast amounts of agricultural produce for local use and trade. The Hohokam sustained a near millennium long development in the southern deserts of Arizona (Haury 1976). This chapter focuses on events and processes that occurred during the Classic period (A.D. 1150–1450). This period includes the

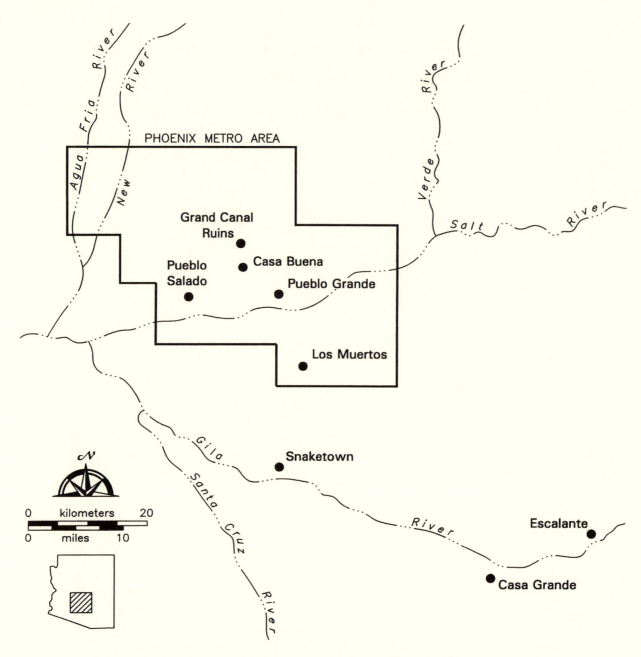

FIGURE 4.1   Map of Southern Arizona Showing Major Hohokam Villages Discussed in This Chapter

Soho phase (A.D. 1150–1300) and the Civano phase (A.D. 1300–1450).

There is little question that the Hohokam were organizationally complex as evidenced by the irrigation canals, settlement hierarchies, and their regional exchange systems. Settlements included small and large villages, villages with public architecture (ballcourts in the earlier periods, apparently replaced by platform mounds in the later periods), and a variety of specialized site types distributed over the landscape. The largest villages also had great houses or towers, in addition to ballcourts and mounds (Fish 1989; Wilcox 1991).

In the Salt River Valley, settlement organization included multiple "irrigation communities," each com-

MITCHELL AND BRUNSON-HADLEY / 47

munity consisting of a group of villages that were located on a network of canals that shared a common intake point from the Salt River (Howard 1987). Villages differed by population size and location; however, the villages with platform mounds appear to have been strategically placed approximately 4.8 km (3 mi) apart (Gregory 1991). Within the larger villages, a standardized pattern also appears for the placement of the homes and other features in relationship to the platform mound and central plazas (Wilcox et al. 1981).

Differentiation and Mortuary Theory

Understanding the nature of the social political organization that best represents Classic period Hohokam society has received a great deal of attention in recent years. Many initial studies utilized information from settlement patterns and trade networks to postulate community hierarchies and networks (Doyel 1981; Upham and Rice 1980; Wilcox 1991; Wilcox and Shenk 1977). More recently, however, these studies have been broadened to include mortuary assemblages as another component in the evaluation of social political organization. This inclusion of mortuary studies is due, in large part, to the excavation of several Hohokam cemeteries in the 1980s and a reanalysis of an assemblage excavated over 100 years ago.

Mortuary studies remain a primary source of information for learning about the populations of the past and how they interacted. Numerous discussions have revolved around the format that a mortuary analysis should take in order to delineate social complexity within a society (e.g., Binford 1971; Goldstein 1976; O'Shea 1984; Saxe 1970; Tainter 1978). The basic assumption for such studies is that a person's burial treatment is a reflection of both his/her personal and social roles. It is quite probable that not all roles can be found through mortuary studies, since some roles may not have had physical representations and some burial goods would not be recoverable through time. Nonetheless, it seems clear that many roles and interactions can be identified through mortuary analyses, as long as a minimal set of data is considered.

Obviously the actual physical remains of the body and accompanying grave goods must be studied, but other factors also must be evaluated. Numerous studies have discussed the importance of evaluating the amount of energy expended during the burial process, the mode of interment, and the location of the burial. Goldstein (1980, 1981) has shown that by identifying discrete ceme-

teries, the social structure of a group can be studied. In addition, she has argued that discrete cemeteries may represent corporate groups that were organized by lineal descent.

In this and other recent studies, we have focused on the concepts of horizontal and vertical differentiation. Elsewhere, we have discussed methods that can be used for identifying horizontal and vertical differentiation within Hohokam society (e.g., Brunson 1989; Mitchell 1994b). Briefly, inequality is assumed to exist in some form in every society since every group has a means to evaluate values and beliefs. Even natural differences of sex, age, and ethnic differences become symbols of inequality at some level. Berreman (1981) has suggested that it is the kind and degree of these evaluations that creates the differential forms of inequality present among different societies.

Various authors have discussed levels of inequality within cultural groups, the factors that create them, and their impact within the social organization of the society (Blanton et al. 1981; Blau 1977; McGuire 1983). For this study, we are assuming that functional differentiation, how each group or person within the society interacts with the others, provides a means of defining the social complexity of a society. That complexity can be defined through the identification of horizontal and vertical differentiation within the society.

Horizontal differentiation is represented by categories whose differences are often considered "non-ranked." Categories of sex, occupation, clan membership, or kin roles can usually be considered representative of horizontal differentiation. In contrast, vertical differentiation represents inequality within categories, where subordination is important and there is a differential access to goods and resources. In terms of rank, horizontal differentiation refers to equivalent ranks within the society, and vertical differentiation refers to social distances, or even stratification, between the ranks.

Hohokam Platform Mounds

Social organizational studies of prehistoric societies must draw on numerous lines of information to learn about the cultures. Studies of platform mounds have shown that these architectural features had distinctive importance among the communities, thereby providing evidence of some level of differentiation. Howard (1992) identified a standardization to their use of space and that many parts of the mound had restricted areas that curtailed public use.

Originally thought of as the private residences of elite individuals, recent arguments have been directed toward an interpretation, first proposed by Cushing (1892), that the mounds had a ceremonial function and the individuals associated with them had religious or ceremonial responsibilities (see Bostwick 1992; Bostwick and Downum 1994; Brunson 1989; Howard 1992; Wilcox 1991).

While it seems clear that the platform mounds had ceremonial importance, that function did not preclude certain individuals from residing on the mound. In fact, the individuals probably had distinctive roles associated with the ceremonial activities. Some roles may have been administrative such as keeping track of material goods, and other roles may have resulted from spousal responsibilities such as cooking, weaving, and cleaning as a support function to those individuals responsible for the ceremonies associated with the platform mound (Crown and Fish 1996).

The enclosure of specific groups by compound walls and the restricted access to some areas argues for some form of differentiation within the society. The presence of platform mounds, their ceremonial importance, and the fact that they occur only at certain large villages also argues for hierarchical differentiation in the culture. Another major source of information for looking at complex social structures is burial studies. For the Hohokam culture, a number of recent mortuary studies have been undertaken to learn if differentiation within specific village communities existed (see Brunson 1989; Brunson-Hadley 1994a, 1994b; Effland 1988; McGuire 1987; Mitchell 1991, 1994a, 1994b; Wilcox 1987).

Hohokam Society

Working with separate data sets from different villages, we independently identified similar levels of differentiation within Classic period Hohokam burial populations. As others (Goldstein 1976, 1981; O'Shea 1984; Saxe 1970) have observed, horizontal differentiation can be identified by discrete cemeteries. Among the Hohokam village sites of the Salt River Valley, cemeteries were identified within which certain types of burial accompaniments could be expected, together with a somewhat standard burial architecture and placement of the body. Many of the cemeteries have distinct boundaries and can often be associated with specific compounds (Brunson 1989; Cushing 1890; Mitchell 1994a).

During the Hohokam pre-Classic era, cremation was the preferred type of burial. However, during the Sed-

entary to Classic period transition, an inhumation style of burial become prevalent and remained throughout the Classic period. During the Classic period, both inhumation and cremation were practiced. Although some differences are present, many of the same burial accompaniments are present with both burial styles, albeit in differing frequencies. In addition, while the inhumation and cremation cemeteries often are spatially distinct within the same village, cemeteries where both styles of burials are present do occur (Mitchell 1991). The fact that the two methods of burial occurred concomitantly provides evidence that some form of differentiation within the culture occurred. Cushing (1890) theorized that the two burial styles reflected the differences between the priestly groups (represented by inhumation burials) and the remainder of the population (represented by cremation burials). Brunson (1989) has discussed a variety of other scenarios, including the proposal (originally proposed by Gladwin et al. [1937] and Haury [1945]) that inmigrating groups brought with them a different religious belief system. Physical anthropological studies also indicate that the results of the Hohokam affinity studies do not always parallel the popular archaeological theories. Affinity issues may be more complex than some archaeological theories would suggest (cf. Matthews et al. 1893; Miller 1981; Turner and Irish 1989). Unless modern genetic tests are completed on human remains, it is unlikely that ethnicity questions concerning the affinitive relationships of the inhumed and cremated burial populations can be positively answered.

Horizontal differentiation can be identified within the burial sets, especially based on age and gender. Distinct cemeteries with similar burial styles and accompaniments also argue for the identification of extended families and kin groups. Most differences in the burial data sets can be explained by horizontal differentiation; however, vertical differentiation is clearly present to some degree at each site. Certain individuals could be identified on the basis of the numbers or distinctiveness of their burial accompaniments, the location of the burials, and sometimes, the energy expenditure and location of the burial pit. Specialized burial accompaniments could be used to identify individuals with specific roles within the society (i.e., potters, weavers, stone tool makers, as well as spiritual or possibly shamanistic roles) (see Mitchell 1994b). While similar vertical differentiation is present at the sites, differences still occur among villages in the mortuary status of people buried on the platform mound.

THE HOHOKAM VILLAGE SITES

Five sites were examined for this study: Grand Canal Ruins, Casa Buena, Pueblo Grande, Los Muertos, and Pueblo Salado. Grand Canal Ruins and Casa Buena are located on the same canal system on the north side of the Salt River. Pueblo Grande is located at the headgates of the canal system that includes Grand Canal and Casa Buena. Pueblo Salado is located on the north edge of the Salt River, west of the canal system that includes Pueblo Grande, Grand Canal Ruins, and the Casa Buena system. Los Muertos is located at the terminus of a large canal system on the south side of the Salt River.

Pueblo Grande, Los Muertos, and Casa Buena each contained a platform mound. Grand Canal and Pueblo Salado do not appear to have associated public architecture and may have been in the next tier of the settlement hierarchy. Most of our information for Grand Canal and Pueblo Salado is based on modern excavations that are delimited by the boundaries of artificially-circumscribed project areas. It is possible that public architecture existed at these sites but was located beyond the project limits. However, there is little historical reference to Grand Canal and Pueblo Salado (in contrast to the other three sites), suggesting that by the early 1900s there was no evidence of public architecture at Grand Canal and Pueblo Salado. There are historical references to public architecture being present at a number of other Hohokam Classic period sites including Pueblo Grande, Los Muertos, and Casa Buena during the same time period.

Pueblo Grande was a primary Hohokam village in the lower Salt River Valley. This site is situated at the head of a major canal system and was probably one of the major centers in the Hohokam core area during the Sedentary and Classic periods (Bostwick and Downum 1994; Laczko et al. 1985), rivaling Casa Grande located to the south on the Gila River. The site was occupied from the Pioneer period through the Classic period, and through time contained two or three ballcourts, a great house or tower, and a large platform mound. Excavations around the platform mound in the 1930s recovered 150 cremations, of which 36 were from the Classic period, and 77 inhumations (Bostwick and Downum 1994; Brunson-Hadley 1994a, 1994b). Excavations away from the mound in 1989 and 1990 identified 12 discrete habitation areas and 16 cemeteries; 809 burials were excavated (Mitchell 1994a, 1994b). The actual village site extended beyond the scope of the modern excavations; but the core area of the site

appears to have been excavated. This large site may have included as many as 20 to 30 compounds during the height of its occupation.

The Los Muertos village site was located on the south side of the Salt River at the end of one of the largest canal systems in this area. Artifactual remains suggest that the site was not settled until the Classic period or during the Sedentary/Classic period transition. The site was excavated in 1887 and 1888 by Frank Hamilton Cushing as part of the Hemenway Expedition. The Los Muertos village was extensive, including at least 34 compounds, together with a large platform mound. Excavated burials included 370 cremations from 18 separate cemeteries and 152 inhumations from within 14 compounds (Brunson 1989; Haury 1945). The large volume of polychrome pottery and the complexity and size of the Los Muertos village architecture suggest that the village was inhabited very late into the Classic period, certainly at the same time as Casa Grande to the south (Brunson 1989).

Casa Buena is another Classic period village within the Phoenix area. Based on archival research, the village had a platform mound and compounds; however, it appears to have been smaller than either Pueblo Grande or Los Muertos. The Casa Buena burials discussed in this study were recovered from an area over 300 m northwest of the platform mound (Wilcox and Howard 1988). Excavations at this site in 1985 revealed portions of several habitation areas and cemeteries. The excavated cemeteries were associated with pithouses and surface structures but not compounds. Five spatially discrete burial areas included 53 inhumations and 9 cremations (Effland 1988; Howard 1988; Mitchell 1991).

The Grand Canal Ruins represent a medium-sized village located in central Phoenix. Excavations in 1986 revealed portions of several habitation areas and cemeteries dating to the Classic period (Mitchell 1989). Burials (79 inhumations and 22 cremations) were recovered from those excavations at seven spatially discrete burial areas. Multiple burials were present including a few instances of secondary cremation burials with inhumations. One possible primary cremation also was found.

The Pueblo Salado community included several compounds within separate loci. The site loci that date to the Classic period include compounds, pithouse clusters, and field house locations. This community was situated close to the Salt River on its own canal system. Recent excavations at one of the compounds identified a Classic period habitation that included 114 burials in five discrete areas, consisting of 59 cremations and 55 inhumations (Mitchell and Jones 1996).

These five sites represent Classic period villages of differing sizes and locations on either side of the Salt River. All sites were occupied during the Soho and Civano phases of the Classic period, but Pueblo Grande had an earlier pre-Classic component, and Los Muertos and Pueblo Salado may have continued to be inhabited longer than the other villages. Associations between village components and the cemeteries also varied from site to site; in some cases, the cemeteries were associated with compounds, and in other cases, the burials were associated with pithouses. Despite the differences, the villagers did exhibit a certain standardized approach to burial practices.

Hohokam Mortuary Patterns

This section presents an overview of burial practices observed at the five study sites as well as other excavated sites in the Hohokam area. The patterns presented here suggest a normative burial program but at the same time acknowledge the rich diversity present at these villages. The causes for this diversity are explored in the next section. One caveat with these data is the nature of the excavation limits, that is, nearly all these cemeteries were located in villages that were excavated as part of a nonarchaeology initiated project, such as highway expansion. Therefore, it is possible that larger or more complete site samples would have altered particular frequencies. However, by looking at a large enough sample of villages and cemeteries, we feel that the impact of this limitation is negligible.

Table 4.1 lists the burial method and demographic profile for the sites discussed. All sites contained both cremations and inhumations. Among the five sites, the percentage of cremations varies considerably from a low of 15% at Casa Buena to over 70% at Los Muertos. The Classic period burial method ratio of cremation versus inhumation styles has been shown to change with time, with an increase in cremations later in the temporal sequence. However, the near contemporaneity of some of the sites, for example Los Muertos and Pueblo Salado, which both had significant Civano components, suggests that these burial style differences were quite real.

Demographic profiles for adults found that roughly equal proportions of adult men and women were represented. Demographic studies for subadults, however, found that infant underenumeration is clearly a problem, and the sites are uneven in this regard. For example, only 11% of the burials at the Grand Canal Ruins were subadults compared to 46% of the burials at Pueblo Grande. This is a common problem in burial studies and can result from poor bone preservation of subadults as well as burying children under a certain age in areas away from the regular cemeteries, such as under house floors.

A normative Classic period inhumation burial consisted of a single individual being placed supine and extended within a pit, oriented east-west, with the head to the east (figure 4.2). The burial pit usually was subrectangular and approximately the size of the extended body. Grave accompaniments usually included pottery that was placed by the head or shoulder, and usually on the right side.

Variation did occur within the standardized form of

TABLE 4.1   Burial Method and Demography for Phoenix-Area Burial Sites

Site	Cremations	Inhumations	Subadults	Adults	Total Style/Age	Reference
Pueblo Grande	189 (23%)	620 (77%)	290 (46%)	335 (54%)	809/625	Mitchell 1994b
	36 (32%)	77 (68%)	34 (54%)	29 (46%)	113/63	Brunson-Hadley 1994a, 1994b
Los Muertos	370 (71%)	152 (29%)	68 (33%)	135 (67%)	522/203	Brunson 1989
Casa Buena	9 (15%)	53 (85%)	14 (26%)	39 (74%)	62/53	Effland 1988
Grand Canal	22 (22%)	79 (78%)	11 (14%)	68 (86%)	101/79	Mitchell et al. 1989
Pueblo Salado	59 (52%)	55 (48%)	28 (29%)	69 (71%)	114/97	Mitchell and Jones 1996

Note: Subadult-adult percents calculated from total number of burials for which age could be determined.

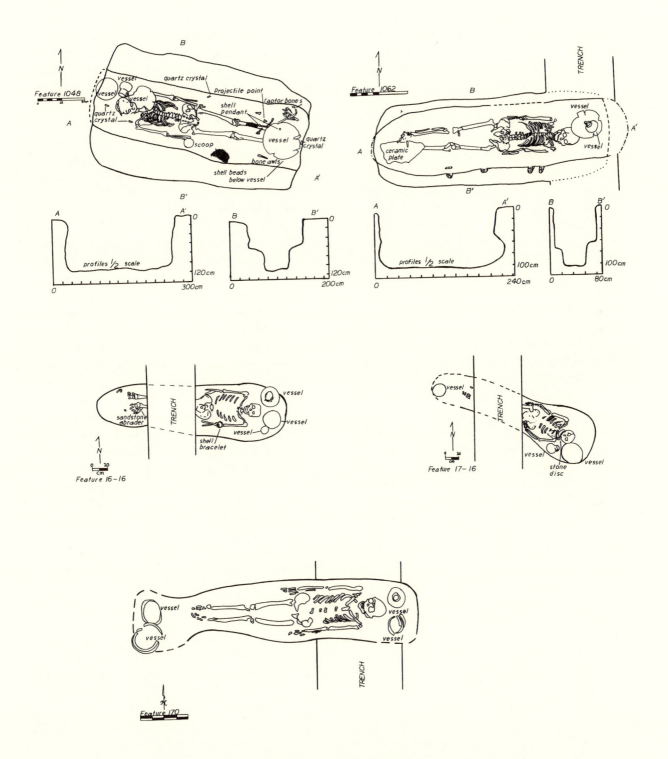

FIGURE 4.2 Typical Inhumation Burials from Hohokam Villages in the Phoenix Basin: (top row) Pueblo Grande, (middle row) Grand Canal Ruins, (bottom row) Pueblo Salado

burial. Although many burial pits exhibit little elaboration, some contained interior earthen shelves over which sticks were placed, covering the individual. This practice was observed for about a third of the inhumation burial pits at Pueblo Grande and for some of the inhumation burial pits at Grand Canal (Allen et al. 1989; Mitchell 1994b). Burials with formal wooden coverings have been identified at a small number of sites throughout the Hohokam area, including Plaza del Tempe and Mesa Grande (Casa Altas) (Brunson 1981; Countryman 1997). At Los Muertos, there is evidence that some inhumations were interred in adobe-lined pits and a few select individuals in adobe sarcophagi (Brunson 1989). A similar adobe sarcophagus was reported at Casa Grande (Andresen 1985; Fewkes 1912), and adobe-lined burial pits also have been reported from Mesa Grande (Placona 1979) and Las Colinas (Saul 1981). Other less common means of burial include placing a person in a seated position, in a face down position, or flexed.

Orientation of the head also varied, although the vast majority of the bodies were placed with their heads to the east. Interestingly, the frequency of head orientations in other directions seems to have varied from village to village, and the side of the body where burial goods were placed was affected by the head orientation (Brunson 1989). Another characteristic that varies from one village to another is the location of vessels around the body. For those sites on the Pueblo Grande canal system, a large percentage of accompaniments was found by the feet (second only to the head), whereas at Los Muertos it was rare to find vessels by the feet. Body painting also occurred in some instances. At Pueblo Grande, for example, 40 burials (out of 664 inhumation remains) included pigment staining. Colors observed on these burials included red, blue, green, white, and yellow (Mitchell 1994b).

For the secondary cremation burials, a person was cremated somewhere in or near the village, and the remains were collected and placed within a jar that usually was covered by a bowl. Usually additional vessels served as accompaniments. Few primary cremations and crematoria have been identified within the core Hohokam area, suggesting that those facilities were insubstantial. Within the Hohokam core area, the majority of the cremations are secondary remains representing the gleaning of the body and some accompaniments that were part of the primary burning. Additional accompaniments (which show no evidence of burning) often are part of the cremation.

Primary cremations found at the Cashion site on the far west edge of the Salt River Valley, appear to date to the Sedentary to Classic transition. Several of the primary cremations were gleaned, but the others were left in place. One burial included evidence of scaffolding and textiles (Antieau 1981). The Gillespie Dam site (Fagan et al. 1989), also located on the western periphery of Hohokam culture, had several Classic period primary cremations. These cremations were interesting because the initial crematory fire of the burials had begun in all cases, but for some reason, the burials were only partially burnt when the burial pits were filled in; thereby extinguishing the fire and preserving much of the burials and their grave goods. Three burials were recovered that had accompaniments suggesting the individuals held important positions within the community. In the burial of a small child (12–18 months), the baby was wrapped in textiles and accompanied by numerous food items (squash, corn, and cotton), baskets, and a multiple copper bell and bead necklace. Remains of the burial scaffolding were clearly present. Another double burial included an adult male with another partial individual associated with a unique headdress, projectile points, and copper fragments, as well as charred wood from the burial scaffolding (Fagan et al. 1989). The headdress looked like a wig, with the hair tendrils made from cotton and vegetable fiber cordage. A topknot on the wig contained antler fragments (see Fagan 1989:576). Ceramics from the burials confirmed their Classic period status (Judy Brunson-Hadley, personal observation), as did radiocarbon dating (Fagan et al. 1989). While the individuals appear to have special status from the type of grave accompaniments, the use of scaffolding at this and the Cashion site suggests that the practice of cremation may have included the building of a scaffold within the primary pit as part of the ceremony. Since similar primary cremations have not been found within the core area of the Hohokam, it may be that the practice represents a variant burial ceremony distinct to the western periphery.

For both burial styles, multiple burials occur at most large sites, but in low frequencies. Inhumation and cremation burials are interred in discrete cemeteries. These cemeteries can be linked directly to adjacent habitation areas (see Mitchell 1992). Inhumations occurred in discrete cemeteries outside of the compounds and often in plazas within the compounds. Subadult inhumations were found in extramural cemeteries and under house floors. In contrast, cremation cemeteries occur primarily in discrete cemeteries outside of the compounds, with a rare cremation being found inside the compound (Brunson 1989). At some sites, cremations and inhumations may both occur within the same cemetery (Mitchell 1991), but at most sites, there were discrete cemeteries for each.

Grave Goods

One of the most tangible means of examining variability among the these populations is through the material culture interred with the deceased. Grave goods are common with burials in the Phoenix area. For example, over 80% of the burials had grave offerings at Pueblo Grande (81%) and Pueblo Salado (82%) (Mitchell 1994b; Mitchell and Jones 1996). Similar high numbers were found at Los Muertos for both inhumations and cremations (Brunson 1989).

A review of the five sites found that grave goods most commonly included ceramic pots but also included shell beads, bracelets and pendants; stone beads and pendants (including turquoise); animal bone awls or hair pins; projectile points; spindle whorls; manos; metates; and other items. Rare items include such things as quartz crystals, painted wands or staffs, turtle shell artifacts, a hawk bone necklace, and painted baskets (table 4.2). Burials from other sites have produced such rare items as textiles, turquoise and shell frog mosaics, a headdress, copper bells, and woven grass mats.

Certain patterns occur with artifact associations through time and space and by age and gender at the various sites. There appears to be more diversity in the types of grave goods interred with the dead during the earlier part of the Classic period (Soho phase), perhaps related to the changing nature of the larger Hohokam exchange networks and the dynamics of the regional system of which this culture was a part. At Los Muertos, the decline in grave good diversity is accompanied by an increase in the numbers of grave goods during the Civano phase. Spatially, there appears to be considerable variation within the types and quantities of goods found in cemeteries at different sites. Unfortunately, the only large Classic period cemeteries examined occur in the Phoenix metropolitan area and may represent a sampling bias when viewing the entire Hohokam culture, since the Hohokam core area encompasses a much larger area. Other large, significant Classic period villages, such as Casa Grande on the Gila River, have never been systematically examined or reported.

Most of the analyses at both large and small cemeteries have concentrated on the distribution of artifacts by age and gender (table 4.3). Gender and age grading are appar-

ent in Hohokam society (see Brunson 1989; Crown and Fish 1996; Mitchell 1991, 1994b). Patterns are beginning to emerge suggesting that, in general, adults have more artifacts than subadults, and there is a difference between male and female adult burial accompaniments. Adult males tend to have more projectile points, polychrome vessels, bone awls or hairpins, and shell and stone jewelry; Hohokam adult females universally tend to have a greater frequency of large numbers of ceramic vessels and utilitarian items. Subadults on average have fewer grave goods, more miniature pots, and more minerals.

There also is a difference in grave goods between burial styles. Inhumations tend to have more *whole* artifacts including more redware and polychrome vessels than cremations. At Los Muertos, however, cremations actually have more vessels than inhumations, if partial vessels are counted. At Grand Canal Ruins, adult female burials included more spindle whorls and manos, and at Pueblo Grande, cremated adult males were buried with more bone awls/hairpins and more projectile points. At Los Muertos, there is some indication that certain items that are gender-linked, differ between the inhumation and cremation burials. For instance, polychrome is associated with inhumed males, but with cremations it appears that it was associated with females.

Many of these associations probably reflect various horizontal levels of differentiation (see Carr 1995; O'Shea 1984), often being linked by age and gender. However, two associations seem to stand out: the abundance of goods and exotic items with certain adult males and subadults (infants and children). These associations can be used to suggest some degree of vertical differentiation also occurred within the society.

Grave goods are certainly one of the most important indicators of the previous relationships of an individual. The measurement of these goods is an issue of some importance. In an attempt to approach the contextual value of goods, McGuire (1987, 1992) developed a measure, the Grave Lot Value or GLV, where each artifact was evaluated for its context, origin, and labor investment. Certain considerations must be evaluated and understood when utilizing this method. As McGuire (1992) has noted, the simplification of ranking the artifacts may also obscure some of the inherent complexity of the record. However, this method of analysis has received a fair amount of attention because it goes beyond both counts and diversity and certainly appears to identify important patterns within the Hohokam population.

TABLE 4.2 Artifacts Found with Burials at Five Hohokam Villages

Artifact Category	Pueblo Grande	Los Muertos	Casa Grande	Grand Canal Ruins	Pueblo Salado
Utilitarian Items					
Plainware/redware pottery	+	+	+	+	+
Red-on-buff pottery	+	+	+	+	+
Polychrome pottery	+	+	+	+	+
Effigy vessel	+	+	+	+	
Spindle whorl	+	+	+	+	+
Stone knife	+	+	+	+	+
Stone axe				+	+
Projectile point	+	+	+	+	+
Mano, metate	+	+			+
Animal bone awl	+	+	+	+	+
Shell awl/needle	+				+
Polishing stone	+	+			
Obsidian nodule	+				
Ornamental Items					
Stone bead (argillite, turquoise, slate)	+	+	+	+	+
Animal bone bead					+
Ceramic bead		+		+	
Shell bead	+	+	+	+	+
Bird bone necklace				+	
Shell bracelet	+	+	+	+	+
Pendant (shell and stone)	+	+	+	+	+
Stone lip/nose plug	+				
Shell and turquoise mosaic	+	+[1]		+	
Ritual and Miscellaneous Artifacts					
Painted wooden stick or staff	+				
Stone concretion	+	+			
Bird wings (golden eagle, raven)	+				
Animal (bird?) bone whistle				+	
Painted turtle shell				+	
Quartz crystal	+				
Painted basket	+				
Stone ring	+				
Stone ball, stone cylinder	+				
Copper artifact					+
Whole Laevicardium shell	+				
Ceramic vessel with charred material	+	+		+	
Corn meal in vessel	+				
Fish bones in vessel	+				
Ceramic figurine		+			+
Copper ore raw material (azurite, malachite, chrysacolla, etc.)	+				
Iron ore raw material (hematite, other?)	+	+			

[1] Turquoise encrusted shell frog was found, but its association is not clear.

TABLE 4.3 Associations of Artifact Categories with Burials from Five Phoenix-Area Sites

Pueblo Grande	Los Muertos	Casa Buena	Grand Canal Ruins	Pueblo Salado
Pottery				
More redware pots with inhumations; more polychrome with adult males; highest number of pots with adult females	Highest number of pots with adult females; more polychrome with male and subadult inhumations, and female cremations; miniature pots and scoops with subadults; pitchers with females and subadults	Polychrome with adult males; highest number of pots with adult females	Miniature pots with subadults; effigy pots with adults; highest number of pots with adult females	Polychrome with adult males
Utilitarian Items				
More bone awls/hairpins with cremations; more bone awls/hairpins with adult males regardless of burial method; more projectile points with male cremations	—	—	More spindle whorls with adult females	More bone awls/hairpins with cremations
Ornamental Items				
More beads with adult males Turquoise with subadults	More ornaments with adult males	—	—	—
Ritual Items				
More of these items with adults	—	—	More charred plant remains with adults	—

For this study, we examined the GLV scores for three of the sites, Pueblo Grande, Pueblo Salado, and Los Muertos. Even though Los Muertos did not appear to have the diversity of burial accompaniments (apart from pottery) that some of the other sites had, distinctive GLV scores still occurred. While the absolute values vary from each site, the shapes of the curves are quite similar (figure 4.3). Many burials have low to moderate scores while only a very few burials have scores considerably beyond the range of most burials. We view this as evidence for the presence of a few individuals at each village who were quite different than the remainder (table 4.4).

At Los Muertos, of the seven inhumation burials with the highest GLV scores, three were adult males, two were subadults, and no information was available for the other two. Among the Los Muertos cremations with high GLV scores, it appears that women tended to have the higher scores (Brunson 1989:420). At Pueblo Grande, for the 12 highest GLV scores, nine individuals were inhumed (two adult males, two adult females, five subadults), and three were cremated (two unsexed adults and one for which age could not be determined) (Mitchell 1994b). At Pueblo Salado, the two burials with the highest GLV scores included a subadult and an adult female (both

inhumations) (Mitchell and Jones 1996). When reviewing information from other sites, in most cases it
appears that adult males, and a smaller number of
subadults, tend to have the higher scores, but not to the
total exclusion of females. There are some high scoring females within the different village populations.
Crown and Fish (1996) have suggested that it is the
older women who are allowed to attain the additional
status.

At Los Muertos, the location of the inhumations
with high GLV scores tends to substantiate their
"uniqueness." The burials were identified in five
different compounds, including two male adults that
were buried in elaborate sarcophagi on the platform
mound. At another compound (not a platform
mound), an adult male burial was placed in the doorway leading into a cemetery room containing other
burials. All three men were associated with polychrome accompaniments placed by their knees. The
other high GLV score burials included two burials each
containing two subadults (different compounds), and
the remaining two individuals were from another
compound (Brunson 1989). The six burials with the
highest GLV scores at Pueblo Grande included an adult
cremation, two adult males, and three subadults. These
burials were interred in four separate cemeteries; three
of the burials were interred in the same cemetery in the
central part of the site.

Special status burials were recovered from the other
three sites. In many cases, the accompaniments suggested that the individuals had spiritual roles (Allen et
al. 1989; Effland 1988; Mitchell 1991, 1994b; see Mitchell
1994b for a further discussion of shamanism and
Hohokam society).

Other unique burials have been reported from a
variety of sites (Morris and El-Najjar 1971; Placona
1979; Wilcox 1987). An adult male was excavated by
Cushing at the Las Acequias site, who he suggested was
a warrior priest. Analysis of the burial accompaniments found the artifacts that were collected included
numerous obsidian flakes, a 12-cm long obsidian knife,
turquoise pendants, mineral paint, and polychrome
vessels, including a bowl that had a twined ceramic
handle over the top like a basket (Brunson 1989;
Brunson-Hadley and Countryman 1998). All of these
individuals provide clear evidence that differential
roles, many of them prestigious, did occur within the
Hohokam society.

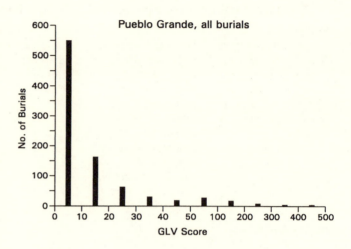
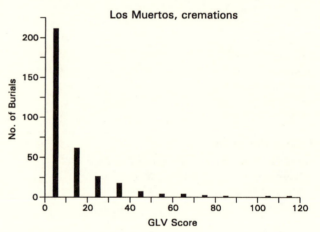
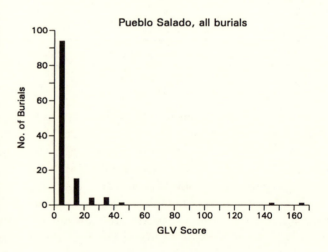

FIGURE 4.3 Grave Lot Value (GLV) Frequency
Distributions for Pueblo Grande, Los
Muertos, and Pueblo Salado

TABLE 4.4 Characteristics of Burials with High Grave Lot Value (GLV) Scores at Pueblo Grande,
Los Muertos, and Pueblo Salado

Burial	Burial Accompaniments
Pueblo Grande	
Infant inhumation, early period (F3419)	2 plainware vessels, 1 redware vessel, 1 stone bead, 44 shell pendants, 1 shell bead, 1 shell bracelet
Infant inhumation, late period (F1402)*	1 plainware vessel, 1 projectile point, 1 stone bead, 1 shell ring, 1 stone spindle whorl, 13 misc. pieces of shell, 24 shell bracelets, 6 stone "gaming pieces"
Child inhumation, early period (F445)	1 redware vessel, 5 turquoise tesserae, 1 stone ornament, 1 shell pendant, 5 shell beads, 55 misc. pieces of shell, 3 shell bracelets, 1 whole Laevicardium shell
Old adult male inhumation, early period (F184)	1 plainware vessel, 1 redware vessel, 2 projectile points, 1 turquoise tesserae, 1 turquoise bead, 10 stone beads, 1 shell bead, 38 misc. pieces of shell
Old adult male inhumation, early period (F938)	8 plainware vessels, 1 decorated vessel, 8 projectile points, 1 casual stone tool, 2 manos, 1 turquoise bead, 1 stone bead, 1 shell bead, 1 bone awl, 62 misc. pieces of shell, 1 shell bracelet, 1 whole Laevicardium shell
Adult (gender indet.) cremation, early period (F1006)	2 plainware vessels, 1 projectile point, 1 stone ornament, 1 stone bead, 1 shell bead, 1 shell ring, 1 shell awl/needle, 3 bone awls, 20 misc. pieces of shell, 14 shell bracelets, 1 quartz crystal, 1 pointed stone
Los Muertos	
Adult male inhumation, Civano (Cmpd I, Sep. 2)	Gila Polychrome bowl, Tonto Polychrome handled beaker
Adult male inhumation, Civano (Cmpd I, Sep. 3)	2 Tonto Polychrome bowls, Gila Polychrome jar, paint materials; 3 large stone slabs bordered the south side of the sarcophagus
Adult male inhumation, Civano (Cmpd II, Sep. 21)	Gila Polychrome bowl contained Tonto Polychrome handled beaker
Double subadult inhumation, Civano (Cmpd XIII, Sep. 46)	Gila Polychrome bird effigy vessel, Gila Polychrome bowl, unidentified bowl, 5+ turquoise beads, 2 turquoise pendants, white shell beads
Double subadult inhumation, Civano (Cmpd XIX)	2 Gila Polychrome bowls, 1 Gila Polychrome jar
Age unknown inhumation, Civano (Cmpd XIX)	Gila Polychrome bowl, Gila Polychrome jar, Salado Polychrome bowl, redware smudged beaker
Adult female cremation, Civano (Crem. 2T)	1 redware bowl, 2 redware jars, 1 Red-on-buff pitcher, 3 plainware jars, 1 Salado Polychrome handle, 21 vessels less than 25% complete (7 redwares, 8 plainwares, 1 Tonto Polychrome, 4 Gila Polychrome, 1 Red-on-buff)
Age unknown cremation, Civano (Crem. 9C)	1 Tonto Polychrome jar, 1 Tonto Polychrome bowl, 1 Tonto Red jar, 1 redware bowl, 1 redware beaker, 2 plainware vessels, 20 vessels less than 25% complete (6 Red-on-buff, 5 redware, 2 polychrome, and 7 plainware)
Age unknown cremation, Civano (Crem 14XXX)	4 redware jars, 3 redware bowls, 1 plainware jar, 1 Gila Polychrome jar, stone beads, chipped river stone implement, 9 vessels less than 25% complete (5 redware, 2 plainware, 2 Gila Polychrome)
Adult female cremation, Civano (Crem 23N)	1 redware double-handled jar, 2 redware bowls, 1 redware vessel, 1 redware chipped base to form a plate, 1 redware plate, 18 vessels less than 25% complete (6 redware, 1 redware punctate jar, 2 Salado Polychrome, 1 Tonto Polychrome, 5 plainware, 1 Red-on-buff, 2 unknown)
Pueblo Salado	
Subadult inhumation (F141)	1 plainware vessel, 2 redware vessels, 187 shell beads, 6 shell bracelets (incl. fragments), 1 shell frog, 1 copper artifact
Adult female cremation (F218)	2 plainware vessels, 1 mano, 1 bone awl, 1203 shell beads

Note: This table is a partial list of high GLV scores; it does not list all individuals. The reader is referred to the original reports for detailed information (Brunson 1989; Mitchell 1994b; Mitchell and Jones 1996).

* It is not clear if this feature represents an infant burial or an artifact cache; two fragmentary pieces of infant bone were found near the artifacts.

DISCUSSION

The cemeteries from these five Classic period sites allow a glimpse into thirteenth and fourteenth century Hohokam society. The sites represent large central villages and smaller peripheral villages. Viewing this variability allows us to make some generalizations about Hohokam social organization from a regional perspective. It appears that the Classic period Hohokam probably attained a level of development commensurate with what some researchers have referred to as middle range societies (Feinman and Neitzel 1984; Kosse 1996; Lightfoot and Upham 1989). Such societies have social political systems that are not simple consensus decision-making organizations nor are they complex chiefdom or state level structures, rather they are something in between (Lightfoot and Upham 1989:16).

The analysis of Classic period burials from the Hohokam villages supports a conclusion that horizontal and vertical differentiation occurred at all the large villages. Several levels of vertical differentiation are present, with a small group of individuals that stand out and may possibly be called "elite" based on the location of their burials, energy expenditure on the grave pit, and the type of accompaniments that were present. Other individuals of distinction could be recognized based on the numbers or types of burial accompaniments but not by location. These individuals were not confined to an "elite" cemetery but instead were scattered throughout the village cemeteries. One or two such individuals would tend to be associated with each cemetery, suggesting they may have had similar leadership roles associated with kin or corporate groups. The evidence suggests that levels of differentiation occurred, distinctive and differing roles were present, and differential access to certain goods occurred. However, any one social level would have access to another level, although the amount, or presence, of certain burial styles or specific items varied between the levels. Certain prestige items, such as polychrome, tended to be found in the more vertically differentiated burials but still were available to other members of the community; albeit, in much smaller quantities. Other items such as obsidian and turquoise also had differential availability for the community members. Polished redware appears to have been a prestige item, appearing more often in burials than within the habitation areas (Abbott 1988; Mitchell 1994b). Certain ritual items such as a hawk bone necklace, copper bells, or eagle wings had a much more restricted availability.

Based on the burial data recovered from these villages, we do not believe that Hohokam society was represented by a chiefdom or a single-leader type of organization. There is no evidence for one chief among the Hohokam culture, or even one chief at each Hohokam village. There also is no evidence that any one individual had total control over the redistribution of material. Storage areas are found, and there is evidence that some materials were stored within platform mounds, but there is no evidence for a tribute system. There was restriction of access to certain structures or rooms within structures, and differential access to many types of artifacts; although some of those artifacts were available to other members of the population in much smaller quantities.

Mitchell (1994b) has proposed that the presence of spatially restricted groups of burials containing more wealth at these Hohokam villages (e.g., Pueblo Grande, Casa Buena, and Grand Canal) indicates a social system with wealthy lineages. Segments of kinship-related groups may have attained sufficient wealth and authority to exert a disproportionate amount of control over other members of the community. This may have largely evolved through economic considerations (Henderson 1987). In this model, Hohokam society was organized around successful lineages. These lineages may have attained their economic success through exchange alliances or perhaps acquisition of the all-important land and irrigation rights.

From a somewhat different perspective, Brunson (1989) has proposed that a similar division of Hohokam society based on kinship or lineages existed, but her argument, based on Cushing's theories and utilizing ethnographic information from Southwest Puebloan groups, is that the mechanism creating the vertical differentiation within the population is a result of ceremonial or religious responsibilities. Such responsibilities allowed certain groups (such as clans, lineages, and kin groups) and specific individuals to acquire power and prestige as an outcome of their religious, and hence social, responsibilities.

An economic model does not negate a religious-authority model. In fact, these models are not mutually exclusive, and it appears that aspects of both of these models are probably quite pertinent to an understanding of Classic period Hohokam society. Community activities would have allowed for power accumulation by certain individuals, including some ceremonial or spiritual leaders, as well as groups. Wilcox has speculated that economically elite family groups were living atop the platform mounds in the Phoenix Basin. He suggests that:

people living on the platform mounds . . . probably were members of high-ranking corporate groups with considerably greater wealth than those in other compounds (corporate groups). They were an elite that probably was invested with sacred authority to mediate for the larger community with the gods, having taken over ritual functions previously handled by religious sodalities. (Wilcox 1991:268)

Based on ethnographic studies, it is likely that the responsibility or power would often continue to reside within specific kin groups. With the number of levels of activity present in Hohokam society—trade networks, marriage alliances, movements of people, and the maintenance of a massive irrigation system to name a few—not all power would have necessarily resided only with religious leaders. It is to be expected that circumstances would occur that would allow individuals on the basis of economics to achieve some level of power. However, the apparent religious structure of the society and the types of artifacts found with certain "elite" burials suggest that religious responsibilities were a key factor in socially recognized differentiation within the community.

Schlegel (1992) has discussed the complex system of hierarchy and kinship for the nineteenth century Hopi villages. During this time Hopi villages had a hierarchical political-ceremonial system where members of one system were also members of the other.

> There may have been a rank order of prestige and authority, for example in the settlement of land disputes, but there is no evidence that each mesa was a chiefdom of villages under the hegemony of one of their number. . . . This was not a stratified system; there was no dominant class imposing its will through the threat of force or deprivation on a subordinate class. (Schlegel 1992:380)

Land was owned by the clans, and there was no obvious difference in material culture or access to wealth between members of high-ranking and low-ranking clans. There were, however, some differences in land holding with the higher ranking clans having better farmlands. While farmlands were controlled by clans, there is no evidence that craft production and trade were clan controlled. An individual who was industrious and clever could probably gain more through trade than his fellows, regardless of clan affiliation (Schlegel 1992:381).

Based on his knowledge of Zuni social organization in

the 1800s, and his excavations at the Hohokam sites, Cushing (1890) suggested that the burial styles and information indicated that a four-tiered hierarchy existed in the Hohokam villages, with the hierarchy being structured by ceremonial and religious obligations. He suggested that a group of six or seven "hereditary" priests/priestesses oversaw each community, and these individuals were buried on the platform mounds. In addition, each compound represented a clan or gens, and "lesser" priests associated with the compound also would have had religious responsibilities (see Brunson 1989 for further discussion of Cushing's views of the Hohokam social structure).

In an in-depth study of social organization at the Zuni protohistoric site of Hawikku, Howell (1994) found that the Hawikku decision-making structure consisted of ascriptive male and female roles. Leadership seems to have been on the village level, although he noted that there was some evidence for a council that may have had representatives from the various Zuni villages (Howell 1994:147). Referring to studies of the Zuni in 1900, he notes that leadership appeared more dependent on specific roles, rather than on wealth, and a greater number of religious/spiritual leaders were drawn from the larger clans.

A review of the Hohokam villages within the Salt River Valley finds some interesting parallels. Within the large villages with platform mounds, there are individuals who are differentiated based on their burial goods, and in some cases, their burial locations and the level of energy expenditure on their burial pit preparation. At Los Muertos, the presence of elite burials in adobe-lined pits or adobe sarcophagi on the platform mound provides further evidence of hierarchical identification. Burials are reported from platform mounds at several sites within the Hohokam culture area. In some cases, it appears that the individuals received special treatment, but this does not seem to be the case in other areas (table 4.5). This variability is consistent with other lines of evidence for midlevel differentiation based on economic, ritual, and probably ethnic divisions.

The presence of two distinct burial styles (inhumed and cremated interment) also provides some evidence of different social beliefs or identification. In some cases, elite cemeteries are present within the village, but more generally, one or two individuals with special grave assemblages can be identified within each of the large discrete cemeteries, for both inhumations and cremations.

TABLE 4.5 Characteristics of Burials Found on the Tops of Hohokam Platform Mounds
(Central mound, does not include burials within the compound wall but off of the mound)

Site	Description	Reference
Pueblo Grande	**HB4**, adult male, extended east; redware bowl and pitcher, both containing clean gravel; scoop containing gravel, charcoal, and burnt corncob; remnants of finely woven cloth around head and torso with a red-painted hide garment; woven grass matting beneath body; string apron	Brunson 1994b
	HB5, adult female, extended east; owl by skull; 2 redware bowls and 1 redware pitcher	
	HB6, subadult, twisted with head to east; jar neck sherd; trace of matting on top of one leg	
	HB46, subadult, body disturbed by rodents, head to east; redware jar and plainware scoop containing shell; Olivella shells in neck area, shell bracelet fragment, perforated shell; obsidian flake; corn kernels and beans; traces of hematite in skull	
	HB47, fragmentary secondary reburial in pit with rocks and sherds; no obvious grave accompaniments	
	SK1, aged adult, extended east; pitcher sherds, redware jar; turquoise beads on left wrist and shell bead and drilled shell associated with right wrist; flat rock on right hip; Polychrome sherd reportedly associated and charcoal	
	Sim1, subadult, partially flexed and head to east; redware bowl, unidentified bowl, and plainware pitcher; 40 small beads	
	Sim2, subadult, oriented south; redware bowl near feet and lower torso, containing charcoal and ashes; mano near right hip	
	Sim3, subadult, fragmentary; no information	
	Sim4, subadult, oriented northeast; plainware bowl with scoop; 6 shell bracelets; small black beads; red pigment	
Los Muertos	**Sep. 1**, 2 adults, oriented N/S; burial disturbed, no artifacts	Brunson 1989
	Sep. 2, adult male, extended east; Gila Polychrome bowl, Tonto Polychrome handled beaker; adobe sarcophagus with the foot area of the grave curved into the central wall of the platform mound	
	Sep. 3, adult male, extended east; 2 Tonto Polychrome bowls and 1 Gila Polychrome jar; paint materials; adobe sarcophagus with the head area curved into the central wall of the platform mound; south side of grave lined with 3 large stones	
	Sep. 4, subadult; burned ceramic "dog" figurine; adobe-lined cist/sarcophagus associated with a columnar structure and a hearth	
	Sep. 5, adult male, extended east; 1 plainware bowl, 1 redware jar, 1 pitcher; paint materials; adobe sarcophagus that abutted the central wall	
	Sep. 6, subadult, semiflexed with head to the east; 1 Gila Polychrome bowl; burial within the central wall	
Las Colinas	**Burial 1**, adult male and subadult*; adobe lined pit; no artifacts recovered; burial extremely disturbed; few remaining bones	Saul 1981 and Harrington 1981
	Burial 2, adult, no artifacts; however, much of burial(upper torso) destroyed by historic feature; individual appears to have been extended	
	Burial 4**, infant; 6 vessels: 4 redware bowls, 1 redware jar, 1 Casa Grande Red-on-buff jar; 1 quartz crystal; 1 shell bracelet frag.; 1 shell ring	
	Burial 5, adult female, extended east; 2 redware vessels	

Table 4.5   *continued*

Site	Description	Reference
Las Colinas continued	**Burial 6**, adult female, extended east; 2 vessels: 1 redware bowl broken with part by right side of head and other part by left shoulder and miniature redware tripod vessel; piece of ochre; 1 stone ball; 1 turquoise bead, 2 shell rings	
	Burial 7, infant*; possibly associated with 2 bone awls; associated with isolated hearth—no other information	
	Burial 8, adult male*, extended east; no artifacts	
	Burial 9, adult female*, extended east; 5 redware vessels	
	Burial 10, adult female*; 2 redware vessels; 5 stone beads	
	Burial 11, adult-probable female*, extended east; 2 redware vessel fragments: worked rim sherd and sherd; Burial may have been disturbed, much of skeleton missing	
	Burial 13, adult-probably female*; partial redware vessel, unknown vessel; 1 stone bead	
	Burial 14, adult-probable female*; redware bowl; possible pouch containing quartz crystal, 1 piece of asbestos, and "other small objects"; hematite on pelvis [not clear if on bone, or was piece of ochre]	
La Ciudad	**X1**, subadult#, head to west; 3 vessels (2 polychrome); 1 shell pendant, 2 shell beads	Wilcox 1987
	X2, infant; no artifacts—disturbed	
	X3, infant, head to east; 1 redware vessel	
	X4, infant; no artifacts	
	X5, infant; no artifacts—disturbed.	
	X6, infant, head to north; 225 shell beads; rodent disturbed	
	X7, subadult#, head to east; 1 polychrome vessel; "high-grade turquoise set"	
	X8, infant, head to east; 3 redware vessels; partially under a wall	
	X9, infant, head to east; 1 redware scoop	
	X18, adult, head to east; 1 redware vessel; turquoise pendant	
	X19 and **X20**, double burial of adult female and adult male; X19 adult female; 1 plainware vessel, 2 redware vessels, 1 polychrome vessel; 2 perforated shells; 1 polished pebble; obsidian projectile point; X20, adult male; 3 redware vessels; axe fragment, mano, discoidal stone	
	X21, adult female, head to east; no artifacts	
	X22, juvenile, head to east; 1 redware vessel; 2 manos	
	X23, adult female, head to east; 1 redware vessel	
	X24, adult male; no artifacts	
Escalante	**Burial 18**, subadult; no artifacts	Doyel 1975
	Burial 19, adult male; no artifacts, buried in a seated position	
	Burial 20, age and gender unknown; no artifacts	

* analysis completed by Birkby in laboratory; otherwise age and sex identified in the field by excavator (see Harrington 1981).

** excavator suggested adult also present; however, Birkby (in Harrington 1981) suggests excavator misidentified the subadult's long bones.

Midvale identified both individuals as female juveniles. Charles Merbs subsequently identified X7 as a young child (Wilcox 1987). See Brunson (1989) for a discussion of the validity of the juvenile female identifications.

These individuals probably held similar leadership positions at each village.

Of interest is a comparison of Pueblo Grande and Los Muertos, both large villages. While Los Muertos had elite burials on the platform mound, Pueblo Grande had burials on its platform mound, but not with the same level of elaborateness or burial accompaniments. Burials were present on the Pueblo Grande platform mound but not with any identified prestigious accompaniments. Los Muertos also had a much higher percentage of polychrome in its burial population (23% inhumed, 14% cremated) than did Pueblo Grande (< 1%)[1] (Brunson 1989; Peterson 1994). This difference suggests that a slightly different mechanism for symbolizing leadership roles was operative at Los Muertos.

Los Muertos appears to have been a late site, without a pre-Classic component, and it is located at the terminus of a large canal system. In contrast, Pueblo Grande was inhabited from the inception of the Hohokam culture until its demise, and it is strategically located at the head of a canal system. Studies of the different villages suggest that compounds often had individuals with leadership roles. In addition, a smaller number of individuals could be identified with apparent religious roles, based on the accompanying grave goods and sometimes unique burial styles. Both types of leaders were identified within the Pueblo Grande and Los Muertos cemeteries. In addition, however, Los Muertos has the elite individuals buried with apparent ceremony on the platform mound. Based on his knowledge of Zuni religious orders, Cushing argued that some of the individuals were priests on the basis of certain grave goods and symbolism on the pottery.

It may be possible that while every village had its leaders, one village had additional religious responsibilities for the entire Salt River Valley community. The fact that Los Muertos was one of the larger communities and flourished at the terminus of the canal system (and therefore could not control the headgates of the system), suggests it held some level of power over many of the other villages on the system. The large numbers of polychrome vessels associated with the community lends further credence to the argument that the village had special status or special trade relationships in comparison to the remainder of the Salt River Valley community. Possibly the village was created primarily for its leadership and ceremonial responsibilities, so that a village location near direct access to canal water was less important (in contrast to Pueblo Grande, which had direct access to canal water). Other large villages had

similar geo-cultural positions: Las Colinas on the Salt River and Casa Grande on the Gila River system.

Based on the presence of Tonto polychrome, it does appear that Los Muertos was inhabited later than some sites; however, it also was inhabited contemporaneously with the other sites discussed in this chapter. Many of the cremation burials containing polychrome also had Casa Grande Red-on-buff pottery, indicating a mid-Classic period time frame for many of the burials.

It is difficult to determine why the village of Los Muertos had such a high percentage of polychrome and a larger number of sarcophagi platform mound burials when compared to the other villages. The population may represent important individuals from each of the village sites (similar to the Zuni council concept), or they may have represented a group that moved into the valley from somewhere else, although we do not know from where. If indeed, Los Muertos had specialized roles in the larger community, we can only speculate at this time as to what its roles may have been. The fact that Los Muertos was similar to other Classic period villages (other than sarcophagi platform mound burials and amount of polychrome in both inhumed and cremated burials) shows it was an integral part of the valley community, albeit unique.

CONCLUSIONS

Despite the possibility of economic power positions, the types of artifacts found with many burials that have been identified as part of the vertical differentiation argues that religious roles had a profound effect on the societal structuring. In addition, certain roles appear to have been ascribed based on evidence from individual subadult burials.

Finally, we would simply reiterate our views on Hohokam society based on our observations at several Phoenix-area villages. Settlement hierarchies, massive irrigation works, and public architecture argue for complexity in Hohokam society. Various studies of Hohokam mortuary patterns suggest that most artifact variability represents horizontal differentiation rather than vertical differentiation. Differentiation did occur on the basis of gender and age; males tended to have more ornamental accompaniments, and women had more utilitarian accompaniments. Children had fewer artifacts than adults, and certain items were more commonly found with the children. The diversity of grave goods appears to have been greater during the early part (Soho phase) of the Classic period, but the numbers of grave goods increased during the later part of the phase. Similar age and gender differentiation were present among both cremations and inhumations, although there is some suggestion that certain items that were gender-linked may have differed between the two burial styles. Apart from the age and gender differences, however, there are enough instances of burials with abundant and unique combinations of artifacts to indicate that some people, young and old, male and female, were distinctive. In particular, male inhumations tend to have the most ceremonial accompaniments and polychrome accompaniments, although some elderly females also appear to have had access to elite items. Certain rich subadult burials would suggest that some roles may have been ascribed through kinship ties.

On the basis of the graves and burial accompaniments, we believe much of the vertical differentiation was due to religious or spiritual responsibilities that not only allowed for individual prestige but brought responsibilities, and hence some additional power, to specific clans or lineages. Despite vertical differentiation occurring, different lines of evidence indicate that mechanisms of the society existed for balancing that power and not allowing for a strict stratified society. Certain individuals and groups held more power or prestige, but they were not separated from the remainder of the population, nor were many of the artifacts that could be used to identify their vertical placement withheld from the rest of the population. There is some evidence, however, to speculate that the site of Los Muertos with its high percentage of polychrome vessels and elite burials on the platform mound served a unique position within the larger Salt River Valley community.

We offer the theory that Classic period Hohokam society included a political structure of powerful religious leaders and wealthy lineages (with some overlap), who together provided the authority and power to direct their people through three centuries of desert life. Differentiation between villages suggests that a hierarchy of responsibilities existed for the different villages, with those villages containing platform mounds having additional religious responsibilities beyond those without platform mounds.

NOTES

1. Some authors have suggested that the fact that Los Muertos was excavated in the 1880s may have con-

tributed to inaccurate information on the number of polychromes from the site. However, Haury's (1945) and subsequently Brunson's (1989) actual analysis of the Hemenway documents and artifacts found that ample evidence for the identification of specific polychrome vessels is confirmed in the record, both by document and actual curated vessels. If anything, some additional accompanying items may not have been catalogued, but there is no question on the contextual location for most ceramic vessels.

REFERENCES CITED

Abbott, David
1988   Form, Function, Technology, and Style in Hohokam Ceramics. In *The 1982–1984 Excavations at Las Colinas: Material Culture*, by D. R. Abbott, K. E. Beckwith, P. L. Crown, R. T. Euler, D. A. Gregory, J. R. London, M. B. Saul, L. A. Schwalbe, M. Bernard-Shaw, C. R. Szuter, A. W. Vokes, pp. 73–198. Arizona State Museum, Tucson.

Abbott, David (editor)
1994   *The Pueblo Grande Project, Volume 3: Ceramics and the Production and Exchange of Pottery in the Central Phoenix Basin.* Soil Systems Publications in Archaeology No. 20. Soil Systems, Phoenix.

Allen, Wilma, T. Michael Fink, and Douglas R. Mitchell
1989   Results of the Grand Canal Project: Burial Descriptions. In *Archaeological Investigations at the Grand Canal Ruins: A Classic Period Site in Phoenix, Arizona*, vol. 1, edited by D. R. Mitchell, pp. 75–167. Soil Systems Publications in Archaeology No. 12. Soil Systems, Phoenix.

Andresen, John M.
1985   Hohokam Murals at the Clan House, Casa Grande Ruins National Monument. *The Kiva* 48:267–77.

Antieau, John M.
1981   *The Palo Verde Archaeological Investigations: Hohokam Settlement at the Confluence: Excavations along the Palo Verde Pipeline.* Museum of Northern Arizona Research Paper No. 20. Museum of Northern Arizona, Flagstaff.

Berreman, Gerald D.
1981   *Social Inequality: Comparative and Developmental Approaches.* Academic Press, New York.

Binford, Lewis R.
1971   Mortuary Practices: Their Study and Their Potential. In *Approaches to the Social Dimensions of Mortuary Practices*, organized and edited by J. A. Brown, pp. 6–29. Memoirs of the Society for American Archaeology, no. 25. Society for American Archaeology, Washington, D.C. (Issued as *American Antiquity* 36(3) Pt. 2, July 1971.)

Blanton, R. E., S. A. Kowalewski, G. Feinman, and Jill Appel
1981   *Ancient Mesoamerica: A Comparison of Change in Three Regions.* Cambridge University Press, New York.

Blau, Peter M.
1977   *Inequality and Heterogeneity.* The Free Press, New York.

Bostwick, Todd
1992   Platform Mound Ceremonialism in Southern Arizona: Possible Symbolic Meanings of Hohokam and Salado Platform Mounds. Paper presented at the Second Salado Conference, Globe, Arizona.

Bostwick, Todd W., and Christian Downum (editors)
1994   *Archaeology of the Pueblo Grande Platform Mound and Surrounding Features: Features in the Central Precinct of the Pueblo Grande Community.* Pueblo Grande Museum Anthropological Papers No.1. Pueblo Grande Museum, Phoenix.

Brunson, Judy L.
1981   The Science Library Site, AZ U:9:87 (ASU). Ms. on file, Department of Anthropology, Arizona State University, Tempe.
1989   *The Social Organization of the Los Muertos Hohokam: A Reanalysis of Cushing's Hemenway Expedition Data.* Unpublished Ph.D. dissertation, Department of Anthropology, Arizona State University, Tempe.

Brunson-Hadley, Judy L.
1994a   Cremation Burials. In *Archaeology of the Pueblo Grande Platform Mound and Surrounding Features: Features in the Central Precinct of the Pueblo Grande Community*, edited by T. W. Bostwick and C. Downum, pp. 145–84. Anthropological Papers No.1. Pueblo Grande Museum, Phoenix.
1994b   Inhumation Burials. In *Archaeology of the Pueblo Grande Platform Mound and Surrounding Features: Features in the Central Precinct of the Pueblo Grande Community*, edited by T. W. Bostwick and C. Downum, pp. 185–216. Anthropological Papers No.1. Pueblo Grande Museum, Phoenix.

Brunson-Hadley, Judy L., and Linda Countryman
1998   Introduction to the Hemenway Expedition Las Acequias Excavations. In *Excavations at Las Acequias, AZ U:9:44 (ASU), Mesa, Arizona*, edited by M. R. Hackbarth, pp. 20–41. Northland Research Technical Report No. 96–4. Flagstaff.

Carr, Christopher
1995   Mortuary Practices: Their Social, Philosophical-Religious, Circumstantial, and Physical Determinants. *Journal of Archaeological Method and Theory* 2:105–200.

Countryman, Linda
1997   A Use-Wear Analysis of Hohokam Burial Ceramics. Unpublished manuscript, Department of Anthropology, Arizona State University, Tempe.

Crown, Patricia L., and S. K. Fish
1996   Gender and Status in the Hohokam Pre-Classic to Classic Transition. *American Anthropologist* 98:803–17.

Cushing, Frank H.
1890   *Preliminary Notes on the Origin, Working Hypothesis and Primary Researches of the Hemenway Southwestern Archaeological Expedition.* Congres International des Americanistes. Compte-Rendu de la septieme session, Berlin, 1888, pp. 151–94. Berlin.
1892   Hemenway Southwestern Archaeological Expedition. Ms. on file, Peabody Museum of Archaeology and Ethnology, Harvard University, Cambridge.

Doyel, David E.
1975   *Excavations in the Escalante Ruin Group, Southern Arizona.* Archaeological Series No. 37. Arizona State Museum, Tucson.
1979   The Prehistoric Hohokam of the Arizona Desert. *American Scientist* 67:544–54.
1981   *Late Hohokam Prehistory in Southern Arizona.* Contributions to Archaeology 2. Gila Press, Scottsdale.

Effland, Richard W., Jr.
1988   An Examination of Hohokam Mortuary Practice from Casa Buena. In *Excavations at Casa Buena: Changing Hohokam Land Use along the Squaw Peak Parkway*, vol. 2, edited by J. B. Howard, pp. 693–794. Soil Systems Publications in Archaeology No. 11. Soil Systems, Phoenix.

Fagan, Brian
1989   The Artifactual Record. In *Cultural Resources Report for the All American Pipeline Project.* New Mexico State University, Las Cruces.

Fagan, Brian, Fred Plog, Elaine J. Struthers, and Jerry William
1989   A Site Sampler. In *Cultural Resources Report for the All American Pipeline Project.* New Mexico State University, Las Cruces.

Feinman, Gary, and Jill Neitzel
1984   Too Many Types: An Overview of Sedentary Prestate Societies in the Americas. In *Advances in Archaeological Method and Theory*, vol.7, edited by M. B. Schiffer, 39–102. Academic Press, Orlando.

Fewkes, J. Walter
1912   Casa Grande, Arizona. In *Twenty-Eighth Annual Report of the Bureau of American Ethnology*, pp. 25–180. Government Printing Office, Washington, D.C.

Fish, Paul R.
1989   The Hohokam: 1,000 Years of Prehistory in the Sonoran Desert. In *Dynamics of Southwest Prehistory*, edited by L. S. Cordell and G. J. Gumerman, pp. 19–63. Smithsonian Institution, Washington, D.C.

Gladwin, Harold S., Emil W. Haury, E. B. Sayles, and Nora Gladwin
1965   *Excavations at Snaketown: Material Culture.* Reprinted. University of Arizona Press, Tucson. Originally published 1937 Medallion Papers No. 25. Gila Pueblo, Globe, Arizona.

Goldstein, Lynn G.
1976   *Spatial Structure and Social Organization: Regional Manifestations of Mississippian Society.* Unpublished Ph.D. dissertation, Department of Anthropology, Northwestern University, Evanston.
1980   *Mississippian Mortuary Practices: A Case Study of Two Cemeteries in the Lower Illinois Valley.* Northwestern University Archaeological Program, Scientific Papers, No. 4. Northwestern University, Evanston.
1981   One-Dimensional Archaeology and Multi-Dimensional People: Spatial Organization and Mortuary Analysis. In *The Archaeology of Death*, edited by R. Chapman, I. Kinnes, and K. Randsborg, pp. 53–70. Cambridge University Press, Cambridge.

Gregory, David A.
1991   Form and Variation in Hohokam Settlement Patterns. In *Chaco and Hohokam: Prehistoric Regional Systems in the American Southwest*, edited by P. L. Crown and W. J. Judge, pp. 159–94. School of American Research Press, Santa Fe.

Harrington, Richard J.
1981   Analysis of the Human Skeletal Remains from Las Colinas. In *The 1968 Excavations at Mound 8, Las Colinas Ruins Group, Phoenix, Arizona*, edited by L. C. Hammack and A. D. Sullivan, pp. 251–56. Archaeological Series No. 154. Arizona State Museum, Tucson.

Haury, Emil W.
1945   *The Excavation of Los Muertos and Neighboring Ruins in the Salt River Valley, Southern Arizona.* Papers of the Peabody Museum of American Archaeology and Ethnology No. 24(1). Cambridge.
1976   *The Hohokam, Desert Farmers and Craftsmen: Excavations at Snaketown, 1964–1965.* University of Arizona Press, Tucson.

Henderson, T. Kathleen
1987   *Structure and Organization at La Ciudad.* Anthropological Field Studies No. 18. Arizona State University, Tempe.

Howard, Jerry B.
1987   The Lehi Canal System: Organization of a Classic Period Community. In *The Hohokam Village: Site Structure and Organization*, edited by D. E. Doyel, pp. 211–22. Southwestern and Rocky Mountain Division of the American Association for the Advancement of Science, Glenwood Springs, Colorado.
1992   Architecture and Ideology: An Approach to the Functional Analysis of Platform Mounds. In *Proceedings of the Second Salado Conference, Globe, AZ*, edited by R. C. Lange and S. Germick, pp. 69–77. Occasional Paper 1992. Arizona Archaeological Society, Phoenix.

Howard, Jerry B. (editor)
1988   *Excavations at Casa Buena: Changing Hohokam Land Use along the Squaw Peak Parkway.* Soil Systems Publications in Archaeology No. 11. Soil Systems, Phoenix.

Howell, Todd
1994   *Leadership at the Ancestral Zuni Village of Hawikku.* Unpublished Ph.D. dissertation, Department of Anthropology, Arizona State University, Tempe.

Kosse, Krisztina
1996   Middle Range Societies from a Scalar Perspective. In *Interpreting Southwestern*

Diversity: Underlying Principles and Overarching Patterns, edited by P. R. Fish and J. J. Reid, pp. 87–96. Anthropological Research Papers No. 48. Arizona State University, Tempe.

Laczko, Gina, David E. Doyel, and David R. Wilcox
1985   Pueblo Grande: A Central Place in the Prehistoric Salt River Valley. Paper presented at the 50th Annual Meeting of the Society for American Archaeology, Denver.

Lightfoot, Kent G., and Steadman Upham
1989   Complex Societies in the Prehistoric American Southwest: A Consideration of the Controversy. In *The Sociopolitical Structure of Prehistoric Southwestern Societies*, edited by S. Upham, K. G. Lightfoot, and R. A. Jewett, pp. 3–30. Westview Press, Boulder.

Matthews, W., J. L. Wortman, and J. S. Billings
1893   The Human Bones of the Hemenway Collection in the United States Army Medical Museum at Washington. *Memoirs of the National Academy of Sciences* 6(7):141–286. Washington, D.C.

McGuire, Randall H.
1983   Breaking Down Cultural Complexity: Inequality and Heterogeneity. *Advances in Archaeological Method and Theory*, vol. 6, edited by M. B. Schiffer, pp. 91–142. Academic Press, New York.
1987   *Death, Society, and Ideology in a Hohokam Community: Colonial and Sedentary Period Burials from La Ciudad*. Office of Cultural Resource Management Report No. 67. Arizona State University, Tempe.
1992   *Death, Society, and Ideology in a Hohokam Community*. Westview Press, Boulder.

Miller, Robert
1981   *Chavez Pass and Biological Relationship in Prehistoric Central Arizona*. Unpublished Ph.D. dissertation, Department of Anthropology, Arizona State University, Tempe.

Mitchell, Douglas R.
1991   An Investigation of Two Classic Period Hohokam Cemeteries. *North American Archaeologist* 12:109–27.
1992   Burial Practices and Paleodemographic Reconstructions at Pueblo Grande. *Kiva* 58:89–106.

Mitchell, Douglas R. (editor)
1989   *Archaeological Investigations at the Grand Canal Ruins: A Classic Period Site in Phoenix, Arizona*. Soil Systems Publications in Archaeology No. 12. Soil Systems, Phoenix.
1994a   *The Pueblo Grande Project, Volume 2: Feature Descriptions, Chronology, and Site Structure*. Soil Systems Publications in Archaeology No. 12. Soil Systems, Phoenix.
1994b   *The Pueblo Grande Project, Volume 7: An Analysis of Classic Period Mortuary Patterns*. Soil Systems Publications in Archaeology No. 20. Soil Systems, Phoenix.

Mitchell, Douglas R., and Dee Jones
1996   Mortuary Practices at Area 6 of Pueblo Salado. In *Life on the Floodplain: Further Investigations at Pueblo Salado for Phoenix Sky Harbor International Airport. Volume 2. Data Recovery and Re-evaluation. Part 1: The Report*, edited by D. H. Greenwald, J. H. Ballagh, D. R. Mitchell, and R. A. Anduze, pp. 369–400. Pueblo Grande Museum Anthropological Papers No. 4. Pueblo Grande Museum, Phoenix.

Mitchell, Douglas R., T. Michael Fink, and Wilma Allen
1989   Disposal of the Dead: Exploration of Mortuary Variability and Social Organization at the Grand Canal Ruins. In *Archaeological Investigations at the Grand Canal Ruins: A Classic Period Site in Phoenix, Arizona*, edited by D. R. Mitchell, pp. 705–73. Soil Systems Publications in Archaeology No. 12. Soil Systems, Phoenix.

Morris, Donald H., and Mahmoud Y. El-Najjar
1971   An Unusual Classic Period Burial from Las Colinas, Salt River Valley, Central Arizona. *The Kiva* 36:30–35.

O'Shea, John M.
1984   *Mortuary Variability: An Archaeological Investigation*. Academic Press, New York.

Peterson, Jane D.
1994   Chipped Stone. In *The Pueblo Grande Project, Volume 4: Material Culture*, edited by Michael S. Foster, pp. 49–118. Soil Systems Publications in Archaeology No. 20. Soil Systems, Phoenix.

Placona, JoAnne
1979   *A Report on the Mesa Grande Ruin: Excavation, Chronology, Research Goals, and Problems*. Unpublished Master's Thesis. Department of Anthropology, Arizona State University, Tempe.

Saul, Marilyn B.
1981   Disposal of the Dead at Las Colinas. In *The 1968 Excavations at Mound 8, Las Colinas Ruins Group, Phoenix, Arizona*, by L. C.

Hammack and A. D. Sullivan, pp. 257–68. Archaeological Series No. 154. Arizona State Museum, Tucson.

Saxe, Arthur A.
1970   *Social Dimensions of Mortuary Practices in a Mesolithic Population from Wadi Halfa, Sudan.* Ph.D. dissertation, Department of Anthropology, University of Michigan, Ann Arbor.

Schlegel, Alice
1992   African Political Models in the American Southwest: Hopi as Internal Frontier Society. *American Anthropologist* 94:376–97.

Tainter, Joseph A.
1978   Mortuary Practices and the Study of Prehistoric Social Systems. In *Advances in Archaeological Method and Theory*, vol. 1, edited by M. B. Schiffer, pp. 105–41. Academic Press, New York.

Turner, Christy G., II, and Joel D. Irish
1989   Further Assessment of Hohokam Affinity: The Classic Period Population of the Grand Canal and Casa Buena Sites, Phoenix, Arizona. In *Archaeological Investigations at the Grand Canal Ruins: A Classic Period Site in Phoenix, Arizona*, edited by D. R. Mitchell, pp. 775–92. Soil Systems Publications in Archaeology No.12. Soil Systems, Phoenix.

Upham, Steadman, and Glen Rice
1980   Up the Canal without a Pattern: Modeling Hohokam Interaction and Exchange. In *Current Issues in Hohokam Prehistory*, edited by D. E. Doyel and F. Plog, pp. 78–105. Anthropological Research Papers No. 23. Arizona State University, Tempe.

Wilcox, David R.
1987   *Frank Midvale's Investigation of the Site of La Ciudad.* Anthropological Field Studies No. 19. Arizona State University, Tempe.
1991   Hohokam Social Complexity. In *Chaco and Hohokam: Prehistoric Regional Systems in the American Southwest*, edited by P. L. Crown and W. J. Judge, pp. 253–76. School of American Research Press, Santa Fe.

Wilcox, David R., and Jerry B. Howard
1988   Casa Buena: Archaeological Background and Site Boundary Definition. In *Excavations at Casa Buena: Changing Hohokam Land Use along the Squaw Peak Parkway*, vol. 1, edited by J. B. Howard, pp. 19–50. Soil Systems Publications in Archaeology No. 11. Soil Systems, Phoenix.

Wilcox, David R., and Lynette O. Shenk
1977   *The Architecture of the Casa Grande and Its Interpretation.* Arizona State Museum Archaeological Series 115. Arizona State Museum, Tucson.

Wilcox, David R., Thomas R. McGuire, and Charles Sternberg
1981   *Snaketown Revisited.* Arizona State Museum Archaeological Series No. 155. Arizona State Museum, Tucson.

CHAPTER FIVE

Mortuary Ritual and Organizational Inferences
at Grasshopper Pueblo, Arizona

Stephanie M. Whittlesey and J. Jefferson Reid

THE GRASSHOPPER REGION IS A CANYON-BORDERED
mountain plateau lying at the heart of central Arizona
north of the Salt River. This rugged, environmentally
diverse region was occupied prehistorically by the Mogollon, and today is home to the White Mountain Tribe of
the Western Apache. Grasshopper Pueblo, dating to the
Pueblo IV period and the largest pueblo in the region, is
one of the most intensively studied prehistoric settlements
in North America. Research sponsored by the University of
Arizona Archaeological Field School began at Grasshopper
in 1963 and continued until 1992. Three decades of research
have resulted in one of the largest, well-provenienced, and
well-documented collections of human remains and burial goods from a single population in the world (Longacre
and Reid 1974:9). The 674 individuals and thousands of
associated artifacts have been studied by physical anthropologists and archaeologists from many perspectives,
resulting in a wealth of knowledge about prehistoric
demography, subsistence, migration, cultural affiliation,
and social organization (Berry 1983, 1985a, 1985b; Birkby
1973, 1982; Clark 1967; Ezzo 1991, 1993, 1997; Fulginiti 1993;
Griffin 1969; Hinkes 1983; Price et al. 1994; Reid and
Whittlesey 1999; Shipman 1982; Whittlesey 1978, 1999).

We focus in this paper on mortuary practices and the
organizational and ritual inferences that can be gleaned
from studying burial treatment. Following an introduction
to Grasshopper Pueblo, we describe mortuary ritual from
two perspectives—normative patterns in burial treatment
and the ways in which mortuary ritual varied among
different groups. Age, sex, and social and ceremonial memberships were the primary variables affecting how the dead
were treated. Next, we present some of the most important
inferences about the organization of Grasshopper Pueblo
that derive from bioarchaeological data. We discuss coresidence and ethnic variation, sodalities, and the relationship
of these organizational features to political authority, status, and leadership. Last, we compare mortuary ritual in
other regions of central Arizona and northern Mexico and
explore some implications of the similarities that we
observe.

GRASSHOPPER PUEBLO

The Grasshopper region is part of central Arizona's rugged
Transition Zone, a mountainous area cut by canyons and
marked by dramatic elevational changes. The region is
bounded roughly by the Salt River on the south and the
Mogollon Rim to the north, Canyon Creek to the west,
and Cibecue Creek to the east. Rich in wild game and col-
lectible plant resources, the Grasshopper region is marginal
for agriculture, with limited arable land, a relatively short

growing season, and unpredictable although abundant rainfall (Reid 1989; see Holbrook and Graves 1982). Grasshopper Pueblo is the biggest Pueblo IV period (A.D. 1300–1450) settlement in the Grasshopper region and the largest site in the mountains west of Kinishba. Grasshopper is located at an elevation of nearly 1,829 m (6,000 ft) in a lush meadow near a spring, adjacent to the broadest expanse of arable alluvium in the area. The original channel of Salt Draw once divided the pueblo and was dammed prehistorically to form a reservoir (Reid 1989).

Grasshopper Pueblo represented 500 rooms distributed among three room blocks forming the main pueblo and associated plazas, along with a number of smaller, outlying room blocks (figure 5.1). The main pueblo consisted of full-standing masonry rooms, some of which were multiple storied. The outlying room blocks, which are thought to be among the latest constructed, had jacal or brush walls above low, masonry foundations. Tree-ring dates and reconstructions of pueblo growth and abandonment (Graves 1991; Reid 1989; Reid and Riggs 1995; Riggs 1994, 1999a, 1999b) indicate that Grasshopper Pueblo was established around A.D. 1300. We think that Grasshopper was founded by families who abandoned the nearby Grasshopper Spring and Chodistaas Pueblos in the last decade of the A.D. 1200s, joining a small group already residing at Grasshopper Pueblo to establish what would become the region's largest settlement (Reid and Whittlesey 1999). Pueblo growth followed a logistic curve (Eighmy 1979), accelerating rapidly as multiple-room construction units were added (Ciolek-Torrello 1978:80–83; Reid 1973; Riggs 1999a). Tree-ring dates from the southern roofed corridor indicate that the main components of the settlement core were completed by the early A.D. 1320s; less than a decade later, Plaza 3 was converted into the Great Kiva (see figure 5.1). The date of this event corresponds to the time when logistic growth reached a plateau (Ciolek-Torrello 1978; Riggs 1999a, 1999b). Longacre's (1975, 1976) simulation of population growth indicated that the peak population could only be accounted for by immigration from other settlements. It is unlikely that the hypothetical immigrants derived solely from aggregation of local settlements, given the small number of Pueblo III period habitation sites in the Grasshopper region (Welch 1996).

The main unit at Grasshopper Pueblo represents an aggregate of three "villages," each corresponding in size (120 to 140 rooms) to the next-largest settlements in the region (Reid and Riggs 1995; Reid and Tuggle 1988). Each room block was associated with a plaza, and the integrity of these residential units was maintained throughout the pueblo's history. Bioarchaeological data suggest that the residents of each room block maintained distinct lifestyles. For example, diets varied, with maize and wild plant foods emphasized in different degrees (Ezzo 1993:56).

There were three types of ritual structures, which integrated households at different levels of organization (Reid and Montgomery 1999; Reid and Whittlesey 1982, 1999). Three households shared one ceremonial room, a type of room that contained some ritual features but lacked the complete complement of formal features that identifies kivas. Rectangular kivas with masonry benches, ventilators, and deflectors occurred in a ratio of one kiva to six households (Reid and Whittlesey 1982). The entire village, and perhaps other regional settlements, used the Great Kiva for ceremonial purposes. Plazas served as ancillary ceremonial features.

Kinship was one foundation of Grasshopper social organization. Variation in size, composition, and "wealth" of households reflects stages in the developmental cycle of domestic groups (Ciolek-Torrello 1978, 1985; Ciolek-Torrello and Reid 1974; Reid 1973; Reid and Whittlesey 1982). We infer that sodalities were the integrative and decision-making units (Reid 1989; Reid and Whittlesey 1982, 1999) and discuss them in detail in a following section. Male religious leaders probably held the strongest role in decision making, with household and kinship groups functioning in matters of social control and discipline. There is no evidence for the operation of true political authority.

Growth in the main pueblo apparently ceased after A.D. 1350 (Ciolek-Torrello 1978:80–81). Reid (1973, 1989:85) proposed that, as the size of Grasshopper Pueblo stabilized, it began to disperse, first into the smaller, less substantially constructed outlier room blocks and later into satellite communities. For example, the Canyon Creek cliff dwelling was established in A.D. 1327 after a period of stockpiling construction timbers (Graves 1983). It was founded just as Grasshopper Pueblo reached its peak size and grew exponentially between A.D. 1330 and 1350, precisely when construction at Grasshopper Pueblo had leveled off. Reid (1989) suggested that such satellite pueblos were established to bring more arable land under cultivation in an attempt to maintain or increase crop production under conditions of resource depletion and chronic nutritional stress (Decker 1986; Ezzo 1993; Hinkes 1983). The ultimate response to these stresses was abandonment (Reid 1989; Reid and Tuggle 1988). The absence of evidence for occupation

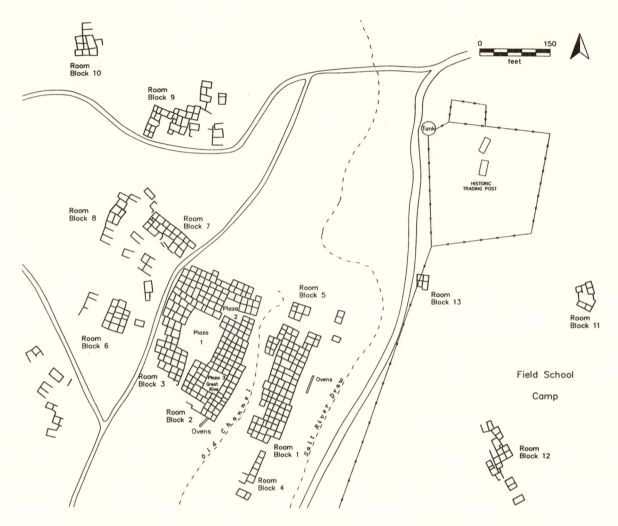

FIGURE 5.1   Map of Grasshopper Ruin

after A.D. 1400 indicates that the entire Grasshopper region was abandoned by that time. A region that for centuries had supported small, relatively mobile populations following a mixed forager-farming strategy could not sustain larger and more stable populations dependent on agriculture (Reid 1989; Reid and Whittlesey 1999; Welch 1994, 1996).

HISTORY OF MORTUARY AND BIOARCHAEOLOGICAL RESEARCH AT GRASSHOPPER

The human skeletal remains from Grasshopper Pueblo consist of 674 individuals distributed among 655 assigned burial numbers. Early in the history of the field school,

burials were excavated as they were encountered within rooms, plazas, and extramural trash deposits. There was no sampling program designed specifically to recover burials. Great care was taken with recovery and recording procedures, and as noted by Hinkes (1983), preservation is excellent. A more complete and well-preserved prehistoric skeletal series probably is not available, and a similar collection is unlikely to be obtained in the future at any southwestern site.

When the junior author assumed directorship of the field school in 1979, a growing awareness of Native American concerns, particularly the values and interests of the White Mountain Apache Tribe upon whose land Grasshopper Pueblo is located, prompted him to establish a policy of no excavation of human remains. In consultation with the Tribal Chairman, Ronnie Lupe, no burials were excavated after that year. For this reason, there are no human remains from proveniences at Grasshopper Pueblo or other sites, such as Chodistaas and Grasshopper Spring Pueblos, that were excavated after 1979. The Grasshopper burials and associated artifacts will be repatriated to the White Mountain Apache under the conditions of the Native American Graves Protection and Repatriation Act (NAGPRA).

The operation of the field school during the nascent years of processual archaeology meant that research was initially oriented toward reconstructing prehistoric social organization, and mortuary data were central to such studies. An excellent overall summary of research is provided by Ezzo (1993).

Bioarchaeological studies were initiated with Birkby's (1973, 1982) analysis of discontinuous, cranial morphological traits. His was the first study to identify the existence of genetic variability among the Grasshopper Pueblo inhabitants, suggesting that at least two different social groups with distinct cemetery areas occupied the pueblo. Birkby also proposed that male exogamy was practiced.

Several studies examined the skeletal series with respect to nutrition and health. Berry (1983, 1985b) found dental pathologies such as caries, alveolar abscesses, and hypoplasia to be more widespread and severe than among other southwestern burial populations. Hinkes (1983) studied the subadult population for stress markers, including porotic hyperostosis, cribra orbitalia, and Harris lines. Her study provided parallel skeletal evidence for previous notions that pueblo growth and abandonment were responses to subsistence stress (Reid 1973, 1978). Hinkes's results indicated that stress was chronic and increased through time. She also found that burials from the outlying room blocks, which were the latest occupied at Grasshopper Pueblo, exhibited evidence of the most severe stress.

Ezzo (1991, 1993) used bone-chemistry analyses to examine human adaptation from ecological and social perspectives. Three variables guided his research: environmental change, dietary change and stress, and nutritional quality of the diet. Ezzo (1993:83) found dietary variability through time, among room blocks, and between males and females. He interpreted spatial variability as reflecting differential access to farmland and resources. Consumption of wild resources decreased, and use of maize increased, through

time. Dietary data also supported higher status for males, although the distinction blurred late in the pueblo's history when nutritional stress was most evident. Ezzo (1993:81) found no evidence for vertical social differentiation or centralized authority based on dietary differences.

A number of researchers have used the mortuary data in studies of prehistoric social organization, beginning with Clark (1967). Clark defined a number of burial clusters based on provenience. Clark then statistically compared the clusters in terms of mortuary treatment and associated artifacts. He concluded that a model of social stratification could explain the tremendous variability he observed. Following Clark's lead, Griffin (1969) attempted to discover ranked social hierarchies using the mortuary data. An alternative hypothesis, that of an egalitarian social system, also was tested. Mortuary, room-floor assemblage, and ceramic data were matched with test implications for each hypothesis. Griffin (1969:171) concluded that there was no evidence for ranking and redistribution at Grasshopper Pueblo, and suggested that further research could more profitably explore the egalitarian adaptation rather than waste effort in attempts to identify hierarchical structure.

The bizarrely contradictory conclusions of Clark and Griffin led Whittlesey (1978) to use these studies as cases in a methodological and theoretical exploration of archaeological correlates (Schiffer 1976). Whittlesey used the Grasshopper mortuary data to demonstrate the effects of correlate derivation and application on behavioral inference. A hypothetical model derived from typical processual approaches and employing deductive methodology was contrasted with a second, inductive model. The results were illuminating—both models were confirmed. The deductive approach yielded evidence consistent with a model of social stratification, whereas the inductive model was congruent with an egalitarian system of social organization. Because both organizational structures could not have operated simultaneously at Grasshopper Pueblo, Whittlesey reached the inevitable conclusion that the results were predestined by the analytic methods. Most important, the diluting influence of weak data was underscored. Both models—ranked and nonranked organization—could be supported when weak data and poorly derived correlates were employed, but when only strong cases were examined and when considerable attention was directed toward correlate construction and use, only one could be confirmed. The theoretical nature of Whittlesey's study was ignored by critics of the Grasshopper model of social organization, who treated it as though it was an inferential reconstruction (e.g., Plog 1985; Upham and Plog 1986).

Mortuary practices were central to the Grasshopper-Chavez Pass debate that emerged in the 1980s. At the heart of the debate was the nature of Mogollon Pueblo social organization. Archaeologists from Arizona State University studying Chavez Pass Pueblo (also called Nuvaqueotaka and Nuvakwewtaqa) attempted to define social complexity at the pueblo, identifying social stratification, managerial elites, and hierarchical rank. Those investigating Grasshopper Pueblo demonstrated an organizational framework similar to the model provided by historic Western Pueblos, in which kinship-based groups were the foundation of land tenure and social organization; social inequality was based in age, gender, and ceremonial rank; and political authority was vested in ceremonial status. Incorrectly known as the "egalitarian model" of social organization (e.g., Lightfoot and Upham 1989), or as Plog (1985) terms it, "the Grasshopper alternative," the Grasshopper perspective, in particular the interpretations based on mortuary data, was widely, acrimoniously, and destructively criticized (see Cordell 1985; Cordell et al. 1987; Plog 1985; Upham 1982; Upham and Plog 1986). For example, Plog (1985) presented a critique of Whittlesey's (1978) dissertation that was at best a gross misunderstanding and at worst a deliberate misrepresentation of that work, accusing Whittlesey of deliberately manipulating data to influence the results.

The negative aspects of the debate, the passionate rhetoric that accompanied it, and the diverting focus on theoretical concepts served to mask effectively the real crux of the matter—the nature of the opposing data sets (Reid 1999). The simplistic approach of the Chavez Pass researchers to behavioral inference can be criticized (see Reid and Whittlesey 1990), but the issue quite simply is the weak nature of the Chavez Pass data. As has been noted (e.g., Downum 1986; Graves 1987; Whittlesey 1984, 1989), the site was tested in an extremely limited fashion. Test pits were placed in rooms; not a single room was excavated completely. The mortuary data are even weaker. The data used by Upham (1978) to construct a five-tiered, hierarchical system of social organization based on the distribution of status markers consisted of 44 vandalized burial loci, some of which contained neither human skeletal remains nor burial goods in situ (Whittlesey 1984). Similar burials are typically excluded by other researchers investigating prehistoric mortuary

practices (e.g., Hohmann 1982; Whittlesey 1978). As Ezzo (1993:22) noted, there was no attempt on the part of the Chavez Pass researchers to control for temporal placement, sample representativeness, or even basic age and sex data. By admission, much of the critical information used in the study of mortuary practice was unrecoverable (Upham and Plog 1986). There can be no question that the Chavez Pass mortuary information does not constitute reliable data. Whereas it always is stimulating for archaeologists to argue the merits of theoretical positions, no resolution of the Grasshopper-Chavez Pass debate is possible with the current data set from Chavez Pass. Any revival of the debate must proceed on the basis of comparable evidence.

MORTUARY RITUAL AT GRASSHOPPER PUEBLO

Discussion of mortuary ritual is based on a sample of 411 complete, relatively undisturbed interments, as revised from Whittlesey (1978). The typical practice at Grasshopper Pueblo was to bury the dead within rooms that were abandoned and filled with refuse, or in the case of young children, in rooms that were still occupied. It appears that there was no method of marking graves, for as rooms continued to be used for interments, the graves of previous burials were encountered repeatedly. When the remains of previous burials were discovered during a subsequent interment, the skeletal remains and associated goods were removed and redeposited without formal reburial, evidently close to the original location. As a result, there were numerous instances of nonarticulated, highly disturbed burials, particularly those of subadults who were buried most often in rooms. Of the 674 individuals in the burial sample, 263 (39.0%) were disturbed in this fashion. Although many of these cases can be used in bioarchaeological research (e.g., Hinkes 1983), they do not constitute strong cases for describing mortuary practices or inferring prehistoric social organization and ritual from mortuary data and for this reason were not used by Whittlesey (1978).

Bioarchaeological data of many kinds have been collected over the years by many different researchers, and the human remains continue to be studied. The present research, like Whittlesey's (1978) original study, used the baseline age, sex, and cranial deformation data collected by Walter Birkby of the Arizona State Museum, University of Arizona. The senior author also made observations on

TABLE 5.1 Age and Sex Distribution of Grasshopper Burials

Age Class and Sex	Total Sample*		Undisturbed Burials	
	Number	*Percent*	*Number*	*Percent*
Fetal	40	6.6%	22	5.4%
Birth to 1 year	116	19.1%	58	14.1%
1–3.9 years	106	17.4%	88	21.4%
4–11.9 years	109	17.9%	63	15.3%
12–14.9 years**	6	1.0%	7	1.7%
Male	3	(50.0%)	1	(14.3%)
Female	3	(50.0%)	1	(14.3%)
Indete.	0	—	5	(71.4%)
15–19.9 years**	30	4.9%	18	4.4%
Male	13	(43.3%)	8	(44.4%)
Female	17	(56.7%)	9	(50.0%)
Indete.	0	—	1	(5.6%)
20–29.9 years	57	9.4%	36	8.8%
Male	20	(35.1%)	12	(33.3%)
Female	37	(64.9%)	24	(66.7%)
30–39.9 years	58	9.5%	48	11.7%
Male	24	(41.4%)	17	(35.2%)
Female	34	(58.6%)	31	(64.6%)
40–49.9 years***	86	14.1%	45	10.9%
Male	34	(39.5%)	22	(48.9%)
Female	52	(60.5%)	23	(51.1%)
> 50 years***	—	—	26	6.3%
Male	—	—	7	(26.9%)
Female	—	—	19	(73.1%)
Total	**608**	**100.0%**	**411**	**100.0%**

* Data from Hinkes (1983:Table 1). Excludes 66 unanalyzable subadult burials.

** Hinkes (1983:Table 1) classified these age groups as 12–14 and 14–20, respectively.

*** Hinkes (1982:Table 1) classified these age groups as 40–45 and 45+, respectively.

cranial deformation for a small number of individuals (Whittlesey 1978).

The nature and representativeness of the complete burial sample have been discussed previously (Ezzo 1993; Hinkes 1983). The sample is biased toward subadults and, among adults, toward females. Of the 674 individuals, only 231 (34.3%) were aged 15 years or older (table 5.1). Hinkes (1983) noted that Grasshopper displayed an extremely high percentage of subadults compared to other prehistoric southwestern sites. Although infant mortality undeniably was great, archaeological recovery procedures also contributed to the high percentage of subadults. Excavation focused on rooms, in which 90%

of the subadults were found (Hinkes 1983:19). Extramural areas, particularly plazas, in which proportionately more adults were buried, were excavated less intensively, contributing to the relatively low proportion of adults.

The striking majority of females (60% of sexed burials) (see table 5.1) has been noted as unusual among burial samples from contemporaneous populations (Berry 1985a). Archaeological recovery techniques probably were not responsible for this disparity. Some areas that yielded higher proportions of female burials (e.g., Plaza 2) were excavated less intensively than other burial areas, and all of the extramural areas that were used as adult burial locales were sampled. The predominance of females does not seem puzzling given the conditions of life at Grasshopper Pueblo. It is probable that mortality rates were much higher for women than men. Ezzo (1993:54–55) presented evidence that diets of men and women differed, at least during the earlier portions of the pueblo's history, when men evidently subsisted more heavily on meat. Late in Grasshopper's occupation, the amount of meat and wild plant foods in everyone's diets declined, as maize became the dietary mainstay. The lesser amount of protein in women's diets combined with the nutritional deficiencies that result from subsisting almost completely on maize (El-Najjar et al. 1976; Ivanhoe 1985; Snow 1990; Walker 1985) may have created impoverished nutrition and poor health, particularly during pregnancy and lactation. For example, Cummings (1995:344) has noted that folate deficiencies can result in megaloblastic anemia, and pregnant women are more susceptible because the body's need for folate doubles during pregnancy. "If the diet was composed largely of corn, megaloblastic anemia undoubtedly increased the death rate among pregnant women and nursing mothers" (Cummings 1995:344). Women no doubt also experienced complications of pregnancy and labor, and the lack of medical care must have resulted in many deaths. It also is possible that, because of hunting, raiding, and long-distance journeys, some men died and were buried away from the pueblo.

The complete burial sample (Hinkes 1983) and the collection of articulated, undisturbed burials are compared in table 5.1. There are some differences due to the methods used. For example, Hinkes (1983) sexed subadults less than 15 years of age, whereas Whittlesey (1978) did not. These considerations aside, the smaller collection appears to differ little in age and sex distributions from the complete sample. The largest differences are in the sex proportions among adults in the 40-to-50-year age interval, which are nearly equal in the undisturbed sample. Ezzo (1993:29) concluded that "the evidence suggests that the burial series may be treated as a viable sample of the inhabitants of the site in terms of age ranges, social/ ethnic affiliations, and probably in status positions." We make a similar claim for the sample of undisturbed interments. Note that, in the discussion that follows, we most often use "sex" in its biological sense, rather than "gender" in its social sense.

Normative Mortuary Ritual

A general pattern in the treatment of the dead at Grasshopper Pueblo has been identified that holds for all age groups, both sexes, and across the social, ethnic, and residential classes that have been inferred. It also changed little through time. This pattern suggests to us the existence of a normative ritual to prepare the residents of Grasshopper Pueblo for the afterlife. Normative treatment involved burial in a simple, rectangular pit without any elaboration or cover. The deceased was placed in a supine, extended position with arms and legs parallel to the body and feet uncrossed. Orientation was typically east-west, with the head placed to the east. There was, however, considerable variation in orientation and head placement.

Accompaniments also were highly standardized, consisting of ceramic vessels—predominantly bowls—presumed to have held offerings of food and water, personal ornaments, and little else. The placement of ornaments upon the body suggests that the deceased was dressed in clothing, although scant evidence of perishable materials has survived. Wrapping the body in blankets or matting and use of powdered pigments were not common, although this may also reflect factors of preservation and archaeological recovery. There is no way to ascertain if the face and body were painted, although pigment staining on skeletal elements of some burials suggests that this took place. The placement of offerings also was standardized. Vessels were placed at the head, feet, and pelvis, and more commonly at the left side of the body. Although some adults were buried with specialized tool kits, the everyday tools used in domestic life, such as grinding equipment, flaked-stone tools, and hammer stones, were conspicuously sparse among the mortuary artifacts. We conclude from these patterns and from the variability in mortuary accompaniments described below that it was the social and ceremonial memberships of the deceased, rather than the daily roles assigned to individuals, that influenced their treatment at death (Whittlesey 1999).

Variability in Mortuary Ritual

The existence of a normative burial pattern does not imply that variability did not exist. Quantitative and qualitative differences among burial treatment are apparent. We think that much of the variability in the ways that people were treated upon death stems from the age and gender of the individual, from the social and ceremonial memberships that they held, and to the less tangible factors of prestige accorded to politicoreligious leaders and skilled artisans and shamans.

Age of the Deceased

The first variable that influenced mortuary treatment was the age of the deceased. Children were treated differently than adults. The burials of children displayed the most variability in aspects of grave type and body positioning, and the least variability in artifactual accompaniments. Standardization in the former and variation in the latter increased with increasing age at death.

Children

Location, Facility, and Position. Subadults were more likely than adults to be buried within rooms. The youngest infants and fetal burials often were placed in pits immediately below the floors of occupied rooms. This has been explained with reference to ethnographically documented Pueblo practices. By keeping the deceased child close to the mother, its spirit may be encouraged to return quickly in the form of another baby (Bunzel 1932:482; Eggan 1950:47; Parsons 1939:71; Voth 1912:103; White 1942:164). Certain types of graves were used more frequently for subadults, including slab-covered pits and stone-lined cists. The majority of slab-covered and stone-lined grave pits occurred with children less than four years of age. The high-energy-expenditure types of graves, such as log-crib-covered pits, were seldom used. Although burial in trash without benefit of a formal pit was not common at Grasshopper, about 90% of these interments represented subadults, and many of these were fetal burials. Children were seldom wrapped in reed matting or other types of body cover.

Children also were variable in body positioning. About three-fourths of the few flexed and semiflexed burials were subadults. There was greater variation in placement of the limbs and extremities as well. The majority of the burials that were oriented with the head to north, south, and west were subadults.

Accompaniments. There was little variability in the artifacts that accompanied children; the types and numbers of accompaniments were limited. Children tended to be buried with ceramic vessels and personal ornaments of particular types. The ornaments that signify membership in sodalities (see below) and the utilitarian and ceremonial items that accompanied adults were not found among subadults. Subadults always were accompanied by fewer grave goods (mean = 2.03 artifacts) than adults (mean = 6.03 artifacts), and these patterns held regardless of burial provenience. We found that the number of associated artifacts increased along with the age of the child at death. Younger children were also buried less frequently with painted vessels. No painted vessels were found with fetal burials; roughly one-third of the burial vessels interred with subadults aged birth to four years were painted. By contrast, about 50–60% of the vessels buried with individuals aged four years and older were painted. Children also had more miniature ceramic vessels than adults.

Life Cycle and Mortuary Ritual. The location of burials inside rooms and the variability in aspects of grave preparation and body positioning suggest to us that it was most likely the deceased child's immediate family and other close kin who prepared the body for burial. It also implies that, whereas it may have been necessary to treat adults in highly normative ways to prepare them for the afterlife, such preparation was not needed for children. We think that the limited number and type of grave goods indicates that children did not participate in the wider circle of social and ceremonial obligations that were criteria of adult status.

We also believe that we can identify particular transitions in the life cycle and social recognition of these changes. The first of these was birth. Infant burials of fetal age differed from full-term infants in location of interment (room floors, trash) and associated grave goods (typically none). This suggests that membership in the natal kinship unit was bestowed on a full-term infant at birth, and premature and stillborn infants were not regarded in the same way (Whittlesey 1989). Cushing reported that a Zuni infant was not considered a living human being until nine days after its birth (Green 1979:205). A second transition took place at about one year of age. The number of ceramic vessels accompanying children increased dramatically at that age. More than two-thirds of children aged less than one year at death lacked ceramic vessels, contrasted with only one-third of children aged one to four years at death. This may indicate a transition in status, perhaps induction into a ceremonial group or formal bestowal of a name. Titiev (1992:129) reported that at Oraibi a child who died prior to its katsina cult initiation was given a distinctive type of burial. Or the pattern may indicate simply that children less than one year of age were not yet weaned and therefore did not require offerings of food and water in the afterlife (Whittlesey 1989).

ADULTS

Patterns among adults are the reverse of those observed with children—there was more standardization in attributes of grave type and body position, and more variability in associated artifacts.

Location, Facility, and Position. Adults were buried in outdoor locales, including plazas and trash deposits outside the pueblo, more frequently than subadults. Abandoned rooms filled with trash occasionally were used, but adult burials apparently were never placed in occupied rooms.

The most energy in grave preparation and body treatment was expended on adults. Adults were much more likely than children to be buried in elaborated grave pits, such as those with cribbed wooden roofs, pits with ledges for accompaniments, and pit-and-chamber graves. Body coverings and grave linings, such as woven reed matting, occurred more frequently than among children, and there was far less variability in body position. Adults, particularly those in the midlife years, were most commonly interred in the extended supine position. It is interesting that among the oldest adults there was a return to greater variation in treatment. Individuals aged 50 years and older at death were buried in slab-covered pits, cists, and log-crib graves more frequently than younger adults, and there was more variation in body position. The sample is relatively small, however, in this age group (21 burials).

Accompaniments. Adults were buried with utilitarian and ceremonial goods in addition to ceramic vessels and ornaments. The quantity of ceramic offerings per burial, particularly painted pottery, was much higher among adults. Utilitarian and ceremonial items typically were found associated together as tool kits and seldom included common domestic equipment such as manos. Tool kits represented diverse items used in making particular kinds of tools or in presumed ritual activities. A flintknapper's tool kit might include an anvil, antler flakers, cores, flaked-stone tools, and debitage. Ritual objects—possible shaman's tool kits—included quartz crystals, animal effigies, unusual natural objects such as concretions, eccentric flaked-stone tools, worked and unworked pigments, and nonutilitarian objects such as polished stone cylinders. Their tightly clustered placement suggests these objects were originally contained in a bag or pouch of perishable materials. Although single projectile points, quartz crystals, or stone effigies were occasionally found with subadult burials, the specialized tool kits and the clusters of projectile points thought to represent quivers of arrows (discussed below) occurred only with adult burials, most of whom were male. Also found with adults were fragments of painted wooden staffs and large sherd plates containing charcoal.

Life Cycle and Mortuary Ritual. We infer from the location of interments, standardization of grave type and body position, and nature of accompaniments that burial of an adult was performed by individuals other than the immediate family and that burial ceremonies may have been public events. Among adults, there was a trend toward increased energy expenditure and additional numbers of accompaniments as age increased. Log-crib-covered graves occurred among almost two-thirds of the adults aged 50 years and older at death, contrasted with less than 10% of younger adults and about 5% of children aged 1–12 years. All of the higher-energy treatments occurred more frequently with increasing age. Persons of advanced age were buried with nearly twice the number of accompaniments as the individuals in the 40-to-50-year age class (excluding the exceptional Burial 140 discussed below). This suggests to us that increasing age was awarded increased respect; the most senior persons in the community also were those most likely to have the largest network of social and ritual obligations.

SEX OF THE DECEASED

The second variable to influence mortuary treatment was the sex of the deceased. The most energy was expended on the interment of men, and they were accompanied by the most grave goods. The treatment of women was intermediate between that accorded adult men and children, and it is striking that many of the same attributes that characterized child burials also applied to women.

Location, Facility, and Position. There was little difference in the burial location among males and females. Like males, adult females tended to be buried in extramural areas more frequently than other proveniences. The exception is the Great Kiva, in which only females and subadults were buried following its abandonment as a ritual facility. Another provenience with a tendency toward more female burials was Plaza 2, whereas proportionately more males were buried in Plaza 1.

Females were more variable in grave type and body position than males. Certain higher-energy grave types occurred more commonly with one sex or the other, although the correlation is not absolute. Females, for example, were buried more often in slab-covered graves, stone-lined cists, and log-crib graves. Only males were buried in pit-and-chamber graves (n = 2) and were more frequently interred in pits with ledges. Males also were buried in lined grave pits and wrapped in some type of body covering more often than females. Flexure and semiflexure were more common among females, but there was little difference in orientation. We do not know the degree to which these patterns were influenced by the significantly larger sample of female burials.

Accompaniments. Males were buried consistently with more associated artifacts than females. Excluding Burial 140, the mean number of accompaniments among males (9.17) was nearly twice that of females (4.95). Types of accompaniments also differed. Whereas males were buried with many more utilitarian and ceremonial objects than females, both sexes had ornaments in similar proportions. There was some variability in particular ceramic types and artifact classes, although as with other variables, there were no absolute differences. Males tended to be buried more frequently with vessels of Roosevelt Red Ware, White Mountain Red Ware, Salado Red Ware, Cibicue Polychrome, and Cibecue Painted Corrugated. Females were accompanied more frequently by offerings of Pinedale Black-on-white, brown plain ware, red ware, and Grasshopper Red Ware vessels. The last is a locally made, painted ware with a brown paste and designs imitative of White Mountain Red Ware (Van Keuren 1999). Certain ornaments were found only with one sex or the other. Bone hairpins, *Conus* sp. shell tinklers, bone beads, and *Glycymeris* sp. shell pendants were found only with male burials, whereas only females had shell ornaments covered with turquoise mosaic and finger rings of bone and shell. Both sexes were buried in stone pendants; strings of disc beads made from stone and shell worn as anklets, bracelets, and necklaces; *Glycymeris* sp. shell bracelets; and turquoise mosaic earbobs.

Certain types of utilitarian objects also were found predominantly with one sex or the other. Although rare in the sample as a whole, the class of stone tools including polishing, pecking, and rubbing stones was found only with female burials. Inferred ritual tool kits, flintknapper's tool kits, and clusters of projectile points were found only with males.

Life Cycle and Mortuary Ritual. It is notable that the more common types of grave elaborations and variants in body position among women also were those found more often with children. Women also were similar to children in the types and quantities of mortuary accompaniments. We do not infer from these data that women necessarily held lower status in the community, but instead that they probably participated less intensively in pueblo religious life and held fewer memberships in nonkinship-based groups. Most women probably were buried by members of their own families and larger kinship groups. Their burial ceremonies were probably less often public events than those held for men and were attended by fewer mourners bringing offerings.

Whittlesey (1999:46) observed that social and ritual memberships seem to have been far more important in determining social identity than gender alone. The near-complete absence in mortuary contexts of the objects that must have marked the everyday activities and roles of men and women—mealing equipment, butchering and processing tools, cooking pots—indicates that these roles were not recognized in either mortuary ritual or the afterlife.

ORGANIZATIONAL INFERENCES FROM MORTUARY RITUAL

Coresidence and Ethnic Variation

Following Reed (1948, 1950), we identify Grasshopper Pueblo as part of the Mogollon Pueblo tradition. This simple heuristic device should not mask the cultural and biological variability of Grasshopper's residents. A long-term research interest has been identifying ethnic coresidence at Grasshopper Pueblo and at earlier settlements in the region (Reid 1989). Available information suggests that migration into the Grasshopper region began in the late A.D. 1200s, probably in response to environmental deterioration on the Colorado Plateau. Excavated settlements occupied immediately prior to Grasshopper Pueblo were characterized by variability in architecture, ceramics, and lifestyles that suggest some were occupied by Plateau Anasazi and others by Mogollon with considerable, long-term contacts with Anasazi people (Lorentzen 1993; Lowell 1995; Montgomery and Reid 1990; Reid 1989; Reid and Whittlesey 1999; Zedeño 1994).

An enclave of Anasazi apparently lived in harmony with the indigenous Mogollon at Grasshopper Pueblo (Reid and Whittlesey 1999; Riggs 1999a, 1999b), continuing a tradition that had characterized the mountains for hundreds of years (e.g., Haury 1940, 1985). This inference is derived from bioarchaeological, architectural, and mortuary data. The majority of burials exhibited the deformed crania thought to stem from binding infants inside cradleboards. More than 80% of the individuals for whom deformation could be determined, primarily adults, exhibited vertical-occipital deformation. This type of skull deformation has long been thought to have characterized the Mogollon (Reed 1948; Reid 1989), who clearly were the majority population at Grasshopper Pueblo.

A small but important group of 28 individuals displayed lambdoidal cranial deformation, which typically has been associated with the Anasazi. These individuals were buried throughout the pueblo except in Room Block 3. Proportionately more of these individuals were found in Room Block 1 and the extramural refuse areas. The percentage of females in the group of lambdoidally deformed individuals was much higher than among the total sample (75.0%). Architectural and mortuary data suggest that Anasazi people may have occupied Room Block 5, a small, detached group of rooms north of Room Block 1 (see figure 5.1). T-shaped doorways, which were rare at Grasshopper Pueblo, occurred in this room block, and the location of a pit-and-chamber grave (unexcavated) in one of the rooms also suggests an Anasazi presence. Both of the excavated pit-and-chamber graves at Grasshopper contained lambdoidally deformed males.

A much smaller group of eight individuals (only one of whom was male) exhibited undeformed skulls, which presumably resulted either from not being placed in cradleboards during infancy or use of a soft, flexible form of infant restraint. We know of no region or culture particularly associated with the absence of cradleboard deformation, although we note that a significant number of the burials from Point of Pines Pueblo exhibited undeformed crania (Bennett 1973). Ezzo (1993:52) linked this feature with desert populations. As with the lambdoidally deformed individuals, the burials with undeformed skulls were distributed throughout the pueblo, although again there were none in Room Block 3. No conclusions can be drawn in light of the small sample size.

Variability in cranial deformation suggesting ethnic coresidence at Grasshopper Pueblo is borne out by analysis of strontium isotope ratios in tooth enamel (Ezzo 1997; Price et al. 1994). The sample is small, but the data indicate that three of seven analyzed individuals likely were born elsewhere, moving to Grasshopper later in life (Price et al. 1994). A Colorado Plateau origin, perhaps in the Little Colorado River Valley or more northern areas, is suggested for these individuals.

There is nothing to indicate that the sojourn of resident Anasazi and other probable immigrants at Grasshopper Pueblo was anything but harmonious. The men were active in the pueblo ceremonial system, and indeed the Anasazi may have enjoyed somewhat greater personal wealth as the result of participation in exchange networks (Ezzo 1997; Triadan 1989, 1997). The predominance of women among the inferred nonlocal groups hints that marriage into Grasshopper Pueblo may have been a mechanism for strengthening economic and other ties with distant relatives.

Sodalities

Sodalities—ceremonial associations that crosscut kinship groups—are inferred to have been another important structural base of Grasshopper social organization and the foundation of political leadership (Reid and Whittlesey 1982, 1999). The mortuary ritual provides us with evidence for the presence of sodalities. Several types of mortuary accompaniments were differentially distributed, placed in the graves or worn by the deceased in extremely standardized ways, and do not appear to reflect simple ornamentation. We think that these objects were worn or carried as part of a ceremonial costume and that they symbolized membership in several sodalities (Reid and Whittlesey 1982, 1999).

Bone hairpins are the first special ornaments and were found only with males. These ornaments were placed at the skull in such a fashion as to suggest that they were thrust through a knot of hair at the top or back of the head. Hairpins were well polished with a long length-to-width ratio. Shorter, less well-polished bone tools, inferred to be awls, were occasionally found in the graves of females but were never placed at the skull.

The second group includes shell ornaments of several types. Shell bracelets (*Glycymeris* sp.), typically worn on the left arm, occurred singly or in groups among male and female burials. Pendants were made by removing the center of a *Glycymeris* shell and perforating it for suspension; these objects have a much smaller opening than bracelets and are too small to have been worn as such. Shell pendants were placed in stylized fashion only with male burials. Their location above the pubic symphysis suggests that they were attached to a belt or loincloth.

Ceramic sculpture from coastal Mexico shows male figures wearing conch shells above a loincloth in a similar position (Kan et al. 1970:figure 16a). Tinklers made by grinding the tips of *Conus* sp. shells and drilling them for suspension were also found only with males. By their location in burials, some tinklers appear to have decorated quivers and others were sewn to clothing. In one case a cluster of tinklers decorated the tip of a painted wooden staff (cf. Tower 1945; see Di Peso et al. [1974b:468] for an illustration of this use).

The third group represents inferred quivers of perishable material. A few males were buried with groups of projectile points placed, with one exception, above the left shoulder with tips projecting upward. Their aligned position and parallel placement against the body suggests that the points were hafted on arrow shafts when interred. The placement of other items, such as bone rasps and shell tinklers, implies that the arrows and other items were contained within a quiver of leather, cloth, basketry, or other perishable material. Quivers carried in this fashion at the shoulder, with tips of points placed upward, are depicted on Mimbres Black-on-white vessels (figure 5.2). Similar perishable quivers have been found with burials from cliff dwellings and rockshelters (e.g., Haury 1950:418, 464, plate 39). For example, a burial at Hidden House in the Verde Valley, Arizona (Dixon 1956) was accompanied by two quivers, bows, and a number of arrows. A decorated cloth quiver containing 12 arrows, a leather quiver containing 10 unfinished arrows, and two bows (one of which also was unfinished) were placed to the right side of the body. The arrows in the cloth quiver were placed with feathered ends down and points projecting from the opening. A bundle of arrow foreshafts, yucca fiber, a feathered stick, and bundles of feather and sinew also accompanied the burial.

Their limited distribution indicates that the quivers did not simply represent the everyday equipment of hunters. Although we can assume with some certainty that most adult men hunted and made their own arrows and other hunting equipment (Whittaker 1984), only seven men were buried with arrow clusters, or about 10% of the male burials.

The distribution of the inferred symbolic objects at Grasshopper is striking. First, the shell ornaments were mutually exclusive. For example, if an individual was buried with a shell pendant, he did not also have shell bracelets or tinklers. Second, bone awls were exclusive relative to all shell ornaments except bracelets; neither shell

pendants nor tinklers co-occurred with bone awls. We think that simple decorative ornaments would be unlikely to have such an unusual distribution, although we recognize that the sample of each ornament group is small. In addition, we note that other types of ornaments, including those most commonly worn by women and children (such as strings of stone and shell beads), do not have similar, exclusive distributions.

If we are correct in our interpretation of the unusual distributions of ornamental objects and projectile points, there were four male sodalities, three of which were exclusive in membership. Because bone awls and shell ornaments were found among the men buried with inferred quivers of arrows (with the same observed patterns of shell ornament exclusivity), we think that the arrow group was a sodality that drew its membership from men belonging to all other groups. The composition and function of the group possibly represented by shell bracelets is less clear, because it included men and women in its membership. It may not represent a sodality but some other kind of group, or the bracelets may represent simple ornamentation, wealth, or prestige. There were men of presumed Anasazi and Mogollon origin in all but the shell tinkler and arrow groups, but because the number of lambdoidally deformed males is small, these patterns are tentative.

Symbolic representations of identity are common among agriculturally based Neolithic peoples. They are particularly widespread in Puebloan iconography and include animals, colors, and directions (Bunzel 1932; Cushing 1883; Eggan 1950; Parsons 1939; Thompson and Joseph 1944; Waters 1963). It is not surprising, therefore, that artifact symbols of sodality membership and leadership occur in Puebloan ethnography. For example, the village chief or *kikmongwi* at Oraibi inherited a wand or stick of authority that was used only during important ceremonies (Titiev 1944:64). The stick was placed in the grave at death, where it "marks the person as a member of a particular society and a leader in that group" (Wright 1979:92). Other types of symbols were also called by the term for "chief stick" and were usually taken to mean the badge of office carried by a sodality member (Wright 1979:92). Fewkes (1896:365) stated that shell tinklers were considered as socioreligious objects representing several Hopi gods (reported by Di Peso et al. 1974b:467; Ravesloot 1994:843). We interpret the unusual patterning in particular ornaments and objects to mean that a sodality member was prepared for burial in ceremonial dress that included those

FIGURE 5.2   Warrior Figure with Quiver, Mimbres Black-on-white Bowl. Drawing by Stephanie M. Whittlesey
(based on Brody 1987:plate 14).

particular symbols associated with the society. As White (1962:215) wrote of Zia Pueblo, "Members of the societies are dressed in the costume worn in their ceremonies. Nonsociety members are dressed in ordinary clothes." At Oraibi, the kikmongwi was painted with face and body symbols for important ritual occasions and to prepare his body for burial (Titiev 1992:64).

Tantalizing evidence for the interpretation that the inferred arrow quivers symbolized sodality membership comes from Hawikuh. Describing a burial, Hodge wrote (Smith et al. 1966:174), "[along the right side of the body] were a collection of 3 bows and 2 flutes, massed together. . . . In the vicinity of the neck and left shoulder were 7 small arrowpoints. . . . The quiver or covering of

the bows seems to be of woven material, an impression of which is seen on the mass of bows." At the left side of the body was "a mass of arrowshafts. An old Zuni says these are the remains of a Priest of the Bow" (Smith et al. 1966:174).

Further support for these inferences and the basis by which we suggest sodalities were the foundation of political authority is Burial 140. Widely characterized in earlier years as a "high-status burial" (e.g., Griffin 1967), this individual indeed is the most richly appointed burial to have been recovered at Grasshopper Pueblo. We think that the abundance of burial goods reflected his leadership of two Grasshopper sodalities and the prestige and authority stemming from this role. Burial 140 was a male aged between 40 and 45 years at the time of his death. He was interred in Plaza 3, which was converted to the Great Kiva midway in the occupation of Grasshopper Pueblo. His grave evidently was a log-cribbed form, although not recognized as such during excavation, which contained two layers of burial accompaniments.

Although the number of ceramic vessels (36) and the presence of ceremonial objects in this burial are striking, most interesting is the unusual character of the other accompaniments. Around the left upper arm were eight *Glycymeris* sp. shell bracelets. Several decorated bone hairpins, including one with a turquoise and shell mosaic handle, were placed at his skull. An elaborately incised and painted wand made from the femur of a grizzly bear was included with the hairpins. These decorated hairpins are unique; no others have been recovered from mortuary or domestic contexts at Grasshopper. About 130 projectile points were found in two layers with the burial. At the right shoulder, signifying perhaps that the man was left-handed, was a cluster of projectile points oriented with tips pointing upward (to the east). Placement suggests that a notched bone tool or rasp was carried in the quiver along with the arrows. Another cluster of points was found at the right ankle, and smaller groups of points were placed along the body. The majority of these points were oriented to the west. In the upper layer, probably representing the log-crib covering, were 54 projectile points, 48 of which were arranged in clusters of two to eight points. Ground specular hematite was distributed among the point clusters.

The unusual character of the burial accompaniments indicates to us that Burial 140 may have been the leader of the sodality symbolized by bone hairpins and the hunting or warrior society represented by arrow quivers. The striking and highly visible decorated hairpins, the other probable symbols of authority such as the incised wand and bone rasp, and in particular the additional clusters of projectile points appear to reflect factors other than simply personal adornment or wealth. The arrow clusters may have been contributed by members of the arrow society as offerings. A discussion of Zia Pueblo mortuary practices by White (1962:215–16) is illuminating in this regard:

> If the deceased was a member of a secret society the head man of the society is notified immediately after death occurs. He notifies all the member of the society, and they gather in their ceremonial house to prepare the costume and paints for the deceased. When they are ready they go to the home of the deceased and prepare him for burial:

> they put on his ceremonial costume, paint him, and wrap him in a blanket. (White 1962:215–16)

White (1962:217–19) also noted that:

> Four days after death, one of the four societies qualified to perform mortuary ceremonies will conduct a ritual for the deceased. The ritual will be carried out by the deceased's own society if he was a member of one of the qualified societies, or by one of the other societies if he was not. The ceremony involves meal paintings, food offerings, prayersticks, and concludes with a meeting in the society house. (White 1962:217–19)

If prestige and wealth are measured by the number of burial accompaniments, then the men belonging to sodalities were accorded great respect and had accumulated more personal wealth than men who did not belong to such groups. The average number of accompaniments was far greater than the adult average, and the number of ceramic vessels was particularly high, even excluding Burial 140. Higher social and religious rank evidently was not accompanied by real economic benefits, however. Based on strontium, barium, and stable-carbon-isotope ratio values, Ezzo (1993:54) inferred that the diets of sodality members did not differ from those of other adult males.

COMPARISONS AND IMPLICATIONS

We have described patterns in mortuary ritual at Grasshopper Pueblo, identified a normative style of burial treatment, and isolated several variables that contributed to variability in treatment. We turn now to comparisons. How do other contemporaneous settlements compare in aspects of grave type, body positioning, and accompaniments? Comparing Grasshopper Pueblo to Roosevelt and Gila phase settlements in the Tonto Basin, Classic period Hohokam settlements in the Phoenix Basin, and Casas Grandes (Paquimé), we discover what appears to be a striking amount of similarity in mortuary ritual. Next, we explore several variables that may have contributed to the adoption of such normative burial ritual among culturally diverse populations.

Comparisons

Recent excavations in the Roosevelt Lake area sponsored by the U.S. Bureau of Reclamation yielded additional data concerning mortuary practices that confirm patterns established in earlier studies (Doyel 1978; Hohmann 1985, 1992; Hohmann and Kelley 1988). At contemporaneous sites—such as the Schoolhouse Point site (Lindauer 1996) and the Cline Terrace mound (Jacobs 1997)—interment locales, grave types, body positioning, and burial accompaniments were similar to those of Grasshopper Pueblo. Subadults were primarily buried below room floors and adults in extramural areas such as plazas (Loendorf 1996:686, 1997a:474). Extensive prehistoric disturbance from repeated interments was common, particularly because a number of grave facilities were used for multiple burials (Loendorf 1996:691, 1997b:557–58, 1998: 202–7). Graves typically were simple, rectangular pits, and orientation of the grave facility tended to be east-west. Grave elaborations were similar to those present at Grasshopper and other mountain communities, such as Kinishba (Cummings 1940): pits covered with stone slabs, pits with undercut sides similar to Grasshopper pit-and-chamber graves, and pits with ledges for offerings. Log-cribbed graves were common (Loendorf 1996: 710–12). At Schoolhouse Point, these graves tended to be used for adults rather than children. Extended supine position was most common, and few flexed and semi-flexed interments were found. The head often was placed to the east, although there was considerable variability (Loendorf 1996:figure 15.16, 1998:figure 10.5).

Ceramic vessels and artifacts representing personal belongings were common accompaniments. Loendorf (1996:721, 1997a:492) noted the absence of domestic implements such as metates, shaft straighteners, and hammer stones among burial accompaniments. Although subadults were found to have markedly fewer accompaniments, only slight differences were found between adult males and females (Loendorf 1998:217). As at Grasshopper Pueblo, some subadults were treated more elaborately than the typical subadult burial (Loendorf 1998:228–29). Painted sticks, suggested to be symbols of authority, were also found (Loendorf 1998:209–10).

These patterns in mortuary treatment evidently were established in the preceding Roosevelt phase. Grave facilities, body position, orientation, and accompaniments were similar to those of later Gila phase burials (Loendorf 1997b; Ravesloot 1994). One distinctive difference between the Roosevelt Lake and Grasshopper patterns is the use of multiple inhumation facilities at the former settlements. At AZ U:8:450/15b, a compound site in the Schoolhouse Point Mesa area of the eastern Tonto Basin, exceptionally

large, log-cribbed burial facilities containing as many as 18 individuals were found (Loendorf 1997b:557–58). Only a few multiple inhumations were found at Grasshopper, and none consisted of more than two individuals.

Turning to the Phoenix area, virtually identical patterns in mortuary treatment have been observed for inhumations at a number of Classic period sites, including Casa Buena (Howard 1988), Pueblo Grande (Bostwick and Downum 1994; Downum and Bostwick 1993), and Grand Canal (Mitchell 1989). Mitchell's (1992, 1994a, 1994b) description of mortuary practices based on the large collection of inhumations recovered from Pueblo Grande is remarkable for its parallels. Among these are extended supine inhumation; log-crib-covered, pit-and-chamber, and niched graves; predominantly eastern orientation; and subfloor inhumation of subadults (Mitchell 1994b). Ceramic vessels, objects of personal adornment, and ritual items were typical accompaniments (Mitchell 1994a). Among the similar nonutilitarian objects were painted wooden staffs (found with adults), quartz crystals, unusual stones, and vessels containing charcoal (Mitchell 1994a:149). Subadults typically had fewer vessels, but there were no significant differences in the number of vessels found with male and female inhumations (Mitchell 1994a:132).

Lastly, we turn to Casas Grandes (Paquimé). The similarities are not as striking at Paquimé, and although there are a number of differences that set Casas Grandes apart, there is also an intriguing cast of similarity. Among Medio period burials, similarities that occur include log-cribbed graves, eastern orientation, multiple burials thought to represent related family members, use of matting, and burial of subadults within rooms (Di Peso et al. 1974a; Ravesloot 1988). Ceramic vessels and ornaments were the primary accompaniments; utilitarian objects were rare and found primarily with adults. Di Peso et al. (1974a) listed several adult male burials with flintknapping tool kits and collections of unusual stones, minerals, and other objects suggestive of medicine kits. Shell ornament types were similar and included shell beads, bracelets, tinklers, and pendants. Males were more frequently interred with jewelry manufactured from nonlocal materials and with polychrome ceramics than females (Ravesloot 1988:54). Differences with the Roosevelt Lake, Grasshopper, and Classic period patterns include the preference for flexed body positions, greater variety in grave facilities, and exotic accompaniments such as copper artifacts and ceramic hand drums. Perhaps the greatest dissimilarity is the inferred deliberate sacrifice of retainers and other elements of Mesoamerican social and ritual complexity—possible trophy skulls, specially prepared burial urns, possible troves of human long bones, and artifacts and ornaments made from human bone (Di Peso et al. 1974a; Ravesloot 1988:25, 30, 36, 56, 70).

On the basis of these comparisons, we must agree with Ravesloot (1994:845) when he noted for a typical Roosevelt phase compound that "the standard burial treatments afforded the dead are very similar to those reported at sites throughout central and southern Arizona during the Classic period (Whittlesey 1978; Reid 1989; Hohmann 1992; Mitchell 1992) and ethnographic descriptions of modern pueblo mortuary treatments." The widespread occurrence of this normative burial ritual across much of central Arizona among groups traditionally attributed to Mogollon, Salado, and Classic period Hohokam has received little attention in the archaeological community.

Explaining Cross-cultural Similarities

Carr's (1994) cross-cultural ethnographic survey demonstrated that social organizational and philosophical-religious factors influence variability in mortuary practices far more than physical or circumstantial factors. If we agree with Carr, we are left with the inescapable conclusion that the residents of Grasshopper Pueblo, the Salado of the Roosevelt Lake region, the Classic period Hohokam—and in certain aspects, also the residents of Paquimé—were similar in the major dimensions of social personae and organization—age, gender, vertical and horizontal social position, personal identity, and social classification. They also evidently shared beliefs about the soul, the afterlife, the nature of the soul's journey to the afterlife, cosmology, and universal order (Carr 1994:67). We should be able to use these factors to explain the observed striking similarities in widely separated geographical and cultural areas. Ethnic group membership, social structure, and ritual and ceremonial organization are three broad areas of ancient life that may have some explanatory potential.

ETHNIC AFFILIATION

We begin with the issue of ethnic diversity. Did the populations sharing normative burial rituals also share ethnic affiliation? Can we exhume the old migration hypothesis to explain what we observe? Beginning in the 1970s, migration was discredited by processual archaeologists as a nonexplanation. The indigenous development theory explaining the sweeping changes of the Classic period in the Arizona deserts, which now enjoys wide-

spread favor (e.g., Doyel 1977, 1981; Effland and Macnider 1991; Wood and McAllister 1982), was developed in direct opposition to Haury's (1945) original Salado migration hypothesis (Whittlesey et al. 1995). Migration has cycled back to receive favorable archaeological attention once again (e.g., Cameron 1995). Bioarchaeologists have been following the ephemeral trail of cultural and genetic affinity through mountains and desert for several years, using comparative studies of dental morphology. Establishing cultural affinity through bioarchaeological research was an important component of the Roosevelt Platform Mound Study (RPMS) (Rice 1992; Rice et al. 1992).

Bioarchaeological data unfortunately have contributed little toward determining if the normative burial treatment of the fourteenth century occurred among different populations. The results of the RPMS bioarchaeological analyses are contradictory and confusing. An initial assessment of Hohokam affinity by Turner and Irish (1987) established a baseline for comparison. A subsequent study (Turner et al. 1989) compared Classic period Hohokam from the Grand Canal and Casa Buena sites (Howard 1988; Mitchell 1989) in the Phoenix Basin, the pre-Classic period Hohokam occupants of La Ciudad in the Phoenix Basin (Henderson 1987), and a number of samples from mountain sites, including Grasshopper. Turner and Irish found that the Classic period Hohokam of the Grand Canal and Casa Buena sites—precisely those groups that participated in a normative mortuary ritual identical to mountain patterns—were dentally more like the Mogollon of Grasshopper Pueblo than the residents of La Ciudad. Neither the pre-Classic nor Classic period Hohokam samples were similar to modern Pima peoples.

Initial studies of the Roosevelt Lake burials compared samples from single sites to the baseline data. Regan et al. (1997) reported that dental morphology of the Schoolhouse Point burials was overall more similar to that of the Mogollon at Grasshopper Pueblo than to the Hohokam. Similar conclusions were drawn for Cline Terrace, although the sample was too small to analyze statistically (Regan and Turner 1997:527). The analysis of Turner et al. (1989), according to Regan et al. (1997:829), "continued to support the idea based on archaeological finds, such as pottery styles and architecture, of a late external migration into the Hohokam area. The Schoolhouse Point Mound odontological findings continue this support. Now, there is a biological smoking gun pointing at the Saladoans."

More recently, the Arizona State University bioarchaeologists grouped all Roosevelt Lake samples and essentially reversed their position. According to Turner (1998:186),

> In previous univariate analyses of small local samples of RPMS teeth, there were some closer relationships suggested between RPMS people and those of the Mogollon samples (Point of Pines and Grasshopper). Those univariate similarities are now viewed as probably erroneous due to small sample sizes, because the larger pooled sample used herein more likely represents the Tonto Basin population better.

We disagree with this conclusion. The Tonto Basin population has been demonstrated to be multicultural and probably multiethnic as well (e.g., Clark 1995; Stark et al. 1995), as discussed more fully below. We would certainly agree with Turner's (1998:190) conclusion that "on epigenetic and cultural grounds" the "Tonto Basin was not a closed, static biocultural system." In lumping all burials from all sites together, Turner has simply homogenized the sample. Turner (1998:190) has stated intriguingly that the Roosevelt phase Saladoans "possessed an external linkage with peoples to the north of Tonto Basin, including the Sinagua and Western Anasazi. Later, in Gila phase times, that connection had ended, and a new dynamic appeared that shifted southward, linking the Tonto Basin Saladoans with the Hohokam communities." This seems to us rather strong, bioarchaeologically based support of the original Gladwin and Haury migration hypothesis.

As for connections with residents of northern Mexico, Turner's (1998) analysis found a close link between the Mimbres Mogollon of Nan Ranch and northern Mexico, represented by Paquimé, and both populations grouped more closely with the Roosevelt Lake burial samples than with either Hohokam or the Mogollon of Point of Pines and Grasshopper (Turner 1998:table 9.1). Rice (1998:233) observed that "Despite the close affinity of Tonto Basin to the Hohokam, the populations of the Hohokam core area were significantly different from those in the Mimbres and Northern Mexico regions;" he goes on to suggest that, because Tonto Basin, Mimbres, and northern Mexico are considered part of the "Salado horizon," this horizon has an unexpected biological component of shared affinity in addition to ceramic and architectural similarities.

Taking the results of these bioarchaeological analyses at face value, the normative burial ritual occurred among

biologically distinct populations, although Grasshopper would appear to be less similar and Paquimé, Tonto Basin, and Classic period Hohokam more similar, among those analyzed by Turner (1998).

SOCIAL ORGANIZATION

If mortuary practices are a mirror of social organization and the social roles that individuals held in ancient society, as many believe (Binford 1971; Carr 1994; Goldstein 1981; Saxe 1970; Tainter 1978; Whittlesey 1978), similarities in normative burial ritual may reflect similar organization. Presence or absence of sodalities; dominance of kinship groups, lineages, or clans; moieties; or nonkinship-based structures should be visible in some fashion in mortuary ritual. This review is too limited to tackle all of the potential organizational forms, so we will restrict our comparison to evidence for the presence of sodalities.

Some artifactual indicators of sodality membership identified in mountain communities have been found in and near the Tonto Basin. At the Schoolhouse Point site (Loendorf 1996), Mazatzal House (Hartman 1987), Togetzoge Pueblo (Hohmann and Kelley 1988), and elsewhere, these included *Glycymeris* sp. pendants, bracelets, and rings and *Conus* sp. tinklers (Reid and Whittlesey 1982, 1999). An inhumation at Schoolhouse Point had a *Laevicardium* disk between the legs, below the pelvis (Loendorf 1996:table 15.1). Given the disturbance among the burials, some of the whole-shell pendants may originally have been placed similarly. An inhumation at AZ U:8:450/14b was accompanied by a cluster of arrow points identical in orientation (clustered and points aligned) to those accompanying Grasshopper Burial 140, but they were located differently with reference to the body—along the right lower leg with tips facing toward the feet (Loendorf 1997b:563, figure 16.7). Clusters of projectile points, like those we infer to be arrow quivers, have not been reported elsewhere in the lower Tonto Basin.

Bone awls worn as hairpins vary in distribution. With one exception, they did not occur among Schoolhouse Mesa or Schoolhouse Point burials (Loendorf 1996; 1997b:587). Instead, bone tools were found in contexts suggesting that they functioned as awls, which is reinforced by their relative width and blunt tips. At Schoolhouse Point, bone awls were recovered in the hands of four burials, three of which were female (Loendorf 1996:721). The single exception was a child approximately 4 years old with a hairpin placed at the cranium (Loendorf 1997b:tables

16.4 and 16.14). By contrast, four of the five males buried at Mazatzal House, an earlier compound site in the upper Tonto Basin, had bone awls placed beside or under the skulls in positions that indicated they were worn as hairpins (Hartman 1987:224). One of these burials also had other accompaniments symbolizing sodality membership, including a shell bracelet around the left humerus, a shell pendant, and two projectile points placed near the left shoulder. At Togetzoge Pueblo (Hohmann and Kelley 1988:76), bone hairpins were associated with adult males as at Grasshopper Pueblo.

Turning to the Phoenix area, we find some possible symbols of sodality membership among the Pueblo Grande inhumations. Projectile points and bone awls were associated with adult males (Mitchell 1994b:144). Whole-shell pendants were found with a number of burials; according to Mitchell (1994b:150), "[t]he burials that had the shells placed over the pelvic area were adult males." The Pueblo Grande burial data are not presented in such a way that associations among artifact types can be evaluated. This is also true for the Casas Grandes burial sample because burials were not illustrated and the position of artifacts in graves was usually not described (see Di Peso et al. 1974a).

On the basis of these data, we can conclude only that there are tantalizing hints of the presence of sodalities in Tonto Basin and Pueblo Grande and that Paquimé remains enigmatic. Certainly further study is required. We might speculate that the differential importance of irrigation among Tonto Basin, Grasshopper, Phoenix, and northern Mexican societies was responsible for the apparently variable presence of sodalities among these groups. The importance of labor organization in irrigation societies has long been posited (Wittfogel 1957; Wittfogel and Goldfrank 1943), and its role in Rio Grande Pueblo society is illustrated by Dozier (1970:127). The moieties of Rio Grande pueblos were tribal sodalities to whom all adults belonged (Jorgensen 1980:227). By contrast, the sodalities of Western Pueblos, whose chief functions were control of rainfall, fertility, and related issues of health and well-being, were restricted— membership was limited to a select group of individuals, and not all males belonged to sodalities (Jorgensen 1980:227). Restricted sodalities may have been weak in the Phoenix Basin, Tonto Basin, and at Paquimé, and well developed at Grasshopper, for similar reasons. Irrigation agriculture created a new set of demands on the social and ritual organizations of irrigation-based communi-

ties; the restricted sodalities of Hopi, with their emphasis on bringing rain and success to the crops, were by contrast welcomed at Grasshopper Pueblo.

RITUAL ORGANIZATION

Last, we consider ritual organization, which also does little to clarify the issue of widespread similarities in mortuary ritual. Ceremonialism at Grasshopper Pueblo was centered on the little kiva-great kiva-plaza-macaw complex that some have linked to the katsina cult (Adams 1991). In the Tonto Basin, kivas were conspicuously absent, and ceremonial architecture was dominated by the platform mound (Rice et al. 1998; Whittlesey et al. 1995). This of course is true of the Phoenix Basin, where the platform mound has an even longer history (Gladwin et al. 1937; Haury 1976). As Lange (1992) observed, the ideological symbols of the katsina cult and the ritual organization represented by platform mounds appear to be mutually exclusive.

We might look to irrigation agriculture to explain these differences in ceremonial organization as we did for sodality organization (Whittlesey et al. 1995). Because irrigation provides people with considerable control over water, ceremonial organization among irrigation societies is directed toward maintaining and directing labor rather than focused on ritual appeals for rain (Dozier 1970:128). Among the irrigation-based Eastern Pueblos, for example, ritual organization was centered around the community and the moieties; the katsina cult was absent or only weakly developed (Adams 1991). By contrast, the katsina cult, with its emphasis on bringing rain and fertility to crops, was an appealing and functional integrative device among the Hopi, who relied on floodwater farming (Adams 1991:121).

Using this correlation, Whittlesey et al. (1995) suggested that the lack of kivas in the Tonto Basin indicates that the katsina cult was also absent there and a village-based type of organization focused on platform mounds that can be linked to irrigation agriculture developed instead. A similar argument could be made for the irrigation communities of the Phoenix Basin with their prominent platform mounds. Another possibility, of course, is that the protokivas and ceremonial rooms identified in the Grasshopper region (Reid and Montgomery 1999) have not been recognized in the Tonto Basin because these rooms lack the full complement of features that identify kivas, and the features that distinguish them from domestic rooms are limited in archaeological visibility.

A MORTUARY CULT?

This review concludes with a consideration of one last possibility. Having been unable to attribute the widespread, normative mortuary ritual of the fourteenth century to biological, cultural, social, or ceremonial factors, this leads us to wonder whether the normative burial treatment might represent a mortuary cult. We begin by noting the sweeping demographic shifts and widespread population relocations that characterized the late A.D. 1200s and early A.D. 1300s. Archaeologists working in the Tonto Basin (e.g., Clark 1995; Stark et al. 1995) have recently rediscovered the original Salado migration theory (Gladwin and Gladwin 1935; Haury 1945), first revived by Whittlesey and Reid (1982) and later developed by Ciolek-Torrello et al. (1994). Ceramic, architectural, and other data indicated that some sites excavated during the Roosevelt Community Development Study were occupied by culturally and ethnically distinct groups with close ties to mountain communities.

We do not have to look far to understand the reasons for such cultural diversity. Farmers of the Colorado Plateau seeking relief from the drought and environmental deterioration of the late A.D. 1200s moved inevitably to better-watered locales below the Mogollon Rim. The demographic, economic, and social consequences of these demographic shifts upon mountain populations have long been recognized (e.g., Haury 1958) and are well documented in the Grasshopper region, where Anasazi and Mogollon lived together from at least the mid-A.D. 1200s (Reid 1989; Reid and Whittlesey 1999). The Tonto Basin and regions farther south were affected by such population movements. There can be little doubt that most of central Arizona was occupied by a multicultural, multiethnic population, and seasonal, logistical movement by these peoples further stirred the cultural melting pot. We cannot assume that even single sites were occupied by a culturally or ethnically uniform population, in light of the clear evidence for coresidence among central Arizona populations (Reid 1989; Reid and Whittlesey 1999).

A mortuary cult, with a consistent set of beliefs about the cosmos and the afterlife, ways in which the dead should be prepared for the afterlife and represented in it, and a set of symbols to provide structural representation for actions and beliefs, could have served as a ready means to integrate culturally and ethnically diverse populations with distinct forms of social and ritual organization. Such a cult could be particularly appealing among populations

already suffering severe environmental, nutritional, and social stress (e.g., Berry 1983, 1985b; Hinkes 1983; Mitchell 1992; Reid 1989; Turner et al. 1994; Van Gerven and Sheridan 1994).

It is interesting that, in direct contrast to some hypotheses (e.g., Crown 1994), there appears to be no ceramic component to this hypothetical mortuary cult. At Grasshopper, Roosevelt Red Ware was the most common painted ceramic in mortuary contexts (Pinto and Pinto-Gila Polychromes were more common than Gila Polychrome) (Whittlesey 1978). At the Schoolhouse Point site, Gila Polychrome was present among burials but not as abundant as black-on-white or painted corrugated pottery (Loendorf 1996:table 15.1). At Cline Terrace, Gila Polychrome was the most common painted mortuary ware, but painted ceramics as a whole were rare (Loendorf 1997a:table 13.1). Roosevelt Red Ware was quite rare at Pueblo Grande; 13 vessels were found with 10 inhumations (Mitchell 1994b:136). Extraordinarily, *none* of the excavated burials from Casas Grandes contained Gila Polychrome vessels (Ravesloot 1988:table 5.1). Noting that Gila Polychrome occurred almost exclusively in mortuary contexts outside of the Salado heartland, Ciolek-Torrello (1987:368) concluded that "the Salado presence may represent in part the spread of a cultural horizon expressed in a form reminiscent of a mortuary cult rather than an actual Salado presence." Mortuary cult it may have been, but Gila Polychrome was not one of its prominent components.

CONCLUDING THOUGHTS

The significance of mortuary ritual at Grasshopper Pueblo is that it raises issues that touch upon culture-historical, processual, and methodological themes and prompts epistemological questions that encompass every aspect of contemporary prehistoric archaeology. We introduce a few of these themes and questions as concluding thoughts to draw attention to areas needing exploration.

Clearly one need is to revisit the culture-historical questions of population movement, ethnicity, and ethnic coresidence. Grasshopper research began in the early 1960s with these questions and continued to investigate them through 30 years of research. Throughout central Arizona, and at Grasshopper in particular, population movement in late prehistory was a principal factor contributing to variability in the archaeological record. It is encouraging that a number of colleagues have begun to examine population movement in detail (see Cameron 1995).

Grasshopper research demonstrates conclusively that rules for structuring the social relations of individuals and the organizational principles of groups are inferred most convincingly from the mortuary ritual (Reid and Whittlesey 1999; Whittlesey 1999). By contrast, the conclusions that result from applying simple linear models directly relating status and material goods (e.g., Hohmann 1982; Upham 1978) or created from rank-size pyramids of archaeological data (e.g., Wood 1989) are shown to be highly suspect (Reid and Whittlesey 1990). A methodological issue to emerge in this regard is whether it is possible to compare prehistoric organization as inferred from mortuary data to inferences from settlement analysis. Certainly any comparison would have to be provisional because of the difference in the relative strength of the inferences.

Our cursory review of mortuary ritual at Grasshopper Pueblo resounds with the possibilities for moving beyond speculation and ethnographic projection in the investigation of ideology. The session "Beyond Eco-Determinism: A Glimpse of the Role of Ritual and Symbolism" at the 1992 Southwest Symposium (Fish and Reid 1996) was a first attempt to explore these research pathways from a contemporary perspective. The papers in that session as well as recent attempts to identify ritual activities (Adams 1991; Crown 1994) point to the importance of the mortuary ritual as the clearest path to understanding the pervasive sacred and symbolic character of prehistoric life in the Southwest. A host of methodological obstacles must be eliminated before archaeologists can reconstruct past ideologies with confidence.

In closing, we underscore the epistemological conundrums that confront our every research moment. The nature of archaeological knowledge is constantly under scrutiny, as should be questions concerning what is worth knowing and what is capable of being known in light of archaeological evidence. In addition to these questions, the mortuary ritual at Grasshopper raises concerns about what should be kept secret and what should be made public about a particular prehistoric past. Having successfully worked out ways to reconstruct paleoenvironments and prehistoric social organization, archaeologists are now at the threshold of developing methods for reconstructing the symbolic content of past behavior—those phenomena that identify us as uniquely human.

REFERENCES CITED

Adams, E. Charles
1991   *The Origin and Development of the Pueblo Katsina Cult.* University of Arizona Press, Tucson.
Bennett, Kenneth A.
1973   *The Indians of Point of Pines, Arizona: A Comparative Study of Their Physical Characteristics.* Anthropological Papers No. 23. University of Arizona Press, Tucson.
Berry, David R.
1983   *Disease and Climatological Relationships among Pueblo III-Pueblo IV Anasazi of the Colorado Plateau.* Unpublished Ph.D. dissertation, Department of Anthropology, University of California, Los Angeles.
1985a   Aspects of Paleodemography at Grasshopper Pueblo, Arizona. In *Health and Disease in the Prehistoric Southwest*, edited by C. F. Merbs and R. J. Miller, pp. 43–64. Anthropological Research Papers No. 34. Arizona State University, Tempe.
1985b   Dental Paleopathology of Grasshopper Pueblo, Arizona. In *Health and Disease in the Prehistoric Southwest*, edited by C. F. Merbs and R. J. Miller, pp. 253–74. Anthropological Research Papers No. 34. Arizona State University, Tempe.
Binford, Lewis R.
1971   Mortuary Practices: Their Study and Their Potential. In *Approaches to the Social Dimensions of Mortuary Practices*, organized and edited by J. A. Brown, pp. 6–29. Memoirs of the Society for American Archaeology, no. 25. Society for American Archaeology, Washington, D.C. (Issued as *American Antiquity* 36(3) Pt. 2, July 1971.)
Birkby, Walter H.
1973   *Discontinuous Morphological Traits of the Skull as Population Markers in the Prehistoric Southwest.* Unpublished Ph.D. dissertation, University of Arizona, Tucson.
1982   Bio-social Interpretations from Cranial Non-metric Traits of the Grasshopper Pueblo Skeletal Remains. In *Multidisciplinary Research at Grasshopper Pueblo, Arizona*, edited by W. A. Longacre, S. J. Holbrook, and M. W. Graves, pp. 36–41. Anthropological Papers No. 40. University of Arizona Press, Tucson.

Bostwick, Todd W., and Christian E. Downum (editors)
1994   *Archaeology of the Pueblo Grande Platform Mound and Surrounding Features: 2. Features in the Central Precinct of the Pueblo Grande Community*. Anthropological Papers No. 1. Pueblo Grande Museum, Phoenix.

Brody, J. J.
1987   *Mimbres Painted Pottery*. School of American Research, Santa Fe and University of New Mexico Press, and Albuquerque.

Bunzel, Ruth L.
1932   *Introduction to Zuni Ceremonialism*. Forty-seventh Annual Report of the Bureau of American Ethnology for 1929–1930, pp. 467–544. Smithsonian Institution, Washington, D.C.

Cameron, Catherine M. (editor)
1995   Migration and the Movement of Southwestern Peoples. *Journal of Anthropological Archaeology* 14.

Carr, Christopher
1994   A Crosscultural Survey of the Determinants of Mortuary Practices. In *The Pueblo Grande Project, Volume 7: An Analysis of Classic Period Mortuary Patterns*, edited by D. R. Mitchell, pp. 7–69. Soil Systems Publications in Archaeology No. 20. Soil Systems, Phoenix.

Ciolek-Torrello, Richard S.
1978   *A Statistical Analysis of Activity Organization, Grasshopper Pueblo, Arizona*. Ph.D. dissertation, Department of Anthropology, University of Arizona, Tucson. University Microfilms, Ann Arbor.
1985   A Typology of Room Function at Grasshopper Pueblo, Arizona. *Journal of Field Archaeology* 12:42–63.
1987   Cultural Affiliation. In *Archaeology of the Mazatzal Piedmont, Central Arizona*, edited by R. S. Ciolek-Torrello, pp. 356–69. Research Paper 33, Vol. 1. Museum of Northern Arizona, Flagstaff.

Ciolek-Torrello, Richard S., and J. Jefferson Reid
1974   Change in Household Size at Grasshopper. *The Kiva* 40:39–47.

Ciolek-Torrello, Richard S., Stephanie M. Whittlesey, and John R. Welch
1994   A Synthetic Model of Prehistoric Land Use. In *The Roosevelt Rural Sites Study: Changing Land Use in the Tonto Basin*, edited by R. S. Ciolek-Torrello and J. R. Welch, pp. 437–72. Technical Series No. 28, Vol. 3. Statistical Research, Tucson.

Clark, Geoffrey A.
1967   *A Preliminary Analysis of Burial Clusters at the Grasshopper Site, East-Central Arizona*. Unpublished Master's thesis, Department of Anthropology, University of Arizona, Tucson.

Clark, Jeffery J.
1995   The Role of Migration in Social Change. In *The Roosevelt Community Development Study: New Perspectives on Tonto Basin Prehistory*, edited by M. D. Elson, M. T. Stark, and D. A. Gregory, pp. 369–84. Anthropological Papers No. 15. Center for Desert Archaeology, Tucson.

Cordell, Linda S.
1985   Status Differentiation and Social Complexity in the Prehistoric Southwest: A Discussion. In *Status, Structure, and Stratification: Current Archaeological Reconstructions*, edited by M. T. Garcia, M. Thompson, and F. J. Kense, pp. 191–95. University of Calgary, Alberta.

Cordell, Linda S., Steadman Upham, and S. L. Brock
1987   Obscuring Cultural Patterns in the Archaeological Record: A Discussion from Southwestern Archaeology. *American Antiquity* 52:565–77.

Crown, Patricia L.
1994   *Ceramics and Ideology: Salado Polychrome Pottery*. University of New Mexico Press, Albuquerque.

Cummings, Byron
1940   *Kinishba: A Prehistoric Pueblo of the Great Pueblo Period*. Hohokam Museums Association and University of Arizona, Tucson.

Cummings, Linda Scott
1995   Agriculture and the Mesa Verde Area Anasazi Diet: Description and Nutritional Analysis. In *Soil, Water, Biology, and Belief in Prehistoric and Traditional Southwestern Agriculture*, edited by H. W. Toll, pp. 335–52. Special Publication 2. New Mexico Archaeological Council, Albuquerque.

Cushing, Frank H.
1883   *Zuni Fetishes*. Second Annual Report of the Bureau of Ethnology for 1880–1881, pp. 3–45. Government Printing Office, Washington, D.C.

Decker, Kenneth A.
1986   Isotopic and Chemical Reconstruction of Diet and Its Biological and Social Dimensions at Grasshopper Pueblo, Arizona. Paper presented at the 1986 meeting of the Society for American Archaeology, New Orleans.

Di Peso, Charles C., John B. Rinaldo, and Gloria J. Fenner
1974a   *Casas Grandes: A Fallen Trading Center of the Gran Chichimeca, Volume 8: Bone, Perishables, Commerce, Subsistence, and Burials*. The Amerind Foundation, Dragoon, Arizona, and Northland Press, Flagstaff.
1974b   *Casas Grandes: A Fallen Trading Center of the Gran Chichimeca, Volume 6: Ceramics and Shell*. The Amerind Foundation, Dragoon, Arizona, and Northland Press, Flagstaff.

Dixon, Keith A.
1956   *Hidden House: A Cliff Ruin in Sycamore Canyon, Central Arizona*. Bulletin No. 29. Museum of Northern Arizona, Flagstaff.

Downum, Christian E.
1986   Potsherds, Provenience, and Ports of Trade: A Review of the Evidence from Chavez Pass. Paper presented at the Fourth Mogollon Conference, Tucson.

Downum, Christian E., and Todd W. Bostwick (editors)
1993   *Archaeology of the Pueblo Grande Platform Mound and Surrounding Features, vol. 1. Introduction to the Archival Project and History of Archaeological Research*. Anthropological Papers No. 1. Pueblo Grande Museum, Phoenix.

Doyel, David E.
1977   *Classic Period Hohokam in the Escalante Ruin Group*. Unpublished Ph.D. dissertation, Department of Anthropology, University of Arizona, Tucson.
1978   *The Miami Wash Project: Hohokam and Salado in the Globe-Miami Area, Central Arizona*. Contribution to Highway Salvage Archaeology No. 52. Arizona State Museum, Tucson.
1981   *Late Hohokam Prehistory in Southern Arizona*. Contributions to Archaeology No. 2. Gila Press, Scottsdale.

Dozier, Edward P.
1970   *The Pueblo Indians of North America*. Holt, Rinehart, and Winston, New York.

Effland, Richard W., Jr., and Barbara S. Macnider
1991   *An Overview of the Cultural Heritage of the Tonto National Forest*. Cultural Resources Report No. 49. Archaeological Consulting Services, Tempe.

Eggan, Fred
1950   *Social Organization of the Western Pueblos*. University of Chicago Press, Chicago.

Eighmy, Jeffrey L.
1979   Logistic Trends in Southwest Population Growth. In *Transformations: Mathematical Approaches to Culture Change*, edited by C. Renfrew and K. L. Cooke, pp. 205–20. Academic Press, New York.

El-Najjar, Mahmoud Y., D. J. Ryan, C. G. Turner, II, and B. Lozoff
1976   The Etiology of Porotic Hyperostosis among the Prehistoric and Historic Anasazi Indians of the Southwestern United States. *American Journal of Physical Anthropology* 44:447–88.

Ezzo, Joseph A.
1991   *Dietary Change at Grasshopper Pueblo, Arizona: The Evidence from Bone Chemistry Analyses*. Unpublished Ph.D. dissertation, Department of Anthropology, University of Wisconsin, Madison.
1993   *Human Adaptation at Grasshopper Pueblo, Arizona: Social and Ecological Perspectives*. International Monographs in Prehistory, Archaeological Series No. 4. Ann Arbor.
1997   Analytical Perspectives on Prehistoric Migration: A Case Study from East-Central Arizona. *Journal of Archaeological Science* 24:447–66.

Fewkes, J. Walter
1896   Antiquities of the Upper Verde River and Walnut Creek Valleys, Arizona. In *Thirteenth Annual Report of the Bureau of American Ethnology, 1891–1892*, pp. 181–220. Government Printing Office, Washington, D.C.

Fish, Paul R., and J. Jefferson Reid (editors)
1996   *Interpreting Southwestern Diversity: Underlying Principles and Overarching Patterns*. Anthropological Research Papers No. 48. Arizona State University, Tempe.

Fulginiti, Laura C.
1993   *Discontinuous Morphological Variation at Grasshopper Pueblo, Arizona*. Unpublished Ph.D. dissertation, Department of Anthropology, University of Arizona, Tucson.

Gladwin, Harold S., Emil W. Haury, E. B. Sayles, and Nora Gladwin
1937   *Excavations at Snaketown: Material Culture*. Medallion Papers No. 25. Gila Pueblo, Globe, Arizona.

Gladwin, Winifred J., and Harold S. Gladwin
1935   *The Eastern Range of the Red-on-buff Culture*. Medallion Papers No. 16. Gila Pueblo, Globe, Arizona.

Goldstein, Lynn G.
1981   One-Dimensional Archaeology and Multi-Dimensional People: Spatial Organization and Mortuary Analysis. In *The Archaeology of*

Death, edited by R. Chapman, I. Kinnes, and
K. Randsborg, pp. 53–70. Cambridge
University Press, New York.

Graves, Michael W.

1983   Growth and Aggregation at Canyon Creek
Ruin: Implications for Evolutionary Change
in East-Central Arizona. *American
Antiquity* 48:290–315.

1987   Rending Reality in Archaeological Analyses:
A Reply to Upham and Plog. *Journal of Field
Archaeology* 14:243–49.

1991   Estimating Ring Loss on Tree-Ring
Specimens from East-Central Arizona:
Implications for Prehistoric Pueblo Growth at
the Grasshopper Ruin. *Journal of Quantitative
Anthropology* 3:83–115.

Green, Jesse (editor)

1979   *Zuni: Selected Writings of Frank Hamilton
Cushing.* University of Nebraska Press,
Lincoln.

Griffin, P. Bion

1967   A High Status Burial from Grasshopper Ruin,
Arizona. *The Kiva* 33:37–53.

1969   *Late Mogollon Readaptation in East-Central
Arizona.* Unpublished Ph.D. dissertation,
Department of Anthropology, University of
Arizona, Tucson.

Hartman, Dana

1987   Burial Analysis. In *Archaeology of the
Mazatzal Piedmont, Central Arizona,* edited
by R. S. Ciolek-Torrello, pp. 216–40. Research
Paper No. 33, Vol. 1. Museum of Northern
Arizona, Flagstaff.

Haury, Emil W.

1940   *Excavations in the Forestdale Valley, East-
Central Arizona.* Bulletin 11(4), Social Science
Bulletin No. 12. University of Arizona,
Tucson.

1945   *The Excavation of Los Muertos and
Neighboring Ruins in the Salt River Valley,
Southern Arizona.* Papers of the Peabody
Museum of American Archaeology and
Ethnology No. 24(1). Cambridge.

1950   *The Stratigraphy and Archaeology of Ventana
Cave.* University of Arizona Press. 2nd
edition, 1975.

1958   Evidence at Point of Pines for a Prehistoric
Migration from Northern Arizona. In
Migrations in New World Culture History,
edited by R. H. Thompson, pp. 1–6. Social
Science Bulletin No. 27. University of Arizona,
Tucson.

1976   *The Hohokam: Desert Farmers and Craftsmen:
Excavations at Snaketown 1964–1965.*
University of Arizona Press, Tucson.

1985   Tla Kii Ruin, Forestdale's Oldest Pueblo. In
*Mogollon Culture in the Forestdale Valley,
East-Central Arizona,* by E. W. Haury, pp.
1–133. University of Arizona Press, Tucson.

Henderson, T. Kathleen

1987   *Structure and Organization at La Ciudad.*
Anthropological Field Studies No. 18. Arizona
State University, Tempe.

Hinkes, Madeleine J.

1983   *Skeletal Evidence of Stress in Subadults: Trying
to Come of Age at Grasshopper Pueblo.*
Unpublished Ph.D. dissertation, Department
of Anthropology, University of Arizona.

Hohmann, John W.

1982   *Sinagua Social Differentiation: Inferences
Based on Prehistoric Mortuary Practices.*
The Arizona Archaeologist No. 17. Arizona
Archaeological Society, Phoenix.

1985   Site AZ U:3:49 (ASU). In *Hohokam and
Salado Hamlets in the Tonto Basin: Site
Descriptions,* by J. W. Hohmann, pp. 216–90.
Office of Cultural Resource Management
Report No. 64. Arizona State University,
Tempe.

1992   *Through the Mirror of Death: A View of
Prehistoric Social Complexity in Central
Arizona.* Unpublished Ph.D. dissertation,
Department of Anthropology, Arizona State
University, Tempe.

Hohmann, John W., and Linda B. Kelley

1988   *Erich F. Schmidt's Investigations of Salado Sites
in Central Arizona: The Mrs. W. B. Thompson
Archaeological Expedition of the American
Museum of Natural History.* Bulletin No. 56.
Museum of Northern Arizona, Flagstaff.

Holbrook, Sally J., and Michael W. Graves

1982   Modern Environment of the Grasshopper
Region. In *Multidisciplinary Research at
Grasshopper Pueblo, Arizona,* edited by W. A.
Longacre, S. J. Holbrook, and M. W. Graves,
pp. 5–11. Anthropological Papers No. 40.
University of Arizona Press, Tucson.

Howard, Jerry B. (editor)

1988   *Excavations at Casa Buena: Changing
Hohokam Land Use along the Squaw Peak
Parkway.* Publications in Archaeology No. 11.
Soil Systems, Phoenix.

Ivanhoe, Francis

1985   Elevated Orthograde Skeletal Plasticity of

Some Archaeological Populations from Mexico and the American Southwest: Direct Relation to Maize Phytate Nutritional Load. In *Health and Disease in the Prehistoric Southwest*, edited by C. F. Merbs and R. J. Miller, pp. 165–76. Anthropological Research Papers No. 34. Arizona State University, Tempe.

Jacobs, David

1997   *A Salado Platform Mound on Tonto Creek, Roosevelt Platform Mound Study: Report on the Cline Terrace Mound, Cline Terrace Complex.* Roosevelt Monograph Series No. 7, Anthropological Field Studies No. 36. Office of Cultural Resource Management, Arizona State University, Tempe.

Jorgensen, Joseph G.

1980   *Western Indians.* Freeman, San Francisco.

Kan, Michael, Clement Meighan, and H. B. Nicholson

1970   *Sculpture of Ancient West Mexico: Nayarit, Jalisco, Colima: Catalogue of the Proctor Stafford Collection at the Los Angeles County Museum of Art.* Los Angeles County and University of New Mexico Press, Albuquerque.

Lange, Richard C.

1992   Pots, People, Politics, and Precipitation: Just Who or What Are the Salado Anyway? In *Proceedings of the Second Salado Conference, Globe, AZ*, edited by R. C. Lange and S. Germick, pp. 325–33. Occasional Paper 1992. Arizona Archaeological Society, Phoenix.

Lightfoot, Kent G., and Steadman Upham

1989   Complex Societies in the Prehistoric American Southwest: A Consideration of the Controversy. In *The Sociopolitical Structure of Prehistoric Southwestern Societies*, edited by S. Upham, K. G. Lightfoot, and R. A. Jewett, pp. 3–30. Westview Press, Boulder.

Lindauer, Owen

1996   *The Place of the Storehouses, Roosevelt Platform Mound Study: Report on Schoolhouse Point Mound, Pinto Creek Complex.* Roosevelt Monograph Series No. 6, Anthropological Field Studies No. 35. Office of Cultural Resource Management, Arizona State University, Tempe.

Loendorf, Chris

1996   Burial Practices at the Schoolhouse Point Mound, U:8:24/13a. In *The Place of the Storehouses: Roosevelt Platform Mound Study: Report on the Schoolhouse Point Mound, Pinto Creek Complex*, Part 2, by O. Lindauer, pp.

681–759. Roosevelt Monograph Series No. 6. Anthropological Field Studies No. 35. Office of Cultural Resource Management, Arizona State University, Tempe.

1997a   Burial Practices at AZ U:4:33/132, the Cline Terrace Mound. In *A Salado Platform Mound on Tonto Creek, Roosevelt Platform Mound Study: Report on the Cline Terrace Mound, Cline Terrace Complex*, by D. Jacobs, pp. 465–504. Roosevelt Monograph Series No. 7, Anthropological Field Studies No. 36. Office of Cultural Resource Management, Arizona State University, Tempe.

1997b   Burial Practices at Schoolhouse Point Mesa Sites. In *The Archaeology of Schoolhouse Point Mesa, Roosevelt Platform Mound Study: Report on the Schoolhouse Point Mesa Sites, Schoolhouse Management Group, Pinto Creek Complex*, by O. Lindauer, pp. 549–630. Roosevelt Monograph Series No. 8, Anthropological Field Studies No. 37. Office of Cultural Resource Management, Arizona State University, Tempe.

1998   Salado Burial Practices and Social Organization. In *A Synthesis of Tonto Basin Prehistory: The Roosevelt Archaeology Studies, 1989 to 1998*, edited by G. E. Rice, pp. 193–230. Roosevelt Monograph Series No. 12, Anthropological Field Studies No. 41. Office of Cultural Resource Management, Arizona State University, Tempe.

Longacre, William A.

1975   Population Dynamics at the Grasshopper Pueblo, Arizona. In *Population Studies in Archaeology and Biological Anthropology: A Symposium*, edited by A. C. Swedlund, pp. 71–74. Memoirs of the Society for American Archaeology, no. 30. Society for American Archaeology, Washington, D.C.

1976   Population Dynamics at the Grasshopper Pueblo, Arizona. In *Demographic Anthropology: Quantitative Approaches*, edited by E. B. W. Zubrow, pp. 169–84. University of New Mexico Press, Albuquerque.

Longacre, William A., and J. Jefferson Reid

1974   The University of Arizona Archaeological Field School at Grasshopper: Eleven Years of Multidisciplinary Research and Teaching. *The Kiva* 40:3–38.

Lorentzen, Leon H.

1993   *From Atlatl to Bow: The Impact of Improved Weapons on Wildlife in the Grasshopper*

Region. Unpublished Master's paper, Department of Anthropology, University of Arizona, Tucson.

Lowell, Julia C.

1995   Illuminating Fire-Feature Variability in the Grasshopper Region of Arizona. *Kiva* 60:351–69.

Mitchell, Douglas R.

1992   Burial Practices and Paleodemographic Reconstructions of Pueblo Grande. *Kiva* 58:89–105.

1994a   An Evaluation of the Spatial Integrity of the Pueblo Grande Burial Groups. In *The Pueblo Grande Project, Volume 7: An Analysis of Classic Period Mortuary Patterns,* edited by D. R. Mitchell, pp. 71–128. Soil Systems Publications in Archaeology No. 20. Soil Systems, Phoenix.

1994b   The Pueblo Grande Burial Artifact Analysis: A Search for Wealth, Ranking, and Prestige. In *The Pueblo Grande Project: Volume 7. An Analysis of Classic Period Mortuary Patterns,* edited by D. R. Mitchell, pp. 129–80. Soil Systems Publications in Archaeology No. 20. Soil Systems, Phoenix.

Mitchell, Douglas R. (editor)

1989   *Archaeological Investigations at the Grand Canal Ruins: A Classic Period Site in Phoenix, Arizona.* Soil Systems Publications in Archaeology No. 12. Soil Systems, Phoenix.

Montgomery, Barbara K., and J. Jefferson Reid

1990   An Instance of Rapid Ceramic Change in the American Southwest. *American Antiquity* 55:88–97.

Parsons, Elsie Clews

1939   *Pueblo Indian Religion,* 2 vols. University of Chicago Press, Chicago.

Plog, Fred

1985   Status and Death at Grasshopper Pueblo: The Homogenization of Reality. In *Status, Structure, and Stratification: Current Archaeological Reconstructions,* edited by M. T. Garcia, M. Thompson, and F. J. Kense, pp. 161–66. University of Calgary, Alberta.

Price, T. Douglas, Clark M. Johnson, Joseph A. Ezzo, Jonathan Ericson, and James H. Burton

1994   Residential Mobility in the Prehistoric Southwest United States: A Preliminary Study Using Strontium Isotope Analysis. *Journal of Archaeological Science* 21:315–30.

Ravesloot, John C.

1988   *Mortuary Practices and Social Differentiation at Casas Grandes, Chihuahua, Mexico.* Anthropological Papers No. 49. University of Arizona Press, Tucson.

1994   Burial Practices in the Livingston Area. In *Archaeology of the Salado in the Livingston Area of Tonto Basin, Roosevelt Platform Mound Study: Report on the Livingston Management Group, Pinto Creek Complex,* part 2, by D. Jacobs, pp. 833–50. Roosevelt Monograph Series No. 3, Anthropological Field Studies No. 32. Office of Cultural Resource Management, Arizona State University, Tempe.

Reed, Erik K.

1948   The Western Pueblo Archaeological Complex. *El Palacio* 55:9–15.

1950   East-Central Arizona Archaeology in Relation to the Western Pueblos. *Southwestern Journal of Anthropology* 6:120–38.

Regan, Marcia H., and Christy G. Turner II

1997   Physical Anthropology and Human Taphonomy of U:4:33/132, the Cline Terrace Mound. In *A Salado Platform Mound on Tonto Creek, Roosevelt Platform Mound Study: Report on the Cline Terrace Mound, Cline Terrace Complex,* by D. Jacobs, pp. 505–28. Roosevelt Monograph Series No. 7, Anthropological Field Studies No. 36. Office of Cultural Resource Management, Arizona State University, Tempe.

Regan, Marcia H., Christy G. Turner II, and Joel D. Irish

1997   Physical Anthropology of the Schoolhouse Point Mound Site, U:8:24/13a. In *The Place of the Storehouses, Roosevelt Platform Mound Study: Report on Schoolhouse Point Mound, Pinto Creek Complex,* by O. Lindauer, pp. 787–840. Roosevelt Monograph Series No. 6, Anthropological Field Studies No. 35. Office of Cultural Resource Management, Arizona State University, Tempe.

Reid, J. Jefferson

1973   *Growth and Response to Stress at Grasshopper Pueblo, Arizona.* Unpublished Ph.D. dissertation, Department of Anthropology, University of Arizona.

1978   Response to Stress at Grasshopper Pueblo. In *Discovering Past Behavior: Experiments in the Archaeology of the American Southwest,* edited by P. Grebinger, pp. 195–228. Gordon and Breach, New York.

1989   A Grasshopper Perspective on the Mogollon of the Arizona Mountains. In *Dynamics of*

Southwest Prehistory, edited by L. S. Cordell
and G. J. Gumerman, pp. 65–97. Smithsonian
Institution, Washington, D.C.

1999   The Grasshopper-Chavez Pass Debate:
Existential Dilemmas and Archaeological
Discourse. In *Sixty Years of Mogollon
Archaeology: Papers from the Ninth Mogollon
Conference, Silver City, New Mexico, 1996*,
edited by S. M. Whittlesey, pp. 13–22.
SRI Press, Tucson.

Reid, J. Jefferson, and Barbara K. Montgomery

1999   Ritual Space in the Grasshopper Region, East-
Central Arizona. In *Sixty Years of Mogollon
Archaeology: Papers from the Ninth Mogollon
Conference, Silver City, New Mexico, 1996*,
edited by S. M. Whittlesey, pp. 23–29. SRI
Press, Tucson.

Reid, J. Jefferson, and Charles R. Riggs, Jr.

1995   Dynamics of Pueblo Architecture. Paper presented at The Life History Approach to the
Reconstruction of Prehistoric Behavior symposium, 60th Annual Meeting of the Society
for American Archaeology, Minneapolis.

Reid, J. Jefferson, and H. David Tuggle

1988   Settlement Pattern and System in the Late
Prehistory of the Grasshopper Region,
Arizona. Ms. on file, Department of
Anthropology, University of Arizona, Tucson.

Reid, J. Jefferson, and Stephanie M. Whittlesey

1982   Households at Grasshopper Pueblo. *American
Behavioral Scientist* 25:687–703.

1990   The Complicated and the Complex:
Observations on the Archaeological Record of
Large Pueblos. In *Perspectives on Southwestern
Prehistory*, edited by P. E. Minnis and C. L.
Redman, pp. 184–195. Westview Press, Boulder.

1999   *Grasshopper Pueblo: A Story of Archaeology
and Ancient Life*. University of Arizona Press,
Tucson.

Rice, Glen E.

1998   Migration, Emulation, and Tradition in Tonto
Basin Prehistory. In *A Synthesis of Tonto Basin
Prehistory: The Roosevelt Archaeology Studies,
1989 to 1998*, edited by G. E. Rice, pp. 231–41.
Roosevelt Monograph Series No. 12, Anthro-
pological Field Studies No. 41. Office of
Cultural Resource Management, Arizona
State University, Tempe.

Rice, Glen E. (editor)

1992   *A Design for Salado Research*. Roosevelt
Monograph Series No. 1, Anthropological
Field Studies No. 22. Office of Cultural
Resource Management, Arizona State
University, Tempe.

Rice, Glen E., John C. Ravesloot, and Christy G. Turner II

1992   Salado Ethnic Identity and Social
Complexity: The Biocultural Approach. Paper
presented at the 57th Annual Meeting of the
Society for American Archaeology,
Pittsburgh.

Rice, Glen E., Charles L. Redman, David Jacobs,
and Owen Lindauer

1998   Architecture, Settlement Types, and
Settlement Complexes. In *A Synthesis of Tonto
Basin Prehistory: The Roosevelt Archaeology
Studies, 1989 to 1998*, edited by G. E. Rice, pp.
55–83. Roosevelt Monograph Series No. 12,
Anthropological Field Studies No. 41. Office
of Cultural Resource Management, Arizona
State University, Tempe.

Riggs, Charles R.

1994   *Dating Construction Events at Grasshopper
Pueblo: New Techniques for Architectural
Analysis*. Unpublished Master's thesis,
Department of Anthropology, University of
Arizona, Tucson.

1999a   *The Architecture of Grasshopper Pueblo:
Dynamics of Form, Function, and Use of Space
in a Prehistoric Community*. Unpublished
Ph.D. dissertation, Department of
Anthropology, University of Arizona, Tucson.

1999b   Spatial Variability in Room Form at
Grasshopper Pueblo, Arizona. In *Sixty Years of
Mogollon Archaeology: Papers from the Ninth
Mogollon Conference, Silver City, New Mexico,
1996*, edited by S. M. Whittlesey, pp. 3–11. SRI
Press, Tucson.

Saxe, Arthur A.

1970   *Social Dimensions of Mortuary Practices in a
Mesolithic Population from Wadi Halfa,
Sudan*. Ph.D. dissertation, Department of
Anthropology, University of Michigan, Ann
Arbor.

Schiffer, Michael B.

1976   *Behavioral Archaeology*. Academic Press, New
York.

Shipman, Jeffrey H.

1982   *Biological Relationships among Prehistoric
Western Pueblo Indian Groups Based on Metric
and Disease Traits of the Skeleton*.
Unpublished Ph.D. dissertation, Department
of Anthropology, University of Arizona,
Tucson.

Smith, Watson, Richard B. Woodbury,
and Nathalie F. S. Woodbury
1966   *The Excavation of Hawikuh by Frederick Webb
        Hodge: Report of the Hendricks-Hodge
        Expedition 1917–1923.* Contributions from the
        Museum of the American Indian, Heye
        Foundation, Vol. 20. New York.

Snow, David H.
1990   Tener Comal y Metate: Protohistoric Rio
        Grande Maize Use and Diet. In *Perspectives
        on Southwestern Prehistory*, edited by P. E.
        Minnis and C. L. Redman, pp. 289–300.
        Westview Press, Boulder.

Stark, Miriam T., Jeffery J. Clark, and Mark D. Elson
1995   Causes and Consequences of Migration in the
        13th Century Tonto Basin. *Journal of
        Anthropological Archaeology* 14:212–46.

Tainter, Joseph A.
1978   Mortuary Practices and the Study of
        Prehistoric Social Systems. In *Advances in
        Archaeological Method and Theory*, vol. 1,
        edited by M. B. Schiffer, pp. 105–41. Academic
        Press, New York.

Thompson, Laura, and Alice Joseph
1944   *The Hopi Way.* University of Chicago Press,
        Chicago.

Titiev, Mischa
1992   *Old Oraibi: A Study of the Hopi Indians of
        Third Mesa.* Reprinted. University of New
        Mexico Press, Albuquerque. Originally pub-
        lished 1944, Papers of the Peabody Museum
        of American Archaeology and Ethnology Vol.
        22, No. 1. Harvard University, Cambridge.

Tower, Donald B.
1945   The Use of Marine Mollusca and their Value
        in Reconstructing Trade Routes in the
        American Southwest. *Papers of the Excavator's
        Club*, Vol. 2, No. 3, Cambridge.

Triadan, Daniela
1989   *Defining Local Ceramic Production at
        Grasshopper Pueblo, Arizona.* Master's thesis,
        Freie Universitat, Berlin.
1997   *Ceramic Commodities and Common
        Containers: Production and Distribution of
        White Mountain Red Ware in the Grasshopper
        Region, Arizona.* Anthropological Papers No.
        61. University of Arizona Press, Tucson.

Turner, Christy G., II
1998   Physical Anthropology Synthesis of the
        Roosevelt Platform Mound Study. In *A
        Synthesis of Tonto Basin Prehistory: The
        Roosevelt Archaeology Studies, 1989 to 1998*,
        edited by G. E. Rice, pp. 181–91. Roosevelt
        Monograph Series No 12, Anthropological
        Field Studies No 41. Office of Cultural
        Resource Management, Arizona State
        University, Tempe.

Turner, Christy G., II, and Joel D. Irish
1987   Affinity and Dietary Assessment of Hohokam
        Burials from the Site of La Ciudad, Central
        Arizona. In *Specialized Studies in the Economy,
        Environment and Culture of La Ciudad*, pts. I
        and II, edited by J. A. E. Kisselburg, G. E. Rice,
        and B. L. Shears, pp. 215–30. Anthropological
        Field Studies No. 20. Office of Cultural
        Resource Management, Arizona State
        University, Tempe.

Turner, Christy G., II, Marcia H. Regan, and Joel D. Irish
1994   Physical Anthropology and Human
        Taphonomy. In *The Roosevelt Rural Sites
        Study: Prehistoric Settlements in the Tonto
        Basin*, edited by R. S. Ciolek-Torrello, S. D.
        Shelley, and S. Benaron, pp. 559–83. Technical
        Series No. 28, Vol. 2. Statistical Research,
        Tucson.
1989   Further Assessment of Hohokam Affinity:
        The Classic Period Population of the Grand
        Canal and Casa Buena Sites, Phoenix,
        Arizona. In *Archaeological Investigations at the
        Grand Canal Ruins: A Classic Period Site in
        Phoenix, Arizona*, edited by D. R. Mitchell, pp.
        775–92. Soil Systems Publications in
        Archaeology No. 12. Soil Systems, Phoenix.

Upham, Steadman
1978   Final Report of the Archaeological
        Investigations at Chavez Pass Ruin, Coconino
        National Forest, Arizona: The 1978 Field
        Season. Report submitted to the U.S.
        Department of Agriculture, Forest Service,
        Coconino National Forest, Flagstaff.
1982   *Polities and Power: An Economic and Political
        History of the Western Pueblos.* Academic
        Press, New York.

Upham, Steadman, and Fred Plog
1986   The Interpretation of Prehistoric Political
        Complexity in the Central and Northern
        Southwest: Toward a Mending of the Models.
        Journal of Field Archaeology 13:223–38.

Van Gerven, Dennis P., and Susan Guise Sheridan
(editors)
1994   *The Pueblo Grande Project, Volume 6: The
        Bioethnography of a Classic Period Hohokam
        Population.* Soil Systems Publications in
        Archaeology No. 20. Soil Systems, Phoenix.

Van Keuren, Scott
1999 *Ceramic Design Structure and the Organization of Cibola White Ware Production in the Grasshopper Region, Arizona.* Arizona State Museum Archaeological Series 191. University of Arizona, Tucson.

Voth, Henry R.
1912 *Brief Miscellaneous Hopi Papers I: Notes on Modern Burial Customs of the Hopi of Arizona.* Anthropology Series No. 11, Publication No. 157. Field Museum of Natural History, Chicago.

Walker, Philip L.
1985 Anemia among Prehistoric Indians of the American Southwest. In *Health and Disease in the Prehistoric Southwest*, edited by C. F. Merbs and R. J. Miller, pp. 139–64. Anthropological Research Papers No. 34. Arizona State University, Tempe.

Waters, Frank
1963 *Book of the Hopi.* Penguin Books, New York.

Welch, John R.
1994 Ethnographic Models for Tonto Basin Land Use. In *The Roosevelt Rural Sites Study: Changing Land Use in the Tonto Basin,* edited by R. S. Ciolek-Torrello and J. R. Welch, pp. 79–120. Technical Series No. 28, Vol. 3. Statistical Research, Tucson.

1996 *The Archaeological Measures and Social Implications of Agricultural Commitment.* Unpublished Ph.D. dissertation, Department of Anthropology, University of Arizona, Tucson.

White, Leslie A.
1942 *The Pueblo of Santa Ana, New Mexico.* Memoirs No. 60. American Anthropologist Vol. 44, No. 4, Pt. 2. American Anthropological Association, Menasha, Wisconsin.

1962 *The Pueblo of Zia, New Mexico.* Bureau of American Ethnology Bulletin No. 184. Smithsonian Institution, Washington, D.C.

Whittaker, John C.
1984 *Arrowheads and Artisans: Stone Tool Manufacture and Individual Variation at Grasshopper Pueblo.* Unpublished Ph.D. dissertation, Department of Anthropology, University of Arizona, Tucson.

Whittlesey, Stephanie M.
1978 *Status and Death at Grasshopper Pueblo: Experiments Toward an Archaeological Theory of Correlates.* Unpublished Ph.D. dissertation, Department of Anthropology, University of Arizona.

1984 Uses and Abuses of Mogollon Mortuary Data. In *Recent Research in Mogollon Archaeology,* edited by S. Upham, F. Plog, D. Batcho, and B. Kauffman, pp. 276–84. Occasional Papers No. 10. University Museum, New Mexico State University, Las Cruces.

1989 The Individual, the Community, and Social Organization: Issues of Evidence and Inference Justification. In *Households and Communities,* edited by S. MacEachern, D. Archer, and R. Garvin, pp. 227–34. University of Calgary, Alberta.

1999 Engendering the Mogollon Past: Theory and Mortuary Data from Grasshopper Pueblo. In *Sixty Years of Mogollon Archaeology: Papers from the Ninth Mogollon Conference, Silver City, New Mexico, 1996,* edited by S. M. Whittlesey, pp. 39–48. SRI Press, Tucson.

Whittlesey, Stephanie M., Richard S. Ciolek-Torrello, and J. Jefferson Reid
1995 Salado: The View from the Arizona Mountains. Paper prepared for the seminar "Prehistoric Salado Culture of the American Southwest." Amerind Foundation, Dragoon, Arizona.

Whittlesey, Stephanie M., and J. Jefferson Reid
1982 Cholla Project Perspectives on Salado. In *Cholla Project Archaeology, Volume 1: Introduction and Special Studies,* edited by J. J. Reid, pp. 63–80. Arizona State Museum Archaeological Series No. 161. University of Arizona, Tucson.

Wittfogel, Karl. A.
1957 *Oriental Despotism: A Comparative Study of Total Power.* Yale University Press, New Haven.

Wittfogel, Karl A., and Esther S. Goldfrank
1943 Some Aspects of Pueblo Mythology and Society. *Journal of American Folklore* 56:17–30.

Wood, J. Scott
1989 *Vale of Tiers, Too: Late Classic Period Salado Settlement Patterns and Organizational Models for Tonto Basin.* Cultural Resources Inventory Report 89–12–280. Tonto National Forest, Phoenix.

Wood, J. Scott, and Martin E. McAllister
1982 The Salado Tradition: An Alternative View. In *Cholla Project Archaeology, Volume 1: Introduction and Special Studies,* edited by J. J. Reid, pp. 81–94. Arizona State Museum

Archaeological Series No. 161. University of
Arizona, Tucson.

Wright, Barton

1979   *Hopi Material Culture: Artifacts Gathered by
H. R. Voth in the Fred Harvey Collection.* The
Heard Museum, Phoenix, and Northland
Press, Flagstaff.

Zedeño, María Nieves

1994   *Sourcing Prehistoric Ceramics at Chodistaas
Pueblo, Arizona: The Circulation of People and
Pots in the Grasshopper Region.*
Anthropological Papers No. 58. University of
Arizona Press, Tucson.

CHAPTER SIX

A Study of Sinagua Mortuary Practices and Their Implications

John W. Hohmann

THIS STUDY SEEKS TO RECONSTRUCT SOCIAL organization and differentiation for the prehistoric population of the Flagstaff, Arizona region. Referred to as the Sinagua, these prehistoric people inhabited the mountainous Central Arizona region between A.D. 500–1400. This chapter focuses on the two critical time periods in Sinagua prehistory where social change is postulated to have occurred. Thus, mortuary analyses are presented for the earlier Angell-Winona phase (A.D. 1050–1100) and the later Elden phase (A.D. 1125–1200), highlighting the differences in mortuary practices and the inferred reflections of differences in social organization.

PROBLEM FORMULATION

Many archaeologists have argued that several prehistoric Southwestern populations had developed hierarchical, complex, sociopolitical structures (e.g., Brunson 1989; Cordell and Plog 1979; Lightfoot 1982; Plog 1979, 1989; Ravesloot 1984; Upham 1979a, 1979b, 1982; Upham et al. 1981; Wilcox and Sternberg 1983). Defining and explaining their establishment, maintenance, and denouement continues to be a major research challenge. Mortuary analysis appears to offer a primary avenue for such investigations because, as Peebles (1971:68) suggested, "per-sons who are treated differentially in life will be treated differentially in death."

Braun (1977, 1979) and Kerber (1986) have observed that archaeological mortuary analysis concerned with the study of prehistoric social organization is founded primarily upon the theoretical perspectives and arguments outlined by Saxe (1970, 1971) and Binford (1971). Extensive discussions of these theoretical perspectives on mortuary analysis can be found in Braun (1977, 1981, 1984), Brown (1971), Chapman and Randsborg (1981), Kerber (1986), Peebles (1974), and Tainter (1975). Of these numerous and varied approaches, I find Braun's (1977, 1981, 1984) theoretical and methodological approaches the most elegant. Therefore, for this paper I accept Braun's general theoretical orientation and employ his central methodological approach (i.e., the separation of qualitative from quantitative distinctions in burial practices).

Braun (1977, 1979:67) has identified three critical aspects of mortuary practice that reflect dimensions of status differentiation in a prehistoric society: (1) the various dimensions of living social persona are represented by recognizable dimensions of archaeological variability in burial treatments found within the total mortuary program, (2) variable dimensions in the archaeological burial record combine and/or crosscut with each other to reflect dimensions of status differentiation in the prehistoric society, and

(3) dimensions of social identities are represented by sets of qualitative distinctions which are redundant within the overall mortuary program.

Thus, Braun (1979:67) argues representation of hereditary ranking will be recognizable archaeologically in one or more qualitative attributes of the mortuary rite such as grave offerings, grave type, energy expended for interment, and grave location/placement. These attributes must be redundant, which assists in defining a "distinct dimension" of the variability of the burial program. Finally, Braun (1979:67–68) notes that these qualitative distinctions will crosscut gender and age classes, along with personal ability and perhaps horizontal differentiations. Braun (1977, 1979:66–68) argues that while qualitative indicators can be symbols of rank, quantitative indicators usually reflect personal wealth and prestige.

For this paper, complexity refers to the vertical and horizontal differentiation of social units. Horizontal differentiation distinguishes groups with similar status and prestige. Different horizontal groups are based on social differences such as clans, sodalities, age, gender, and so forth. Usually, societies that display only horizontal differentiation are considered simple or egalitarian systems. Vertical differentiation distinguishes groups or individuals with unequal status, rank, or prestige. Different vertical groups are ordered hierarchically. Usually, societies that display vertical differentiation are referred to as ranked, stratified, or complex systems.

In summary, we can recognize three major ethnographic patterns that we can expect to be mirrored in archaeological burial data. These are: (1) identification of four levels of leadership that can be distinguished by differences in the way political power and control are exercised, (2) these expressions of leadership are related to forms of social structure and social complexity, and (3) a central distinction between ranked and stratified societies is that in ranked societies, centralized formal authority is limited and control of critical resources is spread among many individuals, while stratified societies have strong, formalized and centralized authority with a select few controlling critical resources.

Braun (1979, 1981, 1984, 1987a) and Brown (1981) suggest that burial attributes (e.g., graves, energy expenditures, pre- and postmortem treatments) and selected artifacts (or artifact sets) can represent badges or symbols of rank or status. When badges of rank are found in all age and gender categories, they are thought to reflect inherited power and/or status (Binford 1971:21; Braun 1979; Brown

1981:29). Braun (1979) argues that rank indicators tend to be qualitative rather than quantitative features of the burial assemblage. Tainter (1978:121–22) argues that only rarely (approximately 5%) will rank indicators be included as grave goods.

In egalitarian or tribal societies, children receive minimal burial rites and few offerings and are buried away from the village or around its periphery since they have not participated significantly within the life of the community (Binford 1971:21–22). Moreover, Saxe (1970:149; 1971), Rathje (1973), and Braun (1979:68) note that elaborate child burials do not always reflect inherited rank and/or status but may instead represent the achieved prestige of their parents, family, or clan. It is possible that the difference between ascribed status and personal wealth, especially for subadults, can be recognized by variation and patterning in type, style, and number of mortuary offerings. Highly stratified societies will be characterized by greater patterned variation in the material wealth accompanying burials and the energy expended for interment. Or, as Braun (1979) suggests, by qualitative features of the burial program.

Previously, I have identified 12 critical bridging principles which assist us in moving from the archaeological record and anthropological reconstruction in mortuary studies (Hohmann 1992:44–46). These are:

1. Afterlife concepts affect burial form and mortuary practices. Moreover, mortuary ritual is a symbolic means of reaffirming extant social structure and organization during and after the trauma and disruption of death.

2. Religious beliefs regarding afterlife affect mortuary ritual and practices. In particular,
   a. cemetery location (relative to both village and natural environment),
   b. cemetery structure,
   c. burial body and head orientations within cemeteries, and
   d. postmortem body treatment and disposition.

3. Excluding atypical deaths, different burial attributes *and* groups of attributes can symbolize different social identities, the roles specific to those identities or aspects of the social organization of the society (although they may also indicate additional factors).

4. Variability in burial attributes indicates factors affecting burial forms.

5. Some selected artifacts or artifact sets which crosscut age and gender categories may be badges of rank that reflect inherited power and/or status.

6. It is conservative to assume that rank indicators are normally more qualitative than quantitative features of the burial assemblage and that they are rare.

7. Highly stratified communities can sometimes be identified by greater patterned variation in material wealth and energy expenditure (or by qualitative features of the burial program) than less stratified groups.

8. There often is a direct correlation between higher rank/status of the deceased and the degree of elaborateness and amount of energy invested in grave and body treatment.

9. As social differentiation increases, site complexity and formal structuring of site areas, such as cemeteries, increases.

10. The total burial program may reflect the totality of community organization.

11. Ethnic variety can be a causal factor in burial variability.

12. Formation processes and archaeological preservation play a critical role in our ability to completely and adequately reconstruct social structure and organization.

METHODOLOGICAL CONCERNS

The theory and concepts discussed above have led to the identification of three principal methodological concerns. First, at the individual level, role theory suggests that burial data expresses the total set of rights and duties defined by social structure and reflected in social persona n, though certain social personas dominate others. Thus, methods are required to segregate burial data that express positions the individual held on both the vertical and horizontal dimensions of the social order of his/her community; the deceased's different social personas; and the deceased's different social identities. At the site or community level, assuming that the burial population is a representative sample of the whole population, ethnographic experience suggests a site's burial data reflects the social structure, social organization, and organizational complexity of the community. Thus, analytic methods are

TABLE 6.1 Sinagua Cremation Classes (after McGregor 1941:262–64)

Type 1	Bones and ashes left on the ground, scattered over an area, not collected, usually including some offerings
Type 2a	Bones and ashes placed in a shallow hole in the old clay surface, with no cover or offerings
Type 2b	Rock slabs placed in a hole, with bones above the rocks, and covered with rocks; no offerings
Type 2c	Rock slab placed in a hole, with bones and ashes in the hole, covered with a rock slab, and this in turn with an inverted bowl
Type 3	Bones and ash placed in a shallow hole in the clay surface, and covered only with sherds
Type 4	Bones and ashes placed in a hole in the old clay surface, with a bowl inverted over them; no other offerings as a rule
Type 5a	Bones and ashes placed in a bowl, and covered with sherds
Type 5b	Bones and ashes placed in a bowl, and not covered
Type 6	Bones placed in a bowl with another bowl inverted over it
Type 7a	Bones and ashes placed in a jar or a pitcher, and covered with a bowl or two bowls; often a small jar besides these, all buried
Type 7b	Bones and ashes placed in a jar or pitcher, and covered with sherds
Type 7c	Bones and ashes placed in a jar or pitcher, and covered with a rock slab
Type 7d	Bones and ashes placed in a jar or pitcher, with no covering

TABLE 6.2   Sinagua Inhumation Grave Forms (after Hohmann 1982:20)

Type 1	Simple hole
Type 2	Clay or adobe-lined pit
Type 3	Clay and stone-lined pit
Type 4	Clay or adobe-lined pit with a clay cap
Type 5	Clay and stone-lined pit with clay cap
Type 6	Clay or adobe-lined pit with stone cap or wood crypt
Type 7	Clay or stone-lined pit with cap or crypt
Type 8	Clay, stone, and wood-lined pit with stone and wood cap/crypt, occasionally with a second burial chamber also capped with stones and/or logs, located above the primary chamber

required that identify these social attributes. At the regional level, assuming that these archaeological cultures were single sociopolitical entities, methods are required that identify the degree of sociopolitical complexity of the regional community. Particularly, it is necessary to determine if the regional community functioned on a tribal or chiefly level; if the society was of the ranked or the stratified type during any given time period; and if the degree of sociopolitical complexity changed over time.

Variable Recognition and Dimension Definition

Variables of gender and age are critical in mortuary analysis. Measurable attributes of vertical differentiation include site types, grave locations, burial associations, offering content, and correlations between gender and age variable states (after Braun 1981). Generally, the number of recognizable rank levels is a measure of vertical differentiation. Measurable attributes of horizontal differentiation include burial location, body and head orientation, quantitative offertory studies, and select gender and age groupings (again after Braun 1981). Circumstances and time of deaths, which can affect patterns of *both* vertical and horizontal differentiation, are often expressed as measurable attributes in burial type and burial position (after Braun 1981; O'Shea 1981).

From Braun (1979), we can assign meaning to various social dimensions by observing the order of variable loading on a given factor component. Next, we can crosstabulate modalities found along a particular dimension against gender and age variables. Dimensions equate with a combination of many visible variables (i.e., the archaeological correlates of behaviors). Thus, we can observe dimensions such as power or wealth, each of which are composed of several different factors. Both Braun (1981, 1984), and O'Shea (1981, 1984) find dimensions are *not* independent, and thus, *not* orthogonal. However, such dimensions are defined relativistically; that is, they are recognized by their contrast to other dimensions—which follows what Goodenough (1965) labels identity relationships. To recognize various dimensions, we can use either principal components or factor analysis. Principal components analysis simply explores patterns having the most variance, whereas factor analysis (with oblique rotations) actually maps out those patterns.

Braun (1981) suggests symbols of rank can be crosstabulated with gender and age to yield variable values which can subsequently be employed to interpret the factor analysis results. Graves, energy expended on ritual and interment, pre- and postmortem treatments, and selected artifacts or artifact sets can equate with badges of rank (cf., Braun 1979, 1981, 1984; Brown 1981). Both Braun and Brown argue that if such rank indicators crosscut age and gender dimensions, then ascription is present.

ADDITIONAL TERMS

Due to the significant variation encountered in the cremations from Winona Village and Ridge Ruin, McGregor (1941:262–64) found it necessary to define 13 cremation types. After reviewing McGregor's data, I found no need to expand or modify the list, and the same classes were applied in this study (table 6.1) (Hohmann 1981:46–56). Similarly, a set of inhumation grave forms was developed that also represents increasing interment energy expenditure levels (table 6.2).

Energy expenditures were ranked for both cremations and inhumations, and a list of compatible descending expenditures was developed (table 6.3). The scheme developed by McGuire (1987) for ranking artifact values was reviewed, but such a direct technique was not applicable to Sinagua burial deposits. For this study, energy expenditure ranking was based upon the amount of effort employed in grave construction, the types of materials used in grave construction, and the depth the burial was placed below ground. Energy expenditure estimates were then calculated for each known burial form encountered. Next, equivalency rates between inhumation grave forms and cremation grave forms were calculated.

TABLE 6.3   Compatible Descending Energy Expenditure Levels for Cremation and Inhumation Class Forms

Energy Expenditure Level	Cremation Class	Inhumation Class
7	7c	7, 8
6	7a	6
5	7b	5
4	4	6, 7d
3	3	4, 5a, 5b
2	2	2b, 2c
1	1	1, 2a

THE STUDY AREA

"Sinagua" is the term applied to the cultural attributes of the prehistoric inhabitants who lived in what is now the mountainous Flagstaff, Arizona region. The Sinagua lived in a region characterized by significant environmental variation. Using Plog's (1989:264–265) definition of the spatial extent of Sinagua, the regional boundaries are the Mogollon Rim to the south, the town of Heber to the east, Sitgreaves Mountain west of Flagstaff, and Wupatki to the north.

A diverse plant and corresponding animal community is associated with the Flagstaff region. This diversity is based largely on elevation, exposure, and amounts of effective moisture. Both Merriam (1890) and Lowe (1964) have identified three primary Life Zones within the Flagstaff region: the Upper Sonoran Life Zone (pinyon,

juniper, and grassland), the Transition Life Zone (Ponderosa pine and Oak Woodlands), and Canadian Life Zone (Douglas fir and blue spruce). Faunal distributions within the Flagstaff region are highly variable and frequently correspond to the plant community.

Sinagua prehistory can be divided into eight chronological phases beginning at A.D. 500 and terminating at A.D. 1400 (table 6.4). The modified dates listed in table 6.4 are based upon the most recent absolute and relative chronometric results (see Downum 1988). Several recent studies (e.g., Baldwin and Bremer 1986; Bremer 1989; Downum 1988; Hohmann 1981, 1982a; Pilles 1979; Plog 1989) have reviewed the Flagstaff chronology, especially with regard to Sunset Crater's eruption sequence, the tree-ring series, and its implication for local cultural reconstructions.

This chronology presumes that (1) there is *no* discernible break in Sinagua regional occupation, (2) that the settlement pattern outlined by Pilles (1978, 1979), Baldwin and Bremer (1986), and Bremer (1989) occurred, and (3) that long-occupied, large site complexes were constructed by Sinagua populations by A.D. 1075. This brief review of the Sinagua physical and cultural environments suggests that a continuum can be observed for the indigenous formation, growth, and decline of ceremonial, ritual, and community activities. Beginning in the Cinder Park phase a combined hunting, gathering, and limited horticulture subsistence system dominated, suggesting a limited level of Sinagua social and political complexity. By the Angell-Winona phase, evidence indicates the Sinagua practiced communitywide, highly structured and organized ceremonial rituals. Evidence for community-level energy expenditures for agricultural purposes can be found as early as the Sunset phase.

Agricultural intensification and concurrent social integration increased and began to formalize during the Padre phase and was fully enacted by the late Elden phase. Many researchers (e.g., Baldwin and Bremer 1986; Bremer 1989; Gratz and Pilles 1979; Henderson 1979; Pilles 1979, 1987; Plog 1989; Upham 1979b, 1980, 1982) suggest Sinagua agriculture was sufficiently successful to derive surpluses. Further, we can observe evidence of increasing complexity in Sinagua settlement and economic systems by the Elden phase (see Gratz and Pilles 1979; Henderson 1979; Pilles 1979, 1987; Plog 1989; Upham 1979b, 1982).

By the late Elden phase (A.D. 1150–1200) and continuing throughout the Clear Creek phase, architectural evidence reflects a formalized pattern of community ritual

TABLE 6.4 The Eight Sinagua Chronological Phases and Associated Dates (A.D.)

Pecos Classification	Colton (1946:17)	Plog (1989:267)	Hohmann (this chapter)	Sinagua Phases
Pueblo IV	1300–1400	1264–1450	1264–1400	Clear Creek
	1200–1300	1150–1200	1200–1264	Turkey Hill
Pueblo III	1120–1200	1125–1150	1125–1200	Elden
	1070–1120	1100–1125	1100–1125	Padre
Pueblo II	1075–1100	1050–1100	1050–1100	Angell-Winona
	900–1070	1050–1075	950–1050	Rio de Flag
Pueblo I	700–900	800–950	700–950	Sunset
Basketmaker III	500–700	675–700	600–700	Cinder Park

architecture suggesting a stratified level of social and political complexity (cf., Plog 1989; Upham 1982). This brief review has suggested that the Sinagua were a sedentary agricultural population who, by A.D. 1130, undertook communal labor to build major field and irrigation systems which resulted in surpluses. We also can observe communal labor being invested in the construction of community religious structures. Moreover, for the Sinagua region, we find a long history of formalized, communitywide religious ritual.

ANGELL-WINONA PHASE BURIAL ANALYSIS

From a regional perspective, the Angell-Winona phase burial assemblage reflects a substantial degree of homogeneity. The regional Angell-Winona phase burial population consists of 99 interments collected from 13 sites. Of these individuals, 96 could be assigned to a specific age group. Subadults account for 33% of this regional burial population, while adults encompass the remaining 67%. Gender could be assigned to only 58 cases due to limitations imposed upon the osteological analysis by the cremation processes and age-grade factors. Of the cases that could be identified, 39.7% are female, while 60.3% are male.

Modes of Interment

There are two principal modes of interment, inhumation and cremation, which occur in near equal proportions (59.6% and 40.4%, respectively). Inhumations are typically primary, extended supine interments. Seven cases of mass inhumation were noted. In five cases, two individuals were

interred together, usually an adult female and a very young subadult (four cases), probably representing a mother who died in childbirth, or a mother and child who died while the child was still nursing. The remaining double interment was that of two adults, an elder male with a younger female, possibly reflecting a mating pair. The other two cases of mass inhumation reflect three and five individuals of all ages and genders being interred within a single earthen burial pit. In all multiple interment cases, no offerings accompanied these individuals, and the graves were at the standard depth (approximately 30 centimeters below present ground surface). Unfortunately, the skeletal remains from both of these mass interments were not available for additional analysis, and therefore, I cannot determine if illness (epidemic), sudden traumatic injury (disaster), or intentional (homicide or suicide) were the cause of death and may account for this particular mode of interment.

Fish et al. (1980:173) noted that cremations and inhumations are clustered in separate mounds as well as in separate sections of the same mound. For example, burials recovered from the Kahorsho site (NA10937), which date from the late Angell-Winona to middle Padre phases, are equally divided into cremations and inhumations. Cremations were found predominately on the eastern side of the site, while inhumations were discovered in trash mounds along the western side (Beeson 1977). A similar pattern has been noted for the Winona Village site.

Component spatial analysis at Winona Village suggests a distinct distribution of small pithouse and trash mound clusters during each phase. For each pithouse cluster, two to four habitation units, an occasional granary, and one or two trash mounds were observed. Most Angell-Winona and Padre phase interments have trash mound associations. Detailed discussions of trash mound stratigraphy by McGregor (1941) indicate the mounds were not built atop previously interred burials, but rather that burial deposits and burial pits were dug into existing mound deposits.

Additionally, inhumations usually occur in adjacent trash mounds whereas cremations are interred in a discrete area reserved for that purpose. Several investigators (Binford 1971; Goldstein 1981; Saxe 1970, 1971) argue that different cemetery areas can represent different social identities such as family or clan affiliations, sodalities, and so forth. Moreover, they suggest spatial proximity of cemeteries to discrete habitation units often reflect a use of these cemeteries by the units' residents. Following these arguments, Winona Village cemetery trash mounds probably contain interments derived from associated, nearby house clusters. Inhumation interment in trash mounds adjacent to residential units could suggest that inhumation mortuary ritual was undertaken primarily on a family or extended family level.

At the regional level, inhumations occur most frequently in trash mounds (n = 38, 63.4% of all inhumations). Also, most subfloor interments are inhumations (22 inhumations versus 2 cremations). Most subfloor inhumations appear to be infants who died within their first year of life. When infant subfloor interment is found, evidence indicates a continuation of room occupation. In those few cases of adult subfloor interment, we find either that room abandonment quickly followed interment or that the room was constructed atop the interment after the interment occurred.

Angell-Winona phase cremations were predominately primary green cremations (n = 27). Such treatment of the dead is found to occur in all gender and age groups, site types and sizes, and burial proveniences. Cremations usually occur in crematorium areas but also are found in subfloor contexts (n = 2), trash mounds (n = 3), cemetery areas (n = 2), and in random localities (n = 2).

From a regional perspective, such patternings suggest that the Angell-Winona phase burial population was divided in a nearly equal occurrence of cremations and inhumations. Further, cremations tend to be interred within a cemetery area, while inhumations are found in trash mounds. Discerning such regional patterns in an earlier study (see Hohmann 1981, 1982a, 1982b) led me to conclude that such configurations and spatial arrangements reflected social units such as moieties and/or clans. The

results of this regional study indicate I may have been incorrect. Such patterning might indicate the community's response to their unique natural environment. The spatial distribution of cremations suggests cremation was undertaken during periods when the ground was frozen. Most cremation deposits are interred within the crematorium area where the ground surface has already been warmed and thawed by the cremation fires. Thus, we find cremations being interred either in small pits or covered over where burned, both more easily accomplished during winter periods when using primitive technology.

Previously, I have contended (see Hohmann 1981: 106–112, 1982a:38–40) that the dual interment pattern of inhumation and cremation is not contingent upon the deceased's status or cultural affiliation as suggested by Colton (1946:255–57, 260–66, 1960:41–45) and Stanislawski (1963:311–13). This re-analysis continues to support my original analysis, as do studies by Fish et al. (1980:173–74).

Grave Forms

For both inhumations and cremations, a full range of variability can be observed in grave forms and in the associated energy levels expended for interment. While both cremations and inhumations were found interred in simple earthen holes, clay-lined pits, stone-lined pits, and in stone- and clay-lined pits with stone caps, only inhumations were found to have clay caps or wooden cribbing above the grave. Further, cremations tended either to be placed in a simple earthen hole or placed within a stone- and clay-lined pit capped by a stone cover. The bimodal distribution between low energy expenditure interments and high energy expenditure interments might reflect a major social division between those individuals of low status and those who may have acquired a higher status.

The range of energy expenditure levels for postmortem body treatment and interment of both cremations and inhumations have parallel ranges of complexity and variability in the Sinagua region. Unlike the Hohokam region where it is considered a high energy mortuary treatment, cremation in the Sinagua region is not considered labor or energy intensive because: (1) there is abundant fuel wood available, (2) less fuel is used, (3) there is less attendance to the remains during cremation, and (4) there is less handling after cremation.

Most Angell-Winona phase cremations were either left upon the crematorium floor and simply covered over by earth, or collected and buried in small shallow pits located around the periphery of the crematorium (see

Fish et al. 1980; Hohmann 1981, 1982a, 1982b, 1984a, 1984b; Hohmann and Reinhard n.d.; Hudgens 1974; McGregor 1941). Angell-Winona phase crematoria appear to be communally used and maintained and might be predecessors of later formalized cemeteries.

Body and Head Orientations

Angell-Winona phase inhumations are almost equally divided between north-south (21.3%) and east-west (27.7%) body orientations. Such body positioning occurs in all age and gender groups, but particular body orientations (e.g., north-south versus east-west) are spatially discrete. Most north-south oriented bodies are not found in the same trash mounds in which one finds east-west oriented bodies. Since each trash mound is associated with a small house cluster suggesting extended family groupings, the body orientation pattern may reflect ritual mandates founded within an extended family or clan.

The heads of north-south oriented burials were fairly evenly divided between north and south orientations. This was not true for east-west oriented individuals.

Heads oriented toward the east (n = 23) far outnumbered those pointed toward the west (n = 3). This unusually high occurrence suggests eastern orientation was possibly a patterned response to religious ritual rather than an indicator of social or status divisions.

General Mortuary Treatment

A major distinction between subadults and adults exists in that subadult burials consistently yield fewer mortuary offerings (figure 6.1) and are interred in less elaborate grave forms. Adults were recovered from all grave forms and all levels of energy expended for interment, while subadults were only found in earthen holes (n = 9), stone-lined pits (n = 2), and stone capped pits if cremated (n = 21). A moderate correlation exists (Pearson's $r = .30$, $p < .0017$, n = 96) between advanced age and the number of status markers, energy expended for interment, and the total number of offerings.

To better determine the percentage of variability accounted for by age in Angell-Winona phase mortuary treatment, factor and principal components analyses were

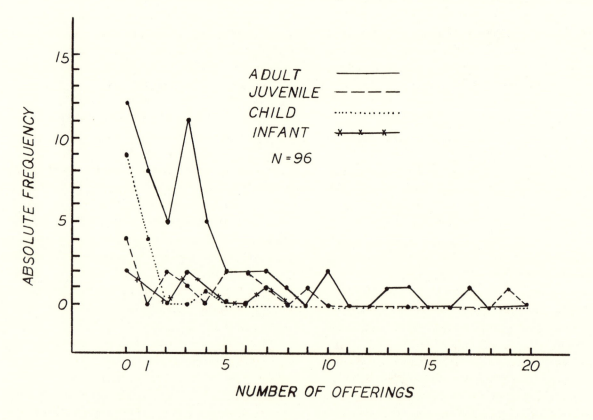

FIGURE 6.1 Comparison of Artifact Offerings by Age Groups for Burials from the Angell-Winona Phase

TABLE 6.5 Angell-Winona Phase Principal Component and Factor Analysis Data Using Orthogonal Rotation Variable

	Communality Factor	Eigen value	Pct of Var.	Cum. Pct
Age	.038091	1.24321	31.1	31.1
Gender	.038842	1.15061	28.8	59.8
Total Offerings	.043183	.82818	20.7	80.6
Grave Type	.039534	.77799	19.4	100.0

Analysis No. 1 Listwise Deletion of Cases with Missing Values

	Mean	Std. Dev.
Age	3.77586	.67650
Gender	1.60345	.49345
Total Offerings	3.68966	4.03583
Grave Type	4.50000	2.54951

Number of Cases = 58

Correlation Matrix:

	V11	V12	V16	V5
Age	1.00000	1.00000		
Gender	.14951	-.08050	1.00000	
Total Offerings	.09616	.09064	-.17221	1.00000

Determinant of Correlation Matrix = .9216692

1-Tailed Sig. of Correlation Matrix: ('.' is Printed for Diagonal Elements).

	V11-Age	V12-Gender	V16-Off.	V5
Age	.			
Gender	.13133	.		
Total Off.	.23635	.27402	.	
Grave Type	.31097	.24930	.09807	.

Extraction 1 for Analysis 1, Maximum Likelihood (ML)

undertaken. While the entire set of Angell-Winona variables was initially reviewed, preliminary testing indicated that variables of age, gender, grave type/energy expended for interment, total offerings, personal offerings, local ceramics, and trade ceramics were most relevant. Of these, gender, age, grave type, and total offerings appear to be the most sensitive. Such variable definition was accomplished for this study by following arguments outlined by Braun (1977, 1979, 1987a, 1987b) and initial data evaluation. The correlation between each pair of variables was calculated through R-factor analysis and orthogonal rotation was employed.

Table 6.5 presents the results of the factor analysis for Angell-Winona phase burial data. This analysis identifies the deceased's age as a major factor in the variation in mortuary treatment. Age accounts for 31.1% of the variation and has an eigenvalue of 1.243.

Gender of the deceased is the second major cause of variation in Angell-Winona phase mortuary treatment (28.7%). Generally, females received fewer offerings, religious objects, and status markers and less elaborate grave forms than males during the Angell-Winona phase. In those instances where females were accorded several offerings, the majority of items was either ground stone (e.g., manos and metates) or shell jewelry. The unique occurrence of an elderly female receiving numerous burial offerings could reflect familial or societal esteem or prestige. When combined, the two variables of age and gender account for 59.8% of the variation.

Offertory Sets

Offering distributions are presented in figure 6.2. Offering distributions indicate a basically bimodal distribution: those with zero to three offerings and those with four or more. One third of the population received no offerings at all. Generally, we find a limited range of variation in number and kind of grave offerings for burials from the Angell-Winona phase.

Fish et al. (1980:167, 173–74) note that earlier studies of Angell-Winona mortuary offerings indicate high and low status individuals in both cremations and inhumations. They conclude that "there is no difference between the kinds of goods found in each group as might be expected if the cremations represent an intrusive population" (Fish et al. 1980:173–174). Within Angell-Winona phase offertory sets, religious items included effigy vessels, clay

figurines, special mineral caches and dyes, and turquoise jewelry. Status indicators included decorated ceramics and formal stone tools, plus turquoise and shell jewelry, whereas personal offerings included plain ware ceramics, shell jewelry, and lithics (both chipped and ground stone).

Gender apparently influenced the distribution of offering sets (figure 6.3). While an elderly female (Case 58, Site NA1600) received the greatest number of offerings for this phase (n = 19; offerings included nine Black Mesa Black-on-white vessels, one Rio de Flag vessel, two ground-stone implements, and numerous pieces of shell jewelry), the next four high status burials were elder males (Case 18 from Site NA2134 with 17 offerings, Case 41 from Site NA2133 with 14 offerings, Case 20 from Site NA2134 with 13 offerings, and Case 61 from Site NA1600 with 10 offerings). Thus, only four males from a total burial population of 99 received elaborate burials. Of these, the top three were dominated by religious artifacts, suggesting these men might have been religious

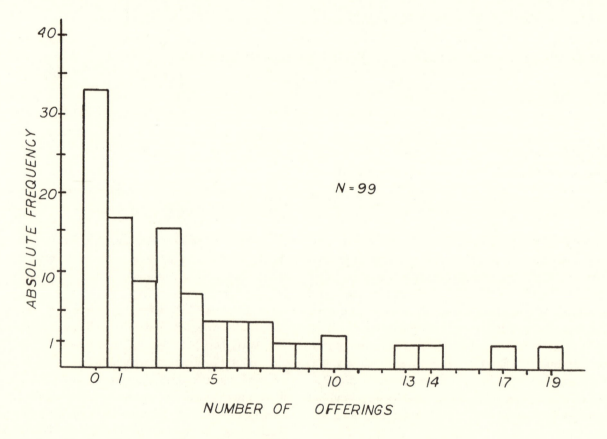

FIGURE 6.2   Absolute Frequency Histogram of Angell-Winona Phase Mortuary Offerings

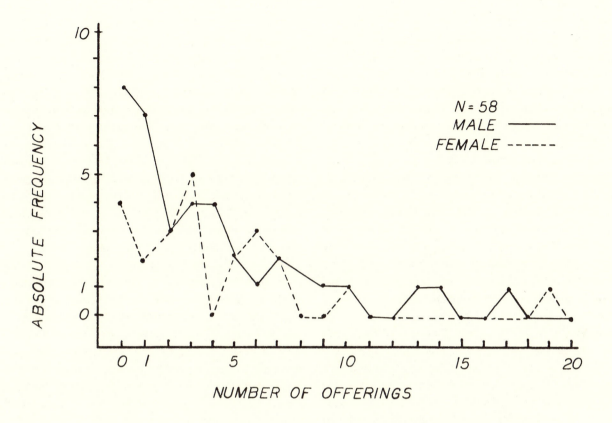

FIGURE 6.3   Comparison of Artifact Offerings by Gender for Burials from the Angell-Winona Phase

leaders (Pearson's r = .815, p < .0001 for religious artifacts and total offerings [n = 99]).

Social Reconstructions

The mortuary data patterns recognized for this phase lead me to infer that the Angell-Winona phase Sinagua were a ranked society, functioning within a limited or simple level of social complexity. Limited variations in material wealth, in energy expended for interment and ritual, and the fact that few grave offerings were associated with subadult interments suggest status was achieved. Braun (1979, 1981, 1984) and Brown (1981) list status indicators as including elaborate graves, high energy expenditures, elaborate pre- and postmortem treatment, and selected/specialized offertory sets or artifacts. The observed association between elder males, religious artifacts, elaborate grave forms, and high energy expenditure levels for interment ritual further supports the contention that the Angell-Winona Sinagua practiced a form of social organ-

ization where elder males could achieve high status. Often, select elder males were interred with numerous religious articles, perhaps reflecting their role as religious or ceremonial leaders. These analyses also indicate that elder females were occasionally afforded burial rites reflecting prestige and esteem, although most females were only interred with personal items.

ELDEN PHASE BURIAL ANALYSIS

Comparison of mortuary practices between the early Elden phase (A.D. 1125–1150) and the Angell-Winona phase suggests that a breakdown of homogeneity occurred in Sinagua burial treatment in the latter phase. This breakdown was initiated during the late Padre phase times (see Hohmann 1992:231–79). Such a breakdown appears more emphatically expressed at the larger sites which appear to have served as regional trade and redistribution centers. Such change then later spread to the smaller village networks.

The development of what might be discrete ranking categories and status levels, coupled with the concurrent increase in mortuary ritual variability, suggests a change in social organization and differentiation. Thus, such variability and change in early Elden phase mortuary practices indicates a time of transition. Indeed, I contend that this phase (A.D. 1125–1150) of the Elden phase is a time of radical and rapid change.

Studies of late Padre phase and early Elden sites and artifacts suggest a significant change in regional trade networks. Close contacts with southern peoples decreased significantly as evidenced by a cessation of Hohokam and Hohokam-like ceramics, pithouses, and ballcourts; only shell remained a substantial trade item from the south. Reviewing evidence collected from both site and burial contexts, an increase in the number and diversity of trade items from the north and northeast can be observed. Investigators in the region (e.g., Bremer 1989; Hohmann 1982a; Pilles 1978, 1979, 1987; Plog 1979, 1989; Upham 1978, 1979a, 1980, 1982) have suggested that the development of new, major exchange and redistribution systems in the Flagstaff region led to a significant change in Sinagua social organization. Archaeological evidence from the early Elden phase also demonstrates an intensification in agricultural subsistence efforts which might have led to food surpluses. Such evidence suggests substantial changes were occurring that could have had significant impacts upon Sinagua social organization and differentiation.

The late Elden phase (A.D. 1150–1200) displays marked changes in particular aspects of mortuary ritual and evidences a formalization and structuring of prescribed mortuary ceremony. The late Elden phase burial population consists of 167 interments collected from 17 sites. All burials could be assigned to a specific age group, with adults constituting 64.7% of the population, while subadults accounted for the remaining 35.3%. Gender designations could be assigned to only 45 individuals (27% of the burial population). Of the identifiable cases, 48.7% are female, while 51.3% are male.

Modes of Interment

Inhumations dominate the Elden phase burial assemblage. Only two (1.2%) secondary green cremations have been discovered postdating A.D. 1150; the remaining burial population was inhumed. Over 95.8% (n = 159) of the burials were interred in an extended, supine fashion.

Variations in this pattern include 17 double or mass inhumations (10.2%), one secondary inhumation, one individual placed extended prone, two placed extended on their sides, and one situated on his side, semiflexed.

Unlike the preceding Padre phase where mass interments were all cremations and were typically interred in groups of five or more individuals, Elden phase mass interments were all inhumations and most were pairs (either male/female couple or woman/infant). Only two of the mass inhumations had three to four individuals interred together. Both of these cases were interred in a simple, shallow earthen hole with only a few personal items (e.g., ceramic vessels and shell jewelry). Unfortunately, the skeletal remains of these individuals were reburied prior to full osteological analysis. Thus, we are unable to establish the causes of death, although the mass interment of several individuals from similar age groups and both genders might indicate some manner of sudden group traumatic death (e.g., fire, natural disaster, warfare, or epidemic).

Mass interments that occurred in groups of twos can be divided into two principal groups: woman/infant pairings, and male/female pairings. In woman/infant pairings, one case collected from Elden Pueblo clearly was the burial of a mother who died during childbirth (given placement of fetus within the mother's skeletal remains). The other two cases also appear to reflect such deaths. When such burials are accompanied by offerings, the offerings are few in number, are personal items, and appear directly associated with the adult female, *not* the stillborn infant.

The second, more common form of pair burial is the male/female grouping. Frequently, the male ranged in age from 33 to 50 years while the female ranged from 18 to 35 years. A range of grave types, energy expenditure for interment, number and type of grave offerings could be observed for these various cases. Individuals interred within the same grave area appear to have shared equally in the joint offerings placed within the grave.

While interments from the Angell-Winona, Padre, and early Elden phase sites are found in both trash mounds and formal cemetery areas, or within discrete, separate sections of the same mound (again see Beeson and Goldfried 1976; Hohmann 1982a, 1992; King 1949; McGregor 1941, 1943), Elden phase interments dating after A.D. 1150 are predominately (77.9%) found in formal cemetery areas. Moderately sized and large Elden phase sites appear to have had several discrete formal cemetery locations.

For example, formal, spatially definable cemeteries were present at Elden Pueblo (figure 6.4). Associated mortuary offerings and interment forms indicate that all age and gender categories, all status levels, and all orientation modes were present within each cemetery unit. The range of ceramic types included as grave furniture suggests all three cemetery areas were utilized at the same time throughout most of the site's occupation. It would appear then that these cemeteries do not represent different time periods, status groups, or social units.

Patterns of infant subfloor burial infrequently observed during the Angell-Winona phase became the dominant practice during the Elden phase. Newborn or stillborn

infants were typically interred under habitation room floors. After subfloor burial, the floors were resurfaced and room occupation continued (Hohmann 1983, 1992).

Grave Forms

There is increased evidence of premortem, prepared burial pits during the Elden phase (see Colton 1946; Hohmann 1980, 1981, 1982a; King 1949). Premortem, prepared burial pits discovered at late Elden phase sites appear as large, formally excavated rectangular pits, frequently already clay-lined. No capping is present, nor are

FIGURE 6.4   Map of Elden Pueblo Showing the Distribution of Architectural Features and Burials

TABLE 6.6   Grave Offerings and Grave Form for the Late Elden Phase

Grave Form

No. of Offerings	Hole	Clay	Stone	Clay Cap	Stone-Clay Cap	Wood Cap	Stone Cap	Total
0	57	4	—	—	—	1	—	62
1	18	1	—	—	1	—	—	20
2	10	1	—	—	—	—	—	11
3	10	—	—	—	1	—	—	11
4	6	3	—	—	—	1	1	11
5	7	2	1	—	—	—	—	10
6	4	—	—	—	—	1	—	5
7	4	—	—	—	—	1	—	5
8	2	—	—	—	—	—	1	3
9	1	—	—	—	—	—	—	1
10	1	—	—	—	—	—	—	1
12	1	—	—	—	—	—	1	2
14	1	1	2	—	—	—	—	4
15	2	—	—	—	—	—	—	2
18	—	1	—	—	—	—	—	1
19	1	1	—	—	—	—	—	2
24	—	—	—	1	—	—	—	1
27	—	—	1	—	—	—	—	1
28	—	1	—	—	—	—	—	1
40	1	—	—	—	—	—	—	1
613	—	—	—	—	—	1	—	1
Total	126	27	4	1	2	5	2	167

Note: Pearson's r =.31672, significance =.0000.

any skeletal remains evident. Indeed, careful examination of stratigraphic fill in several predug burial pits (see Hohmann 1983) indicates that no body had ever been placed in the grave and no fill material had ever been intentionally placed over or within the pit. Fill within the premortem graves consists of washed fill and later cultural fill and/or natural sedimentation. Creation of premortem burial pits would have alleviated difficulties inherent in digging such graves during the winter months when the ground could be both frozen and snow covered. The significantly high frequency of premortem prepared burial pits during the Elden phase, in association with discrete, formalized cemeteries, also argues for a region-wide formalization and standardization of mortuary practices and attendant rituals.

While a full range of variability can be observed in Elden phase grave forms and corresponding levels of energy expended for interment, over 75% of the total regional burial population was interred in simple earthen holes. Table 6.6 reveals a moderate correlation (Pearson's $r = .317$, significance = .00001) between grave type and energy expenditure levels and total offerings. There are also corresponding moderate correlations between elaborate grave forms, energy expended for interment and ritual, and specific artifact types such as wands, special stone/mineral caches, and ceramic effigies. Indeed, most ceramic effigy forms occurred in stone-lined burial cists or in stone-lined tombs capped with wooden cribbing and adobe covers.

The above patterns were further examined employing T-distribution tests (table 6.7). T-tests were performed with energy expended for interment against religious objects, total offerings, status items, and personal objects. The results clearly illustrate a significant difference of the means between simple earthen hole burials, clay-lined pits, and high energy interments with these various offertory subsets. Clearly, three distinct groups are present. It will be argued that these three groups equate to three primary status groupings.

Body and Head Orientations

Elden phase burials demonstrate greater variability in body and head orientations than in all previous phases. While an eastern head orientation is still the most dominant orientation (32.8%), it is closely followed by north (22.4%) and northeast (18.7%) head orientations. As with previous phases, Elden phase orientations can occur in all gender and age groups.

Generally, all body and head orientations are found in each separate and distinct late Elden phase cemetery area. However, there appear to be small clusters of burials oriented in the same direction within each individual cemetery. Regionally, most Elden phase cemeteries seem to be divided by head and body orientations into two major divisions; half of the burials in a cemetery are oriented

east-west while the remaining half are oriented in some other direction.

General Mortuary Treatment

Factor analysis also was conducted for the Elden phase burials (table 6.8). Variables of gender and age account for only 39.2% of the variation when combined. This factor analysis indicates that the mortuary assemblage is the major factor in variability in late Elden phase mortuary treatment; total offerings account for 34%. When additional factors are added, total offerings account for over 57% of the observed variability (table 6.9).

Table 6.8 suggests little correlation between gender of the deceased and total burial offerings and limited correlation between age and total offerings. In this regional analysis, a pattern emerges where for every adult male burial treated in a manner suggesting high or moderate status, there are .60 adult female burials and .44 subadult (combines infants, children, and juveniles) burials treated in equivalent fashion. For example, at Elden Pueblo (NA142) the burial with the second greatest amount of trade ware ceramics included as offerings was a juvenile female. However, only adults received more than 18 total offerings as a portion of their grave furniture. Further, only males received 24 or more offerings in their burials.

The distributions of particular grave good types appear to be correlated to gender and age distinctions within the Elden Pueblo burial population. Pilles (1982) noted the co-occurrence of bone awls and male interments; indeed, upon closer inspection, he found most carved bone awls and many plain awls were placed in unique positions

TABLE 6.7 Results of the T-distribution for Elden Phase Interments with Grave Forms/Energy Expended for Interment Compared with the Total Number of Offerings

	Comparison 1		Comparison 2		Comparison 3	
Variable	Hole	Clay	Hole	High Energy	Clay	High Energy
Number of cases	126	27	126	14	27	14
Mean no. for total offerings	2.61	7.19	2.61	52.14	7.19	52.14
Standard deviation	7.866	6.373	4.866	161.63	6.373	161.63
Standard error	.434	1.227	.434	43.198	1.227	43.198
T value	-3.51		-3.53		-1.46	
Degrees of freedom	32.8		13		39	
2-tail probability	.0013		.0006		.1521	

TABLE 6.8 Late Elden Phase Principal Component and Factor Analysis Data Using Orthogonal Rotation; with Four Critical Variables Examined

Value	Mean	Standard Deviation	Label
V16	7.75000	48.51804	Total Offerings
V5	4.84375	1.48598	Grave Type
V11	1.68125	1.87124	Age
V12	.96875	.20747	Gender

Correlation Matrix:

	V16	V5	V11	V12
V16	1.00000			
V5	.07142	1.00000		
V11	-.04563	.01364	1.00000	
V12	.01234	-.05674	-.34983	1.00000

Initial Statistics:

Variable	Communality	Factor	Eigenvalue	Pct of Var.	Cum. Pct
Total Offerings	1.00000	1	1.35952	34.0	34.0
Grave Type	1.00000	2	1.07473	26.9	60.9
Age	1.00000	3	.91910	23.0	83.8
Gender	1.00000	4	.64665	16.2	100.0

PC Extracted   2 Factors

about many males' heads. Further study led Pilles (1982) to the conclusion that these carved and plain bone "awls" located about adult male heads were not awls but bone hair pieces used as male ornaments.

Age distinctions also are noted within the mortuary complex. Burials recently recovered at Elden Pueblo reveal infants and very young children were interred with miniature offerings, such as miniature or small plain ware and decorated ceramic vessels, miniature projectile points, miniature jewelry, and miniature rattles. Analysis of earlier Elden Pueblo collections suggests this patterned relationship is fairly common. However, there are infants buried without any offerings and young children accompanied with standard-sized grave furniture. Also, adults occasionally will have a miniature or small offering included as a grave good, but always in the accompaniment of other standard-sized offerings; no adult late Elden phase interment has been recovered containing only small or miniature offerings. A similar pattern of infant interments receiving only miniature offerings

was uncovered during excavations at Sunset Pueblo (Hohmann 1982c).

Offertory Sets

Figure 6.5 illustrates a trimodal distribution of total offerings. Over 78% of the total regional burial population received between zero and six offerings, 13.2% received between 7 and 12 offerings, while the remaining 8.4% of the population received over 14 offerings. Both Upham (1979a, 1979b:24–25) and I (Hohmann 1981:155, 1982a:55–56, 1992:321–327) have suggested that these strata can be equated with status levels.

In an effort to determine if such a trimodal distribution was present, or if this distribution simply represents a reverse J-curve with only a few extreme values present, a chi-square and Kolmogorov-Smirnov test were performed. The results of these tests indicate that late Elden phase grave offering distributions are not Poisson or reverse J-curve distributions and that a multimodal distribution is probably present.

Within the lowest status group (zero to six offerings) 47.3% (or 37.1% of the total burial population) received no offerings. Over 91.6% of the total burial population can be accounted for within the first two offertory divisions. Additionally, the highest offertory group can be further divided into two discrete subsets: the first receiving between 14 and 18 offerings (5.4%) and the second with 19 or more offerings (3%) (figure 6.5).

Previous discussions (e.g., Colton 1946; Gratz and Pilles 1979; Hohmann 1980, 1981, 1982a, 1982b, 1984a, 1984b, 1992; McGregor 1943; Pilles 1987) of the Magician's Burial indicate that this individual was probably both a religious leader of a particular clan and a war society leader/priest. The Magician's Burial contained over 613 offerings and was encased within a double-level tomb, which was built under the floor, in the center of an abandoned kiva. The offering assemblage was dominated by religious and ceremonial items including carved, painted, and inlaid wooden wands; special mineral caches; hollow tubes full of dyes and pigments; carved and turquoise inlaid shell jewelry; painted

baskets; matched sets of projectile points; matched sets of turquoise jewelry; nose plugs; breastplates; chaps or pants outlined with *Conus* tinklers; a skull cap; and abundant decorated ceramics.

Another interment from the 3% group discovered at Elden Pueblo (NA142) had 40 grave offerings of which 15 items (or 30.9% of the total offerings accorded the individual) were religious objects. This same individual had only three (17%) trade wares. Moreover, total offerings with high religious object counts appear to identify head priests or heads of religious orders. Other religious leaders appear to receive many fewer offerings. For example, Harrington (1926) encountered at Elden Pueblo a burial which he labeled the Antelope Priest, due to its association with an intact Leupp Black-on-white antelope effigy vessel. Fourteen offerings were recovered with this adult male interment including two turquoise earrings, two carved bone hair pieces, a sandstone nose plug, a shell bracelet (all in situ), three additional pieces of shell (two located just above the burial), and four other decorated ceramic vessels.

TABLE 6.9 Late Elden Phase Principal Component and Factor Analysis Data Using Orthogonal Rotation; with Seven Major Variables Examined

Standard

Value	Mean	Development	Label
V16	20.02222	90.86166	Total Offerings
V5	1.73333	1.42063	Grave Type
V74	.26667	1.35512	Wands
V72	.68889	1.60712	Special Stones
V80	.35556	1.40058	Turquoise
V11	3.91111	.28780	Age
V12	1.53333	.50452	Gender

Variable	Communality	Factor	Eigenvalue	Pct of Var.	Pct
Total Offerings	1.00000	1	4.02202	57.5	57.5
Grave Type	1.00000	2	1.13276	16.2	73.6
Wands	1.00000	3	.91696	13.1	86.7
Special Stones	1.00000	4	.60540	8.6	95.4
Turquoise	1.00000	5	.23469	3.4	98.7
Age	1.00000	6	.07496	1.1	99.8
Gender	1.00000	7	.01321	.2	100.0

PC Extracted   2 Factors

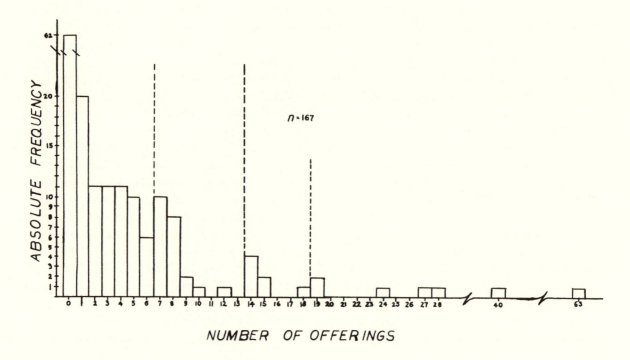

FIGURE 6.5   Absolute Frequency Histogram of Late Elden Phase Mortuary Offerings

While the mortuary set suggests this individual had acquired significant wealth and possible social status or prestige, little evidence is present to suggest a religious role in Elden Pueblo society. The offertory set contained few articles commonly found in Sinagua ceremonial or ritual contexts, such as prayer sticks or wands, rare mineral caches, or painted basketry.

Southwestern ethnographic analogy suggests painted, carved wooden wands are a good indicator of religious rituals and often are associated with religious leaders and/ or priests (e.g., Connelly 1979; Dozier 1970; Eggan 1983; Frigout 1979; Ladd 1979; Lamphere 1983). This regional analysis demonstrates that there is 1 burial with a wand in association with 24 offerings, 1 case with 14 offerings, 1 burial with 8 offerings, 2 interments had 7 offerings each, and 1 burial had 7 offerings which included 2 carved wood wands.

The presence of wands in offering assemblages are only moderately correlated (Pearson's r = .309) with elaborate grave forms. Regression analysis indicates a pattern of differential access to trade and religious items. There is a strong Pearson's r correlation of 90.29 (with alpha = .05) between total offertory count and religious artifacts. Such

differential access to rare or precious goods is commonly cited as a characteristic of highly stratified communities. Selected interments from the 3% group, and all of the 5.4% group, present a pattern markedly different from that discussed above; here, trade ceramics and items of status and personal wealth predominate offertory components, while religious items are rare or absent.

Differential distribution patterns for trade items (i.e., decorated trade ceramics, raw turquoise, special minerals, and unworked shell) suggest particular individuals are associated with particular trade items (r^2 = .7138, alpha = .001). Elden Pueblo (NA142) offers an example where a single burial contains over 78% of all Cibola White Ware recovered in burial contexts from that site. This same pattern holds for Tusayan White Wares, Little Colorado White Wares, and raw, unworked turquoise and shell. Regional Elden phase burial analysis indicates that late Elden phase burials from other sites reveal similar patterns with selected interments containing predominant proportions of such trade items plus rare minerals.

There is a strong correlation between total offerings and special mineral and stone caches (Pearson's r = .788, alpha

= .00001). There is also a strong correlation between shell items and total burial offerings (Pearson's r = .882, alpha = .00001). While raw, unworked turquoise occurs occasionally in bundles or bowls interred with an individual with a high offertory count, finished turquoise jewelry (e.g., pendants and necklaces) occurs most frequently with individuals receiving between seven to 19 offerings, suggesting finished items may be more indicative of personal wealth. Inlaid turquoise mosaic pendants, nose plugs, and other exotic artifact forms are usually associated with offertory sets indicating religious leaders or a select few individuals with extremely high offertory counts indicative of great wealth.

Social Reconstructions

Remembering that redundant burial forms and rituals can symbolize roles and social organization, I suggest that the patterns which I originally discerned for Elden phase Sinagua society (Hohmann 1981, 1982b, 1992) are still evident in this expanded and enhanced regional analysis.

Head and body orientations are not assignable to spatial distributions or any specific age and gender associations, and also include the full range of variability which can be assigned to grave forms, energy expended for ritual and interment, offering types, and offering frequencies. It appears that head and body orientations in Elden phase Sinagua society are likely related more to horizontal social divisions than to vertical distinctions. It is possible such orientation patterning equates with clan or society associations. Evidence for such a contention can also be found in architectural data. Architectural evidence, beginning from the early Elden phase, indicates that moderate to large-sized sites contained both small clan or society kivas (Peter Pilles, personal communication 1994), and simple large structures that functioned as community kivas (see Colton 1946; Hohmann 1981, 1982a; Kamp and Whittaker 1990; McGregor 1941, 1943; Pilles 1987; Plog 1989). While smaller clan/society kivas have now been documented in the Sinagua region as early as the Padre phase, the construction and use of large community rooms or kivas began only after A.D. 1150.

The preceding discussions indicate that mortuary practices and attendant rituals were highly formalized during the late Elden phase. Variability in observed mortuary treatment can be ascribed to the status, rank, and role of the deceased. Unlike the preceding phases, the late Elden phase displays a more complex social system, where status and rank may correlate with formally defined social positions and roles.

Analysis of mortuary offering distributions for the Elden phase delineates a trimodal distribution which appears to equate with discrete status categories. Braun (1981, 1984, 1987a) has argued that status, prestige, and esteem are best identified in the mortuary record by quantitative differences in the offertory assemblage.

The study of status indicator distributions reflects a pattern of differential access to trade and religious items. I have suggested before (see Hohmann 1982a:55–57), and this study further confirms, that such distributional patterning indicates selected individuals appear to have controlled particular trade items or their networks and had differential access to those goods. However, unlike my earlier works (Hohmann 1981, 1982a, 1982b), this new comprehensive study indicates status and prestige distinctions are also afforded selected craftsmen (e.g., obsidian knappers, jewelry manufacturers, etc.) based upon their ability to process raw goods.

Thus, this study identifies four groups: two high prestige groups, a middle group, and a commoner group. The dual division of the highest prestige groups between status indicators and religious items might indicate the presence of a simultaneous hierarchy in late Elden phase society. Such a hierarchy is characteristic of more complex levels of social organization, such as chiefdoms (after Johnson 1978, 1982, 1989).

Binford (1971:21) has suggested that a hierarchically organized society is reflected in mortuary ritual by the association of particular types or large numbers of mortuary offerings which transcend gender and age boundaries. Both Binford (1971) and Braun (1979, 1981, 1984, 1990) observe that selected children's interments having a high frequency of grave offerings reflect high status in an ascribed society. Such patterns are evident in late Elden phase burials.

A lack of patterning between gender, age, offertory sets, and grave forms suggests a nuclear family whose status is ascribed according to the status of the adult male. When the highest status burials, all adult males, are removed from the sample, the remaining high status adult males generally match both numerically and with selected offerings to equivalent high status adult females and subadult burials. This patterning may reflect the development of a wealthy merchant societal class who control various trade items and/or the production of rare or exotic goods. The highest status burials are adult males who appear to hold the highest civil and religious offices.

DISCUSSION AND CONCLUSIONS

This study demonstrates that an indigenous change in Sinagua social organization and differentiation occurred. For the Sinagua, this change began to occur before A.D. 1125 (late Angell-Winona phase) and is formalized by A.D. 1150 (late Elden phase). Early Sinagua populations can be characterized as having simple forms of social organization where elder males could attain high status through an achieved status system.

Sinagua populations after A.D. 1150 display a much more complex social system where status, in one of three levels, was ascribed. The highest status levels appear to represent the heads of civil sociopolitical organizations and/or heads of religious orders and leaders of religious ceremonies. The next status level was ascribed to select individuals, and their nuclear families, who controlled particular regional trade networks. Thus, by the late Elden phase, the Sinagua had a hierarchically organized society with formalized, ascribed leadership positions.

Study Implications

This study strongly supports the position that traditional perceptions of Southwestern prehistoric social organization and complexity must be reconsidered. In particular, this study's results indicate that prehistoric sociopolitical structure in central Arizona was complex and may have been highly variable between various contemporaneous groups.

Cordell and Gumerman (1989:11) suggest Southwestern archaeologists should avoid terms like "chiefdoms" or "ranked societies" since these terms imply specific types of economic and social relationships not known to be present in the prehistoric Southwest. They suggest seeking other terms, models, and regional analogies to move debate and interpretation forward. In particular, Cordell and Gumerman (1989:5) suggest, for the present, employing terms and concepts derived from Johnson's (1973, 1978, 1982) theories and models of social complexity.

Johnson (1982) argues that anthropologists should employ organizational theory when studying social systems. In his studies, Johnson (1982) found organizational change usually occurs when "operating" group sizes increase, resulting in either change to more complex forms of social control and organization or group fissioning and/or dissolution. To explain and classify such change, Johnson (1982) has identified two forms of organizational control: simultaneous and sequential hierarchies.

Johnson defines "simultaneous hierarchy" as decision making undertaken by a small governing body and employed simultaneously through a "number of hierarchically structured levels of control" (1982:396). He also has observed that power sharing is rare and frequently leads to disagreement and confrontations among coequal leaders (1978:104).

Johnson (1982) also developed an alternative to simultaneous hierarchy, sequential hierarchy, for horizontally organized groups. In a sequential hierarchy, nuclear families can operate independently during part of the year and then reform into extended family units when larger-scale labor or communities are needed. Here, decision making occurs on two levels, nuclear and extended family. He also suggested for sequential hierarchies that ceremonial activity is elaborated to assist in reducing scalar stress and to serve an integrative function, helping to promote group cohesion (Johnson 1982:405–6).

Following their own suggestions, Cordell and Gumerman (1989) invited Johnson to review a set of papers addressing issues of sociopolitical complexity in the American Southwest, mostly in the Plateau Southwest. Johnson (1989) found the Southwest examples he reviewed simple and modular. Indeed, Johnson (1989) suggested that prehistoric Southwestern systems were not economically or socially stratified. Cordell and Gumerman write that "A key element in this simplicity is the lack of obvious economic stratification in the Southwest that . . . is a reflection of the relatively low level of environmental productivity" (Cordell and Gumerman 1989:5).

After reviewing summary articles on Mesa Verde, Long House Valley, and Chaco settlement patterns for the Pueblo III period, Johnson (1989:381) found that "multiples of modules in puebloan settlement structure and hierarchies are well within the numerical expectations for sequential organization." Sequential hierarchy "is a structure for the organization of consensus among basically egalitarian aggregates of increasing inclusiveness" (Johnson 1989:378).

Johnson (1989:376–77) also argued that there is no evidence for labor surplus or communal labor as evidenced by monumental architecture in the Southwest. He concluded that "the vast majority of southwestern occupations were those of economically autonomous social units of one or two households, [where] mobility decisions must have rested ultimately with individual households" (Johnson 1989:381). Therefore, Chacoan society was "basically egalitarian" (Johnson 1989:378; 386). This interpretation is supported by long-term Southwestern archaeologists such as

Vivian (1989, 1990) and Toll (1985), although Toll (1991) appears to have moderated his position on this, and others (e.g., Sebastian 1991) still argue Chaco society was complex.

Johnson may have reached such a conclusion due to employment of Judge's (1989) characterization of the Chacoan settlement system as adaptive mobility. Adaptive mobility is the frequent abandonment and resettlement of pueblos based on seasonal subsistence needs and periodic regional crop failures. Using this concept, Johnson argued that since pueblo populations are so mobile, "residential construction could not have been considered a matter of unusual concern" (1989:376).

Although perhaps this is true for the Chaco/San Juan Basin regions, several prehistoric settlement systems in both central and southern Arizona appear quite sedentary and developed substantial monumental architectural achievements. Indeed, even Johnson (1989:377) cannot account for the construction of the Chaco road system nor has he addressed Salado mound construction or Hohokam regional canal networks. Johnson (1989:376) readily dismissed other lines of substantial communal labor such as Hohokam platform mounds (simple "piling behavior") and Plog's (1989) discussions of mortuary ritual which indicated patterns where the very young received elaborate burials, including grave offerings and furniture typically assigned as symbols of status or elite membership. Johnson's (1989:386) brief review led him to conclude that only Casas Grandes appeared to have had ruling elites.

I believe Johnson would have formed a different set of conclusions had he been exposed to a greater range of Southwestern data, especially from late-period central and southern Arizona sites. Johnson's (1989:378) doubts of the existence of Anasazi chiefdoms are echoed by many of today's Southwestern archaeologists. Several researchers (Cordell and Plog 1979; Gratz and Pilles 1979; Hohmann 1981, 1982a, 1992; Hohmann and Kelley 1988; Plog 1989; Redman 1991; Upham 1979b, 1980, 1982) believe that more complex and hierarchically structured prehistoric Southwest societies occurred. These researchers argue that such conditions occur only rarely and only in those habitats and localities where an unusual set of natural and social circumstances combined to allow for the development of surplus goods and labor and where regional trade economies could be established and controlled. I agree with both Johnson (1989) and Cordell and Gumerman (1989) that further studies of Southwest societies which appear to be modular and sequentially structured would add invaluably to our understanding of both Southwest prehistoric social systems and the range of variability actually present and operant in past societies. However, we must also recognize that select areas at particular times had the necessary and sufficient conditions to develop and, at least temporarily, maintain more complex levels of social structure and organization. I would argue that Johnson's conclusions are appropriate primarily for portions of the prehistoric Colorado Plateau and that other regions of the Southwest were, at select periods, more sociopolitically complex. The results of this study suggest that different levels of sociopolitical complexity were present in post-A.D. 1150 central Arizona populations.

REFERENCES CITED

Baldwin, Anne R., and J. Michael Bremer
1986   *Walnut Canyon National Monument: An Archaeological Survey—Archaeological Investigations in the Walnut Canyon Drainage, North Central Arizona.* Publications in Anthropology No. 39. Western Archaeological and Conservation Center, National Park Service, U.S. Department of the Interior, Tucson.

Beeson, William J.
1977   Field Notes from the Kahorsho Site (NA10937). On file at the Department of Anthropology, Museum of Northern Arizona, Flagstaff.

Beeson, William J., and Howard P. Goldfried
1976   *The Kahorsho Site (NA10937) Coconino National Forest, Arizona. An Interim Report.* U.S. Department of Agriculture (USDA), Southwest Region Archaeological Report 12. Santa Fe.

Binford, Lewis R.
1971   Mortuary Practices: Their Study and Their Potential. In *Approaches to the Social Dimensions of Mortuary Practices*, organized and edited by J. A. Brown, pp. 6–29. Memoirs of the Society for American Archaeology, no. 25. Society for American Archaeology, Washington, D.C. (Issued as *American Antiquity* 36(3) Pt. 2, July 1971.)

Braun, David P.
1977   *Middle Woodland-Early Late Woodland Social Change in the Prehistoric Central Midwestern U.S.* Ph.D. dissertation, University of Michigan, Ann Arbor. University Microfilms, Ann Arbor.

1979   Illinois Hopewell Burial Practices and Social
          Organization: A Reexamination of the
          Klunk-Gibson Mound Group. In *Hopewell
          Archaeology, the Chillicothe Conference,* edited
          by D. S. Brose and N. Greber, pp. 66–79. Kent
          State University Press, Kent.

1981   A Review of Some Recent North American
          Mortuary Studies. *American Antiquity*
          46:398–416.

1984   Burial Practices, Material Remains, and the
          Anthropological Record. *Review in
          Anthropology* 11:185–96.

1987a   Selection and Evolution in Nonhierarchical
          Organization. In *Political Evolution and the
          Communal Mode: Resistance and Change in
          Nonhierarchical Societies,* edited by S. Upham.
          Paper presented at the School of American
          Research Seminar, Santa Fe.

1987b   Some Themes in Archaeological Social
          Research. In *Evolving Woodland Society: Social
          Change among Early Sedentary Peoples of the
          Midcontinent.* Manuscript in possession of
          the author.

1990   Selection and Evolution in Nonhierarchical
          Organization. In *The Evolution of Political
          Systems: Sociopolitics in Small-Scale Sedentary
          Societies,* edited by Steadman Upham, pp.
          62–86. Cambridge University Press,
          Cambridge.

Bremer, J. Michael

1989   *Walnut Canyon: Settlement and Land Use.* The
          Arizona Archaeologist No. 23. Arizona
          Archaeological Society, Phoenix.

Brown, James A.

1981   The Search for Rank in Prehistoric Burials.
          In *The Archaeology of Death,* edited by R.
          Chapman, I. Kinnes, and K. Randsborg,
          pp. 25–37. Cambridge University Press,
          Cambridge.

Brown, James A. (organizer and editor)

1971   *Approaches to the Social Dimensions of
          Mortuary Practices.* Memoirs of the Society
          for American Archaeology, no. 25. Society for
          American Archaeology, Washington, D.C.
          (Issued as *American Antiquity* 36(3) Pt. 2, July
          1971.)

Brunson, Judy L.

1989   *The Social Organization of the Los Muertos
          Hohokam: A Reanalysis of Cushing's
          Hemenway Expedition Data.* Unpublished
          Ph.D. dissertation, Department of

Anthropology, Arizona State University,
          Tempe.

Chapman, Robert, and Klavs Randsborg

1981   Approaches to the Archaeology of Death. In
          The Archaeology of Death, edited by R.
          Chapman, I. Kinnes, and K. Randsborg, pp.
          1–24. Cambridge University Press, Cambridge.

Colton, Harold S.

1946   *The Sinagua: A Summary of the Archaeology of
          the Region of Flagstaff, Arizona.* Museum of
          Northern Arizona Bulletin 22. Museum of
          Northern Arizona, Flagstaff.

1960   *Black Sand: Prehistory in Northern Arizona.*
          University of New Mexico Press,
          Albuquerque.

Connelly, John C.

1979   Hopi Social Organization. In *Southwest,*
          edited by A. Ortiz, pp. 539–53. Handbook of
          North American Indians, vol. 9, W. C.
          Sturtevant, general editor. Smithsonian
          Institution, Washington, D.C.

Cordell, Linda S., and George J. Gumerman(editors)

1989   *Dynamics of Southwest Prehistory.*
          Smithsonian Institution, Washington, D.C.

Cordell, Linda S., and Fred Plog

1979   Escaping the Confines of Normative
          Thought: A Re-evaluation of Puebloan
          Prehistory. *American Antiquity* 44:405–29.

Downum, Christian E.

1988   *One Grand History: A Critical Review of
          Flagstaff Archaeology, 1851 to 1988.*
          Unpublished Ph.D. Dissertation, Department
          of Anthropology, University of Arizona,
          Tucson.

Dozier, Edward P.

1970   *The Pueblo Indians of North America.* Holt,
          Rinehart, and Winston, New York.

Eggan, Fred

1983   Comparative Social Organization. In
          Southwest, edited by A. Ortiz, pp. 723–42.
          Handbook of North American Indians vol.
          10, W. C. Sturtevant, general editor.
          Smithsonian Institution, Washington, D.C.

Fish, Paul R., Peter J. Pilles, and Suzanne K. Fish

1980   Colonies, Traders, and Traits: The Hohokam
          in the North. In *Current Issues in Hohokam
          Prehistory,* edited by D. E. Doyel and F. Plog,
          pp. 151–75. Anthropological Research Papers
          23. Arizona State University, Tempe.

Frigout, Arlette

1979   Hopi Ceremonial Organization. In *Southwest,*
          edited by A. Ortiz, pp. 564–76. Handbook of

North American Indians, vol. 9, W. C.
Sturtevant, general editor. Smithsonian
Institution, Washington, D.C.

Goldstein, Lynne
1981   One-Dimensional Archaeology and Multi-
         Dimensional People: Spatial Organization
         and Mortuary Analysis. In *The Archaeology of
         Death*, edited by R. Chapman, I. Kinnes, and
         K. Randsborg, pp. 53–70. Cambridge
         University Press, New York.

Goodenough, Ward H.
1965   Rethinking "Status" and "Role": Toward a
         General Mode of the Cultural Organization
         of Social Relationships. In *The Relevance of
         Models for Social Anthropology*, edited by M.
         Banton. Association of Social
         Anthropologists, Monograph 1:1–24.

Gratz, Kathleen E., and Peter J. Pilles, Jr.
1979   Sinagua Settlement Patterns and
         Organization Models: A Trial Survey. A paper
         presented at the 1979 Annual Meeting of the
         Southwestern Anthropological Association,
         Santa Barbara, California.

Harrington, John P.
1926   Notes on the Excavation of Elden Pueblo,
         Thursday, May 27 to Friday, August 27, 1926,
         Inclusive. Ms. on file at the Bureau of
         American Ethnology Manuscript Collection,
         Smithsonian Office of Anthropology,
         Smithsonian Institution, Washington, D.C.

Henderson, T. Kathleen
1979   Archaeological Survey at Chavez Pass Ruin,
         Coconino National Forest, Arizona: The 1978
         Field Season. Ms. on file, Supervisors Office,
         Coconino National Forest, Flagstaff.

Hohmann, John W.
1980   Sinagua Mortuary Practices: Inferences of
         Prehistoric Social Organization. Paper pre-
         pared for the 27th Annual Meeting of the
         Arizona-Nevada Academy of Science and the
         56th Annual Meeting (Southwest and Rocky
         Mountain Division), American Association
         for the Advancement of Science, Las Vegas.
1981   Sinagua Social Organization: Inferences Based
         upon Prehistoric Mortuary Practices.
         Unpublished Master's thesis, Department of
         Anthropology, Northern Arizona University,
         Flagstaff.
1982a   *Sinagua Social Differentiation: Inferences
         Based on Prehistoric Mortuary Practices.*
         The Arizona Archaeologist 17. Arizona
         Archaeological Society, Phoenix.

1982b   Sinagua Mortuary Ritual: Inferences in
         Prehistoric Social Complexity. Paper pre-
         sented at the 47th Annual Meeting of the
         Society for American Archaeology,
         Minneapolis, Minnesota.
1982c   Excavations at Sunset Pueblo. Manuscript on
         file, Supervisor's Office, Coconino National
         Forest, Flagstaff, Arizona.
1983   Elden Pueblo Mortuary Practices. Ms. on file,
         Coconino National Forest, Flagstaff, Arizona.
1984a   Sinagua Social Organization. Paper presented
         at the 1984 Pecos Conference Symposium,
         Flagstaff, Arizona.
1984b   Variability in Northern Sinagua Mortuary
         Practices. Paper prepared for the Arizona
         Archaeological Council Special Topics Session
         "Burial Ritual and Prehistory: The
         Archaeological Study of Mortuary Practices
         in the Greater Southwest." Pueblo Grande
         Museum, Phoenix.
1992   *Through the Mirror of Death: A View of
         Prehistoric Social Complexity in Central
         Arizona.* Unpublished Ph.D. dissertation,
         Department of Anthropology, Arizona State
         University, Tempe.

Hohmann, John W., and Linda B. Kelley
1988   *Erich F. Schmidt's Investigations of Salado Sites
         in Central Arizona: The Mrs. W. B. Thompson
         Archaeological Expedition of the American
         Museum of Natural History.* Bulletin No. 56.
         Museum of Northern Arizona, Flagstaff.

Hohmann, John W., and Karl Reinhard
n.d.   Archaeological and Physical Anthropological
         Analysis of Winona Village Cremations. Ms.
         on file, Louis Berger and Associates, Phoenix.

Hudgens, Bruce R.
1974   Turkey Hills Community: A Sinagua
         Settlement Pattern Study. Ms. on file at the
         Museum of Northern Arizona, Flagstaff.

Johnson, Gregory A.
1973   *Local Exchange and Early State Development
         in Southwestern Iran.* Anthropological Papers
         No. 37. Museum of Anthropology, University
         of Michigan, Ann Arbor.
1978   Information Sources and the Development of
         Decision-making Organizations. In *Social
         Archaeology: Beyond Subsistence and Dating*,
         edited by C. Redman, M. J. Berman, E. V.
         Curten, W. T. Langhorne, N. M. Versaggi, and
         J. C. Wanser, pp. 87–112. Academic Press, New
         York.

1982   Organizational Structure and Scalar Stress. In *Theory and Explanation in Archaeology*, edited by C. Renfrew, M. J. Rowlands, and B. A. Seagraves, pp. 389–422. Academic Press, New York.

1989   Far Outside-Looking In. In *Dynamics of Southwest Prehistory*, edited by L. Cordell and G. J. Gumerman, pp. 371–89. Smithsonian Institution, Washington, D.C.

Judge, W. James

1989   Chaco Canyon—San Juan Basin. In *Dynamics of Southwest Prehistory*, edited by L. S. Cordell and G. J. Gumerman, pp. 209–62. Smithsonian Institution, Washington, D.C.

Kamp, Kathryn A., and John C. Whittaker

1990   Lizard Man Village: A Small Site Perspective on Northern Sinagua Social Organization. *Kiva* 55:99–126.

Kerber, Richard A.

1986   *Political Evolution in the Lower Illinois Valley: A.D. 400–100.* Unpublished Ph.D. dissertation, Department of Anthropology, Northwestern University, Evanston, Illinois.

King, Dale S.

1949   *Nalakihu.* Museum of Northern Arizona Bulletin, No. 23. Museum of Northern Arizona, Flagstaff.

Ladd, Edmund J.

1979   Zuni Social and Political Organization. In *Southwest*, edited by A. Ortiz, pp. 482–91. Handbook of North American Indians, vol. 9, W. C. Sturtevant, general editor. Smithsonian Institution, Washington, D.C.

Lamphere, Louise

1983   Southwestern Ceremonialism. In *Southwest*, edited by A. Ortiz, pp. 743–63. Handbook of North American Indians, vol. 10, W. C. Sturtevant, general editor. Smithsonian Institution, Washington, D.C.

Lightfoot, Kent G.

1982   *Prehistoric Political Development in the Little Colorado Region, East-Central Arizona.* Northern Illinois University Press, De Kalb.

Lowe, Charles H.

1964   *The Vertebrates of Arizona.* University of Arizona Press, Tucson.

McGregor, John C.

1941   Winona and Ridge Ruin, Part I: Architecture and Material Culture. *Museum of Northern Arizona Bulletin* 18:1–309.

1943   Burial of an Early American Magician. *Proceedings of the American Philosophical Society* 86:270–98.

McGuire, Randall H.

1987   *Death, Society, and Ideology in a Hohokam Community: Colonial and Sedentary Period Burials from La Ciudad.* Office of Cultural Resource Management Report 67. Arizona State University, Tempe.

Merriam, C. Hart

1890   Results of a Biological Survey of the San Francisco Mountains Region and Desert of the Little Colorado in Arizona. *North American Fauna* 3:1–136. U.S. Department of Agriculture, Washington, D.C.

O'Shea, John M.

1981   Social Configurations and the Archaeological Study of Mortuary Practices: A Case Study. In *The Archaeology of Death*, edited by R. Chapman, I. Kinnes, and K. Randsborg, pp. 39–52. Cambridge University Press, Cambridge.

1984   *Mortuary Variability: An Archaeological Investigation.* Academic Press, New York.

Peebles, Christopher S.

1971   Moundville and Surrounding Sites: Some Structural Considerations of Mortuary Practices, II. In *Approaches to the Social Dimensions of Mortuary Practices*, edited by J. A. Brown, pp. 68–91. Memoirs of the Society for American Archaeology, no. 25. Society for American Archaeology, Washington, D.C.

1974   *Moundville: The Organization of a Prehistoric Community and Culture.* Ph.D. dissertation, University of California, Santa Barbara. University Microfilms, Ann Arbor.

Pilles, Peter J., Jr.

1978   The Field House and Sinagua Demography. In *Limited Activity and Occupation Sites*, edited by Albert E. Ward, pp. 119–34. Center for Anthropological Studies, Albuquerque.

1979   Sunset Crater and the Sinagua: A New Interpretation. In *Volcanic Activity and Human Ecology*, edited by Payson D. Sheets and Donald K. Grayson, pp. 459–85. Academic Press, San Francisco.

1982   The Sinagua Area in Mogollon Prehistory. Paper presented in the Symposium: Mogollon Prehistory in Arizona. Spring meeting of the Arizona Archaeological Council, Phoenix.

1987   The Sinagua: Ancient People of the Flagstaff Region. In *Wupatki and Walnut Canyon: New Perspectives on History, Prehistory, Rock Art,* edited by D. G. Noble, pp. 2–12. Exploration, Annual Bulletin of the School of American Research. School of American Research, Santa Fe.

Plog, Fred

1979   Prehistory: Western Anasazi. In *Southwest*, edited by A. Ortiz, pp. 108–30. Handbook of North American Indians, vol. 9, W. C. Sturtevant, general editor. Smithsonian Institution, Washington, D.C.

1989   The Sinagua and Their Relations. In *Dynamics of Southwest Prehistory*, edited by L. S. Cordell and G. J. Gumerman, pp. 263–91. Smithsonian Institution, Washington, D.C.

Rathje, William L.

1973   Models for Mobile Maya: A Variety of Constraints. In *The Explanation of Culture Change: Models in Prehistory*, edited by C. Renfrew, pp. 731–57. Duckworth, London.

Ravesloot, John C.

1984   *Social Differentiation at Casas Grandes, Chihuahua, Mexico: An Archaeological Analysis of Mortuary Practices.* Unpublished Ph.D. dissertation, Department of Anthropology, Southern Illinois University, Carbondale.

Redman, Charles L.

1991   The Comparative Context of Social Complexity. In *Chaco and Hohokam: Prehistoric Regional Systems in the American Southwest*, edited by P. L. Crown and W. J. Judge, pp. 277–92. School of American Research Press, Santa Fe.

Saxe, A. A.

1970   *Social Dimensions of Mortuary Practices.* Ph.D. dissertation, University of Michigan, Ann Arbor. University Microfilms, Ann Arbor.

1971   Social Dimensions of Mortuary Practices in a Mesolithic Population from Wadi Halfa, Sudan. In *Approaches to the Social Dimensions of Mortuary Practices*, organized and edited by J. A. Brown, pp. 39–57. Memoirs of the Society for American Archaeology, no. 25. Society for American Archaeology, Washington, D.C. (Issued as *American Antiquity* 36(3) Pt. 2, July 1971.)

Sebastian, Lynne

1991   Sociopolitical Complexity and the Chaco System. In *Chaco and Hohokam: Prehistoric Regional Systems in the American Southwest*, edited by P. L. Crown and W. J. Judge, pp.

109–34. School of American Research Press, Santa Fe.

Stanislawski, Michael B.

1963   Extended Burials in the Prehistoric Southwest. *American Antiquity* 28:308–19.

Tainter, Joseph A.

1975   *The Archaeological Study of Social Change: Woodland System in West Central Illinois.* Ph.D. dissertation, Northwestern University. University Microfilms, Ann Arbor.

1978   Mortuary Practices and the Study of Prehistoric Social Systems. In *Advances in Archaeological Method and Theory*, vol. 1, edited by M. B. Schiffer, pp. 105–41. Academic Press, New York.

Toll, H. Wolcott

1985   *Pottery, Production, Public Architecture and the Chaco Anasazi System.* Unpublished Ph.D. dissertation, University of Colorado, Boulder.

1991   Material Distributions and Exchange in the Chaco System. In *Chaco and Hohokam: Prehistoric Regional Systems in the American Southwest*, edited by P. L. Crown and W. J. Judge, pp. 77–107. School of American Research Press, Santa Fe.

Upham, Steadman

1978   Final Report on Archaeological Investigations at Chavez Pass Ruin, Coconino National Forest: The 1978 Field Season. Ms. on file, Coconino National Forest, Flagstaff, Arizona.

1979a   Final Report on Archaeological Investigations at Chavez Pass Ruin, Coconino National Forest, Arizona: The 1979 Field Season. Ms. on file, Coconino National Forest, Flagstaff, Arizona.

1979b   Intensification and Exchange: An Evolutionary Model of Non-egalitarian Socio-political Organization for the Prehistoric Plateau Southwest. Paper presented at the 44th Annual Meeting of the Society for American Archaeology, Vancouver.

1980   *Political Continuity and Change in the Plateau Southwest.* Ph.D. dissertation, Department of Anthropology, Arizona State University, Tempe.

1982   *Polities and Power: An Economic and Political History of the Western Pueblos.* Academic Press, New York.

Upham, Steadman, K. G. Lightfoot, and G. M. Feinman

1981   Explaining Socially Determined Ceramic Distributions in the Prehistory Plateau Southwest. *American Antiquity* 46:822–33.

Vivian, R. Gwinn

1989   Kluckhorn Reappraised: The Chacoan System as an Egalitarian Enterprise. *Journal of Anthropological Research* 45:101–13.

1990   *The Chacoan Prehistory of the San Juan Basin.* Academic Press, New York.

Wilcox, David R., and Charles Sternberg

1983   *Hohokam Ballcourts and Their Interpretation.* Arizona State Museum Archaeological Series 160. Arizona State Museum, Tucson.

CHAPTER SEVEN

Salado Burial Practices

Chris Loendorf

INTRODUCTION

CONSIDERABLE VARIABILITY EXISTED IN SALADO mortuary practices (Crown 1994; Hohmann 1985a, 1985b, 1992; Hohmann and Kelly 1988; Rice 1990). Variation in Salado mortuary treatment is apparent within sites, among sites, between regions, and through time. Although substantial variation has been identified in Salado mortuary practices, numerous aspects of burial treatment were remarkably consistent among Classic period sites in the lower Tonto Basin.

Patterning identified in this burial assemblage suggests that Salado social organization is best characterized by a ranked segmentary model (Rice 1992). Segmentary organizations with ranking are comprised of a series of nested units, with lower order segments being linked into progressively more inclusive units (Chang 1989; Fox 1977; Rice 1992). At each level, one segment is ranked higher than its counterparts. The segments, rather than individuals, are given different ranks. Because the segments are not specialized (they duplicate each other in form and some functions), each segment will have its own leaders and nonleaders. The ranking of their respective groups determines the relative rank of the leaders in the society. The leader of the highest ranked segment will rank higher than all other members of the society, but the highest ranked individual in each segment is still part of a segment that includes other lower status positions.

The analysis presented here is based, in part, on the use of two principal assumptions. First, the presence of formal cemeteries is associated with the existence of social units such as corporate groups, and these groups had collective rights (e.g., land use) that were justified through ancestral ties (Charles and Buikstra 1983; Goldstein 1981; Howell and Kintigh 1996; Mitchell 1992; Saxe 1970). Secondly, variability in the burial treatment of deceased individuals is related to their social standing in life (Binford 1971; Carr 1994; O'Shea 1984; Ravesloot 1988; Saxe 1970; Tainter 1978). Southwestern ethnographic research is also used to suggest hypotheses and interpret patterning observed in the burial assemblage.

Archaeologists have come to view sociopolitical complexity as a dimensional phenomenon, with multiple aspects that do not necessarily vary in concert (Blanton et al. 1981; Braun 1981; Gumerman et al. 1994; Nelson 1995; Ravesloot 1988). Therefore in any investigation, it is necessary to specify the particular dimensions of social complexity that are to be modeled (Nelson 1995). This analysis focuses on the nature of ranking in Salado society, which is one key dimension of social organization.

It appears that separate aspects of burial assemblages are related to different dimensions of social organization.

Quantitative and ethnographic data suggest that vessel accompaniments are closely associated with the social relationships of the deceased, whereas most nonvessel artifacts appear to be indicators of wealth.

The data employed in this research were collected during the early 1990s as part of the Roosevelt Platform Mound Study (RPMS), funded by the Bureau of Reclamation, Department of Interior. The RPMS burial assemblage consists of the remains of nearly 480 individuals who were excavated from over 20 Classic period (roughly A.D. 1150–1450) Salado sites in the lower Tonto Basin (table 7.1). The Tonto Basin is located at the confluence of the Salt River and Tonto Creek in the mountainous transition zone of central Arizona (figure 7.1). The Classic period in Tonto Basin is traditionally divided into the Roosevelt (roughly A.D. 1280–1350) and Gila phases (roughly 1320–1450). Major changes in architecture, material culture, demography, and settlement patterns distinguish these phases from the pre-Classic.

Burials were investigated at different kinds of sites including small residential compounds, large room blocks, and integrative sites such as platform mound villages. The interments are largely from two groups of sites—one located on Cline Terrace along lower Tonto Creek and the other on Schoolhouse Point along the Salt River. Based on similarities within and differences between these two locations, each area is inferred to be part of a different dispersed community.

The Tonto Basin-Globe-Miami region has been considered the heartland of the Salado (Doyel 1976; Gladwin and Gladwin 1935; Wood 1983), and this area has therefore played a central role in debates concerning the "Salado culture concept" (Ciolek-Torrello 1987; Doyel and Haury 1976; Lekson 1992; Rice 1985). Detailed discussion

Table 7.1   Roosevelt Platform Mound Study Burial Assemblage

Site Number	Undisturbed	Prehistoric Disturbance	Vandalized or Extreme Disturbance	Juvenile
Tonto Creek Sites				
U:3:128	12	1	—	6
U:4:7	13	1	3	2
U:4:9	9	7	1	8
U:4:10	3	1	4	3
U:4:32	9	—	—	2
U:4:33	25	6	11	15
U:4:75	9	3	—	3
Subtotal	80	19	19	39
Salt River Sites				
U:8:23	4	—	5	—
U:8:24	108	26	69	94
U:8:25	13	5	2	7
U:8:385	1	—	—	1
U:8:450	35	39	1	23
U:8:451	4	4	—	7
U:8:453	1	—	—	1
U:8:454	2	—	—	—
U:8:458	—	2	1	—
U:8:577	1	—	—	—
V:5:66	3	—	1	2
V:5:112	—	2	1	—
V:5:119	12	1	—	3
V:5:121	2	—	3	1
V:5:128	1	—	2	—
V:5:137	1	—	2	1
V:5:139	2	1	4	3
Subtotal	190	80	91	143
Total	**270**	**99**	**110**	**182**

of the nature and validity of the Salado phenomenon is beyond the scope of this chapter, and the term "Salado" is used here simply to refer to the Classic period inhabitants of Tonto Basin.

ROOSEVELT PLATFORM MOUND STUDY BURIAL ASSEMBLAGE

The RPMS burial assemblage consists largely of inhumations, with a smaller sample of cremations. All the features date to the Classic period (A.D. 1150–1450) and are largely Roosevelt phase interments (A.D.1280–1320). This database allows examination of synchronic and diachronic variation in Salado mortuary practices and represents one of the best opportunities available to investigate the nature of Salado social organization in the Tonto Basin.

Post-depositional disturbances to burials in the region are unfortunately severe. The geological substratum throughout much of the basin and the semiarid climate result in poor preservation of organic remains. Organic burial accompaniments were rarely encountered during our investigations, although it is probable that they were commonly interred with individuals.

The most adverse impacts to burial deposits resulted from both prehistoric and historic human activities. Prehistoric cultural disturbance to primary inhumations occurred in over 30% of the cases where it was possible to determine the nature of the disturbance. Prehistoric disturbance usually resulted in the complete disarticulation of inhumed individuals. In some cases, a portion of the skeletal remains of an individual were left articulated and in situ after prehistoric reopening of a facility, but the disturbed portion of these individuals was completely disarticulated.

Adolescent	Female	Male	Adult, sex unknown	
1	2	4	—	Roosevelt phase
—	8	3	4	Integrative site, Roosevelt phase
—	2	5	2	Large site, Roosevelt & Gila phases
—	1	1	3	Large site, Roosevelt & Gila phases
—	4	2	1	Small site, Roosevelt phase
1	8	11	6	Integrative site, Roosevelt & Gila phases
—	1	3	5	Small compound, Roosevelt phase
2	26	29	21	
1	1	2	3	Integrative site, Roosevelt phase
11	27	32	39	Large site, Roosevelt & Gila phases
—	4	6	3	Compounds, Roosevelt phase
—	—	—	—	Small compound, Roosevelt phase
4	16	22	8	Site, Roosevelt & Gila phases
1	—	—	—	Small compound, Roosevelt phase
—	—	—	—	Small compound, Roosevelt phase
—	—	1	—	Integrative site, Roosevelt phase
—	—	—	3	Small compound, Roosevelt phase
—	—	—	1	Small compound, Roosevelt phase
—	1	1	—	Integrative site, Roosevelt phase
—	1	1	1	Compounds, Roosevelt phase
1	2	7	—	Small compound, Roosevelt phase
1	1	1	1	Small compound, Roosevelt phase
—	1	1	1	Small compound, Roosevelt phase
—	—	—	2	Small compound, Roosevelt phase
1	1	—	2	Compounds, Roosevelt phase
20	55	74	64	
22	**81**	**103**	**85**	

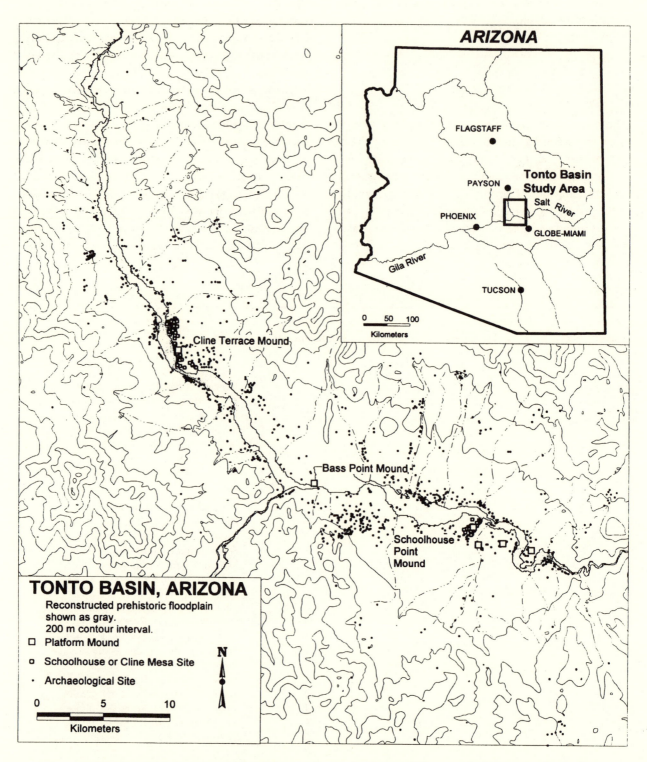

FIGURE 7.1   Tonto Basin Showing Locations of Sites in the Study. The small box on the inset map shows the location of the large scale map within Arizona.

In most cases, a portion of the disturbed individual's skeletal remains was stacked in a pile, with the remaining elements scattered in the fill. Burial accompaniments were frequently placed on or near the bone pile, but additional accompaniments were commonly found broken and scattered in the fill.

Despite severe vandalism in the region, intact or nearly intact Roosevelt phase cemeteries were extensively sampled at 10 sites, and undisturbed burials were excavated from over 50 different burial areas. Data collected during the project are sufficient to characterize the range of variability in mortuary treatment that was once present and to characterize aspects of Salado social organization.

SALADO MORTUARY PRACTICES

The RPMS burial data provide a relatively complete picture of Roosevelt phase burial practices at sites located in the lower Tonto Basin. Gila phase adult burials are underrepresented, and consequently it is more difficult to examine late Classic burial practices in the area. It is possible, however, to observe a number of similarities and differences in burial treatment between the two phases.

Form of Interment

Inhumation was the predominant or exclusive method of interment at Classic period sites throughout Tonto Basin (Hohmann 1992; Loendorf 1996a, 1997a, 1997b, 1997c; Ravesloot 1994). By the advent of the Roosevelt phase, cremation was practiced for only a small segment of the population and appears to have occurred at only a few sites, which also had large inhumation cemeteries. Only two large Roosevelt phase cremation cemeteries were identified; one occurred at the Schoolhouse Point Mound (Loendorf 1996a), and another was identified at the Bass Point Platform Mound (Loendorf et al. 1995). Cremation appears to have been almost entirely discontinued during the Gila phase—only one cremation that may have dated to this phase was identified, and this feature was found in a crypt that also contained the remains of inhumed individuals.

Burial Locations

Classic period burials in the lower Tonto Basin were usually placed in formal cemeteries located within walled areas of the site that were not roofed (i.e., plazas). However, both of the Roosevelt phase cremation cemeteries were outside of compound areas, and several other sites with inhumation cemeteries outside of walled areas were identified. Interments were also occasionally placed in the fill of abandoned pit houses and in the fill of middens. Burials that were placed outside of formal cemeteries were frequently interred in atypical positions and almost always were not associated with any accompaniments.

Subfloor room burial appears to have rarely occurred during the Roosevelt phase, but infant burials appear to have been commonly placed below the floors of rooms during the Gila phase (Loendorf 1996a). Some deceased juveniles were, however, placed in extramural cemeteries during the Gila phase. Burials below room floors were generally infants less than a year old and were frequently not interred with accompaniments. No adult burials were found that clearly appeared to have been placed below the floors of occupied rooms.

Burial Position and Orientation

Inhumations in the lower Tonto Basin were predominately (90%) placed in an extended supine position with the arms generally close along the body. Other burial positions were extremely rare. Inhumations that received the most elaborate treatment were placed in an extended supine position, but some of the individuals in this position were not associated with artifacts. Almost all individuals that were placed in positions other than extended supine (e.g., prone, flexed, on the side) were associated with few or no artifacts (Loendorf 1996a, 1997a, 1997b, 1997c).

Roosevelt phase inhumations were generally orientated with the head to the east, but individuals with roughly northern, southern, and western orientations were also recorded. In contrast, with the exception of the interments from the Cline Terrace Platform mound, all but two of the Gila phase extramural inhumations for which head orientations could be determined had roughly eastern head orientations.

A significant difference existed between Roosevelt phase and Gila phase head orientations for adult burials at the Schoolhouse Point Mound (Loendorf 1996a). Based on the observation that individuals in the same cemetery tended to have similar head orientations, Hohmann (1992) suggested that body orientation is related to kinship and/or societal divisions. A similar pattern was observed in the lower Tonto Basin where burials in a given cemetery were largely orientated in one direction, with a small subset of individuals with head orientations that were roughly 180 degrees opposite of the majority (Loendorf 1996b, 1997b; Ravesloot 1994). If orientation was related to kinship and/or societal divisions, then the greater uniformity in head orientation observed for the Gila phase suggests an increased level of societal integration.

Gila phase infant burials below room floors at the Schoolhouse Point site varied more significantly in head orientations than did Gila phase extramural burials (Loendorf 1996a). Ethnographic sources provide a plausible explanation for this difference. In historic Pueblo mortuary practices, head orientation reflects the direction that the deceased is thought to travel to the land of the dead (Ellis 1968; Parsons 1939; Tyler 1986). Many Southwestern groups buried infants below room floors in the belief that this would facilitate the rebirth of the deceased infant to the parents (Bunzel 1932; Eggan 1950; Ellis 1968; Parsons 1938). If adults are orientated toward their journey to the land of the dead, then young infants who were not thought to make this journey, would not necessarily be positioned toward this location.

Form of Grave Facility

Burial facilities in the basin exhibited substantial variation in form. The morphology of burial facilities appears to have been conditioned, in part, by sediments that underlay sites (Loendorf 1996a). Some sites with similar substrates, however, had different forms of burial pits. Most of the burial pits that contained the remains of only one individual were subrectangular and had U-shaped cross sections. In contrast, most of the more elaborate burial pits contained the remains of more than one individual.

Inward stepping of the long axis side of the pit was one of the most common elaborations to burial facilities in the basin. Several examples where both sides of the pit were stepped also exist. In some instances, the step or steps were used to support a horizontal wooden cap. In other cases, however, individuals were laid directly on the steps, which therefore could not have been used to support wood.

Another common elaboration to burial facilities consisted of undercutting of one or more sides of the pit. Even pits with generally straight walls tended to bell out slightly at the base. In some cases the undercutting was pronounced, and in these instances, inhumed individuals were placed below the undercut. In several examples of pronounced undercutting, wood was set vertically to support the undercut.

Wooden caps occurred in a small proportion of burial facilities, almost all of which contained the remains of more than one individual. The wood generally consisted of small isolated fragments, but several comparatively

well-preserved examples suggest the range of variation present. Cases were found in which the wood was set vertically (along an undercut of the pit edge), horizontally (frequently on steps), and at a roughly 45° angle. In some instances, the wood consisted of a single set of beams laid parallel to the short axis of the pit. In other examples, two sets of beams were laid perpendicular to each other. Clay caps were frequently, but not always, placed over the cribbing. Wood fragments were found in the fill above some inhumations and resting directly on the skeletal material, suggesting that the pits were not filled with sediment below the wooden cap.

Multiple Interments

Both Roosevelt and Gila phase examples of burial features that contained the remains of more than one articulated individual were identified. In addition, cases exist where one or more articulated individuals occurred in the same crypt with one or more disarticulated individuals. These disarticulated individuals, frequently referred to as "secondary burials," appear to have almost exclusively been primary inhumations that were disturbed by the placement of later inhumations in the same pit (Loendorf 1996a).

Some multiple interments consisted of a pit containing two or three articulated individuals who were superimposed (Loendorf 1998). These features were fairly common in Tonto Basin and were found at nine sites. Examples were identified where the two individuals were both male, both female, different sexes, and adults with subadults. This variability suggests that the pairing of individuals was not exclusively restricted to married couples or females with infants. Upper individuals were offset in the pit such that the skeletal material did not fall directly above the cranium of the deepest individual (Loendorf 1996a, 1997a, 1997c). These burial facilities were also generally deeper than burial pits with only one individual.

A less-common type of multiple interment consisted of large and elaborate facilities that contained between five and nine articulated individuals (Loendorf 1998). These features occurred at only three cemeteries near the end of Schoolhouse Point and were not found in any other part of this community. Males, females, and juveniles were interred in each example of this type of burial. These individuals were always placed in different positions (i.e., supine and prone, or with opposite head orientations). In all cases, the individual immediately above the deepest burial was of the opposite sex. Skeletal evidence suggests that individuals in one large multiple

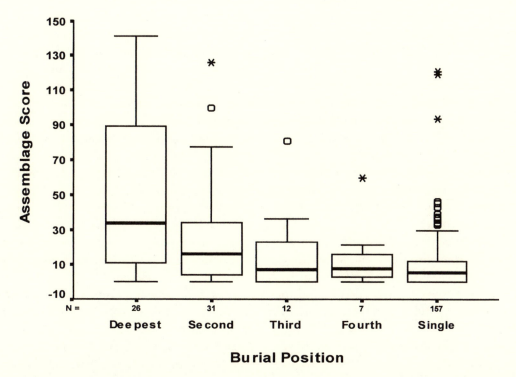

FIGURE 7.2 Boxplots of Assemblage Rarity Scores by Burial Position in Type 1 and Type 2 Facilities and Single Inhumations (excludes side by side multiple burials)

burial facility at the Schoolhouse Point site were closely related genetically (Regan et al. 1996), possibly some type of unilineal descent group. The strong commonalties of these multiple interments suggest that all may have contained groups of closely related individuals.

The deepest articulated individual in multiple interment facilities was generally associated with the largest assemblage (figure 7.2), frequently including possible symbols of authority. The number of accompaniments progressively decreased with distances from the lowest individual, such that burials in the upper portion of facilities were frequently not associated with any accompaniments.

It appears that multiple burial features resulted from unusual burial practices in which deceased individuals were not interred immediately; instead, the remains were kept for a period of time, and groups of individuals eventually were buried together (Loendorf 1998). The extensive and diverse assemblages associated with most multiple burials, the comparatively large size of the pits, and the elaborate nature of the facilities all suggest that only high ranking individuals were interred in these features.

Consequently, the restricted distribution of these facilities among cemeteries in communities suggests that high status positions were not evenly distributed among community segments. The variation observed in the treatment of individuals in multiple burial pits suggests that ranking also occurred within these groups.

Associated Funerary Objects

A relatively limited range of items was interred with burials, and many utilitarian artifacts that were commonly recovered from habitation contexts were infrequently found in burial contexts. Artifact types that were common in habitations but rarely (or never) associated with interments include, metates, manos, tabular knives, polishing stones, shaft straighteners, hammer stones, chipped- or ground-stone axes, unifaces, flakes, and cores. With the prominent exception of ceramic vessels and projectile points, most of the items commonly associated with burials were nonutilitarian artifacts, largely ornaments. Artifacts that were sometimes associated with interments include, ceramic vessels, projectile points, shell or stone ornaments (necklaces, rings, bracelets, armlets, anklets, pendants, tinklers), bone awl/hairpins, ceramic or stone disks, crystals, pigments, ceramic or stone effigies, baskets, painted baskets, matting, cloth, bedding materials, and painted sticks.

Ceramic vessels were by far the most common funerary accompaniment and were generally placed with inhumations that were interred in extramural contexts (79% had one or more vessels). Considerable variation, however, existed in the numbers (counts ranged from 0 to 28) and types of ceramics placed with inhumations. For vessel decoration, red slipped vessels were most common (42% of assemblage), and for vessel form, bowls (70% of assemblage) dominated jars.

Whole vessels were generally placed around inhumations and were rarely set directly on interments. Ravesloot suggests that ceramic vessels "held offerings of food and water that were buried with the deceased for the journey of death to the future world" (Ravesloot 1994). This interpretation is reasonable; however, the placement of some vessels (i.e., inverted vessels, closely nested vessels, and vessels resting on their sides) suggests they could not have held offerings. One possibility to account for the presence of these vessels is they may have been used in the mortuary ritual and subsequently included with the interment.

The source of these funerary objects is a fundamental issue that may provide insight to patterning in the burial assemblage. Do these artifacts represent items made specifically for use in burial rituals, personal possessions of the deceased, and/or offerings brought by friends and relatives? Each of these possibilities has different implications for the interpretation of burial assemblages. They are not mutually exclusive, however, and it appears that the latter two possibilities may have co-occurred.

It is unlikely that most accompaniments were made exclusively for use in funeral ceremonies because many of the burial assemblage artifacts have evidence of use wear, including incomplete artifacts that broke prehistorically (Loendorf 1997b). Further, with the exception of painted sticks and effigy vessels, accompanying artifact types were recovered from a variety of contexts including house floors and midden deposits, suggesting that their use was not restricted to burial rituals.

Based on Pueblo mortuary practices, Whittlesey (1978: 150) suggested that offerings of pottery "reflect the composition of the mourning group, in particular female members of the deceased's household." Simon and

Ravesloot (1994) investigated this possibility by examining patterning in the paste composition of RPMS burial vessels. They concluded that the distribution of vessels made from different clay sources "strongly supports the interpretation that the burial pots and their placements may reflect the social relationships of the deceased within the larger community" (Simon and Ravesloot 1994:12–13).

Ethnographic research concerning native Southwestern peoples suggests that personal possessions were commonly interred with the dead (Ellis 1968; Fewkes 1896; Ortiz 1969; Russell 1975; Tyler 1986). The restricted range of artifact types in the burial assemblage indicates that all of an individual's personal possessions could not have been included; however, it is still reasonable to suggest that some artifacts included with burials were highly prized personal possessions.

Thus, two separate factors may have structured the inclusion of different artifact classes. Some items, largely ornaments, may have been personal possessions that were highly prized by the deceased. Ceramic vessels, on the other hand, may be offerings that more closely reflect the composition of the mourning group. If these observations are correct, then most nonvessel artifacts may be better indicators of personal wealth, whereas ceramic accompaniments may be more closely associated with the social position of the deceased.

Individuals associated with the largest vessel assemblages were generally associated with few nonvessel artifacts. Conversely, burials with large nonvessel assemblages generally had small vessel assemblages. This relationship is presented graphically in figure 7.3 for individuals with more than 15 vessel or nonvessel artifacts. A negative linear relationship is present between these two variables (Pearson correlation coefficient = -.67). With the removal of one outlying individual (Feature 75, AZ U:8:450 [ASM]) the Pearson correlation improves to -.85.

The negative correlation between these variables supports the suggestion that they are related to different aspects of burial treatment. This relatively strong pattern may have resulted from at least two factors, which are not mutually exclusive. First, large assemblages of nonvessel artifacts were interred with individuals because they had few social obligations (as reflected by their small vessel assemblages) and consequently fewer individuals could claim these items. Conversely, for deceased individuals with large vessel assemblages (who by inference had high social status and a larger mourning group), many individuals may have been entitled to the personal possessions of the deceased, which were therefore not interred with them. Second, Salado society may have discouraged the accumulation of wealth (i.e., nonvessel artifacts) by high social status individuals (i.e., individuals with large vessel assemblages).

Symbols of Authority

This section considers ethnographic and quantitative observations that suggest pigment staining on the skeletal material, some painted wood artifacts, and ceramic vessels with effigies were symbols of authority in Salado society. Pigment staining was the most common postmortem body treatment identified, but it occurred on the skeletal material of a small proportion (17%) of inhumations. Despite its rarity, pigment staining was found on individuals of both sexes and all age groups (Loendorf 1996a, 1997a, 1997b, 1997c). Pigment staining of the skeletal material is commonly thought to have resulted from painting or dusting the body with pigments.

Ethnographic observations provide insight into the pos-

sible cultural relevance of this practice. Modern Pueblo groups use facial painting to symbolize leaders of some clans and ceremonial societies (Whittlesey 1978). For example, Tyler (1986:53) reported that Don Talayesva, a Hopi from Oraibi, painted the body of his deceased uncle with white dotted lines on the extremities, and "made a left curve over his left eye with points turned up like a half moon, to signify to the spirit people that uncle was a Special Officer." Another example is provided by the Tewa who painted the bodies of "Made People" (i.e., religious leaders) to distinguish them from the "Dry Food People" (i.e., ordinary individuals) (Ortiz 1969).

Pigment-stained individuals were generally associated with larger burial assemblages. The median counts for vessels are higher for pigment-stained individuals than for individuals without staining (Loendorf 1999). Because these data are discontinuous and non-normal, a Wilcoxon Rank Sum W test was performed comparing vessel counts by the presence or absence of pigment staining. A significant difference exists for vessel counts of individuals with pigment staining and without staining

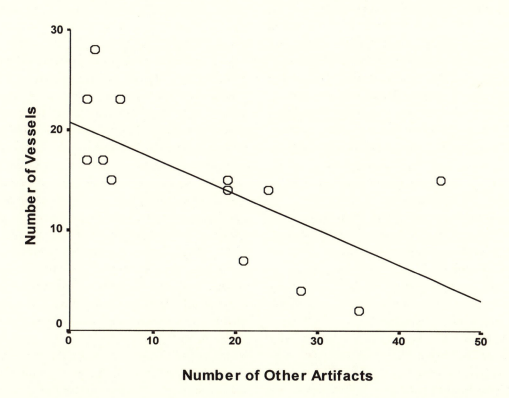

FIGURE 7.3 Scatterplot of Vessel Counts and Nonvessel Counts for Interments with More Than 15 Vessel or Nonvessel Artifacts

(probability < .01). Based on these data and the ethno-graphic observations, it is reasonable to suggest that in some instances the Salado used pigment staining as a symbol of authority.

Titiev (1992:64) reported for the Oraibi Hopi that the "Village chief comes into possession of a symbol of author-ity called a *mongkoho* [chief stick]." These sticks were placed on or in the grave of a deceased leader, and it marked the person as a member of a particular society and a leader in that group (Wright 1979). Most Hopi *mongkoho* differed in appearance from the sticks collected in the Tonto Basin, but "certain prayer sticks [which are more similar in appearance to painted wood in the RPMS assemblage] and small animal effigies may also be called by this term [and] it is usually taken to mean the badge of office carried in the hand of a society member" (Wright 1979:92). These observations suggest that it may be rea-sonable to classify painted sticks in the RPMS assemblage as symbols of authority.

A Hopi *tiponi* is a fetish of stone or wood belonging to a clan or society. Etymologically, *tiponi* is derived from the words for "person," "altar," and "authority" (Waters 1963). A *tiponi* was considered to be the most important item pertaining to rites conducted by the leader (Titiev 1992), and "[a]s a badge of chieftaincy it is carried by the chiefs on certain occasions of initiation and public exhibitions" (Fewkes 1990:267). The Zuni have similar fetishes termed *etowe*. "A large part of Zuni ceremony centers about the veneration of sacred objects. Some of these, like the fetishes of the rain priests, are of indescribable sanctity, and in them rests the whole welfare of the people" (Bunzel 1932:490). Interestingly, these fetishes were given an offering of food each day and were kept with an assort-ment of other items, including pigments, *Olivella* shells, obsidian knives, and arrow points.

Tiponi or *etowe* were not generally interred with deceased individuals and differ in appearance from effigy vessels in the RPMS assemblage. However, the role of these effigies as symbols of authority in Hopi and Zuni society and the general importance placed on fetishes supports the suggestion that ceramic effigies in the RPMS assemblage were symbols of authority.

One way to evaluate if these items were associated with higher social status is to compare vessel counts of indi-viduals associated with effigy vessels or painted wood to those of interments without them. In both instances, individuals with painted wood or effigy vessels were asso-ciated with significantly larger vessel assemblages, which

supports the possibility they were symbols of authority (Loendorf 1999).

Furthermore, the distribution of artifacts thought to be symbols of authority should be restricted primarily to burial contexts or contexts associated with their produc-tion or use (Braun 1981). Painted sticks were only collected from burial contexts and were never found elsewhere (Loendorf 1996b). Similarly, although small fragments of effigy vessels were collected from a variety of contexts, complete or reconstructible vessels were only collected from burial contexts.

QUANTITATIVE METHODS

This analysis employs exploratory data analysis (EDA) techniques and bivariate statistical procedures. The EDA approach emphasizes visual displays of data rather than summary statistics derived from assemblages (Shennan 1990). EDA techniques are used in this analysis because the burial data do not conform to assumptions underly-ing many summary statistics. Furthermore, in contrast to many other statistical analyses, this research is directed toward the identification of outliers in the numbers and types of burial accompaniments, and EDA techniques are well suited for this purpose.

A subset of 270 of the 479 burials was used in the quan-titative analysis of burial accompaniments (see table 7.1). Vandalized and prehistorically disturbed inhumations were excluded from the quantitative sample because it was not possible to ascertain the numbers or types of burial accom-paniments that were originally present. Several potentially important mortuary practices were only considered in descriptive or qualitative terms and were not included in the quantitative analysis because the generally poor preser-vation in burial contexts makes it impossible to consistently determine their presence or absence. For example, evidence that the deceased were associated with organic materials such as basketry was found in some burials with atypical preservation, but in most cases, the nearly complete dete-rioration of organic remains precludes evaluation of whether these accompaniments were once present.

Measures of energy expenditure in construction of the burial facility (Tainter 1978) were not employed in the quantitative analysis, but energy expenditure was con-sidered in more subjective discussions of variability in mortuary treatment. In addition, artifact accompani-ments can be considered as a proxy measure of the energy expended in the construction of the burial pit because artifacts were generally placed beside individuals and the inclusion of substantial numbers of artifacts therefore required the construction of a larger facility. This relationship is most relevant for larger artifact types such as ceramic vessels.

Quantifying the Burial Assemblage

Because this analysis is based on the assumption that higher ranking individuals should have received more elaborate burial treatment, it is necessary to address ways to compare burial assemblages that include different types of artifacts. This process involves the assignment of values to different artifact types. Value is difficult to assign, however, because it is a culturally based construct. This problem is addressed through the use of two different methods for assigning "values" to artifact types.

Artifacts counts are the most straightforward method for quantifying assemblages; the counts of different artifact types are simply added together. Broken artifacts and objects comprised of a number of small pieces are counted as one; for example, a necklace made from hundreds of beads is given a count of one.

The use of artifact counts as a summary of burial assemblages has a fundamental problem: it is unreasonable to assume that all different artifact types had equal value or importance, and under this system all types are weighted equally. As a partial response to these problems, counts of vessels, nonvessel artifacts, and all artifacts are considered independently.

Artifact counts do have important advantages over methods for assigning relative worth to artifact types. First, counts are an objective measure that avoids subjective and potentially circular methods for assessing the value of different types. Second, this method involves the fewest assumptions, and therefore the interpretation of results is more straightforward.

One simple method for assigning values to different artifact types is based on the assumption that more valuable artifacts should occur in lower frequencies than less valuable types. The Assemblage Rarity Score (ARS) approach employs this assumption, which has the advantage that it can be applied objectively (Loendorf 1999). While it may be the case that valuable artifacts were uncommon, it is unreasonable to assume that all rare artifacts were valuable. This method has the potential to assign high values to idiosyncratic items that had little worth. Because of this possibility, broad material classes

are used to group artifacts together. In addition, these broad classes limit the extent to which stylistic change through time is erroneously recorded as variation in burial assemblages. This is particularly evident in the ceramic assemblage where types are known to be chronologically sensitive and their inclusion as variables would complicate comparisons across and between time periods.

In order to assign ARS values, burial assemblages were divided into three categories (vessels, nonvessel artifacts, and symbols of authority), and the weighting factors were calculated separately for types in each category. This was done to allow comparison of these different aspects of burial treatment. Weighted values for artifact types are calculated by multiplying the count of the variable (e.g., projectile points) for a given burial by the inverse of the proportion of that variable within the category (e.g., nonvessel artifacts).

A fairly strong positive linear relationship (Pearson correlation coefficient = .83) exists between the two quantification methods. This suggests that both methods may produce roughly similar results. However, ARS scores discriminate greater variation in the data, which facilitates visual distinctions between burial assemblages using EDA techniques. For this reason, ARS scores are used for graphical comparisons in this analysis. Significance tests for total artifact counts, vessel counts, and nonvessel counts are also presented because they employ fewer assumptions.

ASSEMBLAGE VARIATION BY AGE AND SEX

This section presents evidence that both ascribed and achieved status occurred in Salado society by examining variation in burial treatment based on age and sex differences. Common artifact types were not exclusively restricted to a particular sex or age group, but differences in burial assemblages do exist among these groups which suggest age and sex related patterning in burial treatment.

Table 7.2 presents significance tests for artifact types and assemblage methods by age and sex. Because adolescents are underrepresented, age comparisons were made between juveniles (0–9 years) and adults (18 or more years). All of the vessel types have significant differences between adults and juveniles at the .05 level. In contrast, for the nonvessel types only projectile points and bone awls have significant differences between adults and juveniles. Interestingly, these two types were the only artifact categories that may have been weapons; although bone awls or hairpins are commonly interpreted as ornaments, morphological and contextual evidence suggests that some "awls" were also used as weapons (Loendorf 1996a).

The opposed patterning where all vessel variables have significant differences based on age and most nonvessel variables do not have significant differences based on age suggests, as previously inferred, that these two measures of burial assemblages are related to different dimensions of social organization. This pattern is consistent with the suggestion that vessel accompaniments are better measures of social relationships that are more likely to have

been at least partially achieved and that most nonvessel accompaniments are more closely associated with wealth which may have been more frequently ascribed to juveniles. However, adults also certainly achieved the accumulation of wealth, and some juveniles also appear to have been ascribed social status.

For both temporal phases, adult burials have higher median scores than do juvenile interments, and scores tend to increase with age (Loendorf 1999). This observation is consistent with the achievement of status; however, data also suggest that the ascription of status occurred.

TABLE 7.2 Wilcoxon Rank Sum W Tests for Artifact Types and Assemblage Measures by Age and Sex

Artifact Type	Sex (male = 57, female = 48)		Age (juvenile = 120, adult = 134)	
	Test Statistic	p	Test Statistic	p
Artifact count	U = 1133.0	.13	U = 5082.0	**< .01**
Assemblage rarity score	U = 1108.0	.09	U = 5106.5	**< .01**
Vessel count	U = 1147.0	.15	U = 4797.0	**< .01**
Vessel rarity score	U = 1164.5	.19	U = 4801.5	**< .01**
plain bowl	U = 1345	.82	U = 7214.0	**.02**
plain jar	U = 1314.0	.51	U = 7466.0	**.03**
red bowl	U = 969.0	**< .01**	U = 6345.5	**< .01**
red jar	U = 1277.5	.47	U = 6508.5	**< .01**
corrugated bowl	U = 1365.5	.99	U = 6617.0	**< .01**
corrugated jar	U = 130.0	.54	U = 7200.0	**< .01**
painted bowl	U = 1020.0	**.01**	U = 6407.5	**< .01**
painted jar	U = 1149.0	.07	U = 6765.5	**< .01**
Nonvessel artifact count	U = 1031.5	**.02**	U = 6568.5	**< .01**
Nonvessel rarity score	U = 1030.5	**.02**	U = 7270.5	.14
projectile points	U = 1071.5	**.01**	U = 6794.5	**< .01**
bone awl	U = 1302.0	.54	U = 6990.5	**< .01**
pigment	U = 1167.0	.06	U = 7647.0	.27
shell ornaments	U = 1220.0	.14	U = 7990.0	.89
turquoise ornaments	U = 1213.0	.08	U = 7659.0	.17
other stone ornaments	U = 1334.5	.46	U = 7947.5	.62
disk	U = 1358.5	.85	U = 7999.5	.81
crystal	U = 1330.5	.52	U = 8031.0	.97
Symbols of authority rarity score	U = 1209.0	.20	U = 6987.0	**< .01**
effigy (±)	Fisher's Exact	.62	Fisher's Exact	.22
painted stick (±)	Fisher's Exact	**.04**	Fisher's Exact	**< .01**
pigment staining (±)	Chi-square =.005	.94	Chi-square =.005	.08

Note: Bold items are significant at the .05 level.

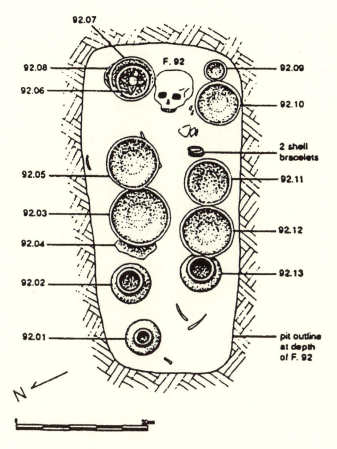

92.07

92.08

92.06

F. 92

92.09

92.10

2 shell bracelets

92.05

92.11

92.03

92.04

92.12

92.02

92.13

92.01

pit outline at depth of F. 92

N

FIGURE 7.4   Plan View of 2–4 Year Old Individual, Feature 92, AZ U:8:450 (ASM)

Although significant differences exist between adults and juveniles for many assemblage measures (table 7.3), some juvenile burials had substantially higher artifact counts than the median count for adults. Feature 92 at AZ U:8:450 (ASM) provides an example of an elaborately treated juvenile burial. This approximately three-year-old child was associated with 13 vessels and 2 shell bracelets (figure 7.4). The presence of comparatively large vessel assemblages with some juveniles suggests they may have been ascribed status.

Although significant differences also exist between Gila phase adults and juveniles in the entire assemblage, many of the Gila phase juveniles were from below room floors. If only extramural inhumations are considered, greater similarity may exist between Gila phase juveniles and adults (Loendorf 1999). The median count is higher for adults, but the distributions are roughly similar. These data suggest that positions of ascribed status existed in both the Roosevelt and Gila phases.

If the burial treatment of children was in some way related to the status of their parents (i.e., ascribed status occurred), then it would be expected that vessel counts for children and adults from the same social segment (cemetery) would be correlated. This relationship can be examined by comparing average juvenile and adult vessel counts for Roosevelt phase cemeteries with five or more excavated burials, of which more than 20% were juveniles (figure 7.5). A positive linear relationship exists for vessel counts of adults and juveniles (Pearson correlation coefficient = .83), supporting the possibility that ascription of status occurred.

Another way to examine juvenile and adult status within corporate groups is to compare the juvenile and adult with the highest vessel count in cemeteries (figure 7.6). As shown in figure 7.6, a strong linear relationship is apparent between the eight Roosevelt phase cemeteries, while the three Gila phase cemeteries fall to the right of Roosevelt phase contexts and may lie along a second regression line. This suggests that Gila phase juveniles buried in cemeteries received more elaborate treatment in comparison to adults, than did juveniles in the Roosevelt phase, and further supports the suggestion that ascribed status existed in Salado society.

In general, males and females do not appear to differ dramatically in burial treatment (see table 7.3). For both phases, the median assemblage score is higher for the males in the sample, but the range of variation is similar (Loendorf 1999). However, significant variation between males and females occurs for some artifact types.

Figure 7.7 is a scatterplot of ARS values by the midpoint of the age estimate for individuals of known sex. Examination of the figure suggests the presence of age-related patterning within the male and female groups, but variation in the burial treatment of similarly aged males and females also occurred. At least two possibilities, both of which may have occurred, could account for this difference: (1) Males and females may have generally attained status in different fashions, and males may have gained higher status earlier in life than females. Male status may also have tended to decline after middle-age, whereas female status increased in later life. These observations are consistent with the achievement of status. (2) Because they were involved in dangerous tasks such as warfare, high ranking males may have had shorter life expectancies than females or low-ranking males. The underrepresentation of old adult males supports this possibility.

To summarize, age related patterning in the RPMS

TABLE 7.3   Wilcoxon Rank Sum W Tests for Phase and Burial Location by Age and Sex

	Sex (male and female)		Age (juvenile and adult)	
	Test Statistic	p	Test Statistic	p
All Roosevelt Phase Interments				
	male = 44, female = 34		*juvenile = 61, adult = 103*	
Artifact count	U = 626.0	.22	U = 2327.0	**< .01**
Assemblage rarity score	U = 593.5	.12	U = 2288.5	**< .01**
Vessel count	U = 625.0	.21	U = 2343.5	**< .01**
Vessel rarity score	U = 643.0	.29	U = 2365.0	**< .01**
Nonvessel artifact count	U = 599.0	.12	U = 2597.5	**.05**
Nonvessel rarity score	U = 576.5	.07	U = 2775.0	.17
Symbols of authority rarity score	U = 689.5	.49	U = 2733.5	.06
All Gila Phase Interments				
	male = 13, female = 14		*juvenile = 59, adult = 31*	
Artifact count	U = 76.5	.48	U = 513.0	**< .01**
Assemblage rarity score	U = 82.5	.68	U = 551.0	**< .01**
Vessel count	U = 78.5	.54	U = 436.0	**< .01**
Vessel rarity score	U = 81.5	.64	U = 421.5	**< .01**
Nonvessel artifact count	U = 54.5	.06	U = 780.0	.21
Nonvessel rarity score	U = 68.0	.21	U = 899.0	.88
Symbols of authority rarity score	U = 75.0	.21	U = 867.5	.44
Gila Phase Extramural interments*				
Artifact count	same as above	—	U = 206.5	.35
Assemblage rarity score	—	—	U = 242.0	.89
Vessel count	—	—	U = 203.0	.31
Vessel rarity score	—	—	U = 192.0	.21
Nonvessel artifact count	—	—	U = 223.0	.55
Nonvessel rarity score	—	—	U = 207.5	.31
Symbols of authority rarity score	—	—	U = 209.0	.20

Note: Bold items are significant at the .05 level. * = excludes juvenile burials from below room floors.

burial assemblage demonstrates that positions of status were partially based on achievement, while several other observations suggest that the ascription of status also occurred in Salado society.

Distribution of Elaborate Burials
Roosevelt Phase Cemeteries

This section evaluates the distribution of status and authority within Salado communities by comparing burial assemblages from different cemeteries. Only the Roosevelt phase cemeteries were considered because representative burial data were collected from too few Gila phase extramural cemeteries to allow comparisons.

Using the assumption that cemeteries represent different social units, these analyses suggest that measurable differences existed in burial treatment between groups that were in close proximity to one another and that these differences continued and even increased through time. During the Roosevelt phase, differences in burial treatment are apparent among sites. Variation in burial treatment during the Gila phase is seen among separate burial locations within sites.

In order to control for temporal variation and differences in regional burial treatment, five contemporaneous Roosevelt phase inhumation cemeteries from the same community are examined first (figure 7.8). These five cemeteries

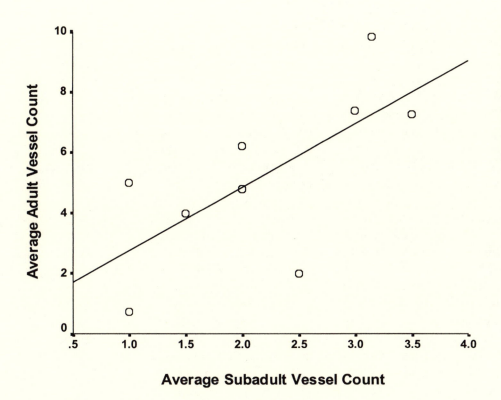

FIGURE 7.5
Roosevelt Phase
Cemeteries Comparing
Average Vessel Counts
for Adult and Juvenile
Burials (includes only
cemeteries with more
than five burials and
20% juveniles)

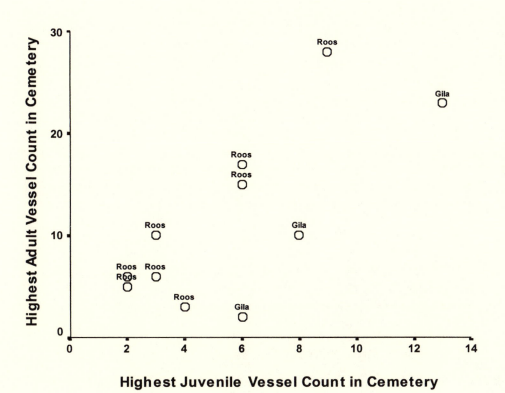

FIGURE 7.6
Comparison of Adult
Versus Juvenile with
the Highest Vessel
Count in 11 Cemeteries
(includes only
cemeteries with more
than five burials and
20% juveniles)

represent a small portion of the entire community, but this sample can still be used to evaluate differences in burial treatment between community segments.

The highest scoring individuals are not randomly distributed but are instead concentrated at AZ U:8:450 (ASM). This site is one of several small contemporaneous Roosevelt phase compounds that were in close proximity to where the Schoolhouse Point mound (AZ U:8:24 [ASM]) was constructed in the Gila phase. The cemeteries that are labeled AZ U:8:24 (ASM) Central and AZ U:8:24 (ASM) Northern are from other compounds in this cluster; the AZ U:8:24 (ASM) Central cemetery was overlain by Gila phase rooms, and subadults assigned to this cemetery include interments that may have been Gila phase juveniles which were placed below room floors—this may have lowered the median score and decreased the interquartile range for this cemetery. The remaining two cemeteries are from more distant Roosevelt phase compounds that were abandoned prior to the Gila phase.

None of these cemeteries was restricted to a single age group or sex, but elaborate burials were concentrated at AZ U:8:450 (ASM). The highest scoring cemetery (AZ U:8:450 [ASM]), however, also included adults that were not associated with any accompaniments. A roughly similar pattern is apparent if juveniles from these cemeteries are compared (Loendorf 1999); the highest scoring individuals were concentrated at AZ U:8:450 (ASM), but high scoring subadults were also present in other cemeteries (the two highest scoring juveniles were from separate cemeteries). In aggregate, quantitative variation in burial assemblages observed among contemporaneous Roosevelt phase corporate groups is consistent with expectations of the ranked segmentary lineage model.

To increase sample sizes and further compare individuals buried in different contexts, it is useful to combine burials from similar site types. All Roosevelt phase interments were assigned to one of three groups, lumping similar sites from different arms of the basin (table 7.4). Although residences on the Tonto and Salt arms were part of separate communities, each area has a similar range of variation in Roosevelt phase burial assemblages, despite the difference in sample size (Loendorf 1999). The similarity of these two populations suggests that it is reasonable to make comparisons across them.

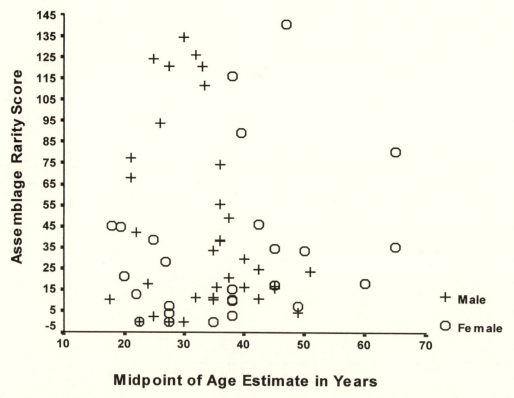

FIGURE 7.7   Scatterplot of Assemblage Rarity Scores by the Midpoint of Age Estimates for Males and Females

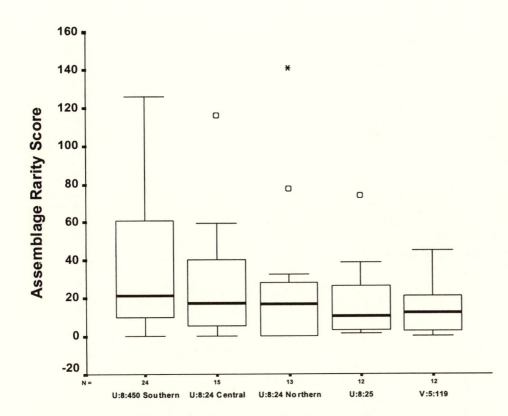

FIGURE 7.8
Boxplots of
Assemblage Rarity
Scores for Roosevelt
Phase Cemeteries in
the Schoolhouse Point
Community with
More Than 10
Inhumations (the sites
are plotted based on
their distance from
U:8:450)

The principal distinction used to group the sites was between integrative sites and residential compounds. A number of observations suggest that integrative sites were central places within multisite communities (Loendorf 1999), suggesting that elaborate burials should be concentrated at these sites. For example, most integrative sites had platform mounds that could not have been constructed within a reasonable time period by the occupants of the site.

Residential compounds were then divided into two groups based on the assumption that aggregation during the Gila phase should have occurred at residential sites where higher ranking corporate groups resided. Aggregation is thought to have been most likely at the settlements of higher ranking groups for two reasons. First, higher ranking groups should have been in better position to control the location of aggregation and are more likely to have chosen their own settlements because of the stress involved in relocating. Second, higher status segments are more likely to have occupied the most favorable locations for habitation which are also generally the locations of aggregation (Kintigh 1985).

The first group consists of Roosevelt phase burials from small residential compounds that were abandoned before the Gila phase. The second group is comprised of Roosevelt phase interments from residential sites where the population eventually aggregated in the Gila phase; these sites were also in areas where several contemporaneous compounds were closely clustered together, whereas compounds in the first category were generally isolated. The terms isolated and clustered are used for convenience to refer to these two groups. The third category consists of burials from integrative sites.

Table 7.5 contains Wilcoxon Rank Sum W tests of assemblage scores for inhumations from these three contexts. For most measures, a greater range of variation exists for individuals from integrative sites and clustered compounds. The most distinct difference between the three groups appears to be in nonvessel counts which suggests by inference that distinctions in personal wealth were most pronounced. As will be more thoroughly considered in the following section, symbols of authority appear to have been relatively evenly distributed among these groups.

These data suggest that all high status positions were not restricted to any one of these groups. At the same time, each site type included individuals of all age and sex groups, but measurable differences existed between segments of the community. It appears that each segment had leaders and nonleaders, but the highest status positions were largely restricted to community integrative sites.

Furthermore, variation occurred in the treatment of males and females buried at isolated compounds and clustered compounds (figure 7.9). Substantial differences exist between males and females from isolated compounds, whereas males and females at clustered compounds received remarkably similar treatment. Significant differences exist between juveniles and adults buried at isolated compounds but not between juveniles and adults at clustered compounds (table 7.6). This pattern where greater similarity in burial treatment occurs between the sexes and age groups in higher scoring cemeteries is consistent with the ascription of status. It

TABLE 7.4 Undisturbed Roosevelt Phase Burials by Cemetery Area and Site Type Assignment

Site Number	Sample Size	Highest Assemblage Rarity Score	Comments
Isolated Sites (abandoned prior to Gila Phase)			
Tonto Creek Sites			
U:4:75	8	Adult male 68	Also vandalized burials at site
U:4:32	9	Adult female 22	Includes 2 midden burials
U:3:128	12	Adult male 52	2 Gila Phase rooms at site
Salt River Sites			
U:8:25	12	Adult male 74	Abandoned clustered? compound
U:8:385	1	Infant 12	
U:8:451	4	Infant 4	Possible subadult cemetery
U:8:453	1	Child 10	
V:5:119	11	Young adult female 45	Roosevelt phase cremation
V:5:121	2	Infant 9	F11 below room floor
V:5:137	1	Infant 0	
V:5:139	2	Infant 10	Abandoned clustered compounds
Subtotal	63		
Clustered Sites (locations of residential population aggregation in Gila Phase)			
Tonto Creek Sites			
U:4:9	1	Infant 8	Cemetery largely vandalized
U:4:9	1	Child 120	Cemetery largely vandalized
U:4:11	1	Adult unknown 0	Isolated burial
Salt River Sites			
U:8:24	1	Adult male 8	Isolated burial
U:8:24	12	Child 33	Northern cemeteries
U:8:24	2	Adult male 121	East cremation cemetery
U:8:24	9	Old adult female 141	All 9 individuals from Type 2 multiple burial
U:8:450	1	Adult male 0	Midden burial
U:8:450	7	Child 43	Also Gila Phase burials in cemetery
U:8:450	23	Adult male 126	Southern cemetery
Subtotal	58		
Integrative Sites			
U:4:7	10	Adult male 135	Also vandalized burials in cemetery
U:4:33	1	Adult male 124	From multiple burial
U:8:24	15	Adult female 116	Central cemeteries
U:8:454	1	Adult male 94	Only 2 burials in cemetery (one was cremated)
V:5:66	3	Adult male 9	Main cemetery vandalized
Subtotal	30		

Note: Some sites have multiple cemetery areas.

TABLE 7.5   Wilcoxon Rank Sum W Tests by Roosevelt Phase Site Type

Assemblage Measures	Test Statistic	p
Isolated Compounds and Clustered Compounds		
Artifact count	U = 1462.5	.29
Assemblage rarity score	U = 1333.5	.08
Vessel count	U = 1459.5	.28
Vessel rarity score	U = 1361.5	.11
Nonvessel artifact count	U = 1360.0	.08
Nonvessel rarity score	U = 1474.0	.27
Symbols of authority rarity score	U = 1537.0	.41
Isolated Compounds and Integrated Sites		
Artifact count	U = 616.5	**.03**
Assemblage rarity score	U = 687.0	.11
Vessel count	U = 770.0	.38
Vessel rarity score	U = 772.5	.40
Nonvessel artifact count	U = 511.0	**< .01**
Nonvessel rarity score	U = 601.5	**.01**
Symbols of authority rarity score	U = 782.0	.32
Isolated Compounds and Integrated Sites		
Artifact count	U = 672.0	.24
Assemblage rarity score	U = 778.0	.85
Vessel count	U = 794.0	.97
Vessel rarity score	U = 746.0	.63
Nonvessel artifact count	U = 583.0	**.04**
Nonvessel rarity score	U = 621.5	.08
Symbols of authority rarity score	U = 770.5	.75

Note: Bold items are significant at the .05 level.

also suggests that achieved status played a more important role in the lower ranking social segments.

SYMBOLS OF AUTHORITY

This section evaluates the distribution of symbols of authority among cemeteries. Ethnographic and quantitative evidence for three probable symbols of authority (pigment staining, effigy vessels, and painted sticks) has already been presented. Examples of other possible symbols of authority (e.g., turquoise mosaics, shell trumpets) are represented in the burial assemblage; however, this analysis is concerned only with the distribution of symbols of authority among community segments which may be done using only a few examples. Furthermore, most other possible symbols of authority occurred with too few individuals for comparisons to be made.

In order to compare the treatment of individuals associated with symbols of authority, the ARS values for vessels and nonvessels were combined. Figure 7.10 is a histogram of these scores in the entire burial population. The distribution is skewed right, discontinuous, and distinct modes are not clearly apparent in the scores.

In order to tabulate the treatment of individuals with different symbols of authority, the population was arbitrarily split into low scores (0–13), medium scores (14–40), and high scores (more than 40) based on the ARS values for vessels and nonvessels (table 7.7). Examination of table 7.7 suggests that although individuals with these symbols generally scored higher, not all individuals with symbols of authority were in the highest scoring group. Table 7.8 lists the counts and proportions of individuals associated with symbols of authority by site type. Painted sticks, effigy vessels, and pigment staining were more common at integrative sites, but they were not restricted to integrative sites.

In summary, the three variables that may represent symbols of authority occurred with a small subset of burials that were distributed among cemeteries at different site types. Individuals associated with these variables generally received more elaborate treatment but variation also occurred in the treatment of these individuals. These observations are consistent with the ranked segmentary lineage model.

SUMMARY

The first portion of this analysis considered variation in burial treatment based on age and sex distinctions, and evidence that both ascribed and achieved status existed in Salado society was identified. Evidence that the ascription of status occurred suggests that simple egalitarian characterizations of Salado social organization must be rejected.

The presence of elaborately treated juvenile burials is generally taken as circumstantial evidence for ascribed status, and juveniles who score substantially higher than the median count for adults are present in the assemblage. The correlation between juvenile and adult burial treatment within cemeteries is also consistent with the ascrip-

tion of status. Furthermore, Peebles and Kus (1977) suggested that societies were organized on the basis of hereditary rank when symbols of authority crosscut age and gender distinctions. Two of three possible symbols of authority in the RPMS assemblage (pigment staining and effigy vessels) crosscut age and gender distinctions (see table 7.7). Although no painted sticks were clearly associated with juveniles, painted sticks were associated with both males and females.

Furthermore, the number of accompaniments is not strongly associated with age or sex at residential sites that contained more elaborate burials; whereas, low-scoring cemeteries had substantial differences between age and sex groups. This pattern is consistent with the ascription of status.

The next part of this investigation considered the distribution of elaborate burials among cemeteries in communities. Elaborate burials were not randomly distributed and were instead found to be concentrated at community integrative sites. However, differences between cemeteries appear to be a continuous gradation rather than modal distinctions.

Qualitative variation in burial treatment among cemeteries also suggests that ranking occurred between corporate groups. The most energy intensive burial facilities (large multiple burials) occurred only at three cemeteries

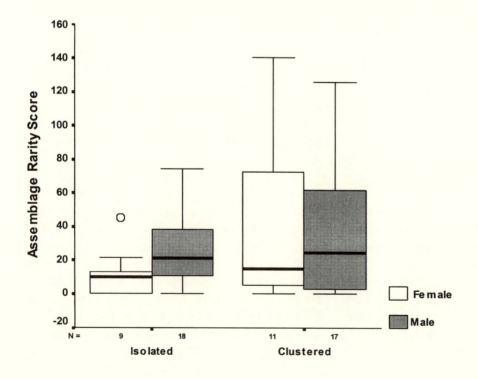

FIGURE 7.9
Boxplots of Assemblage Rarity Scores by Sex for Isolated and Clustered Compounds

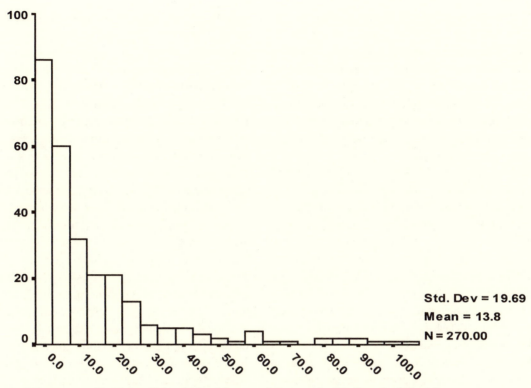

FIGURE 7.10   Histogram of Weighted Vessel Plus Nonvessel Counts for Undisturbed Burials

TABLE 7.6   Wilcoxon Rank Sum W Tests by Age and Sex for Roosevelt Phase Site Types

Assemblage Measures	Age (juvenile & adult) Test Statistic	p	Sex (female & male) Test Statistic	p
Isolated Compounds				
Artifact count	U = 297.0	**.03**	U = 70.5	.11
Assemblage rarity score	U = 285.0	**.01**	U = 76.0	.17
Vessel count	U = 287.0	**.01**	U = 80.5	.24
Vessel rarity score	U = 298.0	**.02**	U = 74.5	.15
Nonvessel artifact count	U = 351.0	.09	U = 69.5	.08
Nonvessel rarity score	U = 363.0	.14	U = 69.5	.08
Symbols of authority rarity score	U = 392.5	.24	U = 100.5	.68
Clustered Compounds				
Artifact count	U = 350.0	1.00	U = 89.5	.85
Assemblage rarity score	U = 316.0	.55	U = 93.0	.98
Vessel count	U = 347.0	.96	U = 87.0	.76
Vessel rarity score	U = 336.0	.81	U = 79.0	.49
Nonvessel artifact count	U = 346.5	.95	U = 73.0	.31
Nonvessel rarity score	U = 344.5	.92	U = 77.0	.41
Symbols of authority rarity score	U = 288.0	.17	U = 90.5	.88

Note: Bold items are significant at the .05 level.

near the end of Schoolhouse Point (a location that included both integrative and clustered compounds, but not isolated compounds) and were not found in any other part of this community. The corporate groups represented by these cemeteries appear to have ranked higher than all other groups in the community, which lacked large multiple burials. Skeletal evidence suggests that the individuals in at least one multiple burial facility were closely related genetically (Regan et al. 1996).

At least four cemeteries also appear to have been used during the Gila phase at the Schoolhouse Point site. However, in contrast to the Roosevelt phase cemeteries at this site, only one of the Gila phase cemeteries appears to have contained large multiple burial facilities (Loendorf 1996a, 1996b). The restriction of large multiple burials to a single Gila phase cemetery suggests that the corporate group represented by this cemetery was ranked with respect to other comparable units at the site. Extensive vandalism of these Gila phase cemeteries precluded more intensive quantitative comparisons.

Two other observations also support the suggestion that important differences existed in burial treatment among community segments. First, Roosevelt phase cremations occurred almost exclusively at integrative sites that also had large contemporaneous inhumation cemeteries, and cremations were not found at residential compounds. Second, Gila phase burials from AZ U:4:33

(ASM) (a large integrative site with a platform mound) were interred at intercardinal positions that differed from Gila phase burials at residential sites.

As a further consideration of the allocation of power and authority in Salado communities, the third part of this considered the distribution of symbols of authority among different site types. Three variables that may represent symbols of authority (pigment staining, effigy vessels, and painted sticks) occurred with a small subset of burials that were not restricted to integrative sites and were instead distributed among cemeteries at different site types. Individuals associated with these variables generally received more elaborate treatment but variation also occurred in the treatment of these individuals.

A number of diachronic changes also occurred in lower Tonto Basin mortuary practices. First, both cremation and inhumation were practiced during the Roosevelt phase, but inhumation was almost exclusively performed during the Gila phase. Second, head orientation also becomes significantly more consistent through time. Third, pigment staining also appears to have been restricted to a smaller segment of the population in the Gila phase; this suggests that the positions represented by pigment staining became more circumscribed through time. Fourth, substantial differences existed between age and sex groups in the Roosevelt phase, but greater similarity existed among these groups in the Gila phase.

TABLE 7.7 Weighted Vessel Plus Nonvessel Rarity Score Group by Symbols of Authority, Sex, and Age

| Category | Vessel plus nonvessel rarity score groups | | | |
	Low (0–13)	Middle (14–40)	High (40+)	Total
Adult with painted wood				
male	0	4	4	8
female	0	0	1	1
Adult with effigy				
male	0	1	2	3
female	0	0	2	2
Individuals with pigment staining				
male	1	1	6	13
female	2	4	4	10
unknown	0	2	1	3
child	5	6	2	13
adolescent	1	1	0	2
Child with effigy	0	1	0	1

TABLE 7.8   Symbol of Authority Presence by Roosevelt Phase Site Type

Roosevelt Phase Site Type	Sample Size	Symbol of Authority		
		Pigment Staining	Effigy Vessel	Painted Wood
Isolated residential compounds	63	12 (19%)	0	3 (5%)
Clustered residential compounds	58	14 (24%)	4 (7%)	1 (2%)
Integrative sites	30	11 (37%)	2 (7%)	4 (13%)

Note: numbers in parentheses are the percentage of individuals from the site type with symbol of authority.

CONCLUSIONS

Insight into Salado social organization provided by this analysis suggests that the prehistoric occupants of Tonto Basin were on a trajectory of increasing social complexity that was truncated by the collapse of the system around roughly A.D. 1450. Substantive variation in burial practices during the Roosevelt phase was replaced by more standardized burial procedures in the Gila phase. Taken at face value, the more standardized burial practices of the Gila phase might be seen as evidence for a decrease in social complexity. However, it is necessary to distinguish between "complicated" and "complex" practices. Hallpike argued that:

> in small-scale, face-to-face societies it is "easier" to develop what are actually more complicated forms of association and classification, but with the growth of size of society, and range of technology and culture, it is necessary for individuals to develop more generalizable forms of order that can transcend local idiosyncrasies and embrace larger numbers and more diverse types of people: that is, to "simplify" in the classificatory sense. (Hallpike 1988:279)

It is in this light that the more standardized and therefore less complicated Gila phase burial practices are seen as evidence for an increase in social complexity.

This analysis has presented compelling evidence that both ascribed and achieved status existed in Salado society. Other observations suggest that vessel accompaniments are more closely associated with the social relationships of the deceased, whereas most nonvessel artifacts may be better indicators of differences in wealth. The negative correlation between vessel count and the count of all other artifact types suggests that any Salado mortuary analysis should at least initially consider these variables separately. Many previous Southwestern mortuary analyses have employed methods that result in an emphasis on nonvessel variables as measures of social status. Observations presented here suggest that it may be wise to reexamine this aspect of these approaches.

Intracemetery variation in burial treatment suggests that ranking occurred within corporate groups during both phases, and all cemeteries included individuals who received nominal treatment. Ranking within corporate groups appears to have been related somewhat to age, but the number of accompaniments is not strongly associated with sex, especially for residential sites that contained more elaborate burials.

Patterning in these data are most consistent with the segmentary lineage model suggested by Rice (1992). He suggests that architectural data and the distribution of rare artifacts both within and between sites are consistent with the structuring principals of a ranked segmentary organization. These organizations are comprised of a series of nested rankings, with the small segments being linked into progressively more inclusive units. At each level, one segment is ranked higher than its counterparts.

Systems that are structured on these principles can amalgamate into more inclusive units by joining lower level segments into a "supra-lineage" (Rice 1992:24). This process of amalgamation accounts for both the diachronic changes in Salado mortuary practices and the distribution of exceptionally elaborate burial facilities.

Most Classic period burial assemblages from throughout the greater Southwest include individuals who received substantially different burial treatment, and it is also possible that the segmentary hierarchy model could provide insight into variation in mortuary treatment for other burial populations.

REFERENCES CITED

Binford, Lewis R.

1971   Mortuary Practices: Their Study and Their
Potential. In *Approaches to the Social Dimensions
of Mortuary Practices*, organized and edited by
J. A. Brown, pp. 6–29. Memoirs of the Society
for American Archaeology, no. 25. Society for
American Archaeology, Washington, D.C.
(Issued as *American Antiquity* 36(3) Pt. 2, July
1971.)

Blanton, R. E., S. A. Kowalewski, G. Feinman, and J. Appel

1981   *Ancient Mesoamerica: A Comparison of Change
in Three Regions.* Cambridge University Press,
New York.

Braun, David P.

1981   Review of Some Recent North American
Mortuary Studies. *American Antiquity* 46:398–416.

Bunzel, Ruth L.

1932   *Zuni Ceremonialism.* Reprinted. University of
New Mexico Press, Albuquerque. Originally
published as three studies: *Introduction to Zuñi
Ceremonialism, Zuñi Origin Myths,* and *Zuñi
Ritual Poetry.* Forty-seventh Annual Report of
the Bureau of American Ethnology, 1929–1930.
Smithsonian Institution, Washington, D.C.

Carr, Christopher

1994   A Crosscultural Survey of the Determinants of
Mortuary Practices. In *The Pueblo Grande
Project, Volume 7: An Analysis of Classic Period
Mortuary Patterns,* edited by D. R. Mitchell, pp.
7–69. Soil Systems Publications in Archaeology
No. 20. Soil Systems, Phoenix.

Chang, Kwang-Chih

1989   Ancient China and Its Anthropological
Significance. In *Archaeological Thought in
America,* edited by C. C. Lamberg-Karlovsky, pp.
155–66. Cambridge University Press, Cambridge.

Charles, Douglas K., and Jane E. Buikstra

1983   Archaic Mortuary Sites in the Central
Mississippi Drainage: Distribution, Structure,
and Behavioral Implications. In *Archaic Hunters
and Gatherers in the American Midwest,* edited
by J. L. Phillips and J. A. Brown, pp. 117–45.
Academic Press, New York.

Ciolek-Torrello, Richard S.

1987   *The Ord Mine Archaeological Project.* Museum of
Northern Arizona, Northern Arizona Society of
Science and Art, Flagstaff.

Crown, Patricia L.

1994   *Ceramics and Ideology: Salado Polychrome

Pottery.* University of New Mexico Press,
Albuquerque.

Doyel, David E.

1976   Salado Cultural Development in the Tonto
Basin and Globe-Miami Areas, Central Arizona.
The Kiva 42:5–16.

Doyel, David E., and Emil W. Haury (editors)

1976   The 1976 Salado Conference. *The Kiva* 42:1–134.

Eggan, Frederick R.

1950   *Social Organization of the Western Pueblos.*
University of Chicago Press, Chicago.

Ellis, Florence Hawley

1968   An Interpretation of Prehistoric Death Customs
in Terms of Modern Southwestern Parallels. In
*Collected Papers in Honor of Lyndon Lane
Hargrave,* edited by A. H. Schroeder, pp. 57–76.
Papers of the Archaeological Society of New
Mexico 1. Museum of New Mexico Press,
Santa Fe.

Fewkes, J. Walter

1896   Antiquities of the Upper Verde River and
Walnut Creek Valleys, Arizona. In *Thirteenth
Annual Report of the Bureau of American
Ethnology, 1891–1892,* pp. 181–220. Government
Printing Office, Washington, D.C.

1990   The Katcina Altars in Hopi Worship. Reprinted.
In *Tusayan Katcinas and Hopi Altars.* Avanyu
Publishing, Albuquerque. Originally published
1926, in *Annual Report of the Board of Regents of
the Smithsonian Institution, 1926,* pp. 463–86.
Government Printing Office, Washington, D.C.

Fox, Richard D.

1977   *Urban Anthropology: Cities in Their Cultural
Settings.* Prentice-Hall, Englewood Cliffs, New
Jersey.

Gladwin, Winifred J., and Harold S. Gladwin

1935   *The Eastern Range of the Red-on-buff Culture.*
Medallion Papers No. 16. Gila Pueblo, Globe,
Arizona.

Goldstein, Lynne

1981   One-Dimensional Archaeology and Multi-
Dimensional People: Spatial Organization and
Mortuary Analysis. In *The Archaeology of Death,*
edited by R. Chapman, I. Kinnes, and K.
Randsborg, pp. 53–70. Cambridge University
Press, New York.

Gumerman, George J., Murray Gell-Man,
and Linda S. Cordell

1994   Introduction. In *Understanding Complexity in
the Prehistoric Southwest,* edited by G. J
Gumerman and M. Gell-Man, pp.3–14.
Addison-Wesley, Reading.

Hallpike, Christopher R.
1988   *The Principles of Social Evolution*. Clarendon Press, Oxford.

Hohmann, John W.
1985a   *Hohokam and Salado Hamlets in the Tonto Basin: Site Descriptions*. Office of Cultural Resource Management (OCRM) Report No. 64. OCRM, Arizona State University, Tempe.
1985b   Status and Ranking as Exhibited in Burial Studies. In *Studies of the Hohokam and Salado of the Tonto Basin*, edited by G. Rice, pp. 211–220. OCRM Report No. 63. OCRM, Arizona State University, Tempe.
1992   *Through the Mirror of Death: A View of Prehistoric Social Complexity in Central Arizona*. Unpublished Ph.D. dissertation, Department of Anthropology, Arizona State University, Tempe.

Hohmann, John W., and Linda B. Kelley
1988   *Erich F. Schmidt's Investigations of Salado Sites in Central Arizona: The Mrs. W. B. Thompson Archaeological Expedition of the American Museum of Natural History*. Bulletin No. 56. Museum of Northern Arizona, Flagstaff.

Howell, Todd, and Keith W. Kintigh
1996   Archaeological Identification of Kin Groups Using Mortuary and Biological Data. *American Antiquity*. 61:537–54.

Kintigh, Keith W.
1985   *Settlement, Subsistence, and Society in Late Zuni Prehistory*. Anthropological Papers No. 44. University of Arizona, Tucson.

Lekson, Stephen H.
1992   Para-Salado, *Perro Salado*, or Salado Peril? In *Proceedings of the Second Salado Conference, Globe, AZ, 1992*, edited by R. C. Lange and S. Germick, pp. 22–30. Occasional Paper 1992. Arizona Archaeological Society, Phoenix.

Loendorf, Chris
1996a   Burial Practices at the Schoolhouse Point Mound, U:8:24/13a. In *The Place of the Storehouses: Roosevelt Platform Mound Study, Report on the Schoolhouse Point Mound, Pinto Creek Complex*, by O. Lindauer, pp. 681–759. Roosevelt Monograph Series No. 6, Anthropological Field Studies No. 35. OCRM, Arizona State University, Tempe.
1996b   Quantitative Analysis of the Burial Assemblage from Schoolhouse Point Mound, U:8:24/13a. In *The Place of the Storehouses: Roosevelt Platform Mound Study, Report on the Schoolhouse Point Mound, Pinto Creek Complex*, by O. Lindauer, pp.767–786. Roosevelt Monograph Series No. 6, Anthropological Field Studies No. 35. OCRM, Arizona State University, Tempe.
1997a   Burial Practices at the Cline Mesa Sites. In *Salado Residential Settlements on Tonto Creek, Roosevelt Platform Mound Study, Report on the Cline Mesa Sites, Cline Terrace Complex*, by T. J. Oliver and D. Jacobs, pp. 769–834. Roosevelt Monograph Series No. 9, Anthropological Field Studies No. 38. OCRM, Arizona State University, Tempe.
1997b   Burial Practices at the Schoolhouse Point Mesa Sites. In *The Archaeology of Schoolhouse Point Mesa, Roosevelt Platform Mound Study, Report on the Schoolhouse Point Mesa Sites, Schoolhouse Management Group, Pinto Creek Complex*, by O. Lindauer, pp. 549–630. Roosevelt Monograph Series No. 8, Anthropological Field Studies No. 37. OCRM, Arizona State University, Tempe.
1997c   Burial Practices at U:4:33/132, the Cline Terrace Mound. In *A Salado Platform Mound on Tonto Creek, Roosevelt Platform Mound Study, Report on the Cline Terrace Mound, Cline Terrace Complex*, by D. Jacobs, pp. 465–504. Roosevelt Monograph Series No. 7, Anthropological Field Studies No. 36. OCRM, Arizona State University, Tempe
1998   Salado Multiple Interments. *Kiva* 63:319–48.
1999   *Salado Burial Practices and Social Organization in Classic Period Tonto Basin*. Unpublished Master's thesis, Department of Anthropology, Arizona State University, Tempe.

Loendorf, Chris, Owen Lindauer, and John C. Ravesloot
1995   Burial Practices at the Bass Point Mound. In *Where the Rivers Converge, Roosevelt Platform Mound Study, Report on the Rock Island Complex*, by O. Lindauer, pp. 401–14. Roosevelt Monograph Series No. 8, Anthropological Field Studies No. 37. OCRM, Arizona State University, Tempe.

Mitchell, Douglas R.
1992   Explorations of Spatial Variability in Hohokam and Salado Cemeteries. In *Proceedings of the Second Salado Conference, Globe, AZ, 1992*, edited by R. C. Lange and S. Germick, pp. 22–30. Occasional Paper 1992. Arizona Archaeological Society, Phoenix.

Nelson, Ben A.
1995   Complexity, Hierarchy, and Scale: A Controlled Comparison Between Chaco Canyon, New Mexico, and La Quemada, Zacatecas. *American Antiquity* 60:597–618.

Ortiz, Alfonso
1969   *The Tewa World: Space, Time, Being, and Becoming in a Pueblo Society*. University of Chicago Press, Chicago.

O'Shea, John M.
1984   *Mortuary Variability: An Archaeology Investigation.* Academic Press, Orlando.

Parsons, Elsie Clews
1938   Relations Between Ethnology and Archaeology in the Southwest. *American Antiquity* 5:214–220.
1939   *Pueblo Indian Religion*, vol. I. University of Chicago Press, Chicago.

Peebles, Christopher S., and Susan M. Kus
1977   Some Archaeological Correlates of Ranked Societies. *American Antiquity* 42:421–48.

Ravesloot, John C.
1988   *Mortuary Practices and Social Differentiation at Casas Grandes, Chihuahua, Mexico.* Anthropological Papers of the University of Arizona No. 49. University of Arizona Press, Tucson.
1994   Burial Practices in the Livingston Area. In *Archaeology of the Salado in the Livingston Area of Tonto Basin, Roosevelt Platform Mound Study: Report on the Livingston Management Group, Pinto Creek Complex,* part 2, by D. Jacobs, pp. 833–850. Roosevelt Monograph Series No. 3, Anthropological Field Studies No. 32. OCRM, Arizona State University, Tempe.

Regan, Marcia H., Christy G. Turner II, and Joel D. Irish
1996   Physical Anthropology of the Schoolhouse Point Mound, U:8:24/13a. In *The Place of the Storehouses: Roosevelt Platform Mound Study, Report on Schoolhouse Point Mound, Pinto Creek Complex,* by O. Lindauer, pp. 787–840. Roosevelt Monograph Series No. 6, Anthropological Field Studies No. 35. OCRM, Arizona State University, Tempe.

Rice, Glen E.
1985   *Studies of the Hohokam and Salado of the Tonto Basin.* OCRM Report No. 63. OCRM, Arizona State University, Tempe.
1990   An Intellectual History of the Salado Concept. In *A Design for Salado Research,* edited by G. E. Rice, pp. 21–29. Roosevelt Monograph Series No. 1, Anthropological Field Studies No. 22. OCRM, Arizona State University, Tempe.
1992   Modeling the Development of Complexity in the Sonoran Desert of Arizona. In *Developing Perspectives on Tonto Basin Prehistory,* edited by C. L. Redman, G. E. Rice, and K. E. Pedrick, pp. 11–26. Roosevelt Monograph Series No. 2, Anthropological Field Studies No. 26. OCRM, Arizona State University, Tempe.

Russell, Frank
1975   *The Pima Indians.* The University of Arizona Press, Tucson. (Originally published 1908 in *Twenty-sixth Annual Report of the Bureau of American Ethnology, 1904–1905,* pp.3–389 Smithsonian Institution, Washington, D.C.)

Saxe, Arthur A.
1970   *Social Dimensions of Mortuary Practices in a Mesolithic Population from Wadi Halfa, Sudan.* Ph.D. dissertation, Department of Anthropology, University of Michigan, Ann Arbor.

Shennan, Stephen
1990   *Quantifying Archaeology.* Academic Press, Harcourt Brace Jovanovich, San Diego.

Simon, Arleyn W., and John C. Ravesloot
1994   Salado Ceramic Burial Offerings: A Consideration of Gender and Social Organization. Paper presented at the 1994 Southwest Symposium, Arizona State University, Tempe.

Tainter, Joseph A.
1978   Mortuary Practices and the Study of Prehistoric Social Systems. In *Advances in Archaeological Method and Theory*, vol. 1, edited by M. B. Schiffer, pp. 105–41. Academic Press, New York.

Titiev, Mischa
1992   *Old Oraibi: A Study of the Hopi Indians of Third Mesa.* Reprinted. University of New Mexico Press, Albuquerque. Originally published 1944, Papers of the Peabody Museum of American Archaeology and Ethnology Vol. 22, No. 1. Harvard University, Cambridge.

Tyler, Hamilton A.
1986   *Pueblo Gods and Myths.* The Civilization of the American Indian Series, No. 71. University of Oklahoma Press, Norman.

Waters, Frank
1963   *Book of the Hopi.* Ballantine Books, Toronto.

Whittlesey, Stephanie M.
1978   *Status and Death at Grasshopper Pueblo: Experiment Toward an Archaeological Theory of Correlates.* Unpublished Ph.D. dissertation, Department of Anthropology, University of Arizona, Tucson.

Wood, J. Scott
1983   *The Salado Tradition of the Tonto National Forest: Ethnic Groups and Boundaries.* Cultural Resources Inventory Report 82–100. Tonto National Forest, Phoenix.

Wright, Barton
1979   *Hopi Material Culture: Artifacts Gathered by H. R. Voth in the Fred Harvey Collection.* The Heard Museum, Phoenix and Northland Press, Flagstaff.

CHAPTER EIGHT

Foundations of Political Power in Ancestral Zuni Society

Todd L. Howell

POLITICAL POWER IS COMMONLY DERIVED FROM ONE of three sources: control over aspects of the economy, military force, or ideology (Earle 1989:86). Research into the nature of prehistoric political organization in the American Southwest has focused largely on economic differentiation as evidence for increased political complexity. This is due, in part, to our ability to measure and record economic differentiation in the archaeological record; leaders may reside in larger or more elaborate houses, enjoy better health (reflecting a superior diet), receive tribute, manage surpluses, or control nonlocal trade. Each of these processes can be measured in the archaeological record. Economic differentiation has also been a focus because of its supposed central role in sociopolitical evolution, especially the development of chiefdoms (Earle 1989; Fried 1967; Sahlins 1963).

Essentially, two contrasting views of prehistoric Pueblo politics have been proposed. One view suggests that prehistoric Pueblo societies were economically egalitarian, employed consensual decision making, and lacked ascriptive ranking and authority beyond a single village (Graves et al. 1982; Reid 1985). A second view proposes that a diverse range of organizational forms developed and that for some groups decision making was centralized in the hands of an ascriptively selected managerial elite who integrated inter-village polities, in some cases, through control over economic processes (Lightfoot 1984; Upham 1982; Upham

et al. 1989). Both views imply that economic differentiation is a key to increased political complexity.

Using mortuary data from the ancestral Zuni settlement of Hawikku (or Hawikuh), the burials of likely community leaders were identified. In order to assess whether these leaders controlled aspects of the economy as a foundation of their power, skeletal indicators of diet and general health are compared between leaders and other Hawikku villagers. These comparisons reveal that leaders did not benefit from their position; they were no healthier than nonleaders. Additionally, an examination of leaders' grave goods suggests that they did not control trade or access to nonlocal material. Rather than control over economic processes, it appears that the foundations of political power at Hawikku stem from access to supernatural forces, esoteric knowledge, and the ability to wield coercive force. Results of these analyses, which de-emphasize the role of economic control as a foundation of power, have dramatic implications for our understanding of political evolution in the Pueblo Southwest.

LEADERSHIP AT HAWIKKU

Hawikku, an 800 room ancestral Zuni village occupied from about A.D. 1325–1680 (Kintigh 1985:61), is located 29 km (18 mi) southwest of modern Zuni, New Mexico. Hawikku was excavated between 1917 and 1923 by the Hendricks-Hodge Expedition (Smith et al. 1966). Mortuary data from 955 burials are used in this analysis. About two-thirds of the burials were inhumations, the remainder, cremations. Burials were found primarily in clusters outside the main room blocks.

Identifying Leaders

The theoretical framework I use to identify leaders is derived from the dimensional approach, most fully articulated by Braun (1979) and Whittlesey (1978). A dimension is defined here as an attribute (or set of attributes) of mortuary treatment that survivors used to symbolize a social role (e.g., mother, weaver, chief, priest, aunt, or warrior). This approach is based on the fact that important social roles are often symbolized by specific ritual mortuary behaviors. For example, in a particular society, the placement of a bow and arrow in a grave might symbolize the role of warrior. The approach presumes that a combination of important social roles held in life, selected by societal rules and norms, are symbolized at death.

In most societies, leaders are important people who maintain a large number of social roles. I use "leader" to refer to individuals that make community (or intercommunity) decisions. Other individuals may exercise power and authority in more limited spheres (e.g., the influence of a lineage head over lineage members), but I focus on leaders at the apex of the decision-making structure. The key to identifying leaders using mortuary data is that they hold a larger number of social roles than ordinary citizens. Leaders wear many "hats," reflecting roles such as war leader, dispute arbiter, ambassador, moral role model, ceremonialist, or controller of trade (Feinman and Neitzel 1984:52–53). Zuni ethnography provides an example of the tendency for leaders to hold a large number of social roles. Zuni leaders hold standard kinship roles like any other community member. Membership in the council of priests, the principal decision-making body at Zuni around 1900, was based on other important positions such as priesthood membership or head of the Bow society. Each of these positions, in turn, was based on other achieved and ascribed roles (Eggan 1950).

The methodological challenge for archaeologists is to be able to measure the number of social roles held in life from mortuary remains. Items placed in the grave, special body preparations, and special grave constructions can all symbolize an individual's social roles. To evaluate the number

of social roles held in life, I used a diversity measure, which is a count of the number of different types of grave goods and special body and grave preparations. Because grave goods and special body and grave preparations are potential symbols of social roles, the diversity score should indicate the number of social roles held in life. The diversity score focuses on qualitative differences in mortuary treatment because it is the presence, not quantity, of mortuary treatments and offerings that appears to symbolize a social role (Braun 1979:67; Ravesloot 1988). Leaders are those individuals in the burial population who exhibit high diversity scores.

Some ritual behaviors intended to symbolize social roles are not archaeologically visible (although the use of more than one mortuary attribute to symbolize a social role may mitigate against missing or underestimating the number of social roles). Aside from social roles, other aspects of life could also be symbolized. These aspects often include idiosyncratic personality traits, circumstances of death, age, gender, and economic roles. Despite the fact that different aspects of one's life may be symbolized at death, the vast number of possible social roles (in any society) provides the greatest number of traits that could be symbolized. The diversity measure should therefore provide a reasonable estimate of the relative number of social roles held by individuals in a burial population.

Over 80 grave goods, grave constructions, and body treatments were coded as present or absent for 955 Hawikku burials (all burials except those recovered from the historic church; see Howell 1994 for a description of the burial population). Table 8.1 lists these variables (each is followed by the number of times it occurs). Additional variables such as age, sex, body position, orientation (direction of the head), degree of flexure, and temporal assignments were also coded but not used in the calculation of diversity scores. Figure 8.1 is a histogram of diversity scores, based on the variables listed in table 8.1. Over 50% of the individuals had a diversity score of zero or one, and the number of burials with higher diversity scores progressively decreases. The highest diversity score in the sample is 36. There is a continuous distribution of scores to 16; only four burials scored higher (Burials 113, 193, 915A, and 927A). Since individuals with a high diversity score were community leaders, the four highest diversity burials are the most likely candidates. Table 8.2 displays some of the attributes which distinguish these individuals.

Three of the four are adult females; all three are inhumations, share a southeast orientation (rare at Hawikku,

TABLE 8.1   Coded Mortuary Variables (Numbers in parentheses indicate the number of graves that exhibited each trait or object.)

Special Grave and Body Preparations

Special lining under body[1] (17)
Special lining over body[1] (3)
Grave lined with matting (63)
Stones over body (19)
Body wrapped with matting (24)

Burial Type

Inhumation/Cremation (637/317)
Multiple/Single interment (54/583)
Primary/Secondary inhumation (622/15)

Grave Furnishings

Bow wrist guard[2] (6)
Turquoise[3] (14)
Prayer stick[2] (28)
Shell[3] (50)
Utility ceramic vessel (118)
Decorated bowl (391)
Decorated jar (227)
Ceramic ladle (25)
Ceramic cup (12)
Worked sherd (17)
Duck-shaped ceramic vessel (28)
Miniature ceramic vessel (12)
Projectile point (15)
Projectile point necklace (6)
Stone concretion (8)
Shaped stone fetish (7)
Weaving tool (11)
Paint grinding stone (9)
Flute[4] (3)
Shell necklace (28)
Shell pendant (30)
Shell wrist ornament (6)
Stone pendant (10)
Necklace[5] (18)
Painted wood object (6)
Bow (9)

War club (3)
Arrow shaft (6)
Pipe[4] (5)
Copper object[6] (3)
Quartz crystal (10)
Iron[6] (13)
Raw clay (7)
Medicine[2] (5)
Human hair (5)
Stone axe (3)
Metate (22)
Mano (36)
Hewe stone[2] (8)
Abrader (8)
Stone flakes (27)
Stone knife (30)
Polishing stone (22)
Hammer stone (10)
Pouch[4] (12)
Antler[6] (5)
Kilt (5)
Bark (15)
Fossil shell (2)
Bone needle (2)
Finger ring[4] (3)

Basket (49)
Feather (3)
Bone awl (56)
Green pigment (37)
Blue pigment (8)
Red pigment (8)
Yellow pigment (5)
Black pigment (4)
White pigment (7)
Corn meal (20)
Squash (41)
Pinyon nut (17)
Corn (227)
Bean (56)
Gourd (21)
Bezoar (18)
Turquoise inlay comb (8)
Turquoise necklace (10)
Turquoise ear pendant (3)
Turquoise ear beads (4)
Plain wood comb (4)
Floor/hair brush[2] (5)
Shaped wood object (20)
Mammal skeleton (9)
Bird skeleton (6)

1 Not including matting
2 Identification based on interpretations made by Zuni workmen who worked on the excavation of Hawikku
3 Form unknown
4 Manufactured from any material type
5 Material other than shell, turquoise, or stone
6 All shapes, forms

accounting for less than 8% of the burials), and each body was in an extended and supine position. All of these burials contained corn, squash, manos, decorated ceramic bowls, utility ceramics, metates, and paint grinding stones. Burial 915A had the most elaborate grave preparation of any burial at Hawikku. Thick matting was placed under the head, and the grave was lined with matting. A portion of the burial pit was also lined with sherds and flat stones (a unique form of grave preparation at Hawikku), and the body was wrapped in fabric. A shrine, interpreted by Zuni excavators as being associated with rattlesnake bite, was also erected in the burial pit. This shrine was composed of upright posts and a painted tablet; attached by a string were four feathers, each a separate species (see Smith et al. 1966:216–17 for a more detailed description of the shrine). The pits of Burials 927A and 193 were partially lined with bark. Each of the three females appear to have held many social roles, including a leadership role.

Burial 113 is an adult male inhumation, extended and supine, with an eastern orientation. Matting lined the grave. Accompaniments differed significantly from the three females and included a bow; arrow shafts; war club; human scalp; and green, red, and black pigment. Also present was a finely crafted tubular ceramic pipe, shaped like a bird, with obsidian inlay eyes, an object unique to the Hawikku grave good assemblage. An associated deposit immediately above Burial 113 contained several round pieces of human scalp, prayer sticks, a ladle handle, and rolls of pigment. Burial 113 also probably represents a leadership role, although one different from the three females.

Assuming that the arguments linking diversity of mortuary treatment to leadership are correct, these four individuals were community leaders at Hawikku. It is likely there were additional leaders, given that Hawikku was occupied for at least 300 years. Other individuals who occupied the same leadership roles should have been accorded treatment similar to the four highest diversity burials. I used cluster and correspondence analysis to identify burials treated similarly to the four highest diversity burials.

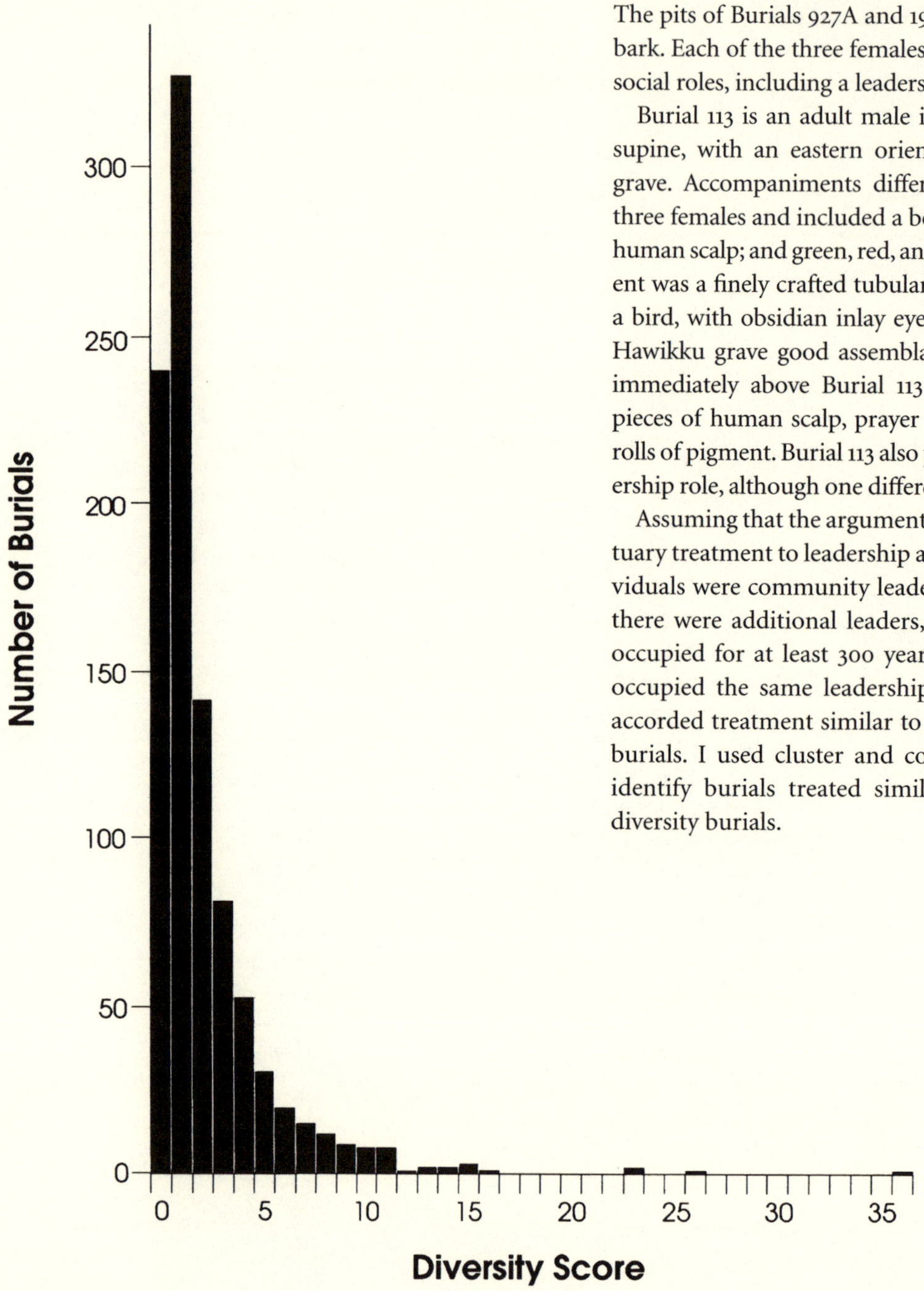

FIGURE 8.1   Histogram of Diversity Scores for 955 Hawikku Burials

TABLE 8.2 Selected Characteristics of High Diversity Burials at Hawikku

	Burial			
Attribute	113	193	915A	927A
Diversity Score	26	23	36	23
Sex	Male	Female	Female	Female
Body Orientation	E	SE	SE	SE
Body Position	E, B1	E, B	E, B	E, B
Grave/Body Preparation				
Grave lined with mat	+2	—	+	—
Other lining under	+	—	+	+
Body wrapped	—	—	+	—
Grave Furnishings				
Corn	+	+	+	+
Squash	+	+	+	+
Utility ceramic	+	+	+	+
Paint grinding stone	+	+	+	+
Mano	—	+	+	+
Metate	—	+	+	+
Human hair	+	—	+	+
Decorated ceramic bowl	—	+	+	+
Arrow shaft	+	—	—	—
Iron object	+	—	—	—
Stone knife	+	—	—	+
War club	+	—	—	—
Prayer stick	+	+	—	+
Pipe	+	—	—	—
Green pigment	+	—	—	—
Red pigment	+	—	—	—
Black pigment	+	—	—	—

1 E refers to extended, B indicates placement on back
2 + indicates item present; — indicates item absent

Searching for Additional Leaders

Since only the highest diversity burials have potential to be leaders, I selected a subset of the original burial population for multivariate analyses. I examined only burials with a diversity score of 8 or higher. This sample includes 50 burials.

Cluster analysis was selected as a means to group similarly treated burials. A number of cluster analyses was performed (based on the variables listed in table 8.1) resulting in groups of similarly treated individuals, including two groups that contained the four highest diversity burials. Four high diversity male burials, including Burial 113 (and Burials 870, 216, and 196) consistently formed an exclusive group. The three highest diversity female burials (Burials 193, 915A, and 927A) consistently

clustered together in a second group, but additional burials in that cluster varied somewhat depending on the clustering algorithm used. However, three burials (Burials 1507, 211A, and 213) were always grouped in this cluster. Two were identified as female; although the skeleton of the third was not sexed, grave goods are consistent with female gender.

The results of the correspondence analysis (CA), using the same set of graves, support the cluster results and suggest the presence of a few additional leaders. CA is mathematically related to principal components and factor analysis but differs from other multivariate techniques by operating directly on raw presence-absence (or count) data rather than on a correlation matrix. It uses a type of chi-square distance as a measure of dissimilarity. CA requires

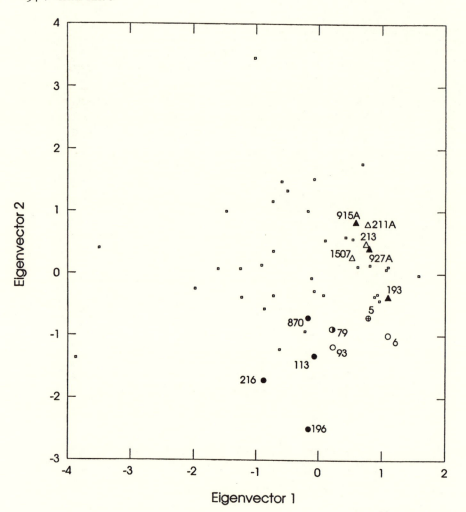

FIGURE 8.2
Correspondence Analysis
Plot of Eigenvectors 1 and 2.
Each dot represents a burial;
those labeled by burial
number are discussed in
the text.

no assumptions concerning the distribution of the data, rendering it a useful archaeological tool (Madsen 1988:14). As with other multivariate techniques, CA attempts to identify a new (and smaller) set of uncorrelated variables from an original (larger) set of variables. The new variables (or eigenvectors) reflect underlying factors which are influenced by more than one of the original variables. Each case (e.g., burial) is assigned a value for each eigenvector. When the eigenvectors are plotted against each other, similar burials will occupy the same space; proximity indicates similarity. Essentially the same data used in the cluster analysis were used in CA, except that two cases with missing data (Burials 916 and 943) were removed from the CA data set because CA is unable to accommodate missing data, and the cremation/inhumation variable was dropped because Burial 943 was the only cremation. Therefore, the CA data matrix contains 48 cases (burials) and 79 variables.

The first three eigenvectors were calculated. Figure 8.2

is a plot of the first two eigenvectors; figure 8.3 plots the second and third eigenvectors. The burials identified by cluster analysis as potential leaders are labeled by burial number, as are a few additional burials, discussed below.

Male Leadership Roles

The four high diversity male burials identified by cluster analysis (Burials 113, 870, 216, and 196) are located in the lower right corner of figures 8.2 and 8.3. They are located near one another (indicating mutual similarity) along the perimeter of the data scatter (indicating dissimilarity to other burials). These four burials are designated Male Group 1. Table 8.3 lists attributes common to these burials. Despite the fact that neither age, gender, or burial type were included in the cluster or correspondence analysis, all four burials are adult male inhumations. All four contained bows, while three of the four contained war clubs, arrows, stone knives, iron objects, corn, green and black pigment, and utility ceramics. Burials 113 and 196 exhibit body wrapping. Traces of black paint were noted on the skull of Burial 196, suggesting the face may have been painted at death. No special body preparation was noted for Burials 870 and 216. Matting lined the graves of Burials 113 and 216; Burials 870 and 196 exhibited no special grave preparation. In addition to the grave furnishings listed in table 8.3, two of the four burials contained shell (a few beads), prayer sticks, decorated ceramic bowls, red pigment, squash, necklaces (other than shell or turquoise), pouches, paint grinding stones, and pipes.

A few additional burials are located in the CA plots near the Male Group 1 burials, indicating mutual similarity. Burials 5, 6, 79, and 93 also appear to represent leaders. All four are adult, but none could be sexed. Accompaniments, however, strongly suggest male gender. Burials 6 and 93 are designated Male Group 1A because of their similarity to

Male Group 1 burials. Burials 5 and 79 are dissimilar to Male Group 1 and 1A burials and differ from each other as well; hence, Burial 5 is designated Male Group 2, and Burial 79, Male Group 3.

The identification of Burials 5, 6, 79, and 93 as probable leaders is based on several factors. Each has a diversity score in the same range as the Male Group 1 burials (table 8.4), and the Male Group 1A burials contained bows and arrows, a hallmark trait of Male Group 1. The strongest indication that Burials 5, 6, 79, and 93 reflect leadership is their association with attributes consistently found with high diversity burials. In order to determine which attributes are most closely linked to leadership, a mean diversity score was calculated for each variable. That is, the diversity scores for every burial (from the sample of 955) in which an attribute was present were summed and divided by the number of burials in which it occurred, resulting in

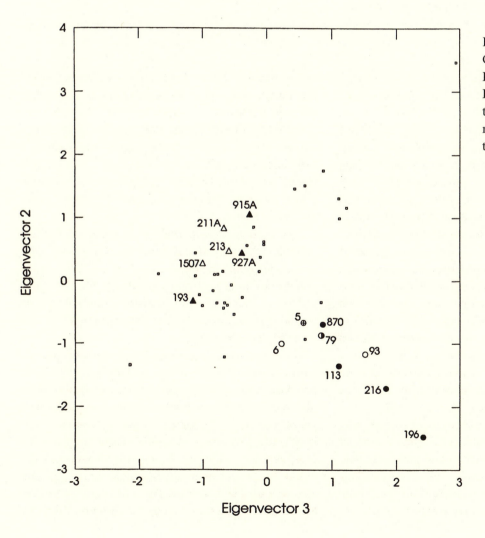

FIGURE 8.3
Correspondence Analysis Plot of Eigenvectors 2 and 3. Each dot represents a burial; those labeled by burial number are discussed in the text.

TABLE 8.3   Selected Mortuary Attributes of Male Group 1 Burials

Attribute	Burial 113	196	216	870
Diversity Score	26	11	11	14
Position	E, B1	E, B	E, B	E, B
Orientation	East	East	East	East
Grave Preparation				
Mat Lining	+	—	+	—
Grave Furnishings				
Bow	+	+	+	+
Arrow	+	—	+	+
War club	+	+	—	+
Corn	+	—	+	+
Utility ceramic	+	+	—	+
Green pigment	+	+	+	—
Black pigment	+	+	+	—
Stone knife	+	—	+	+
Iron object	+	—	+	+

1 E refers to extended, B indicates placement on back.

a mean diversity score for each attribute. This provides a way to identify attributes that are closely linked to high diversity (i.e., leadership). Table 8.5 lists attributes with a mean diversity score greater than or equal to 10 (which I arbitrarily define as high mean diversity values), the number of graves in which the attribute occurs, and the high diversity burials with which it is associated. High mean diversity attributes associated with Burials 5, 6, 79, and 93 are listed at the bottom of table 8.4. The average number of high mean diversity attributes associated with each burial (from the sample of 955) is .21 (with a standard deviation of .94). Less than 1% of all burials are associated with more than 3 high mean diversity attributes. Burials 5, 6, 79, and 93 are associated with between four and seven high mean diversity attributes. By comparison, the number of high mean diversity attributes associated with Male Group 1 burials are equal or higher: Burial 113, 13; Burial 196, 4; Burial 216, 5; and Burial 870, 5. In terms of association with high mean diversity attributes, all eight males are in the upper 1% of Hawikku burials.

Male Group 1 burials share a large number of attributes and probably share a leadership role. Their consistent placement in an exclusive cluster analysis group and their proximity in the CA plots indicate strong similarities. Male Group 1 burials seem to reflect a warfare-related leadership role, as well as a concern with ritual. The triad of bow,

arrow, and war club probably reflects warfare or village defense. War clubs were probably identified as such by Zuni men who worked as excavators for Hodge; they are found exclusively with Male Group 1 burials. The presence of a human scalp with Burial 113 also suggests war leadership. It is conceivable that this role is a precursor to the Bow Priests, who wielded considerable power as the executive arm of the council of priests at Zuni in the 1880s (Pandey 1977; Stevenson 1904).

Zuni excavators recognized Burial 216 as a Bow Priest (as well as Burial 6, discussed below). Stevenson (1904: 315), in describing the burial of a Zuni Bow Priest, notes that the face and neck were painted black (like Burial 196) and that a "war pouch" (similar to ones found with Burials 113 and 196) was among personal belongings buried separately from the Bow Priest.

The presence of pipes, black pigment, and pouches may reflect ritual concerns. Two Male Group 1 burials had pouches containing raw pigments. Pigments, quite possibly used in rituals, were also placed in these graves. Black pigment (described as "sacred" by Zuni excavators) occurs in only four graves—three are Male Group 1 burials. It is possible that the color black (and possibly red, since two of four Male Group 1 burials also contained red pigment) was associated with warfare. These two colors were used by war leaders in a story told to Stevenson regarding the

Pueblo Revolt of 1680: "The keeper [of the Great Shell, a war leader/priest?] and his deputy were nude except for a breechcloth, their bodies and limbs were *painted red . . .* The face of each was *painted black . . .*" (Stevenson 1904:288, emphasis added,). These two colors were also associated with the Bow Priesthood (Stevenson 1904:583, 585). Mortuary ritual associated with the burial of a Bow Priest (observed by Stevenson [1904:315], mentioned above) included wrapping the body with four *red* and *black* blankets.

Male Group 1A includes Burials 93 and 6 and may be temporally antecedent to Male Group 1 (three Male Group 1 burials date to the Historic period, and the fourth could not be dated; based on ceramic associations, Burial 93 is earlier; Burial 6 could not be dated). Bows and arrows suggest a warfare-related role. However, these two burials share very few additional attributes, perhaps indicating that, aside from the war leader role, these two burials shared few

other social roles. Grave offerings associated with Burial 6 not listed in table 8.4 include two flutes, baskets, projectile points, and a grinding stone. Grave construction for Burial 6 was unique; the grave was lined with closely spaced poles, overlaid by bark. Grave furnishings for Burial 93 not listed in table 8.4 include three decorated ceramic bowls, corn, pinyon and squash seeds, a basket, stone flakes, an abrader, and a piece of gypsum.

Male Groups 2 and 3 are more difficult to interpret, although both seem to be concerned with ritual. Burial 5 (Male, Group 2) contained the following high mean diversity variables: gourd, red pigment, painted wood object, kilt, and pouch. Other furnishings not listed in table 8.4 include two decorated ceramic bowls, corn cobs, reeds, a basket, a flute, a bow string guard, and a cord belt. Some of these objects may indicate ritual use. The painted wood object, described as a square, green board, is likely a ceremonial object. Many of the altars described by Stevenson (1904;

TABLE 8.4 Selected Mortuary Attributes of Male Groups 1A, 2, and 3

Attribute	Group 1A		Group 2	Group 3
	93	6	5	79
Diversity Score	16	15	12	11
PositionE, B1	?, ?	E, B	E, B	
Orientation	SE	East	East	East
Grave Preparation				
Mat Lining	+	+	—	+
Common Male Group 1 Grave Furnishings				
Bow	+	+	—	—
Arrow	+	+	—	—
Green pigment	+	+	—	+
Other High Mean Diversity Variables				
Paint grinding stone	+	—	—	—
Fossil shell	+	—	—	—
Shaped wood	—	+	—	—
Bark	—	+	—	—
Medicine	—	+	—	—
Weaving tool	—	+	—	+
Gourd	—	+	+	+
Red pigment	—	—	+	+
Pipe	—	—	—	+
Painted wood	—	—	+	—
Kilt	—	—	+	—
Pouch	—	—	+	—

1 E refers to extended, B indicates placement on back.

TABLE 8.5   Attributes with a High Mean Diversity Score

Attribute	Mean Diversity Score	Number of Graves	Associated High Diversity Burials
Feather	24.3	3	915A, 927A
Human hair	21.2	5	113, 915A, 927A
War club	17.0	3	113, 196, 870
Ring	15.3	3	193, 1507
Floor/Hair brush	14.8	5	113, 1507
Arrow shaft	14.7	6	6, 93, 113, 216, 870
Bone needle	14.5	2	193
Paint grinding stone	14.3	9	93, 113, 193, 927A
Black pigment	13.8	4	113, 196, 216
Kilt	13.2	5	5, 193
Fossil shell	13.0	2	93
Antler	12.9	7	915A, 927A
Painted wood object	12.7	6	5, 915A
Medicine	12.6	5	6, 915A
Pipe	12.4	5	79, 113, 216
Weaving tool	12.3	11	6, 79, 113, 927A
Bow	12.1	10	6, 93, 113, 196, 216, 870
Gourd	11.9	21	5, 6, 79, 113, 193, 915A
Shaped wood object	11.5	22	6, 113, 870, 193, 915A, 927A
Bark	11.1	15	6, 193, 927A
Red pigment	11.0	8	5, 79, 113, 216
Plain wooden comb	10.8	4	213, 927A
Pouch	10.7	12	5, 113, 196, 193
Hewe stone	10.6	8	193, 211A, 213,
Turquoise inlay comb	10.3	8	915A
Raw clay	10.0	7	870, 193

Plates 54, 66, 67, 76, and 77) are composed of similarly shaped and painted wood. The red pigment and gourd (rattle?) could also have ritual uses.

Burial 79 (Male, Group 3) was associated with the following high mean diversity variables: weaving tool (in this case, an entire loom with a blanket attached), gourd, red pigment, and pipe. Other grave furnishings not listed in table 8.4 include three decorated bowls, a basket, squash and pinyon seeds, and corn. Burial 79 may reflect a ceremonial role; pigments, pipe, and gourd could reflect ritual uses.

Female Leadership Roles

The six high diversity females identified by cluster analysis are located near each other in the CA plots in an area that contains the highest density of burials (figures 8.2 and 8.3). Their locations indicate strong similarities with each other and with several nearby burials. None of the attributes common to these six (mano, decorated ceramic bowl, squash, metate, decorated ceramic jar, basket, prayer stick, cornmeal) exhibit a mean diversity score above 10.0 (table 8.6). However, high mean diversity attributes are associated with some of these individuals. Two subgroups can be identified, which I refer to here as Female Groups 1 and 2. Female Group 1 includes the three burials with the highest diversity scores (193, 915A, and 927A). Female Group 2 includes the three with lower diversity scores (1507, 211A, 213). An important distinction between these two subgroups is their strength of association with high mean diversity attributes (listed at the bottom of table 8.6). Female Group 1 burials are associated with between 8 (Burials 915A and 927A) and 10 (Burial 193) high mean diversity attributes. Female Group 2 burials are associated with 3 or fewer high mean diversity attributes (Burial 1507, 3; Burial 211A, 1; Burial 213, 2). Female Group 1 burials are in the upper 1% of the sample in terms of the number of high mean diversity variables with which they are associated; Female Group 2 members are not. The significance of this difference is discussed below.

All six of these burials share a core of traits, including grinding tools (mano, metate), storage and serving vessels (ceramic jars and bowls, baskets), food (squash), and ceremonial items (prayer sticks). Cornmeal is also common and could fall into the category of food or possibly ritual (cornmeal was used in rituals during the 1880s [Stevenson 1904] and probably earlier). Most of these grave furnishings are relatively common. These traits probably reflect a shared social role, or suite of roles, held by all six women. The emphasis on domestic items used in household food preparation, storage, and serving, and on ritual items, suggests that this shared role may be analogous to the head of a matriline or some equivalent role. If this shared role was analogous to a matriline head, it reflects a leadership role with a limited sphere of influence and authority.

In addition to this shared role, Female Group 1 burials appear to exhibit a more important leadership role, based on a strong association with high mean diversity attributes, including shaped wooden objects, feathers, human hair, paint-grinding stones, antler, bark, and gourds. Several of these attributes are probably associated with ritual activities. Paint-grinding stones could reflect secular or ceremonial use. Shaped wooden objects were also potentially ritual objects; the shaped wood from Burial 915A was part of a rattlesnake bite shrine. Zuni excavators identified Burial 915A as a "Medicine Priestess," based on the presence of the shrine and medicinal plants, such as datura (*Datura meteloides*) stalks and roots, and a root the Zuni called *Akwa-Ahona*, which was used to cure stomach ailments. Stevenson (1993:5) observed in 1908 that only rain priests or directors of the Little Fire or Cimex fraternities could administer datura. Gourds may have originally functioned as ceremonial rattles. The feathers associated with 915A were part of the shrine, while the feathers with Burial 927A were the remains of a feather cloth (the only occurrence of such an artifact). These objects suggest individuals in Female Group 1 held a leadership role concerned with ritual or religion.

TABLE 8.6   Selected Mortuary Attributes of High Diversity Female Burials

	Female Group 2			Female Group 1		
Attribute	1507	211A	213	915A	927A	193
Diversity Score	13	9	9	36	23	23
Position E, B1	E, B	E, B	E, B	E, ?	E, B	
Orientation	E	E	E	SE	SE	SE
Body Preparation						
Wrapped	+	—	+	+	—	—
Common Grave Furnishings						
Mano	+	+	+	+	+	+
Bowl	+	+	+	+	+	+
Metate	+	+	—	+	+	+
Ceramic jar	+	+	+	+	—	+
Basket	+	+	—	+	+	+
Prayer stick	+	—	+	—	+	+
Cornmeal	—	+	+	+	+	—
Squash	—	+	—	+	+	+
High Mean Diversity Variables						
Shaped wood	—	—	—	+	+	+
Feather	—	—	—	+	+	—
Human hair	—	—	—	+	+	—
Paint grinding stone	+	—	—	—	+	+
Antler	—	—	—	+	+	—
Gourd	—	—	—	+	—	+

1 E refers to extended, B indicates placement on back

Perhaps the most intriguing attribute associated with Female Group 1 is human hair (as a contributed grave good). Masses of human hair were found along both sides of Burial 927A, along with a human hair cord. Burial 915A contained a band of human hair. Human hair (in the form of scalps, braided cords, or masses) occurred in 5 of 955 burials (0.5%). The significance of human hair as a grave offering is unclear but may point to trophies, similar to scalps, or the use of human hair in craft production.

ASSESSING THE ROLE OF ECONOMIC CONTROL

To what degree did these leaders rely on economic control as a source of power? I assess this possible relationship two ways. First, biological data are used to assess the degree to which Hawikku's leaders depended on economic control as a foundation of power. If certain leaders at Hawikku controlled subsistence production in some way, it may be reflected by better nutrition among leaders (as compared to nonleaders). I also examine the degree to which mortuary offerings in leaders' graves reflect control of trade.

Health and Leadership

If leaders controlled some aspects of subsistence production, it might have been reflected in better health. The economic advantage might also have extended to a leader's kin. If a leaders' kin group could control usufruct rights to the best agricultural land, they might enjoy higher yields than other kin groups. A higher yield could help assure food during lean years. If tribute, in the form of subsistence items such as a portion of the first harvest or portion of deer meat, was owed to leaders, they and their kin also might maintain better nutrition and health. Similarly, if leaders were responsible for the distribution of stockpiled food during lean times, they and their families might obtain better, or more regular, access. Parsons (1929:158) noted that historic Zuni town chiefs had access to corn stores and were responsible for their distribution during times of stress.

Previous research, based on comparisons of dental morphology and other data, indicates that cemeteries at Hawikku were used by specific kin groups (see Howell and Kintigh 1996 and Howell 1994:49–76 for a more detailed presentation of this research). Leaders were found in 2 of 11 cemeteries. Since cemeteries can be equated with kin groups, health data can be used not only to compare leaders with nonleaders but also to compare leader's kin with other kin groups.

Three biological data sets are used here: age at death, incidence of iron-deficiency anemia, and stature.[1] Table 8.7 summarizes these data. Each is a rough measure of overall physiological health and stress, and is described in more detail below. A serious limitation of these data has to do with the available sample size. A total of 266 skeletons from Hawikku is preserved at the National Museum of Natural History, Smithsonian Institution. These data were recorded by Ann Stodder on 185 individuals, of which 156 can be associated with an exact burial number (these data are reported in Howell 1994: 211–213). Preservation of the human remains is variable, which makes age, sex, and biological data impossible to collect in some cases. These small sample size issues are compounded when the sample is divided by sex and cemetery. Sample sizes are, therefore provided for each comparison discussed below.

STATURE ESTIMATES

Adult stature is a measure of overall physiological stress. Adult stature is influenced by a number of different processes, each "acting simultaneously on the human organism" (Hatch 1987:12). Original parameters are genetically determined but are then influenced by nutrition, disease, and psychological fitness (Hatch 1987:12). A more stable and well-rounded diet should be reflected by greater adult height, on average. If leaders and their kin groups enjoyed a more stable and well-rounded subsistence than others, this difference may reflect some form of control over subsistence production. Hatch (1987) used stature as a measure of overall physiological stress to compare individuals from mound interments (believed to be elites) to nonmound interments (nonelites) in Dallas society. He found that adults buried in mounds were taller than nonmound burials but only the difference between males was statistically significant.

Stature estimates are based on the length of the tibia in all but three cases (where femur length was used). The formulae used for the stature estimates is discussed by Santiago (1967). In order to test for stature differences, only adults can be used, and sexual dimorphism requires within-gender comparisons. Stature measurements are available for three of the Male Group 1 interments (Burials 196, 216, and 870). Their average stature is 164.3 cm. All other adult males (for whom stature could be calculated, n = 23) had an average stature of 165.2 cm. Cemeteries 1 and 9 are the cemeteries (kin groups) that furnished male leaders. The mean stature for males in these two cemeteries is 165.5 cm; the mean male stature for males in other cemeteries is 164.4 cm. These results are not statistically significant and suggest no apparent difference in stature between the Male Group 1 burials and other males, or between males in Cemeteries 1 and 9 and males in other cemeteries.

Stature measurements are available for one Female Group 1 Burial (915A), and two Female Group 2 burials (211A, 213). The stature for 915A is 159.8 cm; only two other females were taller. Pooled, the mean stature for these three females is 158.5 cm, compared to 153.6 cm for all other females for which stature could be calculated (n = 44). This difference is statistically significant (T-test, separate variances, p = .001). The mean stature for females buried in Cemeteries 1 and 9 (n = 29) is 154.7 cm; mean stature for females buried elsewhere (n = 16) is 152.9 cm. Although individuals from the two cemeteries that furnished the three high diversity females were, on average, 2 cm taller than females from other kin groups, this difference is not statistically significant (T-test, separate variances, p = .197).

TABLE 8.7 Physiological Health and Stress Data

Burial	Age at Death	Stature (in cm)	Incidence of Anemia
Male Groups 1A, 2 & 3			
5		No data available	
6		No data available	
79		No data available	
93		No data available	
Male Group 1			
113	26–30	n/a	n/a
196	55+	168.2	n/a
216	22–23	167.4	+
870	19–21	157.3	+
Female Group 1			
193		No data available	
915A	25	159.8	+
927A	22–24	n/a	+
Female Group 2			
211A	31–33	158.2	n/a
213	28–30	157.6	+
1507		No data available	
Cemeteries 1 & 9	mean = 24.2*	mean for males = 165.5, std. dev. = 3.38; mean for females = 154.7, std. dev. = 3.79	82.6%
All other cemeteries	mean = 22.2*	mean for males = 164.4, std. dev. = 5.26; mean for females = 152.9, std dev. = 4.24	94.4%

* Calculated for all ages

AGE AT DEATH

Overall life stress can be measured, albeit crudely, by age at death. Differences in diet, disease, sanitation, and work combine to affect one's age at death. Other factors, such as genetic predisposition toward particular diseases or random events such as trauma or accident, are also important. Nevertheless, age at death offers a general, indirect measure of overall life stress.

Estimated age at death takes the form of a single age in years or, more commonly, an age range (e.g., 16–18 years). For those cases exhibiting an age range, an average of the range was calculated and used for comparative purposes. In a few instances, older individuals were given an age range bracketed on the lower end, but not the upper end (e.g., 45+). In these cases, the lower age estimate was used. The mean age at death for males (34.9) is seven years greater than females (27.9). Because of this difference, the data were sorted by sex in order to compare leaders to others. For the males, only the Male Group 1 burials have age estimates. The mean for these four males is 31.4; for all other males (for which there are available data, n = 45) it is 34.9. Based on this overall life stress measure, male leaders did not benefit from their position. For the high diversity females, age at death is available for two Group 1 (915A, 927A) and two Group 2 (211A, 213) burials. Pooled, the mean age at death for these four is 27.3; for all other females (for which there are available data, n = 67) the mean age at death is 28.0. High diversity females, based on age at death, did not benefit from their positions.

In order to compare kin groups of leaders (i.e., Cemeteries 1 and 9) to other kin groups, all available data were used, including individuals of all ages. For Cemeteries 1 and 9, the mean age at death is 24.2, and for the remaining kin groups, it is 22.2. This difference is not statistically significant (T-test, separate variances, p = .44).

IRON DEFICIENCY ANEMIA

Another measure of overall physiological stress is iron-deficiency anemia. In cases of iron-deficiency anemia, abnormal changes occur in the skull, commonly referred to as porotic hyperostosis. The causes of iron-deficiency anemia are varied (Carlson et al. 1974; El-Najjar 1976; Hengen 1971; Kent 1986; Lallo et al. 1977; Palkovich 1987; Reinhard 1988; Stodder 1990; Stuart-Macadam 1992). Each prehistoric case must be examined in light of specific behavioral, ecological, and physiological variables to determine the specific etiology of iron-deficiency anemia in a given population (Carlson et al. 1974:409; Palkovich

1987; Reinhard 1988:362–63; Stodder 1990:205). Endemic patterns of iron-deficiency anemia can be caused by congenital (genetic) factors, a diet low in iron, and infection (skeletal and/or parasitic). Secondary factors include ecology and behavior. No congenital or genetic factors have been found in aboriginal New World populations to account for endemic iron-deficiency anemia (El-Najjar 1976); thus, diet and infection are likely the primary factors in Pueblo groups.

Diets low in meat and high in grains such as maize are iron-deficient. Maize contains little utilizable iron (Dallman et al. 1980:90). Diets high in maize have been characteristic of sedentary agriculturalists in the American Southwest and have been invoked as the primary cause of iron-deficiency anemia and porotic hyperostosis (El-Najjar 1976). Stodder (1990:202) cites ethnographic accounts of culinary ash use, which, if practiced prehistorically, would enhance iron availability in a diet high in maize. Age and physiological status are also important. Pregnant females and children are most susceptible to dietary imbalances because of an increased need for iron.

Infection has also been cited as the primary cause of iron-deficiency anemia (Kent 1986; Stuart-Macadam 1992). Many pathogens require iron for their metabolism yet lack an internal store (Stuart-Macadam 1992:41). Stuart-Macadam suggests that mild iron deficiency may be a physiological response to parasitic infection, i.e., the body withholds iron from parasites. Some parasites, such as hookworms, result in loss of blood and, therefore, anemic conditions.

Reinhard (1988) examined the incidence of helminth parasites from coprolites at Antelope House and Salmon Ruin. The incidence of helminth infection at Salmon was much lower than at Antelope House, and Reinhard attributed this contrast, in part, to behavioral differences. At Antelope House, coprolites were somewhat randomly distributed in rooms, enhancing the probability of disease spread. At Salmon Ruin, specialized rooms were utilized as latrines, which lowered the probability of disease spread. Reinhard also cites ecological constraints which can inhibit or enhance the viability of parasites; moist habitats such as canyon bottoms are more conducive to parasite survival than arid settings (Reinhard 1988:356).

While several factors may effect the incidence of iron-deficiency anemia, it is a good measure of overall physiological stress. At Hawikku, Stodder (1990:220) suggests that both diet and infection influence the incidence of porotic hyperostosis.

Anemia was scored as present or absent. Anemia was coded as present in cases of porotic hyperostosis and cribra orbitalia and includes all states (e.g., active, remodeled, healed). Anemia data are available for two Male Group 1 burials (Burials 216, 870), two Female Group 1 burials (915A, 927A), and one Female Group 2 burial (213). All five of these individuals exhibit iron-deficiency anemia. However, there is a difference in the incidence of anemia between cemeteries that produced leaders (Cemeteries 1 and 9) and other cemeteries. For Cemeteries 1 and 9, 82.6% exhibit iron-deficiency anemia, while 94.4% of individuals in other cemeteries exhibit anemia. This difference is not statistically significant at the .05 level (Person chi-square p = .09, Adeste correction p = .16).

Individuals holding important social roles did not lead longer, healthier lives than their fellow villagers. Statistically, leaders were no better off than other citizens, with the exception of female stature. The fact that women holding leadership and other important social roles were among the tallest in the village may reflect a genetic, kinship link, as suggested by earlier work (Howell and Kintigh 1996). However the overall pattern that emerges suggests that control over aspects of the economy was not a major source of political power.

The kin groups that furnished leaders were generally somewhat better off than other kin groups. Kin groups furnishing leaders lived, on average, two years longer, exhibited less anemia, and had taller females than other kin groups. Although only female stature differences are statistically significant, these results seem to constitute a weak pattern. It is conceivable that kin groups providing leaders enjoyed a small economic advantage of some sort. This may have taken the form of access to better agricultural land, or they may have had access to a broader network of kin from which to rely on in times of need. Cemetery 9 is by far the largest cemetery, and Cemetery 1 is the third largest.

Control of Trade

As indicated above, control of subsistence probably did not form a major foundation of power at Hawikku. A different aspect of control of economic relations that has been linked to Puebloan leadership is differential access to, or control of, trade (Neitzel 1989). Chacoan leaders seem to have controlled trade in some way, as evidenced by the huge quantities of turquoise and shell placed in their graves (Akins and Schelberg 1984:91). If Hawikku leaders controlled trade, their graves do not reflect it. Leaders'

graves do not contain large quantities of turquoise, marine shell, obsidian artifacts, or intrusive vessels. Only one or two intrusive ceramic vessels are associated with leaders' graves. Burial 915A contained a Salado Red vessel, and Burial 915A contained an unusual vessel, typologically unidentifiable, that may be intrusive. Shell was present in only a few high diversity graves in the form of a few beads. Turquoise was rarely found in high diversity graves. One high diversity female had a turquoise inlay comb made from *reused* beads, hardly what one might expect if it functioned as a badge of office. No shell artifacts and only one turquoise artifact class exhibit a mean diversity score above 10 (see table 8.5). Shell and turquoise simply did not function as symbols of leadership in Hawikku society. In fact, shell is found most commonly in subadult graves. If shell, turquoise, obsidian and nonlocal vessels were not symbols of leadership, leaders probably did not control the trade in these commodities.

DISCUSSION

It seems likely, based on the evidence presented above, that economic control was not a primary foundation of power at Hawikku. If leaders did not rely primarily on economic control, what was the foundation of power? The following interpretation is speculative but consistent with what is known about Hawikku society. Within an egalitarian ethos, leaders probably manipulated ideology as a primary foundation of power. Items likely used in rituals are prominent in most of the high diversity burials. It seems likely that many of these individuals (except perhaps for the Female Group 2 individuals) played important roles in religious life. As such, they had the ability to influence ideology as a way to access, reinforce, or legitimize their power (or, conversely, undermine the position of others). Leaders were ascriptively selected at Hawikku (Howell and Kintigh 1996); this may be a result of ideological manipulation. Such manipulation is likely a lengthy process with successive generations of leaders making small changes. Differential access to esoteric knowledge was an important determinant to social status in nineteenth and twentieth century Zuni society. Upham (1982:32) suggests the same processes characterized Zuni leadership during the contact period, based on statements made in contact period documents. Control over access to knowledge is a likely outcome of ideological manipulation.

It appears that by controlling ideology, some leaders were also able to control coercive force. If Male Group 1 and 1A burials represent precursors to the historic Bow Priest roles, they likely wielded considerable force in maintaining social control within the pueblo as well as defense against outside forces. The importance of warfare in male leadership roles seems to have increased through time during the occupation of Hawikku as a response to the Spanish presence and Athabaskan raiding (Howell 1995). Male leadership roles were exclusively linked to warfare after Spanish contact. The results of this analysis suggest archaeologists studying political power should begin to focus on the manipulation of ideology and control of coercive force, rather than economic control. Such a shift in focus should result in a better understanding of political evolution in the Pueblo Southwest, and perhaps elsewhere.

NOTES

1. Dr. Ann L. W. Stodder examined the collection in order to assess the health status of protohistoric populations in the American Southwest. Dr. Stodder has graciously provided me access to data concerning age at death, sex, stature, and iron-deficiency. These data are provided in Appendix B of my dissertation (Howell 1994). I should note that in Smith et al. (1966), 266 individuals are reported to be housed at the National Museum of Natural History, Smithsonian Institution, and 130 are associated with provenience data.

ACKNOWLEDGMENTS

Discussions with Keith Kintigh and T. J. Ferguson helped me to refine some of my thoughts about leadership at Hawikku, and K. Diane Kimbrell Howell provided editorial assistance.

REFERENCES CITED

Akins, Nancy J., and John D. Schelberg
1984   Evidence for Organizational Complexity as Seen from the Mortuary Practices at Chaco Canyon. In *Recent Research on Chaco Prehistory*, edited by W. James Judge and J. D. Schelberg, pp. 89–102. Division of Cultural Research, Albuquerque.

Braun, David P.
1979   Illinois Hopewell Burial Practices and Social Organization: A Reexamination of the Klunk-Gibson Mound Group. In *Hopewell Archaeology, the Chillicothe Conference*, edited by W. J. Judge and J. D. Schelberg, pp. 89–102. Reports of the Chaco Center No. 8. National Park Service, Albuquerque.

Carlson, David S., George Armelagos, and Dennis P. Van Gerven
1974   Factors Influencing the Etiology of Cribra Orbitalia in Prehistoric Nubia. *Journal of Human Evolution* 3:405–10.

Dallman, P. R., M. A. Siimes, and A. Stekel
1980   Iron Deficiency in Infancy and Childhood. *American Journal of Clinical Nutrition* 33:86–118.

Earle, Timothy
1989   The Evolution of Chiefdoms. *Current Anthropology* 30:84–88.

Eggan, Fred
1950   *Social Organization of the Western Pueblos.* University of Chicago Press, Chicago.

El-Najjar, Mahmoud Y.
1976   Maize, Malaria and the Anemias in the Pre-Columbian New World. *Yearbook of Physical Anthropology* 20:239–337.

Feinman, Gary, and Jill Neitzel
1984   Too Many Types: An Overview of Sedentary Prestate Societies in the Americas. *Advances in Archaeological Method and Theory*, vol. 7, edited by M. B. Schiffer, pp. 39–102. Academic Press, New York.

Fried, Morton H.
1967   The Evolution of Political Society. Random House, New York.

Graves, Michael W., William A. Longacre, and Sally J. Holbrook
1982   Aggregation and Abandonment at Grasshopper Pueblo, Arizona. *Journal of Field Archaeology* 9:193–206.

Hatch, James W.
1987   Mortuary Indicators of Organizational Variability among Late Prehistoric Chiefdoms on the Southeastern U.S. Interior. In *Chiefdoms in the Americas*, edited by R. Drennan and C. Uribe, pp. 9–18. University Press of America, Lanham, Maryland.

Hengen, O. P.
1971   Cribra Orbitalia: Pathogenesis and Probable Etiology. *Homo* 22:57–75.

Howell, Todd L.
1994　*Leadership at the Ancestral Zuni Village of Hawikku*. Unpublished Ph.D. dissertation, Department of Anthropology, Arizona State University, Tempe.
1995　Tracking Zuni Gender and Leadership Roles Across the Contact Period. *Journal of Anthropological Research* 51:125–47.

Howell, Todd L., and Keith W. Kintigh
1996　Archaeological Identification of Kin Groups Using Mortuary and Biological Data: An Example from the American Southwest. *American Antiquity* 61:537–54.

Kent, Susan
1986　The Influence of Sedentism and Aggregation on Porotic Hyperostosis and Anemia: A Case Study. *Man* 21:605–36.

Kintigh, Keith W.
1985　*Settlement, Subsistence, and Society in Late Zuni Prehistory*. Anthropological Papers No. 44. University of Arizona, Tucson.

Lallo, John W., George J. Armelagos, and Robert P. Mensforth
1977　The Role of Diet, Disease, and Physiology in the Origin of Porotic Hyperostosis. *Human Biology* 49:471–83.

Lightfoot, Kent G.
1984　*Prehistoric Political Dynamics: A Case Study from the American Southwest*. Northern Illinois University Press, De Kalb.

Madsen, Torsten
1988　Multivariate Statistics and Archaeology. In *Multivariate Archaeology, Numerical Approaches in Scandinavian Archaeology*, edited by T. Madsen, pp. 7–27. Jutland Archaeological Society Publications XXI, Hojbjerg.

Neitzel, Jill
1989　Regional Exchange Networks in the American Southwest, A Comparative Analysis of Long Distance Trade. In *The Sociopolitical Structure of Prehistoric Southwestern Societies*, edited by S. Upham, K. G. Lightfoot, and R. A. Jewett, pp. 149–98. Westview Press, Boulder.

Palkovich, Ann M.
1987　Endemic Disease Patterns in Paleopathology: Porotic Hyperostosis. *American Journal of Physical Anthropology* 74:527–37.

Pandey, Triloki Nath
1977　Images of Power in a Southwestern Pueblo. In *The Anthropology of Power*, edited by R. D. Fogelson and R. N. Adams, pp. 195–215. Academic Press, New York.

Parsons, Elsie Clews
1929　*The Social Organization of the Tewa of New Mexico*. Memoirs of the American Anthropological Association No. 36. Menasha, Wisconsin.

Ravesloot, John C.
1988　*Mortuary Practices and Social Differentiation at Cases Grandes, Chihuahua, Mexico*. Anthropological Papers No. 49. University of Arizona Press, Tucson.

Reid, J. Jefferson
1985　Measuring Social Complexity in the American Southwest. In *Status, Structure and Stratification: Current Archaeological Reconstructions*, edited by M. Thompson, M. T. Garcia, and F. J. Kense, pp. 167–74. The Archaeological Association of the University of Calgary, Calgary.

Reinhard, Karl J.
1988　Cultural Ecology of Prehistoric Parasitism on the Colorado Plateau as Evidenced by Coprology. *American Journal of Physical Anthropology* 77:355–66.

Sahlins, Marshall
1963　Poor Man, Rich Man, Big Man, Chief: Political Types in Melanesia and Polynesia. *Comparative Studies in Society and History* 5:285–303.

Santiago, Genovese
1967　Proportionality of the Long Bones and Their Relation to Stature among Mesoamericans. *American Journal of Physical Anthropology* 26:67–78.

Smith, Watson, Richard B. Woodbury, and Nathalie F. S. Woodbury
1966　*The Excavation of Hawikuh By Frederick Webb Hodge, Report of the Hendricks-Hodge Expedition 1917–1923*. Museum of the American Indian Heye Foundation, New York.

Stevenson, Matilda Coxe
1904　The Zuni Indians: Their Mythology, Esoteric Fraternities, and Ceremonies. In *Twenty-third Annual Report of the Bureau of American Ethnology, 1901–2*, by J. W. Powell, pp. 3–634. U.S. Government Printing Office, Washington, D.C.
1993　*The Zuni Indians and Their Uses of Plants*. Dover Publications, New York.

Stodder, Ann L. W.
  1990   *Paleoepidemiology of Eastern and Western
            Pueblo Communities in Protohistoric New
            Mexico.* Unpublished Ph.D. Dissertation,
            Department of Anthropology, University of
            Colorado, Boulder.
Stuart-Macadam, Patty
  1992   Porotic Hyperostosis: A New Perspective.
            American Journal of Physical Anthropology
            87:39–47.
Upham, Steadman
  1982   *Polities and Power: An Economic and Political
            History of the Western Pueblos.* Academic
            Press, New York.

Upham, Steadman, Kent G. Lightfoot,
    and Roberta A. Jewett (editors)
  1989   *The Sociopolitical Structure of Prehistoric
            Southwestern Societies.* Westview Press,
            Boulder.
Whittlesey, Stephanie M.
  1978   *Status and Death at Grasshopper Pueblo:
            Experiment Toward an Archaeological Theory
            of Correlates.* Unpublished Ph.D. dissertation,
            Department of Anthropology, University of
            Arizona, Tucson.

CHAPTER NINE

Chaco Canyon Mortuary Practices
Archaeological Correlates of Complexity

Nancy J. Akins

A SAMPLING OF THE MORE CURRENT VIEWS ON Chaco Canyon ranges from Chaco being considered ordinary to Chaco representing the apex of a tribute-supported, militant hierarchy maintained by fear and retribution. The Chacoan system is exemplified by monumental architecture, which represents one aspect of a wide-spread settlement system comprised of great houses surrounded by smaller sites and by roads linking sites in Chaco Canyon with other great houses throughout the Four Corners area. This linkage implies a region-wide organization centered around Chaco, in at least the tenth and eleventh centuries. There is a general consensus that developments, as represented by construction of suites of large rooms at Pueblo Bonito, Peñasco Blanco, and Una Vida within the canyon and at a number of outlying sites, had begun by at least A.D. 860 (Windes and Ford 1992:77, 1996:301) and probably had roots stretching back to Basketmaker times (e.g., Fowler and Stein 1992:113; Schelberg 1984:6). There also is some agreement that after A.D. 1150, the focus of the system once centered at Chaco shifted northward (Fowler and Stein 1992:119; Upham et al. 1994:207). Beyond this, there is little consensus.

Archaeologists' views of the local environment are wide ranging. Some see it as impoverished, requiring extraordinary measures to survive; others view it as adequate, while some view the environment as a relative oasis at

certain times in the past. Perceptions of organization or managerial requirements range from no greater than the household level to varying degrees of social inequity. These views on environment and organizational properties combine in almost endless ways. The following are but a sampling of how researchers use one or the other to reach disparate explanations of the system. Numerous other views combine one or more aspects of these as well as additional perspectives.

Judge's view of the system is one initiated by independent communities linked by reciprocity and normal trade (Judge 1989:234–45). Within this framework, Chaco came to dominate turquoise ornament manufacture. The community used this ritually important commodity as a buffer against resource deficiencies brought about by the generally marginal potential for agriculture in Chaco and the rest of the San Juan Basin. Alliance networks between outlying communities, which became formalized through exchange of nonritual goods, came to be controlled by a few elite individuals from a center of ritual dominance at Chaco (Judge 1989:239–40). The great-house sites were scenes of pilgrimage fairs where visitors consumed goods and services under a ritual metaphor (Judge 1989:241–43).

Dean (1992:38) believes that Chaco was one of the best watered locales in the Basin, especially in the tenth and eleventh centuries. His analysis of environmental variability, based on patterns of aggradation and degradation, hydrological variability, effective moisture, dendroclimatic variably, and spatial variability, indicated that beginning around A.D. 925 fluvial aggradation periodically renewed the soil and that groundwater levels were high. Under these conditions, amplified by bedrock geology, Chaco was effectively immune to deficiencies and fluctuations in precipitation. To Dean, the area was capable of supporting a large number of people with simple subsistence technology, at least until the population reached some critical threshold. Once this threshold was reached, water collection and management systems became necessary, and fluctuations in rainfall made a difference. Enhanced predictability between A.D. 900–1150 improved the management of water control and food production while increasing spatial variably in rainfall amplified production differential within the basin, insuring economic interaction and regional-scale behavioral responses to resource stress and economic uncertainty (Dean 1992:38–39, 1996:45).

Others (e.g., Windes and Ford 1992:82–83, 1996:308–9), rely on indications of above normal rainfall in the A.D. 900s for stimulating events in and around Chaco. For them, increased runoff allowed aggregation and greater agricultural production at the sites of side tributaries to the Chaco Wash and other drainages. Local aggregation and agricultural success caused the great houses to be built to store food surpluses. These early communities were essentially independent and no more integrated than in Basketmaker times but became the center of an integrated region in the eleventh century.

Assuming that prehistoric farmers could plant and grow more food than they needed, Sebastian (1991:127–32) sees overproduction and multiyear storage as providing the opportunity for sociopolitical development. During the less productive years of the early A.D. 900s, those commanding the most productive lands were able to create obligations through their generosity and turn those obligations into a labor force for building great houses. More favorable conditions from the A.D. 940s through 990s suppressed their ability to engender obligations. The following 30 years of variable productivity and numerous years of low productivity allowed those with more productive land to convert their relative success into permanent leadership roles and maintain those roles by convincing others that their success was due to special access to the supernatural realm. These leaders were able to mobilize the

labor necessary to expand the great houses, which also served ritual purposes. Competition for followers eventually caused great-house activities to turn inward, and combined with a number of less productive years, weakened the religious power base of the Chaco Canyon leaders as the arena of competition moved elsewhere in the San Juan Basin.

The most extreme view of the Chaco system is that of Wilcox (1993:76–90), who proposed that by the late A.D. 800s, Pueblo Bonito was the domain of suprahousehold elites residing in a "marginal agricultural oasis." By the early eleventh century, Chaco had become a tribute-demanding polity that began to advance against its more agriculturally successful neighbors. An organized force of warriors used the roads radiating out of Chaco to travel to peripheral areas and pillage and collect tribute which was stored in central storerooms. Chacoan outliers served to incorporate a community into the polity and regularize tribute demands. Great kivas were places where the cult was performed. Pueblo Bonito is viewed as the burial place of at least one high-ranking war leader as well as the burial location for tribute or war captives sacrificed during periodic religious ceremonies.

Mortuary practices and the general health of the Chaco burials are seen as strong evidence for inequity, reviewed without comment, ignored completely, or even treated as an aberrance. The remainder of this chapter first describes burial recovery and mortuary practices in the Chaco Canyon, briefly reviews principals derived from cross-cultural studies of mortuary practices, then applies these principals to the workings of the Chaco system. A detailed description of the mortuary practices is included because this information is drawn from many sources and the patterning is important for the understanding of the timing and the nature of the Chaco system.

CHACO BURIALS

Fascination with Chaco burials has a long and often undocumented history. Museum catalogs, and archival and published material document the finding and removal of Chaco Canyon burials from at least 1877 when W. H. Jackson is credited with finding a human skull near Pueblo del Arroyo. Typical of the early years are visits such as that of F. T. Bickford who spent eight days searching for burials or Richard Wetherill who stayed long enough to collect 40 pieces of pottery in 1895 (letter to Talbot Hyde dated December 1895) (Akins 1986:7; McNitt 1966:113; Vivian 1990:44). Warren K. Moorehead, a curator at Ohio State University, stopped and excavated in a few rooms at Pueblo Bonito and in a small cemetery to make a collection of skeletons and pottery vessels (McNitt 1966:178; Moorehead 1906). Histories of excavation in Chaco Canyon can be found in Judge (1991:11–14), Lister and Lister (1981), and Vivian (1990:37–69), and a history of burial removal in Akins (1986:7–12).

In spite of numerous amateur and professional forays into Chaco Canyon, amazingly little information exists on Chaco burials. Much has been lost, and the surviving documentation is dispersed and varies in the quality of information recorded. The bulk of the information comes from work done by the School of American Research/University of New Mexico (SAR/UNM), the American Museum of Natural History, the National Geographic Society, the National Park Service (NPS) Ruin Stabilization Unit, and the Chaco Project. Documentation of the SAR/UNM and NPS work is largely archival and often contains conflicting information concerning dating, the age and sex of the individual, positioning, and objects associated with the burial. Published accounts are often incomplete and require review of field notes and catalog cards to compile a description.

In analyzing Chaco burial practices, all information, published and archival, was amassed along with current assessments of the age and sex. Tom Windes of the NPS examined the burial vessels housed at the Maxwell Museum of Anthropology (SAR/UNM collections) and those at the Chaco Center (NPS and Chaco Project) to insure accuracy of those identifications. Field sketches of ceramic designs and photographs also were used to establish chronology. Context and sherd counts were checked for those individuals buried without diagnostic objects to at least bracket the time span.

The above study resulted in a sample of 179 burials, 153 from small sites and 26 from great houses. Approximately 130 individuals from small sites and many of the great-house burials lacked essential information and were eliminated from at least some aspects of the analysis. For instance, a good number of burials were described as disturbed (about 40), many consisting of only a few elements. In other instances, some burials from middens of multicomponent sites frequently had no associated vessels or sherd counts and could not be dated. Other burials had vessels but the vessels were not described. Chronological placement was considered essential for the analysis; therefore, burials that could not be dated were not used in the analysis. A complete listing of the date, age, sex, location, position, grave preparation, ceramics, ornaments, other objects, comments, and information source for each burial can be found in Akins 1986:table B.1.

Burials in the resulting sample were assigned dates based on the associated ceramics, sherd counts, and context. Since the predominant black-on-white ceramic types overlap the traditional Pecos chronology, these were divided into burials associated with Basketmaker to early Red Mesa Black-on-white ceramics (pre A.D. 925), those associated with Red Mesa Black-on-white ceramics (A.D. 900–1050), those associated with Gallup Black-on-white ceramics (A.D. 1030–1150), those associated with McElmo Black-on-white ceramics (A.D. 1100–1175), and those associated with Mesa Verde Black-on-white and related wares (A.D. 1175–1300). When ceramics of more than one of these types was present, a burial was assigned to the latest dated ware group. The following section briefly describes the burials from each of these associations. These data are summarized in table 9.1.

Pre-Red Mesa (before A.D. 925)

Shabik'eschee Village, the Three C site, Bc 50, Bc 51, and Bc 59 had 34 burials dating before A.D. 925. Most burials were in middens (88.2%), usually identified as scattered shallow excavations containing few accompanying objects. Shabik'eschee Village (n = 14) had a more regular burial program than the other early sites. Nearly all skeletons were semiflexed on the left side (92.9%) with heads to the west (85.7%). Eleven burials had no burial goods, and the few that had goods were high in the fill and probably were some of the latest at the site. Significance tests suggest that only the orientation at Shabik'eschee differs statistically from the other sites (Fisher's exact p = .005).

In general, burial in structures (11.8%) was rare and appears to be unrelated to the age, sex, or number of items buried with an individual. The usual accompaniment was no offerings (55.9%), followed by a single vessel (29.4%), then a vessel fragment (8.8%). Only one individual had more than one vessel, and offerings other than ceramics have not been reported. Semiflexed positions were the most common (52.9%) followed by flexed (14.7%) and extended (8.8%). Orientation was most often west, largely because of Shabik'eschee which had 12 oriented west, one east, and one north. Sites other than Shabik'eschee had a more even distribution (n = 3 for south, west, northwest, and southwest, n = 2 for north).

TABLE 9.1 Summary of Mortuary Variables by Period and Site Type (% of total individuals)

Variable	Pre-Red Mesa	Red Mesa		Gallup		McElmo		Mesa Verde
		small	*Bonito*	*small*	*Bonito*	*small*	*Kin Kletso*	*small*
Sample size	34	7	7	66	13	35	6	11
Age/sex								
unknown	41.2	—	—	—	—	—	—	—
infant	—	—	—	19.7	7.7	17.1	66.7	54.5
child	14.7	28.6	14.3	15.1	23.1	14.3	16.7	—
adolescent	2.9	—	—	7.6	15.4	5.7	—	—
male	2.9	42.8	57.1	15.1	—	31.4	—	27.3
female	2.9	28.6	28.6	31.8	—	20.0	16.7	9.1
adult	35.3	—	—	10.6	53.8	11.4	—	9.1
Location								
structure	5.9	—	57.1	30.3	100.0	68.6	83.3	54.5
subfloor	5.9	14.3	42.8	21.2	—	17.1	16.7	45.4
midden	88.2	85.7	—	43.9	—	14.3	—	—
other	—	—	—	4.5	—	—	—	—
Position								
extended	11.5	14.3	71.4	3.0	76.9	17.1	—	9.1
flexed	88.5	57.1	28.6	78.8	7.7	60.0	50.0	45.4
back	34.6	71.4	57.1	21.2	84.6	25.7	16.7	36.4
face	7.7	—	—	18.2	—	17.4	—	27.3
left side	50.0	—	—	27.3	—	8.6	50.0	18.2
right side	7.7	—	28.6	13.6	7.7	22.9	—	9.1
Orientation								
north	10.7	—	14.3	10.6	—	5.7	—	27.3
south	10.7	28.6	—	16.7	7.7	14.3	—	9.1
east	3.6	14.3	48.2	19.7	69.2	31.4	50.0	9.1
west	53.6	28.6	—	10.2	7.7	20.0	33.3	36.4
other	21.4	14.3	14.3	13.6	7.7	5.7	—	9.3
north-south	21.4	28.6	14.3	27.3	7.7	20.0	—	36.4
east-west	57.2	42.8	57.1	37.9	76.9	54.1	83.3	45.4
Preparation								
pit	?	14.2	—	9.1	—	5.7	50.0	—
stones	8.8+	57.1	?	18.2	?	8.6	?	45.4
matting	—	—	28.6+	34.8	30.8+	45.7	16.7	9.1
feather cloth	—	—	28.6+	7.6	—	5.7	—	—
textile	—	—	28.6+	7.6	7.7	11.4	—	9.1

Red Mesa (A.D. 900–1050)

Burials dating from the Red Mesa period are rare with only 14 recorded. These are from Pueblo Bonito (n = 7), Bc 51 (n = 3), 29SJ 627 (n = 2), and 29SJ 629 (n = 2). Many sites with Red Mesa components have long occupations that could have disturbed the earlier burials. Additionally, if vessel accompaniments were as rare as in the previous period, they could have gone undated, especially since middens continued to be the preferred burial location at the small sites.

Burials from small sites include two females, three males, and two children. Only one was found in a structure, and burial position was fairly standard with four semiflexed and one extended. All were on their backs with much variability in orientation. Two of the males had no offerings, and the third had only a quarter of a bowl. One

TABLE 9.1 *Continued*

| Variable | Pre-Red Mesa | Red Mesa | | Gallup | | McElmo | | Mesa Verde |
		small	Bonito	small	Bonito	small	Kin Kletso	small
Sample size	34	7	7	66	13	35	6	11
Number of vessels								
none	64.7	42.8	28.6	31.8	15.3	28.6	33.3	27.3
one	29.4	14.3	57.1	25.8	—	31.4	33.3	54.5
two	—	—	14.3	22.7	7.7	17.1	16.7	9.1
three	2.9	28.6	—	9.1	15.3	5.7	16.7	9.1
four	—	14.3	—	3.0	30.8	14.3	—	—
five or more	—	—	—	7.6	23.1	2.9	—	—
Miniature vessel	5.9+	14.3	—	15.1	—	8.6	?	?
Effigy vessel	—	—	—	6.1	7.7	5.7	—	—
Number of bowls								
none	70.6	57.1	42.8	59.1	15.4	48.6	50.0	63.6
one	20.6	28.6	57.1	25.8	23.1	17.1	33.3	36.4
two	2.9	14.3	—	10.6	15.4	25.7	—	—
three	—	—	—	4.5	23.1	8.6	16.7	—
four or more	—	—	—	—	15.4	—	—	—
Black-on-red bowl	—	—	—	4.5	—	11.4	—	—
Smudged bowl	—	—	14.3	10.6	—	14.3	—	—
No. of pitchers								
none	91.2	71.4	71.4	68.2	23.1	68.6	83.3	69.2
one	2.9	28.6	28.6	28.8	38.5	28.6	16.7	18.2
two	—	—	—	3.0	23.1	2.9	—	—
three or more	—	—	—	—	7.7	—	—	—
Culinary vessel	11.8	14.3	—	19.7	—	5.7	16.7	9.1
Ladle	—	—	—	16.7	—	8.6	—	27.3
Turquoise	—	—	28.6	7.6	23.1	2.8	—	9.1
Shell	—	—	42.9	6.1	7.7	8.6	—	—
Ornament/cylinder	—	—	28.6	9.1	7.7	11.4	—	—

Note: The unknowns are included in the totals but are not given in this table.

child was buried with a small bowl, and the other with two miniature bowls, a miniature pitcher, and two ground stone items. The two females had the most artifacts. The one from Bc 51 was buried with four vessels, and the 29SJ 627 burial had three vessels, a vessel fragment, and ten well-made projectile points.

Seven burials from Pueblo Bonito had late Red Mesa ceramic vessels in association. These vessels could have been made during those years when Red Mesa and Gallup ceramic designs overlapped (A.D. 1030–1050) or, since similar vessels occur with burials that also had Gallup vessels, these 7 burials could represent either period. Five of 7 burials were recovered by Neil Judd (Judd 1954) and 2 by George Pepper (Pepper 1909, 1920). Two are females, 4 are males, and 1 a child. The 2 females were side by side, extended on their backs, with their heads to the east. Both lay on the same reed mat, and each was covered by feather cloth, cordage, and textiles. A Red Mesa Back-on-white pitcher, half a bowl, and 2 baskets were placed nearby (Judd 1954:325–26). One of the males was similarly positioned with his knees spread. He was accompanied by a Red Mesa Black-on-white bowl, 25 well-made projectile points arranged in a triangle between his knees, and a bundle of arrow shafts, some with projectile points. Also in this room was a child placed in a small adobe bin constructed for that purpose. Beneath the room floor was another male lying on his back with his knees up. With him were a Red Mesa Black-on-white bowl, a pitcher, and on his chest a shell necklace made of discoid and cylindrical beads with pendants of cut *Olivella* shell and a pair of shell pendants (Judd 1954:93, 333–334). The other 2 burials (AMNH Catalog) (Pepper 1909:197–252; 1920:163–78) were males found beneath a plank floor in Room 33, lying on a layer of clean sand covered with wood ash and associated with large numbers of ornaments and other objects, including a Red Mesa Black-on-white vessel and a black bowl. These are by far the most lavishly accompanied burials recovered from Chaco. Above the plank floor were 14 to 15 disarticulated individuals (equal numbers of males and females, and an infant) and a large number of goods that could not be associated with any particular individual. Among these were a corrugated and probably smudged bowl, 5 pitchers, 6 bowls, a corrugated jar, and a cylindrical vessel. Ornaments include 512 pendants, 24,932 beads, 1,052 pieces of matrix, and 451 sets of turquoise; 2,042 shell beads, 98 worked shell pieces, 10 shell discs, 89 shell bracelet fragments, 2 *Olivella* beads, an inlaid shell pendant, 173 inlays of jet and stone, a jet ring, and 2 iron pyrite sets. Also in the room were 6 flageolets, 12 ceremonial sticks, 2 throwing sticks, a reed object, 2 jar covers, walnuts, piñon nuts, seeds, textiles, quartz crystals, a chipped quartz crystal knife, minerals and pigments, 6 projectile points, gizzard stones, a circular yucca mat, and an awl fragment. At least 3 of these burials were mostly intact, 2 others had articulated vertebrae attached to the skull, and an articulated foot and leg were found along a wall. Only 1 skull was crushed, and crania were spread fairly evenly throughout the room. Ceramics included Red Mesa, Puerco, Gallup, Chaco, and McElmo black-on-white vessels reflecting a time span anywhere from 50 to 175 years.

Once these upper burials were removed, Pepper found a floor constructed of planks laid east-west. The eastern end of 1 board had a hole 10 cm in diameter. Removing the planks revealed 2 burials with offerings placed in all four corners of the room. Around a post in the northeastern corner were 983 turquoise beads and pendants, 26 pieces of turquoise, 27 turquoise sets, 6 stone and jet sets, a shell bead, and 2 fragmentary reed arrows with wooden foreshafts. In the northwestern corner were 51 beads, 5 pendants, and 5 worked pieces of turquoise, a piece of malachite, a *Haliotis* shell disc, and a fragment of a reed arrow shaft. The southeastern corner held 589 beads, 57 pendants, 7 sets, and 65 pieces of matrix and worked turquoise, a jet inlay, and a pendant of *Haliotis* shell. The southwestern corner offering consisted of 42 pieces of malachite, shell bracelet fragments, and a bone bracelet. The Red Mesa Black-on-white vessel and smudged bowl rested against the northern wall.

Burial 13 was extended on his right side with his head to the northeast. Scattered around his lower legs were 2,997 turquoise beads, another 698 were around his right ankle. The upper left arm was surrounded by 1,628 beads, a large pendant, and a small set of turquoise. Also in association were an additional 567 beads, 3 sets, and 9 pendants of turquoise, a piece of turquoise matrix, 3 shell beads, and a small piece of shell.

Burial 14 was semiflexed, probably on his back with his head to the north and his feet resting against the southern wall. He has chop marks in his left partial and temporal, a gash in the right parietal, and cuts and chops on the distal left femur, suggesting death in a confrontation. Burial 14 had more goods than others in this room. On his chest was an turquoise ornament composed of 1,980 beads, and 1 large and 8 small pendants. A deposit of 2,642 small beads, 168 small pendants, 3 sets, 2 rabbit-shaped pendants, a shoe-shaped pendant, and an unfinished pendant of turquoise, and 5 jet inlays lay on his abdomen. Around his right wrist were 617 beads, 147 small pendants, and 4 sets of turquoise, a shell bead, and 2 stone beads. The left wrist was surrounded by 2,384 disc beads, 4 cylindrical beads, 194 pendants, 5 pendants shaped as birds, a foot, a bifurcated form, an irregular form in turquoise, and 5 irregularly shaped shell pendants. Around his right ankle were 322 disc beads, 2 cylindrical beads, and 5 pendants of turquoise. The left ankle was surrounded by 434 beads and 8 pendants of turquoise, 8 small stone and shell beads, and a cylindrical shell bead. At his right knee was a shell trumpet, 4 complete *Haliotis* shells, and 26 complete and 15 fragments of shell bracelets. Under 1 *Haliotis* shell were the remains of an 8 x 15 cm cylindrical basket covered with 1,214 pieces of turquoise mosaic. The basket was filled with 2,150 beads, 152 small and 22 large pendants of turquoise, 3,317 shell beads and small pendants, 78 cylindrical shell beads, 68 large shell pendants, 5 shell pendants with turquoise inlay, and an animal form stone pendant with turquoise inlay. Near the body were the remains of a turquoise and shell mosaic on basketwork composed of rows of turquoise beads (over 500) alternating with double rows of thin overlapping pieces of shell. Other objects in the area were a long inlay of red stone, fragments of shell ornaments, pieces of turquoise matrix, small turquoise sets, and a part of a bivalve shell.

Needless to say, the placement of Burials 13 and 14 in the Red Mesa period is debatable. The presence of large amounts of turquoise could support or contradict a Red Mesa date depending on who is right about when it was most available. While most (see Judge 1989:235–40) feel that its presence is synonymous with the peak of the system, Windes (1992:162) maintains that it was most widespread with more evidence of jewelry manufacture in the A.D. 900s through the early A.D. 1000s. Regardless, the only statistically significant contrast between the small-site and Pueblo Bonito burial samples is in the presence of ornaments (p = .03). Three individuals from Pueblo Bonito had some ornamentation while none from the small sites did.

Gallup (A.D. 1030–1150)

More sites have burials associated with Gallup Black-on-white ceramics. These include Pueblo Bonito, Casa Rinconada, Pepper's Mound 2, the Three C site, Turkey House, Bc 50, Bc 51, Bc 52, Bc 53, Bc 59, Bc 192, Bc 362, and 29SJ 597, 29SJ 626, 29SJ 627, and 29SJ 1629. The sample consists of 66 individuals from small sites and 13 from Pueblo Bonito. Few burials came from any one site, and excavations at some concentrated on rooms without investigating exterior, midden, or subfloor proveniences, possibly injecting bias into the sample.

When the Gallup small-site burials were examined for evidence of differential treatment based on age or sex, few of the comparisons resulted in statistically significant differences. Few or no patterns relate to the age and sex of the individual, and placement within a structure or a midden does not appear to condition what was interred with the individual.

Burials were primarily found in structures (51.5%) and middens (43.9%). The only significant age-related difference in burial location is between infants and chil-

dren, where infants (less than 3 years of age) were usually buried in structures while children (3 to 10 years of age) were found in midden areas (chi square = 3.29, p = .047). Males were found in structures (70.0%) more often than females (47.6%) and adults only slightly more often than subadults (53.5 and 52.2%, respectively). Extended burials are rare in the small-site sample (3.7%). When broken down by age or sex, the numbers are small and none of the statistical tests significant. However, there is a tendency for females to be buried on their sides (73.7%) in both structures and middens. Extended burials in rooms tend to be on the back while those in midden areas are face down. Orientation was not patterned, although males were usually oriented east or west (85.7%) and females more equally divided (43.7% east or west).

Few age or sex related differences were observed in the presence of stone coverings, mats, or textiles; although, an unusually high proportion of older females were buried with mats (60.0%), and females had all but one of the feather cloths. Burial location made little or no difference in regard to the presence of these objects. Up to five vessels were interred with individuals. The quantity of vessels did not depend on the age or sex of the individual; however, when only the presence or absence of vessels is considered, males are more likely to have vessels (80.0%) than females (61.9%). The structure verses midden distribution of vessels is not statistically significant, although those buried in structures had vessels less often (61.8%) than those in midden areas (75.9%). Few ornaments were found with burials. Turquoise was found as pendants, beads, and a nodule; shell as pendants and a bracelet fragment; hematite as a pendant and small cylinders; and jet as a pendant. Three projectile points were found at the neck of females suggesting they were part of a necklace, and an infant had 12 tubular bone beads and five nut shell beads. Turquoise was found with females (n = 4) and an infant; shell with an infant, an adolescent, a female, and an adult of unknown sex. Cylinders of hematite were the only form of ornament found with males. Adults were more likely to have ornaments than children (26.7 and 13.0%, respectively). Burials in structures were more likely to have ornaments (26.5%) than those in middens (10.3%).

While many of the disturbed burials found in Pueblo Bonito probably date to this period, only 13 could be used in this analysis, 12 excavated by Judd and 1 by Pepper. All burials (an infant, 3 children, 2 adolescents, and 7 females) were in rooms, and position and orientation was quite standard. All of the adults, the adolescent, and 2 of the children were extended, on their backs, with heads oriented east. One adolescent was buried with the head to the west, an infant was semiflexed, a child was semiflexed on the side with the head northeast, and another child's head was to the north. The adolescents and all of the adults, except the 1 excavated by Pepper, were placed on one or more mats; none of the children were. Only 2 Pueblo Bonito burials were without vessels, the infant and a child, with the number of vessels ranging from 2 to 14. Three adult females had turquoise, and 1 had 2 hematite cylinders. The only child with an ornament had 2 shell pendants. Other materials associated with these individuals included cylindrical and bifurcate basket parts placed just above the infant, oval baskets with humerus scrapers with 4 adult females, 2 digging sticks with another female, and a bifurcated and 2 cylindrical baskets as a joint offering for 2 females.

When burial practices between the small sites and Pueblo Bonito were compared, several variables produced statistically significant results. Differences in burial position (extended verses flexed) are highly significant (chi square = 40.55, p <.0000) as is the north-south versus east-west orientations when only structure burials are considered (p = .0468). Fewer Pueblo Bonito burials were without ceramic vessels than in the small-site sample, but the differences are not statistically significant. The Pueblo Bonito burials with vessels had more vessels (90.0% had three or more) than those of the small sites (28.8%). On a presence or absence basis, differences in distributions of turquoise and ornaments are statistically significant (p = .03 for each). Shell ornaments were rarely found and the distributions similar (7.7% of the Pueblo Bonito and 6.1% of the small-site burials had shell ornaments).

Comparing Gallup and Red Mesa burials in the small-site sample, the only nearly significant trend was the presence of stone or slab covers. Fewer Gallup associated burials were covered with stones (18.2% versus 57.1%, respectively). For Pueblo Bonito, distributions were similar, differing only in the number of pitchers, which were more frequent in the later burials (p = .07). Quantities of ornaments were not compared.

In summary, small-site burial practices for the Gallup period remained variable with no differences that would suggest differentiation among individuals based on age or sex. A greater variety of material was buried with individuals than in previous periods, including mats, feather cloth, textiles, ornaments, and other objects that may represent personal possessions or individual achievement.

The Pueblo Bonito burials generally followed the standardized plan begun in the previous period with some deviation for some infants and children. Most interments had accompanying vessels, and most adults had mats and ceramic vessels. Turquoise was found only with adults, and quantities were less than in the Red Mesa sample. The most important differences between the small-site and great-house mortuary practices are in the organization of the interment and greater quantities of bowls, pitchers, turquoise, and ornaments at the great-house sites.

McElmo (A.D. 1100–1175)

Sites that had burials associated with late carbon-painted wares, such as McElmo Black-on-white, are Bc 50, Bc 51, Bc 53, Bc 57, Bc 59, 29SJ 721, and Kin Kletso. Of the 35 small-site burials, almost all (85.7%) were found in structures, due in part to excavation bias. Burial position varied with a significant (p = .0017) difference in positioning. Infants and children were more often buried extended (71.4%) when compared to adults (5.3%). Orientation was more often east or west (51.4%) and varied little between age groups. In these burials, matting was equally likely to be found with males, females, adults, or subadults. Children were more likely to have vessels than were infants (80.0% and 50.0%, respectively), and children had more vessels. Males had up to 5 vessels, and more males had vessels (81.8%) than females (57.1%), who were never buried with more than 2 vessels. Adults were slightly more likely to have been buried with vessels than subadults (72.7% and 63.6%, respectively). Ornaments were rare, and males were the most likely group to have ornaments (27.3%). Turquoise was found with a probable male who was reported to have a pendant and an earring. Shell artifacts and bone artifacts were both found with 3 burials. The individual with the most ornamentation for this period is probably a female with a necklace of 103 jet beads and 52 shell beads, a jet bird effigy, 2 quartz crystals, 4 steatite cylinders, a bone tube, and 2 small stone objects. Adults (27.3%) were more likely to be buried with ornaments than subadults (18.2%), but the difference is not significant. A wide variety of other materials occurred in McElmo burials. These included ground stone, bone tools, food items, baskets, cordage, a wooden object, a hammer stone, a flake, and a projectile point.

Again, while the disturbed burial rooms at Pueblo Bonito had carbon-painted vessels, individuals and their associated objects could not be isolated for analysis, leaving only the 6 Kin Kletso burials to represent the great houses during this period. This sample is comprised of 4 infants, a child about 10 years of age, and a young adult female about 17 years of age, hardly a representative sample. Three of these were at least partially disturbed, and none of the 3 undisturbed burials were extended. Orientation was usually east or west, and matting was found with 1 infant. One infant and the child lacked vessels, and the other infants had a variety of vessels. The female was associated with a bowl. No ornaments were found, although a projectile point and squash seeds may have been associated with 1 infant.

No significant differences were found between the McElmo small and great-house samples. However, when the Gallup and McElmo small-site samples are compared, there is a significant increase in the number of extended burials (chi square = 5.01, p = .02) but not in any particular orientation. Differences in the presence or absence of vessels or ornaments are not significant. Shell ornaments were slightly more common in the McElmo burials (8.6%) than in the Gallup burials (6.1%); whereas turquoise was more often found with Gallup burials (7.6% and 2.9%, respectively). Comparing Pueblo Bonito Gallup burials with those from Kin Kletso produced significant differences in extended verses flexed burials (p = .004) and the presence of pitchers (p = .03). No significant differences were found between the Kin Kletso and the Gallup small-site sample.

Burials associated with McElmo Black-on-white ceramics were similar to those with Gallup Black-on-white ceramics. Males continued to have slightly more vessels than females, but no significant distinctions based on the age or sex of the individual are indicated.

Mesa Verde (A.D. 1175–1300)

Few burials were recovered from the late occupation of Chaco Canyon; only eleven, all from small sites (Bc 236, Leyit Kin, a small site east of Pueblo Bonito excavated by Roberts, and 29SJ 633). No great-house burials could be identified from this period, although some of those from Pueblo del Arroyo have carbon-painted ceramics.

The age and sex distribution in this small sample is fairly unusual, six infants, three males, a female, and an undetermined adult who may not be representative of this period. Burials were most often semiflexed (36.4%) and generally oriented west for infants and north for adults (p = .04). Stones were placed over three of the infants, and matting and textiles were found with the burial from Leyit Kin. Up to three vessels were found associated, with one

vessel being the most frequent number. All individuals had at least one sherd buried with them. Three infants had only sherds, one male had two vessels, and the female had three vessels. A turquoise chip was found with one infant and a quartz crystal with a male. Other materials recovered with these burials included a lithic found with one infant and seeds and a turkey carcass with another infant.

Sample size for this group is too small for meaningful comparisons. Bowl and vessel distributions are fairly similar to the preceding sample. McElmo adults tend to be oriented east or west while all four of the Mesa Verde adults were oriented north or south.

Aztec Ruin, a great-house site to the north near the Animas River, has a substantial burial population from this period (a least 149). All but four of these were found in rooms. Most were found in abandoned rooms filled with debris, but a fair number were in subfloor pits (about 12%). Most of the burials were placed on their side, and a few (three or four) were extended. Orientation was most commonly east followed by north, west, and south. Morris doubted that orientation had any particular significance since it seemed to relate to the slope of fill in the room and position of doorways. Even the subfloor burials had no uniformity. Wrappings of cloth, feather cloth, or plaited rush mats were noted for 66 (44.3%). Pottery was found with only 78 of the individuals (52.3%) and beads with 32 (21.5%) (Morris 1924:221–23).

As with Pueblo Bonito, considering only the presence or absence of classes of materials, does not tell the whole story. Several Mesa Verde era burials at Aztec contained significant amounts of material that imply differential treatment. In Room 52 of the eastern wing, Morris (1924:151–53) found the remains of at least 15 infants and small children scattered along the eastern wall. Also along the eastern wall were 6 bowls, 3 dippers, a mug, 19 stone beads in the process of manufacture, 27 complete beads of the same material, a string of 3,100 black beads, a string of 16,600 black beads, 88 white, gray, and black beads, 8 crystal beads, 65 turquoise beads, a hematite animal effigy, 46 *Olivella* shell beads, 18 other shell beads, a hematite paint stick, 3 cylindrical stone beads, 16 rectangular slabs of bone that served as backings for beads of fragile materials, galena crystals, worked green stone, hematite, polished stones, a gray quartzite knife, 297 bone tubes and tube fragments, and 2 worked sandstone slabs. The bone tubes were in bundles of 6 to 30 tubes of nearly equal length. Some bundles had traces of cloth wrappings indicting they were enclosed.

Nearby, Room 41 held at least 2 adults and 3 children; probably more had been present (Morris 1924:155–161). The room was burned, and scattered bits of calcined bone raise the possibility of additional interments. One of the adults, partially flexed on the right side in the southeastern corner, had a large quantity and a variety of objects. A pitcher rested against the chest, and the body was completely covered from throat to thighs with *Olivella* beads, abalone shell, and mosaic pendants. An *Olivella* shell anklet was on the left leg. In the southwestern corner of the room, near the partial remains of a child, was a mound of pottery vessels, bowls, mugs, and bird effigies. In one bird effigy were 31,000 tiny black beads. Charred and broken bone tubes, beads, turquoise inlay, and mosaic fragments were scattered throughout. In the northwestern corner, with the remains of 2 children were a number of ceramic vessels, including a set of 4 nested bowls with a mug in the smallest bowl, 7 additional bowls, 3 mugs, a small corrugated pot, pigment, *Olivella* shells, shell beads, pendants and pendant fragments, mosaic fragments, bits of shell and turquoise, galena, many bone tubes, and a pile of 200 quartzite projectile points.

In Room 111 of the northern wing, Morris (1924:163–67) found associated with two adult burials a wealth of vessels; turquoise, shell, lignite, and stone beads; ornaments; cloth; sandals; matting; ceremonial sticks; a bone tube scraper recessed for inlay; bits of turquoise, galena, and shale; and perforated discs of squash shell. The burials were originally covered with plaited rush mats but no soil. Some agent smashed one skull, numerous other bones, and almost all of the vessels then scattered these, along with necklaces and pendants, throughout this and the adjoining two rooms. Morris surmised that human marauders and looters visited the room soon after the bodies were placed there and removed some of the ornaments and possibly other material.

Also in the northern wing, Room 178 held the remains of a male referred to by Morris as the warrior (Morris 1924:192–95). He was mostly extended with his head to the east and when measured from the top of the head to the feet was about 6 feet 1 inch tall. The entire body was enveloped in a feather cloth with an outer covering of rush matting. Above the wrappings was a coiled basket shield with the outer coils coated with pitch holding minute flakes of selenite, the next band of coils was stained dark red, and the remaining coils stained greenish blue. At the back of the skull was a coiled basket and a small bowl. Another bowl was behind the pelvis and

another between the hips and heels. Between his feet and the wall was another bowl, and a pitcher and its cover had been broken and scattered over the skull and behind the body. In the angle formed by the knees were five bone awls, an antler flaker, a sandstone rasping tool, a knife blade, and several pieces of chipped stone. Two axes were below the knees, one was painted red and the other was made from hematite or another ore. Both had wooden handles. With one axe was a knife of red quartzite positioned so that it may have been in a belt. On the chest was an ornament of lignite and on the right forearm a strand of 29 beads (black, white, red, and turquoise). Three wooden sticks lay on his chest.

Mesa Verde era burials at Aztec are quite different from those at Chaco during this period. In fact, these bear a strong resemblance to earlier burials at Pueblo Bonito, especially Judd's burials dating to the Gallup and possibly the McElmo period. While the warrior may well represent achieved status, the same cannot be said for the infant and child burials associated with numerous bowls and ornaments.

Summary of Chronological Differences

Given that so few burials from Chaco Canyon have good information and there was a significant bias toward excavation of rooms at many of the sites, it is far from certain that this sample accurately reflects burial practices in the Canyon. Yet, there are trends in the data.

Midden burials slowly decreased over time, although some of this may be due to excavation bias in favor of rooms in the later sites. More burials from midden contexts were eliminated from this analysis because of disturbance or lack of information on associated ceramics.

Extended burials were relatively rare at the small sites in Chaco Canyon, but they were frequent at Pueblo Bonito. Placement of the body on the back, face, left, or right side shows no chronological trends, although Pueblo Bonito has the greatest regularity with most buried on their back. Overall, the orientation of burials from small sites, with the head to the east, increases in frequency until the Mesa Verde sample. West orientation shows the opposite trend, starting high in frequency and decreasing. The great-house samples have the highest proportion of burials oriented in a single direction, in this case east. Thus, body positioning is more consistent in great-house sites, indicating a more formal mortuary system than found at the small sites.

Grave preparation is especially susceptible to preservation, disturbance, and the vagaries of archaeological recording. In this sample, stone coverings appear to decrease with time until the Mesa Verde sample, but this could be related to the increase in structure burials compared to midden burials. Mats, feather cloth, and textiles are most common in burials associated with Gallup or McElmo ceramics.

The number and form of vessels associated with burials show some temporal trends. Small-site burials with no vessels decreased over time while the number of vessels per person increased for adults through the McElmo sample. Subadults usually had fewer vessels than adults, and subadults at Pueblo Bonito had more vessels than those at the small sites. The largest difference in vessel counts was in the Gallup sample where Pueblo Bonito adults had an average of six vessels compared to 1.5 vessels for adults from small sites. Bowls and pitchers followed the same general pattern. Culinary and corrugated vessels were never numerous as mortuary offerings but tended to increase through the Gallup sample then decline.

Ornaments, particularly those of turquoise, were more often found with great-house burials. Shell occurrence increased between the Gallup and McElmo samples while turquoise decreased.

Summary of Demographic and House Types

In the small-site burials, there is little to suggest differentiation based on age or sex of the individual. The few variables that have statistically significant differences in distribution are almost all between subadults and adults and are related to body position or orientation. These two variables may well reflect a combination of practical and ritual matters. Smaller bodies require a smaller pit so infants and children may be less likely to be flexed than full sized adults. Similarly, orientation could be conditioned by variables such as slope, room orientation, and doorway location. Burial parallel to a slope may diminish the chance of it washing out, while orientation in rooms could reflect the long axis of the room, room size, or the location of the doorway. Some historic Pueblos orient burials to the east because the spirit must begin its journey from that direction (Ellis 1968:65), suggesting there could be a ritual aspect to orientation of prehistoric burials as well.

Adults buried at small sites had vessels more often and had more vessels than subadults, suggesting a system of age grading. Some individuals had more grave goods than others, but none are suggestive of more than achieved status or personal possessions. In general, burial goods in small-site interments seem to correspond to their availability within the system at that time.

The majority of the significant differences in the sample are between the great-house and small-site burials, and it is reasonable to infer some sort of differentiation. Burial at Pueblo Bonito was more standard, and those interred there had more goods of all kinds.

A wide range of objects were found in Chaco graves, but many of these occur infrequently and are more consistent with achieved status or personal possessions. The two most common burial goods are ceramic vessels and ornaments. Ceramics are the single most frequent offering found in burial contexts. The quality of vessels could not be assessed without examining the actual vessels, which are housed at a number of institutions and some of which have been lost. Certain vessel forms may have been at least somewhat exclusive. Cylindrical vessels are almost all from Pueblo Bonito, and a good many of those found came from Room 28 (slightly offset from Pepper's Room 33). This form was found with both Pepper's and Judd's burials but not at any small-site burials.

To assess whether the vessels found with burials are a representative sample of available vessels, rim sherd percentages from five of the Chaco Project sites are compared with percents of the burial vessel types (tables 9.2 and 9.3). Recognizing that using rims sherds as a measurement under represents forms with small orifices while over representing bowls and culinary jars, it still appears that culinary jars and ollas are the most underrepresented forms in burials while pitchers may be over represented. Only two ollas were found with the burials in this sample, both from one of Judd's rooms at Pueblo Bonito. This could indicate that larger items such as ollas and culinary vessels used by a family or a group were less likely to be placed in mortuary contexts than forms such as bowls, pitchers, and ladles which may represent more personal possessions or offerings.

Ethnographically documented inventories of vessels in west Mexican villages range from between 3 and 25 for Huichol households to 62 for Tarascan households, and breakage rates range from .15 to 1.29. Estimated vessel inventories for prehistoric groups include 18 to 25 vessels for Cebolletta region households and 42 vessels for Dolores area households (Nelson et al. 1994a:133–134). One structure at 29SJ 1360 in Chaco Canyon had at least 9 corrugated jars, 4 ollas, 5 pitchers, 4 bowls, and a dipper or 23 vessels on the floor (McKenna 1984:110–111).

Estimates of vessel consumption, or the number of vessels discarded or broken annually range from 7.7 to as many as 28.4 vessels per family at the small sites, and from 1.2 to 125.5 per family at the great-house site of Pueblo Alto (Toll 1985:186). Given theses rates, the inclusion of one or even a few vessels with a burial was not a great loss to the group and suggests that ceramic vessels could be considered as relatively unvalued utilitarian offerings.

While ornaments were found with burials at both small and great-house sites, their presence and quantity is greater at great houses, or at least at Pueblo Bonito during the Red Mesa, Gallup, and possibly into McElmo times. This was especially true of long-distance transport items such as turquoise and shell. Furthermore, there is an important distinction in how these materials entered the archaeological record at the two site types. At small sites, it is predominantly as debris from workshops, loss, discard of broken items, and on rare occasion with a burial (Mathien 1984). Ornaments were available to the small-site population, yet these objects were passed on rather than retired from the system by inclusion with a burial. Few Chaco small-site burials had more than a few beads, although there were exceptions. At one small site, a woman who was accidentally buried in a pit structure wore a necklace of almost 4,000 shale beads (McKenna 1984:357), far more than recovered with any intentionally interred individual in the other small-site burials. The only comparable find with a burial was an adult, probably a female, from Bc 59 who had a necklace of 103 jet and 52 shell beads as well as a McElmo Black-on-white pitcher, a smudged bowl, quartz crystals, and stone cylinders. Ellis (1968:67) has observed that present-day Keresans remove a few beads from a necklace the family wishes to keep and place these with offerings

of food and other personal possessions in burials. The same may have been true in the past.

At the great houses, ceremonial deposition (sealed in niches or boxes in kivas) and burial contexts are the more frequent sources of ornaments. Large showy items are not found at the small sites. Shell trumpets, turquoise mosaic encrusted baskets, inlaid pendants, and shell discs occur only at Pueblo Bonito with burials and as ceremonial deposits. Some of these items appear to have served as symbols of office rather than prestige goods, but the quantity of goods certainly indicates greater access to such materials and higher, probably ascribed, status. Unlike individuals buried at the small sites, these individuals were considered sufficiently important to merit retiring large amounts of valued nonutilitarian goods from the system at their deaths. To some, notably Toll (1991:85–86), Pueblo Bonito was aberrant, perhaps a repository of sorts; however, the turquoise ornaments (between 56,000 and 500,000 pieces) and other exotic items do not exist in numbers that are any more unusual than for more mundane items; that is, it is merely a question of scale, and Pueblo Bonito had lots of everything. This view completely ignores context, fails to distinguish items related to status from those based on wealth (e.g., Wason 1994:126), and does nothing to explain why so much is clustered in a small portion of the site.

BURIAL DISTINCTIONS WITHIN PUEBLO BONITO

Even within Pueblo Bonito there are distinctions. Burials in the northern or Pepper's burial rooms (figure 9.1) had the bulk of the ornaments, most of which were concen-

TABLE 9.2 Vessel Forms Based on Rim Sherd Counts

Vessel form	29SJ 629 Red Mesa	29SJ 1360 Red Mesa -Gallup	29SJ 627 Red Mesa -McElmo	Pueblo Alto Red Mesa -McElmo	29SJ 633 Mesa Verde
Bowl	66.1	59.9	61.0	49.2	58.6
Jar/pitcher	1.6	3.0	3.3	3.4	.4
Ladle	3.7	4.5	4.9	4.6	6.0
Olla	1.9	3.2	2.7	3.3	.8
Culinary jar	17.6	21.9	20.5	35.1	28.5
Other	9.0	7.5	7.5	4.4	5.6
Total sherds	1110	1434	5464	4006	249

Source: Adapted from Toll 1984:Table 4.

TABLE 9.3 Whole Vessel Forms from Burials

Vessel form	pre Red Mesa	Red Mesa		Gallup		McElmo		Mesa Verde
		small	Bonito	small	Bonito	small	Kin Kletso	
Bowl	69.2	36.4	66.6	40.8	63.2	61.1	71.4	36.4
Jar/pitcher	7.7	18.2	33.3	23.5	28.6	22.2	14.2	18.2
Ladle	—	—	—	12.2	—	5.5	—	27.3
Olla	—	—	—	—	2.0	—	—	—
Culinary jar	23.1	9.1	—	13.3	—	3.7	14.2	9.1
Other	—	36.3	—	10.2	6.2	7.5	—	9.1
Number of vessels	13	11	6	98	49	54	7	11

trated in Room 33. Besides those burials already described, Pepper found the partial remains of at least 1 individual in the southeastern corner of Room 32 associated with fragments of wooden implements, a hematite bird with turquoise and shell inlay, cloth, cordage, 2 pitchers, and a jar nearby. Also in the room were 3 pitchers, 10 bowls, a corrugated redware bowl, a water jar, 3 mugs, a dipper, 3 cylindrical jars, jar covers, 9 turquoise beads and 2 shell beads in one of the cylindrical jars, a circular object of jet, well over 300 ceremonial sticks, unfinished wooden objects, a painted slab of wood, a quiver with over 81 arrows, an elk antler club, at least 3 sandals, 2 baskets, galena, gypsum, a drilled piece of squash, reeds, and a metate (Pepper 1920:129–63). Room 28, which leads into Room 32, had no burials. However, within this room was a cache of 114 cylindrical vessels, 8 bowls, and 18 pitchers, 121 sandstone jar covers, a shell bracelet, pieces of worked and unworked turquoise, a piece of hammered copper, an obsidian projectile point, a jet object, fossils, sulphur, and ochre. Among the cylindrical jars and bowls were 12 pendants, bead fragments, inlays, beads of turquoise, 69 figure-eight-shaped beads, 43 *Olivella* beads, 9 bracelets, and 400 disc beads of shell.

Room 53 was partially excavated by Moorehead (1906) who entered the room by tearing down the northern and eastern walls. Cleaning up after Moorehead, Pepper found two pitchers, a small bowl, and a cylindrical jar fragment against the eastern wall and a child's cranium with a deposit of over 4,000 turquoise beads and 30 shell beads and pendants nearby. A skeleton missing only the cranium (probably one of those collected by Moorehead) was found at the southern end of the room. Pieces of feather cloth, portions of cradle boards, ceremonial and gaming sticks, fragments of vessels, and turquoise beads were recovered from the

general debris (Pepper 1920:210–13). Human bone from this room, now housed at the American Museum of Natural History, consists of mandibles from two adult males and a female, a child's cranium, and two mixed groups that represent a newborn infant, at least one and possibly two adolescents, and three adults (a male, a female, and another adult).

In Room 56, Moorehead (1906:34) found the "splendidly preserved skeleton of a young woman wrapped in a large feather robe." Some pottery is noted as accompanying the burial. Pepper, cleaning up after Moorehead, commented (Pepper 1909:216–18) that there were two subfloor graves as well as bones scattered throughout the dirt piled in the northeastern and northwestern portions of the room. One of the graves had a bottom formed by sticks and sides made of boards. It also was covered by boards or matting, fragments of both were found in Room 53. The Phillips-Andover catalog lists a reed mat and feather robe which covered a burial found in the northwestern corner of Pueblo Bonito. This individual, a male about 42 years of age, is probably one of the individuals from this room.

The American Museum of Natural History catalog lists materials purchased from O. H. Buck, hired by Pepper for unspecified duties (McNitt 1966:141). Among those materials, which may have come from Room 61, just north of Room 53, are *Haliotis* shell pendants, shell beads, a turquoise bead fragment, and shell bracelets found with a skull. Pepper (1920:222–23) found fragments of a burned human skull in the southeastern corner of this room as well as a few unburned human bones. He does not mention prior disturbance other than noting that part of the western wall had been demolished.

Judd found burials in four adjacent interior rooms in

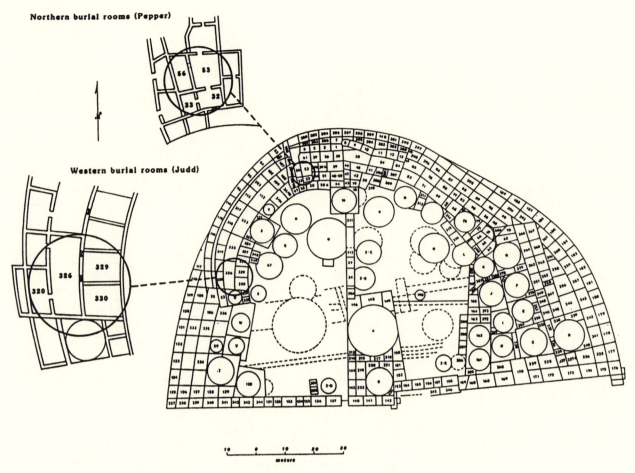

FIGURE 9.1   Clusters of Burial Rooms at Pueblo Bonito (Courtesy of the National Park Service)

the western portion of Pueblo Bonito (figure 9.1). By his estimation, almost 70% of the burials were disturbed by prehistoric vandals who looted stores of corn and ornaments (Judd 1954:340). Unfortunately, Judd's accounts of the material found in these rooms are incomplete. His sections on dress and adornment and on ceramics illustrate objects found with the disarticulated burials but not mentioned in the burial section. Much of the information on possible associations comes from the U. S. National Museum catalog.

Room 320 is a small storage room with a flagstone floor that could be entered and sealed from Room 326. A four-strand turquoise necklace and 2 pairs of pendants were plastered between 2 of the stones. Judd (1954:325–26), based on crania, reports that 8 women and 2 girls were buried in Room 320. By analyzing all elements, Palkovich (1984:106) determined that 21 individuals are represented

from Room 320 (an infant, 2 children, 2 adolescents, 2 young adults of unknown sex, a young male, and 13 females ranging from young adults to over 50 years of age). These include the 2 females described earlier and an older woman missing her cranium and associated with 2 ring baskets and a mat of peeled willows.

The intact and disturbed burials were covered with debris, drifting sand, and finally a collapsed ceiling. Judd does not detail, and the catalog does not distinguish, which material recovered from this room could have been associated with the burials. In addition to the goods associated with the 3 intact burials were 7 bowls, 14 pitchers, 6 Chaco Black-on-white cylindrical vessels, a ladle, a pipe, turquoise ornaments (6 rectangular beads, 7 pendants, 126 disc beads), a handful of shell and stone beads and pendants, galena, malachite, azurite, sulphur, bone awls, a bone scraper, projectile points, 6 cylindrical baskets, a basket cup, a bifurcated basket with a painted design, a sandal and sandal fragments, other basket and matting fragments, 2 willow mats, 2 sets of 4 loom sticks, at least 4 ceremonial sticks, and a bow. If these vessels and ornaments were associated with the disturbed burials, each person averaged 2 to 4 vessels, most had a turquoise bead or pendant, and some a basket.

Room 326 (Judd 1954:326–31) was a habitation room that held the remains of 10 adults (1 male and 9 females) and an infant by Judd's count and 18 by Palkovich's (2 children, an adolescent, 4 males, 10 females, and a young adult of undetermined sex) (Palkovich 1984:106). Three of the burials in Judd's count were only slightly disturbed by being moved a short distance because they were fairly intact and could have been disturbed by placing other burials in the room. The 7 additional individuals counted by Palkovich are probably those cataloged as recovered from in front of the doors in the western wall and detached bones in the middle of the room.

Burials in Room 326 (7 of which were included in the burial analysis as Gallup burials) were placed on mats and most had at least ceramic vessels as offerings. Other materials interred with these burials include a turquoise pendant, a 3 strand turquoise bead bracelet, an oval tray and bone scraper, and 15 vessels with 1 female. A dual burial had a joint offering of 3 bowls, 2 humerus scrapers and oval tray sets, and a cylindrical basket. One of these females also had 3 additional bowls, a pitcher, and 2 pendants of jet and turquoise. The other had a bowl, 2 pitchers, and a turquoise pendant. Three other undisturbed burials had offerings of ceramic vessels and other utensils. Also in the room were at least 34 bowls, 7 pitchers, 6 turquoise pendants, small turquoise pendants and fragments, worked turquoise fragments, stone beads, a hematite bead, a quartz crystal, a fluorite crystal pendant, a cylinder of green stone, hematite fragments, tubular bone beads, a bone button, 8 projectile points, 2 cylindrical and 2 bifurcated baskets, wooden staves, and fragments of cotton cloth and baskets. If objects were evenly distributed, individuals buried in this room all had burial mats, at least 3 or 4 vessels, and a turquoise pendant.

Room 329 (Judd 1954:331–33) had only a ventilator and central fireplace leading Judd to surmise it was a council or secret society chamber that was abandoned after Room 326 was used for burials. It is accessible only through Room 326 and had a partially plugged doorway leading Judd to suggest there also was a ceiling hatchway. Judd counted 17 females, 1 male, and 6 children in this room while Palkovich (1984:106) counted 12 children, 2 males, and 10 females. Only 5 burials were not disturbed, and they were all child burials. These undisturbed burials included: an 8 year old with a mat, 3 pitchers and a bowl; a 12 year old with a willow screen, 2 pitchers, and a bowl; a child under 6 with 2 pitchers, a small bowl, and a duck pot; and another child under 6 with 3 bowls and 2 shell pendants. The other child had no offerings. A unspecified child had a turquoise pendant.

The other individuals were scattered everywhere with parts missing. Material that could have been associated with the disarticulated individuals includes 17 to 19 bowls, 3 to 8 pitchers, a Gallup Black-on-white effigy pitcher, an effigy in a bifurcate basket form, a reddish brown pitcher, 6 cylindrical vessels, beads, undrilled beads, mosaics and fragments of turquoise, a turquoise duck effigy, azurite and malachite pellets, shell pendants, shell bracelet fragments, shell beads, a jet bead, cotton cloth fragments, 10 awls, and copper bell fragments. If burial goods were equally distributed, individuals in Room 329 were accompanied by fewer vessels (up to 2 each) than those in Rooms 320 and 326 and may have had fewer ornaments.

The final room, Room 330 (Judd 1954:333–335), was square with a central firepit and was entered through a ceiling hatchway, possibly another council or ceremonial chamber. Judd counted 23 individuals from this room, 13 males, 4 females, and 6 children. In contrast, Palkovich (1984:106) identified 32 individuals: 5 children, 2 adolescents, 16 males, and 9 females. Only 3 of the males and a child were undisturbed. Two of the males and the child were included in the burial sample as Red Mesa burials. A male in his late twenties was buried under the floor. He was not described in the text, but a photograph shows a burial with at least a bowl and a pitcher, and a note indicated that a shell necklace and paired pendants were found on his chest. No information is given on one of the intact burials other than it was an older male with a pair of *Haliotis* shell discs at his side buried above the floor. Other undisturbed burials were the child buried in an adobe bin and the male with 28 projectile points arranged in a triangle between his knees, a bundle of reed-shafted arrows under his right hip, and a bowl. Other subfloor, possibly disturbed individuals also are indicated. Judd's Skeleton 24, originally though to represent a second undisturbed subfloor burial, turned out to be miscellaneous bones from various skeletons.

Judd describes the remaining individuals as "callously pulled and kicked about" (Judd 1954:333), and photographs indicate that the disturbance occurred while many elements were held in place by ligaments. Artifacts found with parts of individuals include paired pendants of an unspecified material with a child, a lignite disc with an adult male, 4 jet rings with another male, 8 projectile points with an adult male, a bulrush mat with an adolescent male, a fiber mat with another male, a shell necklace and 2 zoomorphic pendants with a male, and fragments of shell pendants with a child. Catalog cards and other text identify 16 bowls; 14 to 16 pitchers; a duck pot; a canteen; 6 cylindrical vessels; a double stirrup canteen; a ladle; a turquoise-on-shell mosaic; a few turquoise beads, mosaics, and fragments; a jet effigy with turquoise inlay; 3.45 m of stone beads at the head of a skeleton; other stone beads; 7 or so shell pendants; shell beads; shell mosaic fragments; a shell and shell bead necklace measuring 6.91 m; unfinished shale pendants; galena; a garnet; kaolin; pigment; azurite pellets; fragments of cotton cloth and willow mats; a cylindrical basket; basket fragments; and 3 bone awls. This material would have furnished the disarticulated individuals with as many as 2 vessels and most with some form of ornamentation, probably more than found in Judd's other rooms.

Comparing the 2 burial clusters is a rather daunting task given that the number of individuals involved is uncertain, quantification of grave goods often lacking, and associations, even by room, difficult to determine. Demographic profiles for the 2 groups are quite different. My notes on collections at the Museum of National History, taken many years ago for purposes other than demography and paleopathology, indicate that Room 53 held at least 4 males (1 young and 2 middle age—based on dental wear), an older female, and 2 infants (1 probably a newborn). Room 33 housed 9 males (5 middle age, 3 older, 1 undetermined), 6 or 7 females (1 young, 1 middle age, 2 older, the rest unknown), and an infant. In both rooms, the infants were represented by only a few small fragments. The combined total for the northern rooms (13 males, 7–8 females, and 3 infants) is quite different from that in the western rooms (23 males, 42 females, 27 subadults). Unfortunately, it is unclear just how Palkovich arrived at her numbers, whether she considered each catalog number, each room, or the entire assemblage. Counts are given by room, and if some of the disturbed burials were spread between rooms, her counts could be high. It is probably safe to say that the northern cluster had proportionately more males and fewer children.

In terms of vessels, on average, neither group had many.

While individuals may have had up to 14 vessels, the mean is closer to 2 or 3 for the western cluster and only 1 for the northern group. Ornamentation is far more difficult to quantify. In the western cluster, only Room 330 averaged more than 2 ornaments per person. This compares to thousands for the 2 Room 33 subfloor burials, and hundreds to thousands for those above the floor. Some form of distinction between the 2 burial clusters is clearly indicated.

COMPLEXITY AND CROSS-CULTURALLY DERIVED PRINCIPALS

The view that prehistoric societies were uniformly egalitarian agriculturalists is being replaced with one that sees the Pueblos as having evolved toward complexity, collapsed, abandoned their territories, and again evolved toward complexity (Stuart and Gauthier 1981:12; Tainter and Plog 1994:167). However, some researchers reach this view only by redefining complexity to include a number of intermittent steps such as nonhierarchical organization in basically egalitarian societies (Hill et al. 1996:109) or periodic alliances precipitated by some form of situational stress (Creamer 1996:99–101). Others, notably Brandt (1994:19–20), challenge the notion that the ethnographic pueblos were egalitarian, finding them stratified and hierarchical with varying degrees of centralized political power and unequal access to and control over resources.

Complex societies are typically defined as those exhibiting ascribed status differentiation, regional organization of the economy on one or more levels above the domestic sphere, and relatively large populations with some form of regional sociopolitical integration and having chiefs with the power to manipulate the labor of their supporters (Arnold 1992:61). These are distinguished from big-man societies which do not have permanent organizational changes in labor and do not generate dependable surpluses. Control over resources is limited, and big-men only occasionally command labor beyond the extended family. Leaders in a complex society have more or less permanent control over investments in resource management, procurement, processing, and storage (Arnold 1992:63).

Central to the definition of a complex society is ascribed status, that is, inequity based on heredity. One means of recognizing inequity is through mortuary data since cross-cultural studies have shown that mortuary practices are heavily influenced by social organization. If anything, mortuary ritual will under represent the degree and complexity of a status hierarchy (Wason 1994:67–68). Wason argues that dimensions observable in the archaeological record include those concerned with the treatment of the body; the preparation of a disposal facility; the content of the grave; biological dimensions including age, sex, health, and disease; circumstances of death; and genetic relationships. Biological dimensions provide independent confirmation that status was hereditary when high status individuals were consistently healthier and more robust than others in the population (Wason 1994:71, 73–74). Status differences can be inferred from major variation in the quantity of grave goods; however, in hierarchical examples, inclusion of large numbers of items is uncommon even for those of very high status. More important than quantity is the range of variation and complexity of the assemblage in terms of artifact types, quality of workmanship, material types and sources, and whether these are utilitarian or nonutilitarian. Restricted access to some items or materials presupposes distinctions (Wason 1994:93–95). Where status is achieved, prestige and power positions will be held by males. When status is hereditary, women often are included. Thus, equal proportions of male and female high status burials and the inclusion of infants and children indicates that heredity was important, while a predominance of adult males, generally in their prime, indicates hereditary factors were less important. When some children appear to have higher status than most adults, status must be acquired by something other than personal achievement (Wason 1994:98–100).

RETURNING TO CHACO

Others have made compelling arguments for regional organization of the economy, relatively large populations with regional sociopolitical integration, and for chiefs or leaders with the power to manipulate the labor of the supporters. Doyel and Lekson (1992:16–19) use the community pattern, which includes the great houses, great kivas, and road segments, to define the Chacoan region but find that the system, so defined, is almost pan-Anasazi. They find the roads and interaction with other Southwestern systems (the Hohokam and the Mimbres) indicate shared world views and access to resources as well as providing structure for interaction with those outside the system. Upham, Crown, and S. Plog find evidence for a regional alliance in the massive amounts of labor

required for great house, road, and outlier construction. Dogoszhi-style ceramics are viewed as stylistic markers indicating participation in the network extended beyond the area defined by roads and outliers (Upham et al. 1994:205–6).

The presence of public architecture in the form of great houses, roads, and great kivas implies not only integration and communication of social status and political power (Stein and Lekson 1992:93) but some form of surplus to maintain the labor forces necessary for their construction (Sebastian 1992:121). Whether this surplus came from within the productive oasis of the Canyon (Sebastian 1991:130), from more productive areas without, or from bartering some commodity such as ritual knowledge or turquoise (Judge 1989:235–40; Weigland 1992:171) is still a matter of debate. Examining the Chacoan road system for evidence of an economic function, Roney (1992:124–25) found that labor investment was greatest in the vicinity of Chacoan structures, great kivas, and shrine-like features, and their primary purpose was to link Chacoan sites into a regional system rather than to move goods.

Population in the San Juan Basin peaked in the Pueblo II era (A.D. 900–1050) (Dean et al. 1994:65; Judge 1989: 215–16). Between A.D. 1030–1090, population increased beyond what can be explained by local changes in fertility or mortality in virtually every part of the northern Southwest. The lack of significant correlations between environmental conditions and this growth suggests that change during this period was largely a cultural phenomenon involving local, regional, and interregional alliance formation (Upham et al. 1994:204–5).

Just how large the Chaco Canyon population was is still a matter of debate. Estimates range from a low of 2,100–5,652 or even 10,000 (e.g., Judge 1989:220–21; Lekson 1991:52; Schelberg 1992:63–64). Even the low number, concentrated in the area of the Canyon, would be sufficient to support an inference of complexity. Communities larger than 500 persons generally have centralized political leadership and must work out strategies for resource allocation and mate selection. When communities larger than 500 persons exist in regions with populations of 10,000 the potential for emergent social and political hierarchies increases greatly (Nelson 1995:600; Upham 1994:249–50).

Presuming that a good case has been made that the other indices of complexity are met, the mortuary evidence is examined in greater detail. As pointed out by Wason (1994:7), major differences in burial practices are not found unless there were substantial status differences. And there were substantial differences in burial practices between Pueblo Bonito and the small sites within the Canyon. Both the quantity and the variety and complexity of the mortuary assemblages were greater for those buried at Pueblo Bonito. Material, artifact types, and quality of workmanship indicate a higher status, particularly for those buried in the northern rooms. Similarly, the labor invested in preparing for the Room 33 subfloor burials, the layer of clean sand, the ashes, and the plank covering, is greater than seen elsewhere. Interment in rooms or structures is not unique to Pueblo Bonito, but converting suites of rooms into cemeteries may be.

Evidence for two different hereditary status groups at Pueblo Bonito is found in the presence of two clusters of room burials, the demographic composition of the two clusters, and biological dimensions. Communal or clustered burials with indications that these represent several burial events are almost always associated with social groupings of considerable importance and unambiguous membership, most likely kin groups. The status of those within such clusters is ranked, but high status and leadership positions can still be achieved within a rank (Wason 1994:89–92).

Burial 14, the most elaborate in both burial treatment and burial goods, is a male with slight to moderate dental wear suggesting an age of around 25 years at death. While he appears to have been the most important person buried at Pueblo Bonito, the circumstance of his death, probably caused by the wounds received, may have altered practices to the extent that treatment represents his status in death rather than that in life (e.g., Wason 1994:69–70). In other words, his placement in the northern burial cluster indicates he was a person of high status, but an inference that he was the highest ranking individual may be unwarranted given the unusual circumstances surrounding his death. Death in battle or defending something of value may have altered the group's perception of this individual and the typical burial practice. Alternatively, he may have became a renowned leader through individual achievement, although this is less likely given his relatively young age, or he could have become a leader through hereditary assent. In either of the latter cases, the treatment would reflect his position as a leader regardless of how he died. He was, undoubtedly, more than just a warrior or even a war leader because his mortuary assemblage does not suggest this was his primary role. The Aztec Ruin "warrior" was a large individual buried in what could be considered battle dress (described in an earlier section of this chapter). Another possible warrior (Wilcox 1993:80), the Magician from Ridge Ruin in Arizona, had an obsidian knife blade, 2 other large knife blades, 3 heavy blades that are probably knives, 420 projectile points, a cap with a point on the top, and club-like objects (McGregor 1943:273, 295). An apparent "warrior" from Pueblo Bonito Room 330 was buried with 28 finely chipped projectile points arranged in a triangle between his knees, a bundle of arrows at his hip, and a bowl, the same vintage as that beneath the plank floor in Room 33. Most importantly, Burial 14 was a member of a closely related group that had already achieved its rank, not merely a big-man who commanded temporary control of resources.

A healthier more robust population is an indication of access to more or higher quality resources (Wason 1994:73), although this is not invariably true. Powell found no patterned significant correspondence between the biological and social dimensions of ranked status at Moundville (Powell 1991:50). Palkovich's (1984:107, 111) much cited contention that the age profile and high rates of nutritional and infectious disease in Judd's Pueblo Bonito burials indicate these individuals were not buffered from the effects of dietary inadequacy characteristic of Anasazi groups does not stand up to scrutiny (Nelson et al. 1994b:89; Stodder 1989:179). When compared to other Southwestern populations, the Pueblo Bonito rates for porotic hyperostosis (25% for infants and children) indicative of iron deficiency anemia, are among the lowest reported and far lower than for the small-site population (83%). Furthermore, nutritional deficiency is not the only cause of anemia. Coprolites from Pueblo Bonito indicate a high rate of helminth parasitism, a consequence of communal living, poor sanitation, and contamination of food and drinking water (Reinhard and Clary 1986:184). One of these parasites causes anemia and may very well be the source of some or all of that at Pueblo Bonito (Stodder 1989:182). Similarly, the life table for Judd's Pueblo Bonito population indicates that this group had a relatively high mean age of death, higher than others reported from the Southwest (Martin et al. 1995:Table 3.181; Stodder 1989:176). The Pueblo Bonito population may have enjoyed a relatively favorable status concerning access to resources (Nelson et al. 1994b:90).

Perhaps the best indication of better health over a number of generations and for differences between the two Pueblo Bonito burial clusters is the attained growth, or stature, since this is one of the more sensitive indicators of nutritional status (Nelson et al. 1994b:97). Both the males and the females from the northern rooms are the tallest reported for Southwestern populations (Stodder 1989:184–85). Femur lengths for the northern room burials average 44.5 cm for males, 41.6 cm for females; for the western room burials the male mean is 43.6 cm and female 41.3 cm; while the small-site males average 42.8 cm and females 39.1 cm (Akins 1986:136).

Although the proportions differ, males, females, and children are found in both burial clusters, and some children were buried with quantities of turquoise. This, too, indicates that ranking was hereditary rather than achieved (e.g., Brown 1981:29; Wason 1994:98). Ceramic types associated with both clusters indicate use as burial facilities from at least late Red Mesa into the McElmo period, minimally from A.D. 1020–1150.

Further evidence of distinct kin groups within Pueblo Bonito is found in craniometric studies employing discriminate analysis. When compared to each other and to crania from Pueblo del Arroyo and small sites around Fajada Butte, the analysis indicates that the two Pueblo Bonito burial clusters are distinct populations, but they are more closely related to each other than to other groups in Chaco Canyon (Akins 1986:75).

Finding distinct kin groups with indications of ranking is antithetical to Wilcox's contention that the disarticulated burials in Pueblo Bonito had been sacrificed in periodic religious ceremonies and may have entered the site as tribute or war captives. He also maintained that slitting the throat and opening the breast during sacrificial rites would leave no physical traces on the skeletal remains (Wilcox 1993:80–81). This is highly unlikely given the stone tools available, and although no one has specifically looked for this type of evidence, neither Hrdlička (n.d.) nor Palkovich (1984) note damage that could be attributed to sacrificial rites.

If we accept a date based on the late Red Mesa Black-on-white vessel found with Burials 13 and 14, this places the two burials at around A.D. 1020–1050, when many see the Chaco system as formalizing with evidence for large-scale construction in the central Canyon (e.g., Judge 1989:237–38) and the use of great kivas (Windes and Ford 1996:308). A relatively early date for these burials and continued use of Pueblo Bonito as a family burial facility until at least A.D. 1100–1150 fit well with at least some reconstructions of the system's origin and duration. These individuals, especially Burial 13 who was the second largest of the Bonito males, had already lived for 25

to 35 years under conditions that allowed for optimal growth implying that privileged access to resources and political centralization were in place by A.D. 990–1020, if not earlier. Dean (1992:38–39) credits the hydrologic transformation occurring around A.D. 925 with benefiting floodplain farming, especially in Chaco Canyon, and enhanced predictability between A.D. 900–1150 with stimulating population growth. These conditions, combined with spatial variability in climate, reinforced the redistributive aspects of the Chaco economy and ensured the success of long-term planning and of accumulating excess production from favored areas for redistribution to less favored locales. Prolonged and serious summer drought between A.D. 1130–1180 would have particularly impacted production dependent on rainfall and undermined the systems ability to sustain itself. This particular sequence fits well with an early date for the burials and for the duration of burial at Pueblo Bonito.

Arguments over whether the system was social, economic, political, or religious based presumes it could be one without the others. As Upham et al. (1994:206) point out, there are strong interrelationships between religion, politics, and economics in virtually every society to which Chaco can be reasonably compared, whether prehistoric, ethnographic, or contemporary. Mortuary practices and the burials themselves tell us that there was ranking and those of rank had access to more or higher quality resources as well as material goods. They also tell us a little about the nature of the political control, that is, whether it was managerial and cooperative, or coercive. Chronological aspects of the mortuary and burial data fit well with the managerial and cooperative role as suggested in Dean's (1992) model derived from a consideration of independent environmental variables and the advent of big rooms at several great houses (Windes and Ford 1996). Wilcox's (1993) model also fits well, but then it was built around the known chronology. Most consider surpluses from times when conditions were optimal as the basis for construction episodes (e.g., Windes and Ford 1996). For Wilcox, it was tribute that provided for construction within the canyon, much of which went into building storage rooms for the tribute and to sustain an organized force of 500–1000 warriors sent out on roads built for the rapid movement of armies to collect more tribute (Wilcox 1993:83–84). But coercion leaves a trail, and there is virtually no evidence of coercion within the Canyon. With the exceptions of burned and broken long bones in a disturbed subfloor context at 29SJ 2358 excavated by Frank

H. H. Roberts and burned and broken long bones at Peñasco Blanco (Akins 1986:140, 165), there is little evidence of violence, especially considering the almost 200 years when Chaco was the center of a regional system. At Pueblo Bonito, there are the chops and cuts on Burial 14 and a lumbar vertebra with an embedded projectile point from one of the disarticulated skeletons in Room 330 (Judd 1954:257). Trauma in the small-site population is exceedingly rare, and none suggests any more than overextension or simple accidents (Akins 1986:34).

Comparing Chaco with La Quemada, Zacatecas, both of which have monumental architecture, extensive road systems, and a settlement hierarchy, Nelson concluded that Chaco organization was collaborative while that at La Quemada was coercive. Evidence for coercive violence at La Quemada is in the form of hundreds of bones, mainly from adult males, piled on the floor of the main ceremonial hall, shallowly buried at the foot of a small pyramid, suspended outdoors on walls or racks, and suspended from the ceiling of a temple. Bone was often mutilated, and displays were a constant reminder of the coercive power of the organization (Nelson 1995:613–15). One room at Casas Grandes similarly held six human trophy skulls, mostly males. Worked human bone includes awls, wands, a skull cap dish, and a human phalange necklace (Ravesloot 1988:36, 47). Several individuals also had pathologies that could represented battle wounds (Ravesloot 1988:76). Although less obvious than at La Quemada, these too may have served as reminders of coercive force. Nothing similar has been reported for Chaco.

Nor is it necessary to invoke coercion of that magnitude. If we accept Brandt's (1994:13) proposition that there are status differences and social inequities in the ethnographic pueblos and view differential resource potential and increasing population as setting the stage for integration and stratification, Chaco can be viewed as the progenitor or an apex of long overlooked patterns seen in the ethnographic record. Brandt's (1994:14–18) analysis of stratification in the ethnographic pueblos has many observations pertinent to prehistory. She finds that all of the pueblos were hierarchically ranked with relatively permanent positions and show well-developed organizational and bureaucratic systems that must have developed to control much larger populations. Ranking can be through religious societies, clan groups, lineages, and households with either hereditary or appointed leaders. Ranking is justified ideologically and can be based on the order of emergence, order of arrival, or the impor-

tance of ceremonial property owned. Sources of power result from factors that include the importance of ceremonial property or objects symbolically identified with authority, groups size, timing of the particular ceremony controlled, the possession of important knowledge, or the quality of resources and land controlled by the group. Differential access to resources can be controlled through ceremonial knowledge and ceremonial property; control of societal technology important in regulating food production, such as the lunar and solar calendrical systems; knowledge regarding and access to specific minerals, plants, and animals used for curing; access to shrines and to land for agriculture; regulation of trade within and between communities; and guarantees of exclusivity of production. Secrecy is essential for preserving the value of this "property" while public display of power and ideology serve to solidify the positions of leaders. Leadership is considered an onerous burden, and this combined with tight control of information discourages others from seeking positions and keeping the number of elites relatively small.

Brandt (1994:18–19) suggested several archaeological manifestations of ranking. Leaders often control storehouses of goods or food, some have larger homes, often with special rooms for storing ritual paraphernalia and for the performance of nonpublic ceremonies. Control of goods often leads to status burials. Specialized buildings, such as kivas, society houses, and space for storage of ritual material and performance of ceremonies not open to the community, should be differentially distributed and found in some but not all sites. Some portion of the population should have evidence of better nutrition. Finally, patterns of destruction or defacement may indicate resistance to hierarchy or increasing inequity.

The Chaco system, centered at Pueblo Bonito, fits well with many of these propositions/observations. Evidence for ranking in the mortuary practices, better access to food and certain material goods, and a settlement hierarchy all point to a complex system. Rather than an aberrance, Pueblo Bonito can be viewed as the seat of authority occupied by hereditary leaders who controlled access to ritual knowledge and paraphernalia and where nonpublic and public ceremonies were performed. Control of resources, either access to land, a commodity such as turquoise, trade, or even ritual knowledge, maintained the system for at least 150 years before evidence of disruption, perhaps indicated by the desecration of the burial rooms, indicate a shift in authority and a less central role for Chaco Canyon.

REFERENCES CITED

Akins, Nancy J.
1986   *A Biocultural Approach to Human Burials from Chaco Canyon, New Mexico.* Reports of the Chaco Center No. 9. National Park Service, Santa Fe.

Arnold, Jeanne E.
1992   Complex Hunter-Gatherer-Fishers of Prehistoric California: Chiefs, Specialists, and Maritime Adaptations of the Channel Islands. *American Antiquity* 57:60–84.

Brandt, Elizabeth A.
1994   Egalitarianism, Hierarchy, and Centralization in the Pueblos. In *The Ancient Southwestern Community: Models and Methods for the Study of Prehistoric Social Organization*, edited by W. H. Wills and Robert D. Leonard, pp. 9–23. University of New Mexico Press, Albuquerque.

Brown, James A.
1981   The Search for Rank in Prehistoric Burials. In *The Archaeology of Death*, edited by R. Chapman, I. Kinnes, and K. Randsborg, pp. 25–37. Cambridge University Press, Cambridge.

Creamer, Winifred
1996   Developing Complexity in the American Southwest: Constructing a Model for the Rio Grande Valley. In *Emergent Complexity: The Evolution of Intermediate Societies*, edited by Jeanne E. Arnold, pp. 91–106. International Monographs in Prehistory, Ann Arbor.

Dean, Jeffrey S.
1992   Environmental Factors in the Evolution of the Chacoan Sociopolitical System. In *Anasazi Regional Organization and the Chaco System*, edited by D. E. Doyel, pp. 35–43. Anthropological Papers No. 5. Maxwell Museum of Anthropology, Albuquerque.
1996   Demography, Environment, and Subsistence Stress. In *Evolving Complexity and Environmental Risk in the Prehistoric Southwest*, edited by J. A. Tainter and B. Bagley Tainter, pp. 25–56. Santa Fe Institute Studies in the Sciences of Complexity. Proceedings Vol. XXIV. Addison-Wesley, Reading.

Dean, Jeffrey S., William H. Doelle, and Janet D. Orcutt
1994   Adaptive Stress, Environment, and Demography. In *Themes in Southwest Prehistory*, edited by G. J. Gumerman, pp. 53–86. School of American Research Press, Santa Fe.

Doyel, David E., and Stephen H. Lekson
1992   Regional Organization in the American Southwest. In *Anasazi Regional Organization and the Chaco System*, edited by D. E. Doyel, pp. 15–21. Anthropological Papers No. 5. Maxwell Museum of Anthropology, Albuquerque.

Ellis, Florence Hawley
1968   An Interpretation of Prehistoric Death Customs in Terms of Modern Southwestern Parallels. In *Collected Papers in Honor of Lyndon Lane Hargrave*, edited by A. H. Schroeder, pp. 57–76. Papers of the Archaeological Society of New Mexico No. 1. Museum of New Mexico Press, Santa Fe.

Fowler, Andrew P., and John R. Stein
1992   The Anasazi Great House in Space, Time, and Paradigm. In *Anasazi Regional Organization and the Chaco System*, edited by D. E. Doyel, pp. 101–22. Anthropological Papers No. 5. Maxwell Museum of Anthropology, Albuquerque.

Hill, James N., W. Nicholas Trierweiler, and Robert W. Preucel
1996   The Evolution of Cultural Complexity: A Case from the Pajarito Plateau, New Mexico. In *Emergent Complexity: The Evolution of Intermediate Societies*, edited by J. E. Arnold, pp. 107–27. International Monographs in Prehistory, Ann Arbor.

Hrdlička, Aleš
n.d.   Brief Report on the Skeletal Material from Pueblo Bonito and Nearby Ruins, New Mexico, collected by Neil M. Judd. Ms. On file, Maxwell Museum of Anthropology, Chaco Archives, Albuquerque.

Judd, Neil M.
1954   *The Material Culture of Pueblo Bonito.* Smithsonian Institution Miscellaneous Collections Vol. 124. Smithsonian Institution, Washington, D.C.

Judge, W. James
1989   Chaco Canyon—San Juan Basin. In *Dynamics of Southwest Prehistory*, edited by L. S. Cordell and G. J. Gumerman, pp. 209–62. Smithsonian Institution, Washington, D.C.
1991   Chaco: Current Views of Prehistory and the Regional System. In *Chaco and Hohokam: Prehistoric Regional Systems in the American Southwest*, edited by P. L. Crown and W. J. Judge, pp. 1–30. School of American Research Press, Santa Fe.

Lekson, Stephen H.
1991   Settlement Patterns and the Chaco Region. In *Chaco and Hohokam: Prehistoric Regional Systems in the American Southwest*, edited by P. L. Crown and W. J. Judge, pp. 31–55. School of American Research Press, Santa Fe.

Lister, Robert H., and Florence C. Lister
1981   *Chaco Canyon: Archaeology and Archaeologists*. University of New Mexico Press, Albuquerque.

Martin, Debra L., Nancy J. Akins, Alan H. Goodman, and Alan C. Swedlund
1995   *Harmony and Discord: Bioarchaeology of the La Plata Valley*. Office of Archaeological Studies, Museum of New Mexico Press, Santa Fe.

Mathien, Frances J.
1984   Social and Economic Implication of Jewelry Items of the Chaco Anasazi. In *Recent Research on Chaco Prehistory*, edited by W. J. Judge and J. D. Schelberg, pp. 173–86. Reports of the Chaco Center No. 8. National Park Service, Albuquerque.

McGregor, John C.
1943   Burial of an Early American Magician. *Proceedings of the American Philosophical Society* 80:270–98.

McKenna, Peter J.
1984   *The Architecture and Material Culture of 29SJ 1360, Chaco Canyon, New Mexico*. Reports of the Chaco Center No. 7. Division of Cultural Research, National Park Service, Albuquerque.

McNitt, Frank
1966   *Richard Wetherill: Anasazi: Pioneer Explorer of Ancient Ruins in the American Southwest*. University of New Mexico Press, Albuquerque.

Moorehead, Warren K.
1906   *A Narrative of Explorations in New Mexico, Arizona, Indiana, etc.* Andover Press, Andover.

Morris, Earl H.
1924   *Burials in the Aztec Ruin*. Anthropological Papers of the American Museum of Natural History Vol. 31, Part 3. American Museum Press, New York.

Nelson, Ben A.
1995   Complexity, Hierarchy, and Scale: A Controlled Comparison between Chaco Canyon, New Mexico and La Quemada, Zacatecas. *American Antiquity* 60:597–618.

Nelson, Ben A., Timothy A. Kohler, and Keith W. Kintigh
1994a   Demographic Alternatives: Consequences for Current Models of Southwestern Prehistory. In *Understanding Complexity in the Prehistoric Southwest*, edited by G. Gumerman and M. Gell-Mann, pp. 113–46. Addison-Wesley, Reading.

Nelson, Ben A., Debra L. Martin, Alan C. Swedlund, Paul R. Fish, and George J. Armelagos
1994b   Studies in Disruption: Demography and Health in the Prehistoric American Southwest. In *Understanding Complexity in the Prehistoric Southwest*, edited by G. J. Gumerman and M. Gell-Mann, pp. 59–112. Addison-Wesley, Reading.

Palkovich, Ann M.
1984   Disease and Mortality Patterns in the Burial Rooms of Pueblo Bonito: Preliminary Considerations. In *Recent Research on Chaco Prehistory*, edited by W. J. Judge and J. D. Schelberg, pp. 103–13. Reports of the Chaco Center No. 8. National Park Service, Albuquerque.

Pepper, George R.
1909   The Exploration of a Burial Room in Pueblo Bonito, New Mexico. In *Putman Anniversary Volume* by his friends and associates, pp. 196–252. G. E. Stechert, New York.
1920   *Pueblo Bonito*. American Museum of Natural History Anthropological Papers No. 27. American Museum Press, New York.

Powell, Mary Lucas
1991   Ranked Status and Health in the Mississippian Chiefdom at Moundville. In *What Mean These Bones: Studies in Southeastern Bioarchaeology*, edited by M. L. Powell, P. S. Bridges, and A. M. W. Mires, pp. 22–51. University of Alabama Press, Tuscaloosa.

Ravesloot, John C.
1988   *Mortuary Practices and Social Differentiation at Casas Grandes, Chihuahua, Mexico*. Anthropological Papers No. 49. University of Arizona Press, Tucson.

Reinhard, Karl J., and Karen H. Clary
1986   Parasite Analysis of Prehistoric Coprolites from Chaco Canyon. In *A Biocultural Approach to Human Burials from Chaco Canyon*, edited by Nancy J. Akins, pp. 177–186. Reports of the Chaco Center No. 9. National Park Service, Santa Fe.

Roney, John R.
1992 Prehistoric Roads and Regional Integration in the Chacoan System. In *Anasazi Regional Organization and the Chaco System*, edited by D. E. Doyel, pp. 123–31. Anthropological Papers No. 5. Maxwell Museum of Anthropology, Albuquerque.

Schelberg, John D.
1984 Analogy, Complexity, and Regionally-Based Perspectives. In *Recent Research on Chaco Prehistory*, edited by W. J. Judge and J. D. Schelberg, pp. 5–21. Reports of the Chaco Center No. 8. National Park Service, Albuquerque.
1992 Hierarchical Organization as a Short-Term Buffering Strategy in Chaco Canyon. In *Anasazi Regional Organization and the Chaco System*, edited by D. E. Doyel, pp. 59–71. Anthropological Papers No. 5. Maxwell Museum of Anthropology, Albuquerque.

Sebastian, Lynne
1991 Sociopolitical Complexity and the Chaco System. In *Chaco and Hohokam: Prehistoric Regional Systems in the American Southwest*, edited by P. L. Crown and W. J. Judge, pp. 109–34. School of American Research Press, Santa Fe.
1992 *The Chaco Anasazi: Sociopolitical Evolution in the Prehistoric Southwest*. Cambridge University Press, Cambridge.

Stein, John R., and Stephen H. Lekson
1992 Anasazi Ritual Landscapes. In *Anasazi Regional Organization and the Chaco System*, edited by D. E. Doyel, pp. 87–100. Anthropological Papers No. 5. Maxwell Museum of Anthropology, Albuquerque.

Stodder, Ann Lucy Wiener
1989 Bioarcheological Research in the Basin and Range Region. In *Human Adaptations and Cultural Change in the Greater Southwest*, by A. H. Simmons, A. L. W. Stodder, D. D. Dykeman, and P. A. Hicks, pp. 167–90. Arkansas Archeological Survey Research Series No. 32. Wrightsville.

Stuart, David E., and Rory P. Gauthier
1981 *Prehistoric New Mexico: Background for Survey*. New Mexico Historic Preservation Bureau, Santa Fe.

Tainter, Joseph A., and Fred Plog
1994 Structure and Patterning: The Formation of Puebloan Archaeology. In *Themes in Southwest Prehistory*, edited by G. J.

Gumerman, pp. 165–81. School of American Research Press, Santa Fe.

Toll, H. Wolcott
1985 *Pottery, Production, Public Architecture and the Chaco Anasazi System*. Unpublished Ph.D. dissertation, University of Colorado, Boulder.
1991 Material Distributions and Exchange in the Chaco System. In *Chaco and Hohokam: Prehistoric Regional Systems in the American Southwest*, edited by P. L. Crown and W. J. Judge, pp. 77–107. School of American Research Press, Santa Fe.

Upham, Steadman
1994 Systems Modeling and Political Evolution: A Position Paper. In *Understanding Complexity in the Prehistoric Southwest*, edited by G. J. Gumerman and M. Gell-Mann, pp. 245–64. Addison-Wesley, Reading.

Upham, Steadman, Patricia L. Crown, and Stephen Plog
1994 Alliance Formation and Cultural Identity in the American Southwest. In *Themes in Southwest Prehistory*, edited by G. J. Gumerman, pp. 183–210. School of American Research Press, Santa Fe.

Vivian, R. Gwinn
1990 *The Chacoan Prehistory of the San Juan Basin*. Academic Press, New York.

Wason, Paul K.
1994 *The Archaeology of Rank*. Cambridge University Press, Cambridge.

Weigland, Phil C.
1992 The Macroeconomic Role of Turquoise within the Chaco Canyon System. In *Anasazi Regional Organization and the Chaco System*, edited by D. E. Doyel, pp. 169–73. Anthropological Papers No. 5. Maxwell Museum of Anthropology, Albuquerque.

Wilcox, David R.
1993 The Evolution of the Chacoan Polity. In *The Chimney Rock Archaeological Symposium*, edited by J. McKim Malville and G. Matlock, pp. 76–90. U.S. Department of Agriculture, Forest Service, General Technical Report RM-227. Fort Collins.

Windes, Thomas C.
1992 Blue Notes: The Chacoan Turquoise Industry in the San Juan Basin. In *Anasazi Regional Organization and the Chaco System*, edited by D. E. Doyel, pp. 159–68. Anthropological Papers No. 5. Maxwell Museum of Anthropology, Albuquerque.

Windes, Thomas C., and Dabney Ford

1992   The Nature of the Early Bonito Phase. In *Anasazi Regional Organization and the Chaco System*, edited by D. E. Doyel, pp. 75–85. Anthropological Papers No. 5. Maxwell Museum of Anthropology, Albuquerque.

1996   The Chaco Wood Project: The Chronometric Reappraisal of Pueblo Bonito. *American Antiquity* 61:295–310.

CHAPTER TEN

Morbidity and Mortality in a Classic-Period Hohokam Community

Susan Guise Sheridan

THIS CHAPTER DESCRIBES THE ANALYSIS OF A large prehistoric population from the Hohokam village of Pueblo Grande. The purpose of this investigation was to analyze the adaptive success of the inhabitants of Pueblo Grande, using the biological and cultural records to reconstruct life in this Classic period community. The first step in the analysis proceeded from a demographic perspective, analyzing mortality and survivorship patterns (Van Gerven and Sheridan 1994a). To test the paleodemographic patterns, morbidity was assessed using a variety of factors such as childhood stress, nutritional status, and adult patterns of disease. These subsequent analyses included an investigation of enamel hypoplasias (Karhu and Amon 1994), porotic hyperostosis and diploic thickening of the cranium (Mittler and Van Gerven 1994), chemical analysis of bone for diet and disease reconstruction, and a study of cortical bone maintenance (Kuzawa and Van Gerven 1994). These analyses were synthesized into a biocultural reconstruction of life at Pueblo Grande. A detailed body of information was gathered, and these independent lines of circumstantial evidence supplied a coherency of outcome that corroborated the demographic patterns. In addition, the corpus of data provided possible insight into why a population which survived over a thousand years eventually declined and disappeared with the close of the Classic period.

THE HOHOKAM CLASSIC PERIOD AND PUEBLO GRANDE

Hohokam refers to a culture that thrived in the Sonoran Desert of Arizona for nearly 1,500 years, the first agriculturalists in North America to utilize intensive irrigation techniques (Haury 1974). Some believe the Hohokam to be the descendants of indigenous peoples of the Phoenix Basin (Lipe 1983), while others have suggested that they migrated from Mesoamerica (Gumerman and Haury 1979). Evidence of their influence begins between 300 B.C. and A.D. 500, and vanishes by A.D. 1450 (Doyel 1991; Houk 1992).

One of the largest Hohokam villages in the Phoenix Basin was Pueblo Grande, located in the northern Sonoran desert (Foster 1994). A collection of over 600 inhumations from this site was utilized in the present analysis. The inhumations date to the Classic period and represent the peak population size for this site. The remains have been divided into early and late Classic phases based upon seriation of whole-vessel attributes and sherds from across the project area (Abbott et al. 1994). In the project area, the early Classic or Soho phase, is thought to date between A.D. 1150–1275. The Late Classic period, including the Civano and Polvorón phases, dates to between A.D. 1275/1300–1425/1450.

PALEODEMOGRAPHY

The fundamental measures of natural selection are differential mortality and fertility; therefore, it is not surprising that the analysis of biocultural adaptation in ancient populations often proceeds from a demographic perspective. Analysis of the age and sex structure of a community provides a starting point for detailed investigations of morbidity and mortality in the past.

Paleodemographic analyses of archaeological populations have generated both praise and criticism. Yet, a detailed demographic profile as the first step in developing an accurate biocultural perspective is useful when such analysis is possible. Therefore, this portion of the investigation assessed the feasibility of generating life tables, mortality curves, and survivorship projections for a Classic Hohokam population from Pueblo Grande. These data were then compared to a reference population, as well as to related Southwestern groups to provide a demographic context against which subsequent biocultural analyses of growth and development, nutrition, health, and disease were assessed.

Although it provides an important database for analyzing life in ancient times, demographic analysis has become the subject of considerable debate due to serious concerns regarding its ability to accurately portray population structure. In a critique of Lovejoy and coworkers' (1977) reconstruction of the Libben site population from Ohio, Nancy Howell (1982) addressed many of the problems of paleodemography. She argued that the population structure recreated from Lovejoy's life table analysis would have been both dysfunctional and virtually without ethnographic precedent. By fitting Lovejoy's life table to the "Model West I Life Table" (Cole and Demeny 1966), Howell determined that working-aged adults would have endured an extremely heavy work load, with numerous dependents (elderly and young) to support. In addition, she found that kinship relations would have differed from any known living group, because only two generations appear to have been alive at any one time.

The effect of errors in age estimation on paleodemographic reconstructions were given intense and negative scrutiny by Bocquet-Appel and Masset (1982). Having assessed several paleodemographic reconstructions, they concluded that age distributions derived from skeletal populations were simply copies of the original modern "reference" populations by which the archaeological remains were aged. They further argued that while sub-adults may be aged accurately, skeletal aging of adults is too imprecise, producing only two or three broad age categories—wholly inadequate for demographic reconstructions.

Van Gerven and Armelagos (1983) responded by demonstrating that age distributions of Nubian skeletal populations from Wadi Halfa and Kulubnarti, Sudan were not passive reflections of their reference populations. They established that bone loss and fracture rate patterns assessed independently of estimated age, produced a highly coherent age relationship. They further argued that such patterns could not be explained if the underlying age structure of the skeletal samples involved were erroneous.

Subsequently, several investigators mounted a strong defense of aging techniques, especially those applied to adults, and suggested that population sampling biases may be of greater consequence than the limitations inherent in age and sex estimation (Buikstra and Mielke 1985; Lovejoy et al. 1985; Meindel et al. 1983; Mensforth 1990). Martin et al. (1991) conducted an extensive demographic analysis of a skeletal sample from Black Mesa, Arizona and reached a similar conclusion. Survivorship at Black Mesa fell well within the boundaries of high and low mortality anthropological populations reported by Weiss (1973) and showed little sign of either forensic (age and sex estimation) or sampling bias.

More recently, Wood et al. again questioned the utility of paleodemographic reconstructions, stating that "demographic non-stationarity, selective mortality, and individual heterogeneity" (Wood et al. 1992:343) confuse statistical interpretations. Goodman's (1993) subsequent response to their concerns detailed the need to properly define the goals and parameters of paleodemography. He argued that the indirect nature of relationships between diseases and skeletal lesions makes it impossible to equate "'n' lesions per bone/individual/population sample" directly with "mortal effect(s) of the disease(s) represented" (Goodman 1993:282); thereby making survivorship the only reliable indicator of adaptive success. While agreeing that further research is necessary in documenting specific osseous responses to disease, Goodman demonstrated that Wood and coworkers' (1992) analysis was inherently flawed because they focused on individual-level analysis, overemphasized morbidity/mortality interdependence, and ignored the importance of cultural processes and ecological constraints. Konigsberg and Frankenberg further summarized the debate over paleodemography's utility by stating that, while appreciating the criticisms of such analyses, they feel "it is time to move beyond the methodological problems and return to answering the interesting larger issues" (Konigsberg and Frankenberg 1994:104).

Paleodemography's limitations are of less concern when well-preserved and well-excavated skeletons are used. However, the question continues whether poorly preserved remains can provide adequate samples for paleodemographic reconstructions. Therefore, the purpose of this phase of analysis was to address the utility of paleodemography using poorly preserved remains by: (a) documenting the methods by which estimates of sex and age were determined, (b) comparing the age structure of Pueblo Grande and the reference population by which it was aged, and (c) analyzing the demographic structure of the Pueblo Grande population from a biocultural perspective utilizing model life tables, comparable prehistoric Southwestern populations, sex ratio patterns, and diachronic changes in life expectancy from early to late Classic times.

PUEBLO GRANDE DEMOGRAPHY

The majority of the Pueblo Grande inhumations were extremely fragmentary. Fracturing and erosion of all skeletal elements resulted from natural cycles of moisture and drying in a caliche soil substrate, as well as from extensive disturbance by agriculture and construction activity. The majority of the remains recovered at Pueblo Grande came from discrete cemeteries, or "burial groups," associated with a habitation area (Mitchell 1994). Of the 17 burial groups, all but one contained inhumations, and all but four contained cremations.

Age Estimation Methods

The fragmentary nature of the inhumations created a number of difficulties in the most fundamental aspects of analysis—most particularly the assessment of age at death. Among the subadult segment of the population, the most consistently preserved elements appropriate for age determination were the teeth. Surprisingly, infants frequently had intact or largely intact long bone diaphyses. It appears that their smaller size reduced the distortion and fracturing experienced by the larger bones of older children and adults.

Although most infants had preserved skeletal and dental elements, there was little consistency in which elements were preserved, making it difficult to produce a

seriation by any common developmental feature. The potential for a seriation based on multiple criteria was even more limited. A solution to this difficulty was provided by comparing the Pueblo Grande subadults to a well-preserved, extensively studied skeletal collection dating to a similar time period.

For comparative aging purposes, the University of Colorado's collection of over 400 mummified human remains excavated from two Medieval Nubian cemeteries at the site of Kulubnarti in Sudan were utilized (Van Gerven et al. 1995). The two Christian-period groups will be referred to as "Early" (A.D. 550–750) and "Late" (A.D. 750–1500) in this chapter. Although sequencing the Hohokam remains within the Nubian developmental pattern no doubt introduced some error due to population differences in growth rates, such errors were certainly smaller than those that would have been produced had only modern growth standards been applied on a burial-by-burial basis. Both groups bear some similarity in temporal and environmental conditions—although of different ancestry, both subsisted in desert environments inimical to cultivation, thereby experiencing recurrent stresses unlike modern reference samples.

Interred in one of the driest environments on Earth, the Kulubnarti remains are in a remarkable state of preservation. Due to an almost total lack of rainfall (less than 1 mm per year), a process of natural mummification in most cases preserved soft tissues in addition to the skeletal remains. This degree of preservation has made the assessment of age at death as well as sex extremely reliable. In virtually every case, age could be estimated using multiple indicators, and sex could often be established on the basis of preserved soft tissues (Mittler and Sheridan 1992; Van Gerven and Armelagos 1983).

Given the availability of this large Kulubnarti sample, the fragmentary Hohokam subadults were seriated using the Nubians as a reference population. Placing them in the graded Nubian series allowed utilization of the developmental continuity of the Nubians, not observable in the modern standards. The Hohokam subadults were accordingly assigned a developmental age based upon position within the Nubian series. This made it possible to age a large number of individuals (193 subadults) when only isolated portions of the skeleton or dentition were present.

The Nubian adults likewise provided a large comparative series. While use of the Nubian series certainly introduced some bias into the data, the advantages clearly outweighed the liabilities. Multiple aging criteria were seldom available for an individual Hohokam case, the Nubian series therein provided a developmental context created from virtually complete skeletons.

Sex Determination Methods

Diagnosis of sex was based upon standard osteological features of the pelvis, appendicular skeleton, and cranium such as morphology of the pubic arch and sciatic notch, elevation of the auricular surface, sacral morphology, overall robusticity, and mastoid, nuchal, supraorbital, and menton development (Bass 1995; Mittler and Sheridan 1992; Schwartz 1996; Weaver 1980). While metric criteria would have provided an ideal extension to the more subjective assessments of pelvic shape and skeletal robusticity, the remains were far too fragmentary to provide a reliable sample of sufficiently precise measurement values.

Paleodemography Results

Calculations of the frequency of age at death for the Pueblo Grande individuals indicate a population experiencing high infant mortality. The modal age at death was birth, with nearly 20% of the total sample falling into that

category. This pattern indicates that the youngest inhabitants at Pueblo Grande were not under represented in the sample, since bone preservation is generally quite poor for this age cohort.

The mean age at death for the total sample was 20.1 years, with a mean adult age of 36.9 years. Cast as a survivorship curve, the Pueblo Grande population displays a Class II pattern characteristic of modern, nonindustrial, high mortality populations. While this pattern is not surprising, a number of issues must be addressed before the plausibility of the outcome can be assessed. For example, Bocquet-Appel and Masset's (1982) contention that archaeological samples inevitably mimic the age structure of the reference populations by which they were aged must be evaluated. In the present case, it is important to determine whether Pueblo Grande emerges as a passive reflection of the Nubian reference population against which it was seriated.

Nubian Demographic Comparison

A comparison of survivorship curves between Pueblo Grande and the Early Nubian sample (figure 10.1) revealed a clear similarity among the subadults. However, adult

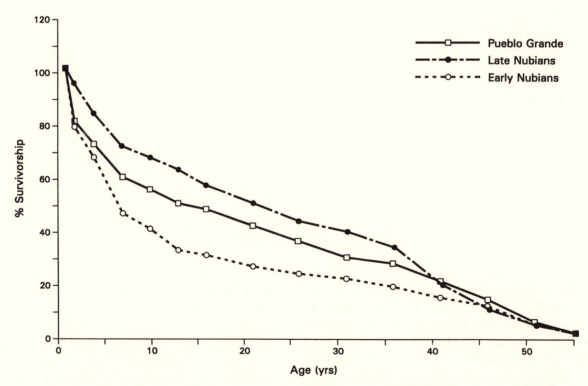

FIGURE 10.1   Comparison of Survivorship Curves between Pueblo Grande and the Early and Late Kulubnarti Nubian Sample

TABLE 10.1   Composite Life Table for the Combined Pueblo Grande Sample

x	d'x	dx	lx	qx	Lx	e⁰*x	e⁰x
0	72	199.5	1000.0	19.9	900.3	6.3	15.2
1	32	88.6	800.6	11.1	756.2	6.7	20.7
3	45	124.7	711.9	17.5	649.6	6.5	23.6
6	23	63.7	587.3	10.9	555.4	6.8	26.9
9	7	19.4	523.6	3.7	513.9	6.6	27.8
12	4	11.1	504.2	2.2	498.6	5.8	25.9
15	9	24.9	493.1	5.1	480.6	4.9	23.5
20	21	58.2	468.1	12.4	439.1	4.1	20.7
25	20	55.4	410.0	13.5	382.3	3.7	18.3
30	22	60.9	354.6	17.2	324.1	3.2	15.7
35	10	27.7	293.6	9.4	279.8	2.7	13.5
40	23	63.7	265.9	24.0	234.1	1.9	9.6
45	25	69.3	202.2	34.3	167.6	1.4	6.9
50	32	88.6	133.0	66.7	88.6	0.8	4.2
55	16	44.3	44.3	100.0	22.2	0.5	2.5
TOTAL	361	1000.0	0.0				

Note: % < 15 = .51; %15–50 = .45; % > 50 = .04; mean age = 19.3; crude birth rate = .07.

x = Ages (years)
d'x = No. of deaths at age x
dx = No. of deaths based on 1000
lx = No. of individuals living at beginning of each age class
qx = Probability of dying at age x
Lx = No. of individuals surviving between x and x + 1
e⁰*x = Mean life expectancy at the beginning of each age class
e⁰x = Mean life expectancy in years

mortality profiles differed considerably. In contrast, a comparison to the Late sample indicated a substantial difference from earliest childhood through middle age, with the most notable differences found during the subadult years. In neither comparison did the Pueblo Grande remains mimic the Nubian reference populations. This independence in age structure of the Pueblo Grande population was more clearly seen when the data were subjected to life table analysis.

A composite life table (table 10.1) for the total Pueblo Grande sample reinforced the Class II quality of high infant mortality. Mean life expectancy (e⁰x) at birth was 15.2 years and reached a peak of 27.8 years at age 9. The probability of dying (qx) reached a minimum of 2.2% just prior to the age 15 category as expected for a stable population (Weiss 1973).

Probabilities of dying revealed two childhood peaks, at birth (19.9%) and at age three (17.5%). The second 3-year peak, followed by a substantial decline to a low of 2.2%

at age 12, suggested the trauma of weaning followed by improved health during the postweaning childhood years. This pattern has been reported for other archaeological, as well as modern nonindustrial populations. Indeed the point of lowest mortality in the Pueblo Grande life table (near age 10) corresponded precisely to the pattern observed in modern anthropological populations (Weiss 1973).

Profile Plausibility

Having established the independence of Pueblo Grande's mortality profile from the Nubian reference populations, as well as a correspondence to modern nonindustrial populations, the most fundamental question can be addressed—is the demographic profile for this Hohokam population biologically plausible? By comparing salient features of the Pueblo Grande life table to model life tables derived from contemporary populations, the likelihood of demographic plausibility can be assessed.

A comparison of survivorship between the Pueblo Grande population and three "West" model life tables (figure 10.2) produced by Cole and Demeny (1966) provided a useful perspective. The three model curves are for populations with life expectancies at birth of 20, 30, and 40 years. As discussed by Howell (1982), the lowest life expectancy curve based on 20 years (CD-20/West 1) reflects a pattern of mortality more severe than that observed in any contemporary population. The Pueblo Grande population, however, fell on or above the curve for a life expectancy of 30 years from birth through age 25 and slightly above the CD-20/West 1 curve through age 40. The drop below CD-20/West 1 following age 45 was an artifact of an inability to age older adults—the 55+ category is likely to contain a percentage of individuals who lived well beyond their 50s.

As a second basis of comparison, salient features of the Pueblo Grande life table were compared to model life tables constructed by Weiss (1973) from a series of anthropological populations. Since Weiss also contended with incom-

plete reporting of data, small sample sizes, and errors in age estimation, his model tables seem particularly appropriate.

A comparison of Pueblo Grande to Weiss's model table MT 20.0–40.0 (table 10.2) revealed a number of similarities. In both cases the proportion of the population under 15 years was approximately 50%, with 45% between 15 and 50 years. While the proportion over 50 was about 2% lower in the Pueblo Grande population, the dependency ratio was virtually the same (1.23 and 1.21, respectively). The crude birth rate $(1/e^\circ x)$ of .066 at Pueblo Grande was slightly higher than the MT: 20.0–40.0 value of .064.

If these values provide a true reflection of the Pueblo Grande population, it is clear that the population was under stress. The large number of consumers (those under 15 and above 50 years) relative to producers reflected in the dependency ratio implies a heavy burden on the young adult segment of the population. Also, the crude birth rate (equal to the death rate) necessary to maintain the population was above the upper limit (approximately .055) observed among contemporary populations.

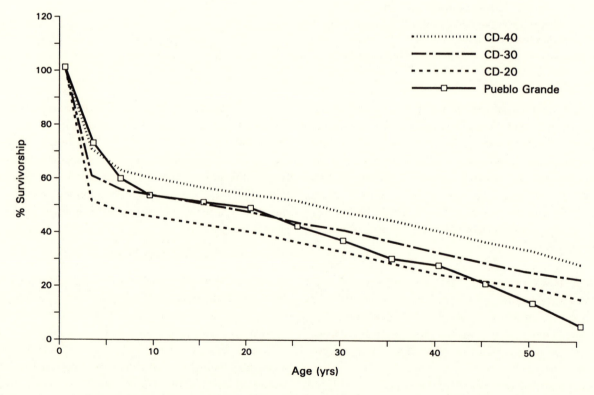

FIGURE 10.2   A Comparison of Survivorship between the Pueblo Grande Population and Three West Model Life Curves

Since gender determination could only be made on postpubescent individuals, this aspect of the analysis excluded all individuals younger than 15 years of age. The male/female ratio of 270 sexable individuals (including those for which age could not be adequately determined) was 1.11. The ratio in the life table sample was .90. Male-female mortality patterns were strikingly similar (table 10.3) with females experiencing slightly higher mortality during the reproductive years. This pattern was reflected in survivorship, probability of dying, as well as mean life expectancy. It appears that with the exception of reproduction, the stresses imposed on the adults at Pueblo Grande were experienced by males and females equally.

While it is difficult to determine whether the age and sex structure of the Pueblo Grande inhumations mirror that of the living population that created them, the pattern is sufficiently plausible to warrant further investigation. This conclusion gains further support when the Pueblo Grande population is compared to other ancient populations in the region.

Regional and Diachronic Comparisons

Regional comparison of the age structure of the Pueblo Grande population to that of other prehistoric groups (table 10.4) showed that for subadults, mortality at Pueblo Grande was high but not extreme. Infant (< 1 year) mortality was higher than that observed at Black Mesa, Casas Grandes, Pecos Pueblo, and Libben but lower than Tlajinga or Arikara. The percentage of individuals between ages one and nine was only slightly higher than Black Mesa, Casas Grandes, Arikara, and Libben. Between ages 10 and 18, only Pecos Pueblo demonstrated a lower mortality than Pueblo Grande. The appearance of lowest mortality in the 10–18

age group is consistent with stable population theory and supports the plausibility of the Pueblo Grande pattern. The percentage of individuals surviving beyond the 18 year category was low at Pueblo Grande, an expected consequence of the higher rate of infant and subadult mortality. Overall, it appears that compared to other prehistoric groups, the people of Pueblo Grande were experiencing high levels of subadult stress and mortality. If, as has been argued, subadults are a sensitive barometer of the biological

TABLE 10.3 Male and Female Life Tables for Pueblo Grande Sample

Males

x	d'x	dx	lx	qx	Lx	e⁰*x	e⁰x
15	1	13	1000	1.3	993.5	5.3	26.3
20	8	104	987	10.5	935.0	4.3	21.6
25	8	104	883	11.8	831.0	3.8	18.8
30	9	117	779	15.0	720.5	3.2	16.0
35	2	26	662	4.0	649.0	2.7	13.4
40	14	182	636	27.0	545.0	1.8	8.8
45	15	195	454	43.0	356.5	1.3	6.4
50	213	169	259	65.3	174.5	.9	4.2
55	7	90	90	100.0	45.0	.5	2.5
Total	77	1000	0				

Females

x	d'x	dx	lx	qx	Lx	e⁰*x	e⁰x
15	1	12	1000	1.2	994.0	5.0	25.2
20	11	128	988	13.0	924.0	4.1	20.5
25	11	128	860	14.9	796.0	3.6	18.1
30	11	128	732	17.5	668.0	3.2	15.9
35	7	81	604	13.4	563.5	2.7	13.7
40	9	105	523	20.1	470.5	2.1	10.4
45	10	116	418	27.8	360.0	1.5	7.4
50	17	197	302	65.2	203.5	.9	4.2
55	9	105	105	100.0	52.5	.5	2.5
Total	86	1000	0				

Note: Overall male/female ratio = 1.1; male/female ratio for tables = .9

x = Ages (years)
d'x = No. of deaths at age x
dx = No. of deaths based on 1000
lx = No. of individuals living at beginning of each age class
qx = Probablitiy of dying at age x
Lx = No. of individuals surviving between x and x + 1
e⁰*x = Mean life expectancy at the beginning of each age class
e⁰x = Mean life expectancy in years

TABLE 10.2 Comparison of the Combined Pueblo Grande Sample to Weiss's Model Table MT 20.0–40.00

Proportion (by age)	Population	
	Pueblo Grande	MT: 20.0–40.0
Under 15 years	.51	.49
15 to 50 years	.45	.45
Over 50 years	.04	.06
Dependency ratio	1.23	1.21
Crude birth rate	.07	.06

TABLE 10.4 Regional Comparison of the Pueblo Grande Sample Subadult Age Structure to Other Prehistoric American Groups

Population	n	< 1 yrs	1–9 yrs	10–18 yrs	> 18yrs
Pueblo Grande	361	20.0	29.4	9.5	40.9
Black Mesa	165	10.4	24.2	14.5	50.9
Casa Grandes	612	10.0	22.0	14.0	54.0
Pecos Pueblo	1722	18.7	14.0	8.0	59.0
Tlajinga	166	41.3	10.3	10.6	38.6
Arikara	1487	31.5	24.0	9.5	45.5
Libben	1239	18.0	22.0	14.0	46.0

Source: Martin et al. 1991, except Pueblo Grande data.

well-being of the general population, then Pueblo Grande appears to have experienced a high level of stress.

This interpretation is reinforced by a comparison to several other ancient Southwestern populations (table 10.5). Within the region, crude mortality at Pueblo Grande was exceeded only by the sites of Grasshopper and Salmon Ruin and was substantially above that of Black Mesa, Chaco Canyon, and Point of Pines. Mean age at death was less extreme at 20.1. Pueblo Grande's comparatively less extreme mean age at death in spite of a high crude death rate is a likely result of the concentration of deaths in infancy with improved survivorship among older children and adolescents. Given this general consistency of the Pueblo Grande age structure with other populations and the overall plausibility of the life table values, the final phase of the demographic analysis considered mortality at Pueblo Grande with time.

A comparison of survivorship between the early and late Pueblo Grande components revealed a small but consistent difference (table 10.6). From midchildhood forward, the late phase of the population experienced a lower rate of survivorship. From age 10 onward, mean life expectancy averaged 8% lower during the late Classic period (table 10.6). This consistent shift in mortality may reflect a decline in the effectiveness of the population's adaptation and a subsequent rise in stress that ultimately led to abandonment of the site.

Paleodemography Summary

Several conclusions can be drawn from the demographic analysis of the Pueblo Grande population. First, in spite of the errors that inevitably occur in age estimation and the truncation of older age categories, the shape of the demographic profile is consistent with known anthro-

pological populations. The Pueblo Grande profiles do not represent artifacts of the reference Nubian population, and although high, they fall within the range of related Southwestern communities. Comparison to modern anthropological populations indicates a Class II pattern consistent with nonindustrialized populations. Young adults were highly stressed; males and females appear comparably stressed, although females show a trend toward greater stress in the reproductive years.

Childhood mortality was analyzed since it provides a sensitive measure of a population's adaptive success. Demographic analysis and comparison to regional counterparts and modern populations indicated a high level of subadult stress at Pueblo Grande. Although infant underenumeration in samples of poorly preserved archaeological remains is the rule, this portion of the

TABLE 10.5 Regional Comparison of Crude Mortality Rates and Mean Age at Death

Population	Crude Mortality Rate	Age at Death
Pueblo Grande	66.2	20.1
Black Mesa	39.6	25.4
Chaco Canyon	37.7	26.5
Point of Pines	43.7	22.9
Houck	51.0	19.6
Turkey Creek	51.0	19.6
Navajo Reservation	59.5	16.8
Grasshopper	70.6	14.2
Salmon Ruin	78.4	12.7

Source: Martin et al. 1991, except Pueblo Grande data.

TABLE 10.6   Life Table for the Early and Late Classic Periods at Pueblo Grande

Early Classic

x	d'x	dx	lx	qx	Lx	e⁰*x	e⁰x
0	26	193	1000	19.3	903.5	6.65	16.6
1	9	67	807	8.3	773.5	7.12	22.6
3	17	126	740	17.0	677.0	6.72	24.6
6	8	59	614	9.6	584.5	6.97	27.9
9	3	22	555	4.0	544.0	6.69	28.5
12	1	7	533	1.3	529.5	5.94	26.7
15	2	14	526	2.7	519.0	5.02	24.1
20	8	59	512	11.5	482.5	4.14	20.7
25	9	67	453	14.8	419.5	3.61	18.1
30	9	67	386	17.4	352.5	3.15	15.8
35	3	22	319	6.9	308.0	2.71	13.6
40	9	67	297	22.6	263.5	1.87	9.4
45	12	89	230	38.7	185.5	1.27	6.4
50	14	104	141	73.8	89.0	.76	3.8
55+	5	37	37	100.0	18.5	.50	2.5
Total	135	1000	0				

Late Classic

x	d'x	dx	lx	qx	Lx	e⁰*x	e⁰x
0	21	206	1000	20.6	897.0	6.12	14.5
1	13	128	794	16.1	730.0	6.58	19.9
3	10	98	666	14.7	617.0	6.75	24.7
6	5	49	568	8.6	543.5	6.83	27.2
9	1	10	519	1.9	514.0	6.43	27.2
12	2	19	509	3.7	499.5	5.54	24.7
15	2	19	490	3.9	480.5	4.74	22.7
20	5	49	471	10.4	446.5	3.91	19.6
25	7	69	422	16.4	387.5	3.31	16.6
30	7	69	353	19.6	318.5	2.85	14.3
35	2	20	284	7.0	274.0	2.43	12.2
40	8	78	264	26.6	225.0	1.57	7.9
45	11	108	186	58.1	132.0	1.02	5.1
50	6	59	78	75.6	48.5	.74	3.7
55+	2	19	19	100.0	9.5	.50	2.5
Total	86	1000	0				

Note: Overall male/female ratio = 1.1; male/female ratio for tables = .9.
x = Ages (years)
d'x = No. of deaths at age x
dx = No. of deaths based on 1000
lx = No. of individuals living at beginning of each age class
qx = Probablitiy of dying at age x
Lx = No. of individuals surviving between x and x + 1
e⁰*x = Mean life expectancy at the beginning of each age class
e⁰x = mean life expectancy in years

population sample was well represented. As a sample, the Pueblo Grande remains have undergone enormous degradation due to both natural and cultural forces, yet even infants were numerous.

Finally, diachronic analysis between early and late Classic times showed a consistent temporal decline in adaptive response which may have contributed to site abandonment. In addition, the difference in survivorship between the early and late samples also reaffirms both the archaeological evidence of increased stress (changed settlement densities) and the improbability that the samples mimic the reference group.

As argued elsewhere (Greene et al. 1986), the shape of paleodemographic profiles such as those generated for Pueblo Grande are more important than the exact numbers. An important contribution of this analysis is that it provides a biologically plausible framework for further specific analyses of health at Pueblo Grande. The patterns of mortality illustrated in the paleodemographic analysis are therefore tested in the remainder of this chapter, using a variety of childhood and adult stress indicators to assess health and nutrition in this Classic Hohokam community.

SUBADULT STRESS

The paleodemographic reconstruction was conducted to provide a context of mortality and population structure important to the interpretation of adaptation-related phenomena such as childhood stress, growth and development, and diet and disease. Although several adult stress indicators were available for this collection, only one direct assessment of subadult stress was possible—an analysis of dental defects known as enamel hypoplasias.

Enamel Hypoplasias

As seen in figure 10.3, enamel hypoplasias appear as bands of depressed enamel resulting from the disruption of ameloblast (enamel-forming cell) activity and a corresponding deficiency in enamel thickness (Goodman et al. 1980). Although too generalized to permit diagnosis of specific disease or dietary conditions, hypoplasias have been clearly associated with periods of physiological stress and interrupted growth.

A wealth of research on enamel hypoplasia frequency across numerous populations has shown a relationship between interrupted growth and diet/disease-related factors (Cutress and Suckling 1982; Duray 1996; Goodman and

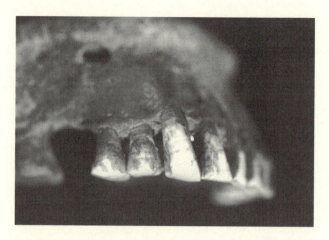

FIGURE 10.3   Enamel Hypoplasias on a Mandibular Canine, a Generalized Indicator of Childhood Physiological Stress

Capasso 1992; Goodman and Rose 1991; Goodman et al. 1987; Scrimshaw 1964; Shaw and Sweeney 1980). Hypoplastic activity reflects a syndrome of early childhood stress, combining chronic nutritional difficulty with repeated bouts of infectious disease. Although the etiology of the specific stressors which produced the dental defects cannot be directly assessed, it is clear that they played a role in early childhood morbidity and mortality.

Teeth were the best preserved tissue at Pueblo Grande; therefore, hypoplasias were analyzed to exploit the relative abundance of well-preserved dental remains. Enamel hypoplasias form sequentially with age along the tooth crown; therefore, their position can be measured and the data used to estimate age of occurrence. Thus, these age data add an important demographic dimension to the analysis of childhood stress.

HYPOPLASTIC PATTERNS AT PUEBLO GRANDE

A study by Karhu and Amon (1994) on hypoplasia frequency at Pueblo Grande provided a measure of both the timing and duration of childhood stresses. They utilized permanent maxillary central incisors and canines, and mandibular canines. Enamel development for these tooth types sample a wide period of the childhood growth and development and are generally the most sensitive to hypoplastic events. They are also the most commonly utilized teeth for hypoplasia studies, thereby providing abundant comparative literature.

Karhu and Amon selected 216 teeth representing 114 individuals for analysis. The teeth were cleaned, scored for wear according to Smith (1984), and measured using Helios needle-point calipers under magnification. Measurements were converted into six-month age intervals using Goodman and Rose's (1990) regression formulae.

Karhu and Amon (1994) found that 94% of the teeth examined exhibited hypoplastic activity. The average frequency of occurrence represented approximately "33 months of interrupted growth between birth and 7 years of age" (Karhu and Amon 1994:29), with peak hypoplasia occurrence at age five years. Temporal changes in hypoplasia frequency were minimal, although a slight trend toward increasing stress with time was indicated. Ninety-eight percent of the early Classic individuals demonstrated hypoplasias, while all from the late Classic period demonstrated hypoplastic enamel. While statistically insignificant, a pattern of early occurrence and longer duration of hypoplastic activity was noted among the late Classic individuals.

The authors also found that comparison of hypoplasia frequencies between Phoenix-area Hohokam sites (table 10.7) demonstrated a greater number of dental defects at Pueblo Grande. Figure 10.4 compares developmental age intervals and relative frequency for the four Hohokam groups. Although each demonstrated a peak between 2.5 to 5.0 years, a range consistent with other archaeological and modern populations, Pueblo Grande was the clear outlier.

As the first test of the patterns seen in the demographic analysis, the hypoplasia study of Karhu and Amon, provided some intriguing support. The enamel defect distributions indicated that during the Classic period, children were consistently experiencing prolonged periods of growth interruption. Mortality rates and hypoplasia frequencies were high for children up to approximately five years of age; hypoplasia frequencies and probability of dying values revealed a configuration common to highly stressed populations (Unicef 1986).

In addition, they found that Pueblo Grande demonstrated greater hypoplastic activity than its regional counterparts, indicating an overall pattern of greater stress in this Classic Hohokam community. Karhu and Amon postulated variation in population densities, with heightened diet and disease stress, as contributing factors. These data suggest that the Pueblo Grande population experienced both a higher hypoplasia prevalence and higher peak frequency than the other Phoenix Basin Hohokam groups, a pattern in agreement with the demographic profile.

Finally, although not statistically significant, there was a trend toward greater stress in the late Classic period. A trend toward greater subadult stress indicated in the teeth provides a tentative affirmation of the consistent reduction in survivorship with time seen in the demographic profile.

Nutritional Stress

Interpretations of the demographic and childhood stress data described above, gain additional support from the analysis of nutritional stress at Pueblo Grande. This aspect of the Pueblo Grande project provided a critical link in the analysis of population adaptation, using indirect measures of nutritional status such as skeletal lesions of the skull, as well as direct measurement of inorganic bone chemistry patterns.

POROTIC HYPEROSTOSIS AND DIPLOIC THICKENING

The first analysis of nutritional status at Pueblo Grande was a study of anemia in children and adults by Mittler and Van Gerven (1994). They investigated iron deficiency using monitors of anemia found in the skull. The first involved a porous lesion of the cranial vault generally associated with childhood known as porotic hyperostosis (figure 10.5a). Evidence of the subadult lesion persists into adulthood and thereby allows for a measure of childhood stress in mature bone.

The second monitor involved a thickening of the bones of the cranial vault (figure 10.5b). Such thickening occurs

TABLE 10.7   Comparison of Hypoplasia Frequencies between Pueblo Grande and Other Phoenix-Area Sites

Population	n	%	References
Pueblo Grande	113 of 114	99	Karhu and Amon 1994
La Lomita	1 of 10	10	Fink 1990
Grand Canal Ruins	16 of 65	25	Fink 1989; Fink and Merbs 1991; Turner and Irish 1989
Casa Buena	9 of 28	32	Barnes 1988; Turner and Irish 1989
La Ciudad	7 of 16	44	Fink and Merbs 1991

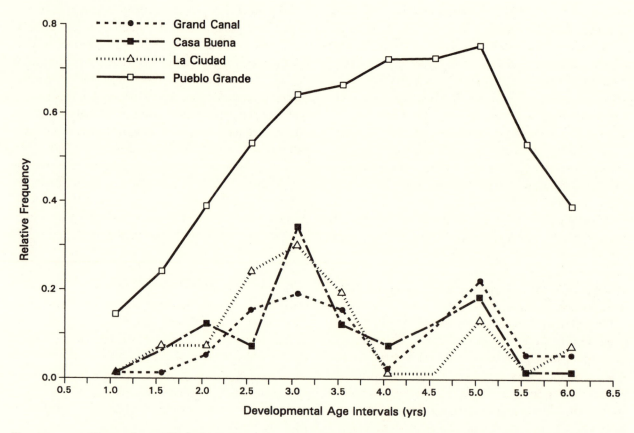

FIGURE 10.4   Comparison of Relative Frequencies of Enamel Hypoplasias and Developmental Age for Four
Hohokam Groups

when cancellous bone (diploe) expands relative to the surrounding compact bone (external and internal tables).

Porotic hyperostosis and diploic thickening are both likely indicators of iron-deficiency anemia. However, porotic hyperostosis seems to be an exclusively childhood skeletal lesion (Stuart-Macadam 1985), while diploic thickening occurs in response to anemia throughout the life cycle (Sebes and Diggs 1979). In adults, thickening of the diploe appears to be localized on the parietal bone. Thus, analysis of the childhood lesion combined with changes in diploic thickness make it possible to trace patterns of anemia across the human age range. The interactions between diet, disease, and parasitism have been studied in clinical and archaeological populations, linking such cranial changes with iron deficiency (Carlson et al. 1974; El-Najjar et al. 1976; Hengen 1971; Lallo et al. 1977; Sandford et al. 1983; Von Endt and Ortner 1982).

Porotic hyperostosis has been extensively documented in archaeological populations throughout the American Southwest (El-Najjar 1976; Merbs and Vestergaard 1985; Palkovich 1985; Stodder 1990; Walker 1985). Mittler and Van Gerven's (1994) exhaustive analysis of anemia at Pueblo Grande added significantly to that database by incorporating a quantitative analysis of diploic thickening with a systematic consideration of porotic hyperostosis. This provided an opportunity to assess the cumulative effect of anemia at Pueblo Grande and compare these patterns to other stressors found in the skeleton, as well as the demographic profile.

ANEMIA AT PUEBLO GRANDE

Mittler and Van Gerven utilized 191 male and female crania ranging in age from birth through 55+ years. Diachronic classification into Classic categories was possible for 110 of the samples.

Porotic Hyperostosis. Mittler and Van Gerven found that over 50% of the crania revealed early and late traces of the childhood porotic lesion, a frequency comparable to that observed in other Southwestern groups (El Najjar et al. 1976; Stodder 1990). Although the group suffered from high levels of porotic hyperostosis, no signs of difference were found in lesion frequency by age, sex, or time period.

Diploic Thickening. Clinical studies (Reynolds 1962; Sebes and Diggs 1979) indicate that anemia is reached when the diploe is at least 2.3 times thicker than the combined thickness of the external and internal tables (1:2.3). Mittler and Van Gerven (1994) found that adult diploic thickness averaged 1:2.17 at Pueblo Grande, only 6% below the clinical boundary. When analyzed by sex, females significantly exceeded male ratios across the adult age range. During the reproductive years, the female ratio exceeded the clin-

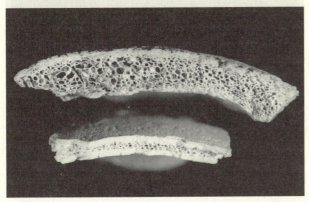

FIGURE 10.5 Cranial Indicators of Anemia, Expressed as (a) Porotic Hyperostosis of the Parietals and (b) Diploic Thickening of the Parietals (upper cross-section illustrates above normal thickening, compared with lower cross-section of normal thickening)

ical boundary by 11%. Overall diploic thickness for young adult women was 48% higher than for similarly aged males (figure 10.6), illustrating the impact of iron deficiency on woman during the child-bearing years. The combined effects of menstruation, pregnancy, and lactation likely contributed to this pattern of anemic response, a factor which may in part explain the demographic trend toward higher female mortality in this age cohort. A temporal increase in thickening from the early to late Classic period was also noted for both sexes. Females increased by 20%, while males jumped 34%.

Porotic Hyperostosis/Diploic Thickness Interactions. Mittler and Van Gerven also found that the relationship between age, porotic hyperostosis and diploic thickening differed by sex. Among males, only those individuals with the childhood manifestation of porotic hyperostosis exceeded the critical diploic thickness ratio in adulthood. Among females, those without the lesion developed thicker diploes with age in the same manner as the males; however, women with the childhood lesion significantly increased their diploe significantly earlier, during the reproductive years. Mittler and Van Gerven argued that individuals, particularly females with childhood porotic hyperostosis, developed an earlier, more severe anemia than those without the lesion. Furthermore, females with the childhood lesion not only had thicker diploes earlier than their female counterparts without the lesion, they also had significantly reduced mean life expectancy. No comparable difference in life expectancy was observed among males.

The interaction between porotic hyperostosis and diploic thickening by age and sex intensified with time. Late Classic adults with the lesion averaged 34% thicker diploes than their early counterparts, those without porotic hyperostosis increased by only 14%. Diachronic changes in diploic thickness in males with porotic hyperostosis increased by 47% compared to 37% among females.

The anemia study of Mittler and Van Gerven was highly consistent with the demographic and hypoplasia patterns of high childhood stress during the Classic period at Pueblo Grande. They found that women showed chronic anemia, exacerbated during the childbearing years—a pattern which worsened with time. Among men, a chronic, age-related trend was seen, with a severe increase during the late period. A pattern of worsening health as the Classic period progressed, with greater susceptibility among reproductive-aged women, again fits the paleodemographic findings. The analysis of porotic hyperostosis and diploic

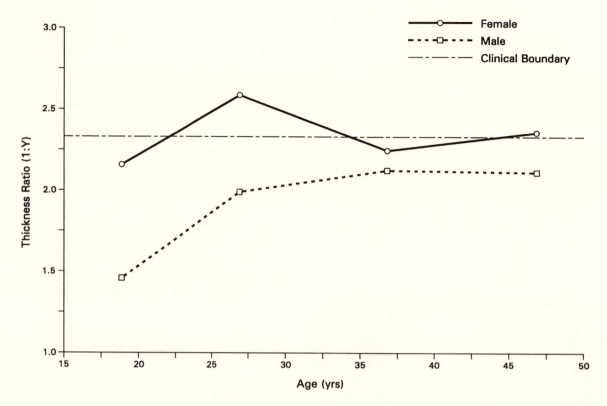

FIGURE 10.6   Comparison of Male and Female Diploic Thickness for the Pueblo Grande Collection. (The clinical boundary is also illustrated.)

thickening, individually and in tandem, provided an important tool of analysis in the assessment of morbidity at Pueblo Grande. However, these measures supply an indirect method of assessing a nutritional deficiency. The next study will explore a direct measure of nutritionally important elements.

MINOR AND TRACE ELEMENT ANALYSIS

Anthropologists and clinicians alike have become actively involved in the analysis of minor and trace elements in human bone. Bone is not affected by short-term changes in elemental abundances—as are blood, hair, and urine—and is therefore well suited for reconstructions of health and nutrition. Bone is a dynamic, living tissue which provides the body support, leverage, protection, and storage (Shipman et al. 1985). It is this last function with which elemental analysis is most interested.

In its capacity as a reservoir, bone has provided anthropologists with a means for reconstructing past diet and dis-

ease. Whereas physiology, internal crystal chemistry, and environmental factors may all influence elemental concentrations, Schroeder (1965) found that diet played the largest role in element uptake in humans. In this manner, bone provides a composite record of lifetime metabolic interactions. Therefore, "the same features that make [bone] resistant to degradation, make it an excellent repository of past biological activity" (Armelagos et al. 1989:232).

Unquestionably, the most frequent application of minor and trace element analysis to archaeological bone has been for studies of prehistoric diet (Klepinger 1984). Chemical analysis of human bone therefore was undertaken to reconstruct dietary patterns in the adult segment of a Hohokam population from Pueblo Grande. Nine elements and three elemental ratios were used in this analysis—strontium (Sr), barium (Ba), magnesium (Mg), iron (Fe), zinc (Zn), vanadium (V), calcium (Ca), phosphorus (P), and manganese (Mn); and strontium/zinc (Sr/Zn), calcium/phosphorus (Ca/P), and strontium/calcium (Sr/Ca).

In addition to biological factors, such as age, sex, diet, and disease, producing variation in minor and trace element values, postmortem alteration can also influence element concentrations. Diagenesis, the process of post-depositional change in bone mineral, is of major concern to the chemical analysis of archaeological remains.

Bone mineral is composed of an inorganic phase consisting of crystals of hydroxyapatite [$Ca_{10}(PO_4)_6(OH)_2$] forming a relatively large surface area for ion exchange. Over time, elements may enter interred bone filling minute voids and fissures, become part of the crystal structure through substitution, or adsorb to the bone surface (Lambert et al. 1985). The extent and varieties of change are a product of the chemical environment in which the bone is buried—temperature, pH, EH (oxidation-reduction), and moisture are major contributors (Hare 1980; Ortner et al. 1972; Parker and Toots 1980).

Research indicates that diagenesis may result in homogenization of elemental values in ancient remains (Price 1988). Elements likely to enrich bone include Fe and Mn (Buikstra et al. 1989; Lambert et al. 1979, 1984, 1985; Sheridan 1992). Mixed results have been obtained for Mg, Ba, and V (Buikstra et al. 1989; Kyle 1986; Lambert et al. 1983, 1984, 1985; Price 1989; Sheridan 1992). In addition, contradictory results for the same elements appear in the literature: Toots and Voorhies (1965) and Parker and Toots (1970, 1980) stated that Sr is stable over time. However, numerous investigators have demonstrated that Sr levels are affected differentially depending on the depositional context (Lambert et al. 1985; Pate and Brown 1985; Price 1989; Radosevich 1993; Sillen 1981; White and Hannus 1983).

The presence of diagenetic alteration may not obliterate paleodietary signatures however. Ezzo et al. (1995) point out that antemortem dietary patterns may still be interpretable even when diagenesis is clearly evident. Therefore, the purpose of this portion of the Pueblo Grande investigation was to determine whether elemental patterns indicative of antemortem reality could be found along the dimensions of age, sex, and time using this poorly preserved bone.

Elemental Analysis of the Pueblo Grande Remains

Sixty adults were utilized for the chemical analysis, based on age (over 18 years), degree of preservation, and the proviso that the femur had to be broken during interment to minimize destruction of the remains, in agreement with the Tohono O'odham Council which initially approved this research. Thirty-four of the 60 samples could be placed into either the early or late Classic period for diachronic analysis. All samples were analyzed using Inductively Coupled Plasma-Atomic Emission Spectroscopy (ICP-AES), according to the methods outlined in Sheridan (1992) and Jones and Sheridan (1994). Table 10.8 lists descriptive statistics for the nine elements and three ratios, and table 10.9 compares the Pueblo Grande concentrations to other populations from the region, including the Black Mesa Anasazi (Martin et al. 1991), Pecos Pueblo (Spielmann et al. 1990), and the Virgin Branch Anasazi (Zaino 1968).

DIAGENESIS

To directly test the degree of diagenesis, postdepositional alteration in these remains was analyzed. First, quality of bone preservation was assessed using solubility profiles to test the adequacy of the cleaning procedure. Fracalacci (1989) and Sillen (1989) suggested using the Ca/P solubility profile to monitor the degree of calcium carbonate ($CaCO_3$) intrusion. They contend that when $CaCO_3$ contamination is present, the samples need to be washed until the Ca/P ratio approaches 2:1. The Pueblo Grande bone was buried in a caliche-rich deposit, producing a chalk-like consistency to the bone mineral. When samples were placed in deionized water for cleaning, dissolution of this $CaCO_3$ matrix was visible, as a milky-white residue which leached from the bone immediately upon immersion in water. The Ca/P Hohokam wash water ratio did reach a 2:1 ratio, although as reported below, this did not fully eliminate diagenetic Ca contamination.

Comparison of modern bone composition to archaeological bone is another measure employed for assessing quality of preservation. By dry weight, fresh bone consists of approximately 70% mineral and 30% organic materials such as collagen. Bone ash constitutes about 67% of whole bone, consisting largely of a 2:1 Ca/P mixture in the form of hydroxyapatite crystals (Price 1989). Therefore, comparison of Ca/P ratios, percentage of Ca, and percentage of P to modern values provides an estimate of the quality and preservation of archaeological bone mineral (Hancock et al. 1987; Kyle 1986; Price 1989; White and Hannus 1983).

According to published estimates, the Ca/P ratio of modern bone is 2.16 (Hancock et al. 1987; Kyle 1986; White and Hannus 1983), Ca content of bone ash by weight (10,000 ppm = 1% ash weight) is approximately 37% (Tanaka et al. 1981), and P is about 15–17% (Price 1989). The Pueblo Grande Ca/P ratio equaled 1.98, percentage of Ca was 33.9%, and percentage of P was 16.9%, indicating some diagenetic alteration in the two major inorganic components of bone.

TABLE 10.8 Chemical and Nutritional Properties of the Elements and Ratios Used in This Study

Elements	Mean (ppm)	CV
Ba	109.9 ± 90.6	82.4
Ca	338678.6 ± 20603.0	6.1
Fe	149.0 ± 76.2	51.1
Mg	1951.5 ± 824.3	42.2
Mn	21.5 ± 14.7	68.5
P	169555.4 ± 9248.8	5.5
Sr	171.6 ± 47.3	27.6
V	24.9 ± 16.6	67.4
Zn	141.6 ± 36.1	25.5
Ca/P	2.0 ± .2	8.9
Sr/Ca	.5 ± .1	29.0
Sr/Zn	1.4 ± .9	63.9

Although diagenesis was indicated by all measures, comparisons by sex and time were conducted to determine whether biologically plausible demographic and diachronic patterns were still identifiable. Elemental patterns by sex provided the first evidence for this plausibility.

Variation by Sex. Descriptive statistics for bone element values by sex are listed in table 10.10. Ba (p = .002), Fe (p = .04), Mg (p = .0008), V (p = .05), Zn (p = .02), and the Sr/Zn ratio (p = .02) showed significant to highly significant variation by sex. Females had higher concentrations of Fe (p = .04), V (p = .05), and Sr/Zn (p = .02) than their male counterparts, and highly significant differences were found for Ba (p = .002) and Mg (p = .0008). Most of the elements found in higher concentrations in females, such as Ba, Mg, Sr, and V, were elements which have been associated with plant consumption (Brown 1973; Lambert et al. 1979, 1982). As an alternative explanation for high Sr values in females, it has been suggested that pregnancy and lactation produce elevated Sr levels in females independent of dietary factors (Sillen and Kavanagh 1982). While this may be a contributing factor at Pueblo Grande, the elevated Ba, Mg, and V levels coupled with significantly lower Zn levels than males, seem to support a dietary hypothesis.

Associated archaeological evidence from Pueblo Grande and the surrounding region appear consistent with this dietary interpretation (Gasser and Kwiatkowski 1991; Szuter 1991). The plant remains (both domesticated and wild) found at the site include agave, chenopodium and amaranthus (green, leafy weeds), maize, squash, beans, mesquite, mustards, grasses, and cactus. With the exception of maize, many of these plants are good sources

TABLE 10.9 Comparison of Pueblo Grande Elemental Values to Three Other Prehistoric Southwest Populations

Elements and Ratios	Pueblo Grande		Black Mesa	Pecos Pueblo		Anasazi
	mean	*cv*	*mean*	*mean*	*cv*	*mean*
Ba	109.9 ± 90.6	82.4	21.0	—	—	—
Ca	338678.6 ± 20603.0	6.1	270000.0	—	—	—
Fe	149.0 ± 76.2	21.1	29.4	—	—	208 ug/g
Mg	1951.5 ± 824.3	42.2	2258.0	—	—	—
Mn	21.5 ± 14.7	68.5	1.6	—	—	—
P	169555.4 ± 9248.8	5.5	138000.0	—	—	—
Sr	171.6 ± 47.3	27.6	149.0	340.0±60.0	17.0	—
V	24.9 ± 16.6	67.4	—	—	—	—
Zn	141.6 ± 36.1	25.5	101.5	—	—	—
Ca/P	2.0 ± .2	8.9	2.0	—	—	—
Sr/Ca	.5 ± .1	29.0	.1	—	—	—
Sr/Zn	1.4 ± .9	63.9	1.5	—	—	—

Note: All values in parts per million (ppm) unless otherwise indicated. Formats for reporting concentrations follow those used in each study. Standard deviation and coefficient of variation are included when available. Data for comparative collections were gathered from Martin et al. (1991:76 [Black Mesa]), Spielmann et al. (1990:752 [Pecos Pueblo]), and Zaino (1968:434 [Anasazi]).

TABLE 10.10   Elemental Comparison by Gender among the Adults at Pueblo Grande

Elements and Ratios	Males		Females		Students' T-test		
	mean	*cv*	*mean*	*cv*	*p*	*t*	*df*
Ba	74.8 ± 64.1	85.6	153.3 ± 100.1	65.3	**.002**	-3.0	38
Ca	339435.9 ± 19976.2	5.9	337688.3 ± 22178.8	6.6	.4	.2	28
Fe	132.7 ± 64.1	48.3	171.6 ± 89.2	52.0	**.04**	-1.7	44
Mg	1653.4 ± 629.7	38.1	2399.7 ± 894.0	37.3	**< .001**	-3.4	45
Mn	20.7 ± 12.6	61.1	18.6 ± 8.7	46.8	.1	1.3	35
P	170228.0 ± 9309.0	5.5	169131.8 ± 9664.7	5.7	.4	.4	45
Sr	166.7 ± 47.9	28.7	179.0 ± 46.7	26.1	.2	-.9	43
V	19.2 ± 13.1	68.3	27.6 ± 16.6	60.2	**.05**	-1.7	34
Zn	150.5 ± 25.8	17.2	127.4 ± 45.7	35.9	**.02**	2.1	42
Ca/P	2.0 ± .1	6.8	2.0 ± .2	11.3	.4	.3	29
Sr/Ca	1.1 ± .4	36.2	1.5 ± .6	43.6	**.02**	-2.2	39
Sr/Zn	.5 ± .2	33.1	.5 ± .1	23.6	.5	-.1	27

Note: All values in parts per million (ppm).

of Sr, Mg, and V. Given their higher levels of Mg, V, and Sr, females may have been consuming such foods in greater quantity than were their male counterparts.

Males demonstrated significantly higher Zn levels, a pattern often associated with the intake of animal protein (Hatch and Geidel 1985; Lambert et al. 1983; Rheingold 1983). Numerous archaeological and modern studies have indicated a stratification of dietary intake among agricultural communities, wherein males receive preferential access to limited meat resources. It should be noted that Ezzo (1994) regarded variations in Zn concentrations as artifacts of bone mineralization (Ezzo et al. 1995). Preliminary work by Goodman and coworkers (personal communication 1996) with living populations on controlled diets, however, points to a strong association between animal protein intake and bone Zn levels.

When considered in concert, the pattern of high plant-associated elements in females, and the high, possibly protein-associated Zn in males, may point to a relative difference in the acquisition of food resources. It appears that females may have consumed greater quantities of plant materials than their male counterparts. This becomes clearer when analyzed diachronically.

Variation by Time. Individuals were then compared between the early and late Classic period. Descriptive statistics for each element by time period are listed in table

10.11, as are the results of between group comparisons using Students' t-test.

Several elements demonstrated a change when viewed temporally, more fully illustrative when compared by sex within (table 10.12) and between (table 10.13) each period. For example, moving from early to late Classic times, V levels increased significantly, possibly indicating an increasing reliance on plant material. For the element Mg, females maintained higher levels than males, also indicating higher plant consumption among women during both periods. Ba was also found in higher concentrations among the late Classic females compared to their male counterparts. Conversely, while overall levels decline, late Classic males were higher in Zn when compared to females. It appears from these combined data that the male/female differences in diet were exacerbated in the late Classic.

Archaeological evidence, as well as the various studies of physiological stress for the Pueblo Grande Hohokam, indicated that individuals were under greater stress in the late Classic (see articles in Van Gerven and Sheridan 1994a). Pueblo Grande was eventually abandoned during this time—changes in dietary patterns indicating greater reliance on plant materials among females and increased discrepancies between the sexes may have eventually contributed to (or at least be indicative of) the site's decline.

Variation by Age. Finally, elemental differences were

TABLE 10.11   Elemental Comparisons by Time Period among the Adults at Pueblo Grande

Elements and Ratios	Early Classic		Late Classic		Students' T-test		
	mean	*cv*	*mean*	*cv*	*p*	*t*	*df*
Ba	107.4 ± 93.6	87.1	95.5 ± 24.9	90.2	.4	.4	30
Ca	326387.0 ± 21345.2	6.5	348267.6 ± 15671.5	4.5	**.01**	-2.5	19
Fe	144.6 ± 73.3	50.7	130.7 ± 75.0	57.3	.3	.5	31
Mg	1969.5 ± 936.8	47.6	2005.0 ± 922.7	46.0	.5	-.1	32
Mn	18.3 ± 10.7	58.8	25.3 ± 11.6	45.7	.1	-1.6	24
P	167428.8 ± 9250.4	5.5	170794.0 ± 8658.2	5.1	.1	-1.1	33
Sr	182.8 ± 50.9	27.8	156.6 ± 36.9	23.6	.1	1.6	30
V	16.0 ± 11.0	68.8	29.1 ± 17.1	58.9	**.01**	-2.3	23
Zn	146.6 ± 30.5	20.8	136.3 ± 49.2	36.1	.2	.7	30
Ca/P	2.0 ± .2	11.5	2.0 ± .1	5.5	.2	-1.0	26
Sr/Ca	1.3 ± .5	38.7	1.1 ± .6	55.9	.2	1.0	26
Sr/Zn	.6 ± .1	25.4	.4 ± .1	27.2	**.04**	1.9	18

Note: All values in parts per million (ppm).

analyzed across the adult age range. Each element was regressed on age for the entire population, then examined for gender differences (table 10.14). The only significant changes with age were among the females in Fe levels (p = .05) and the Ca/P ratio (p = .05). Iron increased while Ca/P decreased. In addition, analysis of variance (ANOVA) by age groups showed that the greatest Fe increase and Ca/P decrease (p = .05) were in the 50+ age group.

The reduction in Ca/P with age indicated one of two processes at work. First, it may provide evidence for osteopenia—as women aged, there was a significant decrease in the concentration of the two main mineral components of bone. Or alternatively, due to the more porous nature of older bone resulting from osteopenia, more of the diagenetically introduced Ca from the caliche-rich soil was washed from the bone during the cleaning process. An overall increase in Ca alone with time, appears to point to the later possibility, especially when combined with the other indicators of significant diagenetic alteration related to burial in a high $CaCO_3$ environment.

In a similar pattern, Fe values indicate alteration. Iron levels were significantly higher in women compared to men during both time periods. Although a possible reflection of an aberrant antemortem pattern, the Pueblo Grande Fe concentrations seem to reflect diagenetic alteration instead. This hypothesis gains credence based upon several factors. First, Fe is known to be sensitive to diagenetic alteration (Ezzo 1994; Lambert et al. 1985;

Sheridan 1992), and diagenesis clearly occurred. Also, higher female Fe levels do not coincide with the other biological monitors in this population—namely the analysis of anemia which demonstrated significantly higher rates of iron deficiency in reproductive-aged women (Mittler and Van Gerven 1994). Furthermore, this pattern is inconsistent with other archaeological populations, which regularly demonstrate depleted iron in females (Sheridan 1992). Although circumstantial, there is strong evidence that the iron pattern seen at Pueblo Grande is the result of postdepositional alteration and not nutritional reality (table 10.15).

A more plausible indicator of a remnant antemortem Fe pattern was reflected in the age-on-element regression and ANOVA comparisons illustrating increased Fe levels with age. Higher Fe levels in women may result following menopause and a cessation of the demands of pregnancy, lactation, and menstruation. The significant rise in the 50+ age category may indicate either increased porosity with age allowing an influx of Fe from the soil or indeed represent a measure of an expected increase in women following the reproductive years. However, the strong circumstantial case for diagenetic alteration of this element hints at the former hypothesis.

SUMMARY

The results of the elemental analyses provide evidence for several patterns at Pueblo Grande. First, diagenesis did

TABLE 10.12 Elemental Comparisons by Time Period and Gender at Pueblo Grande

Early Classic

Elements and Ratios	male mean	cv	female mean	cv
Ba	86.0 ± 90.8	105.5	133.5 ± 95.4	71.4
Ca	327645.1 ± 20253.6	6.2	324374.2 ± 25313.1	7.8
Fe	131.2 ± 67.1	51.2	158.1 ± 80.3	50.8
Mg	1603.3 ± 813.5	50.7	2417.2 ± 920.4	38.1
Mn	20.0 ± 13.4	67.0	16.0 ± 6.2	38.8
P	167045.2 ± 7979.4	4.8	167850.8 ± 10910.2	6.5
Sr	171.4 ± 42.2	24.6	198.7 ± 60.1	30.3
V	13.8 ± 6.5	46.9	20.2 ± 17.1	84.7
Zn	150.7 ± 25.7	17.1	140.9 ± 37.1	26.3
Ca/P	2.0 ± .2	9.1	2.0 ± .3	15.0
Sr/Ca	1.2 ± .4	35.5	1.6 ± .6	39.0
Sr/Zn	.5 ± .1	27.1	.6 ± .1	25.2

Late Classic

Elements and Ratios	male mean	cv	female mean	cv
Ba	55.0 ± 29.0	52.8	176.6 ± 109.9	62.3
Ca	353195.1 ± 9244.7	2.6	343340.1 ± 20563.2	6.0
Fe	105.3 ± 42.6	40.4	171.4 ± 101.6	59.3
Mg	1535.6 ± 583.0	38.0	2630.9 ± 956.5	36.4
Mn	31.5 ± 9.7	30.9	19.2 ± 10.7	55.5
P	70014.4 ± 9987.5	5.9	171838.7 ± 7279.2	4.2
Sr	148.3 ± 39.2	26.4	169.8 ± 32.3	19.0
V	23.3 ± 16.3	70.0	37.8 ± 16.4	43.4
Zn	161.4 ± 25.3	15.7	96.0 ± 53.4	55.6
Ca/P	2.0 ± .1	5.5	2.0 ± .1	5.8
Sr/Ca	.9 ± .3	30.4	1.6 ± 1.1	69.6
Sr/Zn	.4 ± .1	32.3	.5 ± .1	22.8

Note: All values in parts per million (ppm).

occur in the bones, as evidenced by the altered Ca/P ratio and, quite likely, the heightened female Fe levels. However, patterns demonstrated by several other elements may represent biological reality, and it should not be assumed that every element is equally affected in the postdepositional environment. Next, variation in elements by sex may point to a relative difference in the acquisition of food resources, where males enjoyed preferential access to the more limited animal protein while females consumed greater quantities of plant material. The dietary asymmetry becomes amplified from early to late Classic times in each sex. The only significant correlations with age were in female Fe

and Ca/P levels. Iron increased with age, while the Ca/P ratio decreased. Although increasing Fe levels with age may result following menopause, the higher female-to-male Fe levels probably indicate diagenesis. It is quite possible that the increased Fe found in the 50+ individuals resulted from more porous bone often associated with older individuals. Conversely, the Ca/P reduction with age may indicate either: (a) evidence for osteopenia—as women aged, these two main mineral components of bone decreased significantly or (b) because older bone is often more porous due to osteopenia, more of the diagenetically-introduced Ca from the soil was washed out during the cleaning process. These data indicate that, even in poorly preserved bone, some echo of biological reality may be extracted from the remains. When synthesized with a variety of skeletal indicators indicative of health status, the elemental data may provide some insight into an overall assessment of morbidity and mortality at Pueblo Grande.

ADULT STRESS

Given the archaeological evidence for site abandonment in the late Classic, this segment of the research was designed to reveal changing patterns of adult stress during the final phases of occupation. Adults are the primary food-getters, nurturers, and individuals responsible for establishing

TABLE 10.13 Students' T-test Comparison of Elemental Values (from Table 10.12) by Time Period and Gender at Pueblo Grande

Elements and Ratios	Early Classic male vs. female			Late Classic male vs. female			Male early vs. late			Female early vs. late		
	p	t	df	p	t	df	p	t	df	p	t	df
Ba	.1	-1.1	18	**.01**	-3.1	10	.2	.9	17	.1	-1.1	10
Ca	.4	.3	11	.2	.9	6	**.02**	-2.4	10	.1	-1.2	7
Fe	.2	-.8	18	.06	-1.7	11	.2	.9	16	.4	-.3	13
Mg	**.02**	-2.1	18	**.01**	-2.7	12	.4	.2	17	.3	-.4	12
Mn	.2	.7	14	**.05**	1.9	8	.06	-1.7	12	.3	-.7	10
P	.4	-.2	19	.4	-.4	12	.2	-.7	17	.3	-.4	13
Sr	.1	-1.2	17	.2	-1.0	11	.1	1.2	17	.2	.8	10
V	.2	-1.1	13	.1	-1.4	8	.06	-1.7	14	.08	-1.6	7
Zn	.3	.7	17	**.01**	3.0	11	.2	-.9	17	.06	1.8	11
Ca/P	.5	-.06	12	.3	.7	6	.4	-.4	10	.4	.1	8
Sr/Ca	.08	-1.5	15	.07	-1.6	9	.08	1.4	17	.5	-.02	7
Sr/Zn	.4	-.4	10	.2	-1.0	6	.06	1.7	10	.2	1.0	6

TABLE 10.14 Age-on-Element Regressions for the Combined Sample and by Gender at Pueblo Grande

Elements and Ratios	All				Males				Females			
	p	r	F	n	p	r	F	n	p	r	F	n
Ba	1.0	.008	.003	42	.3	.2	1.0	24	.4	.2	.7	16
Ca	.7	.08	.2	30	.2	.3	1.6	17	.1	.4	2.4	13
Fe	.1	.2	2.4	48	.9	.36	.02	26	**.05**	.4	4.4	20
Mg	1.0	.001	5.80E-05	49	.6	.1	.3	27	.7	.09	.16	20
Mn	.8	.05	.09	35	.9	.04	.03	19	.9	.04	.03	16
P	.6	.08	.3	49	.4	.2	.6	27	.07	.4	3.6	20
Sr	.5	.1	.4	47	.9	.04	.04	27	.13	.4	2.6	18
V	.8	.05	.09	36	1.0	.01	.004	23	.5	.2	.5	13
Zn	1.0	.01	.003	46	1.0	.004	2.98E-04	26	.6	.1	.2	18
Ca/P	.09	.3	3.0	30	.9	.04	.03	17	**.05**	.5	4.7	14
Sr/Zn	.6	.09	.3	42	.9	.01	.004	26	.2	.4	2.0	14
Sr/Ca	.8	.06	.1	29	.7	.1	.1	17	.8	.07	.04	12

p = significance
r = regression
F = F ratio
n = sample size

TABLE 10.15 Comparison of Iron Values from Several Archaeological Collections Sampled at the Midshaft Femur

Population	Occupation Dates (A.D.)	Bone	n	Fe Value	References
Black Mesa (Arizona)	1100–1300	femur midshaft	10	29.4*	Martin et al. 1991:69
Pueblo Grande (Arizona)	1050–1400	femur midshaft	60	148.9 ± 76.2	table 10.8
Mayview (Pennsylvania)	1400	femur	1	44.0*	Becker et al. 1968:329
Kulubnarti (Sudan)	750–1550	femur midshaft	70	33.3 ± 15.9	Sheridan 1992:71
Chancay (Peru)	1300	tibia, femur	5	11–100	Becker et al. 1968:329

Note: Fe values reported in parts per million (ppm).
* standard deviation not available in the published article.

cultural buffers which permit society's adaptation; analysis of their well-being is therefore of paramount importance to a complete biocultural reconstruction of the population.

Despite the errors that inevitably occur in age estimation and the truncation of older ages into the 55+ year age category, the shape of the demographic profile for Pueblo Grande was consistent with known anthropological populations. And as argued earlier, the shape of a paleodemographic profile is more important than the exact numbers. Thus, using the profile as a first step in generating a hypotheses about life in this Hohokam community, the adult segment of the collection was next analyzed for evidence of physiological stress using age-related bone loss (Kuzawa and Van Gerven 1994).

Osteopenia

The Pueblo Grande remains were ideal for an investigation of age-related bone loss given the diversity of analyses available for comparison. The demographic study indicated high infant mortality and severe reproductive demands on Pueblo Grande females, while a high prevalence of diploic thickening suggested nutritional problems among reproductive-aged females. This was supported by the elemental analysis indicating reduced animal protein intake among women. Archaeological evidence further indicated (Breternitz and Robinson 1995) that increased population density combined with depletion of resources seriously taxed the population as a whole. Age-related bone loss served as yet another avenue of investigation to assess adaptive success at Pueblo Grande (Kuzawa and Van Gerven 1994).

The most direct evidence for adult age changes in cortical bone maintenance was provided by a thorough investigation of femoral bone loss (osteopenia). Age-related loss of bone in adults (figure 10.7) is an example of the overall process of deterioration seen throughout the body with time in response to a variety of environmental and physiological stressors. During life, bone is removed and replaced through a process known as remodeling, an inefficient method which leads to a net reduction in bone mass with age. This gradual decline is known as osteopenia; if the loss becomes sufficient to jeopardize structural integrity of the bone, it is called osteoporosis.

During childhood, bone deposition outpaces loss thereby increasing the mass of the skeleton. Peak skeletal mass is attained when this pace reaches equilibrium, representing an opening adult bone balance available for use throughout life. If growth is hindered during childhood, recovery is difficult. Deficit upon entry into adulthood is often carried through the remainder of an individual's life. Such appears to have been the case at Pueblo Grande (Van Gerven and Sheridan 1994a; Van Gerven et al. 1993). Persistent bone loss and reduced cortical areas were found in the children at Pueblo Grande until age four. It is likely that the childhood deficit in bone growth at Pueblo Grande contributed to a pattern of reduced bone mass that continued into adulthood.

Some diminishment in mass occurs in all humans across the adult age range; however, several physiological mechanisms can exacerbate the process. Dietary and/or disease processes that enhance calcium or protein deficiency, as well as the demands of reproduction, often accelerate loss with age. Calcium is an important mineral to proper bone growth and maintenance because it is the major component of the hydroxyapatite crystal matrix. Archaeological and botanical analyses of Classic period diets in the Phoenix Basin found a high prevalence of

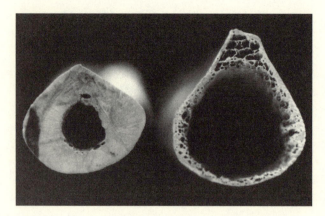

FIGURE 10.7   Femoral Cross-Section Illustrating Healthy Bone Maintenance (left) and Severe Age-Related Bone Loss or Osteopenia (right)

maize use (Gasser and Kwiatkowski 1991), a notoriously poor calcium source. Dietary calcium may have been limited if the population relied heavily upon maize as a staple crop. In addition, the demands of reproduction increase the need for, while draining the supply of, calcium in pregnant and lactating women. When nutritionally stressed, these demands lead to maternal skeletal depletion that may persist if birth spacing is short or breast feeding is protracted.

Several features of osteopenia appear ubiquitous among human populations. Females, for example, show a seemingly universal pattern of hormonally driven loss following menopause, even in the most nutritionally-rich settings. Males on the other hand, rarely lose significant mass unless gravely stressed. As young adults, however, patterns of loss can vary substantially between populations, especially among females. Premenopausal loss appears to be a response to nutritional and reproductive stressors rather than hormonal and age-related changes (Martin et al. 1987; Mensforth and Lovejoy 1985). It is the contribution of these differences with which paleopathologists are most interested, because they provide an indication of the diet and disease stresses acting upon an ancient population (Goodman et al. 1988; Huss-Ashmore et al. 1982; Larsen 1987). Factors contributing to the Pueblo Grande pattern likely included chronic malnutrition beginning in childhood, differential access to food resources by sex, calcium-poor dietary components, and significant demands upon reproductive-age women.

Osteopenia at Pueblo Grande

To measure the degree of osteopenia in this Hohokam collection, percent cortical area, defined as the percentage of the total cross-sectional area containing bone tissue, was measured as detailed in Frost (1962) and Kuzawa and Van Gerven (1994). This measure provides an index of bone loss and gain, independent of body-size effects (Martin and Armelagos 1979; Moore 1987). Kuzawa and Van Gerven (1994) sampled 53 femora ranging in age from 18 to 55+ years. Of these, 24 could be placed in the early Classic period, and 23 females placed in the late Classic period.

As expected, females demonstrated greater loss than males (figure 10.8). Both sexes maintained bone well into their 30s, then diverged markedly with a 24% female reduction compared to a 10% loss by males. Females showed a highly significant (p < .0002) decline of approximately 30% versus a 12.5% loss in cortical area by men (p > .05).

When compared by time period, Kuzawa and Van Gerven found that loss in percentage of cortical area increased significantly from the early to late period for women, and even more markedly so for men. While early Classic men maintained bone in a manner typical for most prehistoric and modern populations, late Classic men demonstrated a severity of loss rarely seen in human males, past or present.

Van Gerven and Sheridan (1994a) showed a percentage of cortical area bone loss pattern in the Pueblo Grande adolescents consistent with, although at the low end of, many archaeological populations (Martin et al. 1987). This early loss may have produced a continuing effect which lasted into adulthood. Although Kuzawa and Van Gerven (1994) found normal patterns of loss among the combined adult Pueblo Grande sample, levels were higher than often encountered in an archaeological setting.

Females showed greater cortical decline, with premenopausal loss evident especially in the late Classic. Also, late Classic males demonstrated a pattern of severe loss. Nutritional and reproductive stresses have been implicated as contributors to premature cortical thinning in other studies and were likely effects at Pueblo Grande. Van Gerven and Sheridan (1994b) showed a mean life expectancy at birth and crude death rate which would have required significant population replacement resulting in extreme reproductive stress. Porotic hyperostosis and diploic thickening patterns likewise indicated a high rate of anemia in the population, especially among reproductive-aged females (Mittler and Van Gerven 1994). Greater reliance on plant material and an overall reduction in nutritional quality with time were indicated by the elemental analysis. Furthermore, if maize was a staple crop, as it was elsewhere in the region (Gasser and Kwiatkowski 1991), then calcium intake may have been minimal. These factors, in concert with the reduced cortical maintenance among women and with time, point to a population under increasing nutritional and reproduction stress as the Classic period progressed.

CONCLUSIONS

Unlike human adaptability research conducted on modern populations, the paleopathologist has only the cryptic information concealed within the skeleton available for study. While many details of life at Pueblo Grande disappeared with the Hohokam, the biological consequences of adaptation left an indelible mark on the skeletal tissues, providing a powerful analytical tool.

When viewed within a bioarchaeological context, these skeletal indicators of population stress, nutrition, and disease prevalence provide a surrogate for the information available to the epidemiologist or human biologist and provide an informative window on the ability of past populations to adapt to environmental, genetic, and cultural challenges.

The osteological analyses conducted on the inhumations from Pueblo Grande illustrate the rich potential for combining modern analytical techniques with an integrative concern for the changing patterns of adaptation and biological well-being of an ancient community. Several traditional investigations were not conducted, such as morphometric analysis, detailed dental examination, distance studies, and analysis of population patterns of infectious disease and trauma. Such investigations were hampered by the fragmentary nature of the material and premature reburial of the remains. Interestingly however, one result of this study was a workable model of analysis which maximized the study of biocultural adaptation, under the time constraints often imposed by the pressures of reburial. Nevertheless, taken

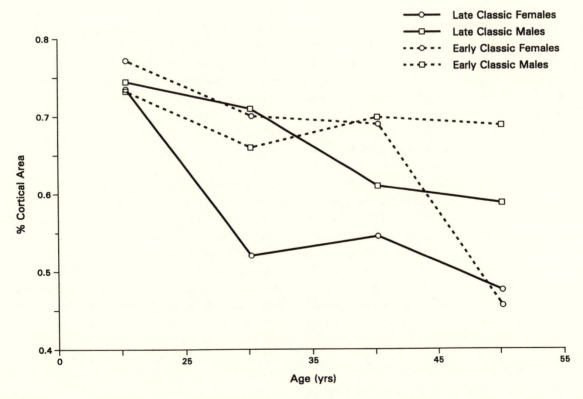

FIGURE 10.8   Comparison of Percent Cortical Thickness for Males and Females through Time at Pueblo Grande

together there is a continuity of result crosscutting each of the separate investigations.

Paleodemographic Reconstruction

Outstanding reconstructions, such as Martin and coworkers' (1991) analysis of Black Mesa, proceed from a demographic perspective. Whether presented in the form of simple survivorship curves or more elaborate composite life tables, mortality patterns provide an essential context describing risk of death throughout the life cycle, from which other interpretations can be made.

Viewed from either perspective, the rate of mortality at Pueblo Grande was high. The modal age at death was birth, with the mean life expectancy of a newborn only slightly above 15 years. Sixty-six people per thousand died each year requiring a comparable birth rate to simply replace the population. Such a birth rate is beyond that observed in any contemporary population and implies a population either in decline or dependent upon immigration to maintain its numbers. Adding to the difficulty of everyday survival, there would have been a large number of consumers (those under 15 and over 50) relative to producers imposing a heavy burden on the young adult segment of the population. Nevertheless, the greatest burden fell on infants and subadults. Infant mortality was higher than that observed at Black Mesa, Casas Grandes, or Pecos Pueblo, and the percentage of individuals surviving beyond 18 years was low for populations in the region (Martin et al. 1991).

As time passed and the population entered its late Classic phase, these severe conditions appear to have spread to the adult segment of the population. One can never know with certainty if this is an accurate depiction of mortality and population structure at Pueblo Grande, but a series of testable hypotheses can be framed based on the demographic evidence. For example, if this demographic profile is accurate, then evidence for a high level of stress and morbidity among infants and children would be expected, as well as a decline in the health of adults between early to late Classic times. Evidence for this decline should appear in the form of generalized indicators of dietary and disease stress. Each phase of the above investigation confirmed these expectations, thereby supporting the demographic patterns.

Childhood Stress at Pueblo Grande

A critical measure of childhood stress and morbidity at Pueblo Grande was provided by enamel hypoplasias (Karhu and Amon 1994). While a number of stress factors may underlie the appearance of these dental defects, it is clear that poor nutrition and bouts of infectious disease during tooth development are major contributors. As a result, patterns of childhood stress reflected in hypoplasias among the Pueblo Grande children corresponded precisely to that predicted from the demographic evidence. As with infant and childhood death rates, subadult stress was extreme by both absolute and regional standards. Approximately 99% of the Pueblo Grande population exhibited hypoplasias compared to 25% reported for Grand Canal, 10% at La Lomita, 32% at Casa Buena, and 44% at La Ciudad.

Furthermore, the average Pueblo Grande child was sufficiently stressed to experience 33 months of interrupted enamel formation during its first seven years of life. To truly appreciate the severity of this stress, it must be realized that the sample contains only individuals who lived to at least age seven and thereby had teeth sufficiently developed for study.

Finally, the lack of evidence for a diachronic shift in subadult mortality was also reflected in the hypoplasia information. While the late Classic children experienced an earlier peak frequency of hypoplastic activity and maintained that frequency longer than their early Classic counterparts, there was no significant difference between the two groups. In short, the severe childhood stress at Pueblo Grande evidenced in the hypoplasia data is consistent with the demographic profile. Also, as reflected in the demographic evidence, the level of subadult stress does not appear to have increased significantly between early and late Classic times.

Nutritional Stress

Among ancient populations, evidence for nutritional anemia appears among children as a cranial lesion (porotic hyperostosis) and among adults as progressive diploic thickening. Mittler and Van Gerven's (1994) analysis of the Pueblo Grande remains revealed evidence for extensive iron deficiency anemia among both sexes across the entire age range. Here again, the ubiquity of the condition, as well as its severity, is consistent with the hypothesis of extreme population stress and mortality.

Lesion frequency among adults reached 54% with reproductive-aged females consistently more effected than their male counterparts. This pattern of heightened female anemia also appeared in their analysis of diploic thickening. Thickening of the diploic space between the internal and external cranial tables has been associated with the expansion of blood-producing tissue. The pattern of age changes in diploic thickening reinforced the hypothesis of high reproductive stress based on the demographic data.

A large body of research on living populations has demonstrated a consistently higher rate of anemia among women related to menstruation, pregnancy, parturition, and lactation. Most importantly, pregnancy results in an average loss of up to 2.5 mg of iron per day. Among the women of Pueblo Grande, the period of greatest diploe expansion corresponded precisely to the middle of the reproductive years. Pueblo Grande males, on the other hand, responded like their modern male counterparts. Diploic thickening developed progressively and became most pronounced as part of old age and senescence. Diachronic changes were also consistent with the demographic evidence for heightened adult stress prior to abandonment of the area. Overall, there was an 18% increase in diploic thickening between early and late Classic times.

Arguments for nutritional stress in ancient populations typically rest on the indirect evidence provided by bones and teeth. Elemental analysis of Pueblo Grande remains provided a body of direct dietary information based on the actual chemical composition of bone tissue.

An observed pattern of female-male difference suggests that females were consuming more plant resources, while males had greater access to meat. These conditions, combined with high reproductive demands, would have exacerbated female dietary stress and increased the likelihood of mortality during the reproductive years as observed in the demographic data.

The elemental data also provided insight into the adaptive decline at Pueblo Grande. Over time, a general decrease in animal protein consumption combined with an increased reliance on plants appears to have occurred. These changes are precisely what the skeletal evidence for a diachronic increase in iron-deficiency anemia would predict. The most important source of iron in the human diet comes in the form of heme-iron provided by animal protein. Maize is a poor source of both iron and calcium.

Taken together, the evidence for poor nutrition and disease at Pueblo Grande provides an extremely coherent picture of dietary stress. Weaning diarrhea produced high rates of anemia among children that continued as a progressive and chronic malady among adults. This condition no doubt contributed importantly to the high rates of infant and reproductive-age female mortality. In addition, the availability of animal protein became diminished over time, and an increasing reliance on cultigens such as maize compounded the nutritional stresses acting on the population. The consequences of life under these conditions is expressed ultimately in the progress of aging and the appearance of age-related degenerative conditions.

Age-Related Bone Loss

As is typical for all human populations, patterns of adult age-related bone loss at Pueblo Grande showed a substantial sexual dimorphism. While males typically maintained cortical bone through old age, female losses were significant. The average female at Pueblo Grande lost over 30% between her second and fifth decade of life, especially during the reproductive years. Unlike modern, well-nourished women who typically maintain bone tissue until menopause, the young, reproductive-aged females at Pueblo Grande were literally mining their skeletons for nutrients—nutrients vital to pregnancy and lactation.

While the pattern of female bone loss is typical of many poorly nourished populations, past and present, a diachronic analysis of bone loss at Pueblo Grande produced results that could have been anticipated only from the mortality, morbidity, and dietary information. Whereas bone loss among females increased slightly between early and late Classic times, the male transformation was pronounced. While early Classic males maintained their cortical bone with advancing age in a manner consistent with most ancient and modern populations, their late Classic counterparts experienced a significant degree of bone loss.

SUMMARY

In his book *Bone, Bodies, and Disease*, Calvin Wells (1964) observed that:

> The pattern of disease or injury that affects any group of people is never a matter of chance. It is invariably the expression of stresses and strains to which they were exposed, a response to everything in their environment and behavior . . . It is influenced by their daily occupations, their habits of diet, their choice of dwellings and clothes, their social structure, even their folklore and mythology. (Wells 1964:17)

This reconstruction of life and death at Pueblo Grande has proceeded in the spirit of Wells's view, based ultimately on

Wells's belief in the connection between human culture and biology. Archaeologists often marvel at the tenacity of the Hohokam, who successfully inhabited an arid desert environment for upward of a millennium. By the Colonial period, they had reached their greatest geographical extent and relied upon intensive agricultural techniques and vast canal networks to sustain regionally concentrated populations within a demanding environment. By some accounts, the Hohokam are viewed as having been successful and well adapted to the unpredictable and fluctuating climatic conditions of the Sonoran desert. For instance, Fish (1989) notes that the "Maintenance of a comparatively stable trajectory for at least 1,000 years argues for a system which anticipated and could absorb large amounts of climatic variability through customary and effective patterns of response" (Fish 1989:44). The facts of prehistory tell us that the Hohokam were effective environmental managers who created a stable culture for upward of 1,000 years (Fish 1989).

The current investigation suggests that this tenacity was not without biological cost. The human remains tell us that by Classic period times, the Hohokam of Pueblo Grande had lost much of that effectiveness. The patterns of bone loss at Pueblo Grande were severe in comparison to all previously reported archaeological and modern populations and suggest not only nutritional problems but also high reproductive demands. The diachronic trends indicate that these costs may have become severe by the late Classic and that the inhabitants of Pueblo Grande were a population on the decline. Whether or not these high levels of stress and poor health played a role in site abandonment, it is clear that the effectiveness of the Hohokam adaptation at Pueblo Grande had diminished by the late Classic. They were a people living on the edge of survival, nutritionally and reproductively stressed, and struggling to maintain their numbers. By the end of the Classic, it would appear that the struggle was lost.

ACKNOWLEDGMENTS

The author would like to thank Dr. Dennis Van Gerven, Diane Mittler, Debra Jones, Julie Sansoni, Julie Amon, Sandra Karhu, and Christopher Kuzawa for their participation in the Pueblo Grande Hohokam project. Additional thanks to Drs. Mark Schurr, Debra Martin, Michael Foster, Christy Turner, and Ms. Jennifer Richtsmeier for their many helpful comments in the preparation of this manuscript. Special thanks to Scott Kolbrenner and Debra Jones for their help in the preparation of the samples for chemical analysis. This work was supported by funds from Soil Systems, Inc., the Center for Indigenous Studies in the Americas, the University of Notre Dame's Institute for Study in the Liberal Arts and Undergraduate Research Opportunities Program, and the Wenner-Gren Foundation for Anthropological Research (#5656).

REFERENCES CITED

Abbott, David R., Douglas R. Mitchell, and J. A. Merewether
1994 Chronology. In *The Pueblo Grande Project, Volume 2: Feature Descriptions, Chronology, and Site Structure,* edited by Douglas R. Mitchell, pp. 157–524. Soil Systems Publications in Archaeology No. 20. Soil Systems, Phoenix.

Armelagos, George J., B. Brennto, M. Alcorn, Debra L. Martin, and Dennis P. Van Gerven
1989 Factors Affecting Elemental and Isotopic Variation in Prehistoric Human Bone. In *The Chemistry of Prehistoric Human Bone,* edited by T. D. Price, pp. 230–44. Harvard University Press, Cambridge.

Barnes, Ethne
1988 Inhumations Recovered from Casa Buena: Skeletal Analysis. In *Excavations at Casa Buena: Changing Hohokam Land Use along the Squaw Peak Parkway,* vol. 1, edited by J. B. Howard, pp. 619–91. Soil Systems Publications in Archaeology No. 11. Soil Systems, Phoenix.

Bass, William M.
1995 *Human Osteology: A Laboratory and Field Manual of the Human Skeleton.* 4th ed. University of Missouri Archaeological Museum Society, Columbia.

Becker, R. O., J. A. Spadaro, and E. W. Berg
1968 The Trace Elements of Human Bone. *Journal of Bone and Joint Surgery* 50-A:326–34.

Bocquet-Appel, J., and C. Masset
1982 Farewell to Paleodemography. *Journal of Human Evolution* 11:321–33.

Breternitz, Cory D., and C. K. Robinson
1995 The Hohokam Collapse as Viewed from Pueblo Grande: What Was So Classic about the Classic Period? Paper presented at the Arizona Archaeological Council Fall meeting, Flagstaff.

Brown, Annette B.
1973   *Bone Strontium Content as a Dietary Indicator in Human Skeletal Populations.* Unpublished Ph.D. dissertation, Department of Anthropology, University of Michigan, Ann Arbor.

Buikstra, Jane E., S. Frankenberg, Joseph B. Lambert, and L. A. Xue
1989   Multiple Elements: Multiple Expectations. In *The Chemistry of Prehistoric Human Bone,* edited by T. D. Price, pp. 155–210. Cambridge University Press, Cambridge.

Buikstra, Jane E., and J. H. Mielke
1985   Demography, Diet, and Health. In *The Analysis of Prehistoric Diets*, edited by R. I. Gilbert and J. H. Mielke, pp. 359–422. Academic Press, New York.

Carlson, David S., George J. Armelagos, and Dennis P. Van Gerven
1974   Factors Influencing the Etiology of Cribra Orbitalia in Prehistoric Nubia. *Journal of Human Evolution* 3:405–10.

Cole, A. J., and P. Demeny
1966   *Regional Model Life Tables and Stable Populations.* Princeton University Press, Princeton.

Cutress, T. W., and G. W. Suckling
1982   The Assessment of Non-Carious Defects of Enamel. *International Dental Journal* 32:117–22.

Doyel, David E.
1991   Hohokam Cultural Evolution in the Phoenix Basin. In *Exploring the Hohokam: Prehistoric Desert Peoples of the American Southwest,* edited by G. J. Gumerman, pp. 231–78. University of New Mexico Press, Albuquerque.

Duray, S. M.
1996   Dental Indicators of Stress and Reduced Age at Death in Prehistoric Native Americans. *American Journal of Physical Anthropology* 99:275–86.

El-Najjar, Mahmoud Y.
1976   Maize, Malaria, and the Anemias in the Pre-Columbian New World. *Yearbook of Physical Anthropology* 20:329–37.

El-Najjar, Mahmoud Y., D. J. Ryan, C. G. Turner II, and B. Lozoff
1976   The Etiology of Porotic Hyperostosis among the Prehistoric and Historic Anasazi Indians of the Southwestern United States. *American Journal of Physical Anthropology* 44:447–88.

Ezzo, Joseph A.
1994   Zinc as a Paleodietary Indicator: An issue of Theoretical Validity in Bone-Chemistry Analysis. *American Antiquity* 59:606–21.

Ezzo, Joseph A., Clark S. Larsen, and James H. Burton
1995   Elemental Signatures of Human Diets from the Georgia Bight. *American Journal of Physical Anthropology* 98:471–81.

Fink, T. Michael
1989   The Human Skeletal Remains from the Grand Canal Ruins, AZ T:12:14(ASU) and AZ T:12:16(ASU). In *Archaeological Investigations at the Grand Canal Ruins: A Classic Period Site in Phoenix, Arizona,* edited by D. R. Mitchell, pp. 619—704. Soil Systems Publications in Archaeology No.12. Soil Systems, Phoenix.
1990   Analysis of the Human Skeletal Remains from La Lomita (AZU:67[ASM]). In *The La Lomita Excavations: 10th Century Hohokam Occupation in South-Central Arizona,* edited by D. R. Mitchell, pp. 67–83. Soil Systems Publications in Archaeology No. 15. Soil Systems, Phoenix.

Fink, T. Michael, and Charles Merbs
1991   Paleonutrition and Paleopathology of the Salt River Hohokam: A Search for Correlates. *Kiva* 56:293–318.

Fish, Paul R.
1989   The Hohokam: 1,000 Years of Prehistory in the Sonoran Desert. In *Dynamics of Southwest Prehistory,* edited by L. S. Cordell and G. J. Gumerman, pp. 19–63. Smithsonian Institution, Washington, D.C.

Foster, Michael S. (editor)
1994   *The Pueblo Grande Project, Volume 1: Introduction, Research Design, and Testing Results.* Soil Systems Publications in Archaeology No. 20. Soil Systems, Phoenix.

Fracalacci, P.
1989   Dietary Reconstruction at Arene Candide Cave (Liguria, Italy) by Means of Trace Element Analysis. *Journal of Archaeological Science* 16:109–24.

Frost, H. M.
1962   *Microscopy: Optical Sectioning and Integrating Eyepiece Measurement.* Henry Ford Hospital Medical Bulletin 10(2).

Gasser, Robert E., and Scott M. Kwiatkowski
1991   Food for Thought: Recognizing Patterns in Hohokam Subsistence. In *Exploring the Hohokam: Prehistoric Desert Peoples of the*

American Southwest, edited by G. J. Gumerman, pp. 417–59. University of New Mexico Press, Albuquerque.

Goodman, Alan H.
1993 On the Interpretation of Health from Skeletal Remains. *Current Anthropology* 34:281–88.

Goodman, Alan H., L. H. Allen, G. P. Hernandez, A. Amador, L. V. Arriola, A. Chavez, and G. H. Pelto
1987 The Prevalence and Age at Development of Enamel Hypoplasias in Mexican Children. *American Journal of Physical Anthropology* 72:7–19.

Goodman, Alan H., George J. Armelagos, and Jerry Rose
1980 Enamel Hypoplasias as Indicators of Stress in Three Prehistoric Populations from Illinois. *Human Biology* 52:515–28.

Goodman, Alan H., and Luigi L. Capasso
1992 *Recent Contributions to the Study of Enamel Developmental Defects*. Journal of Paleopathology, Monograph Publication 2. Associazione Antropologica Abruzzese, Chieti, Italy.

Goodman, Alan H., and Jerry C. Rose
1990 Assessment of Systematic Physiological Perturbations from Dental Enamel Hypoplasias and Associated Histological Structures. *Yearbook of Physical Anthropology* 33:59–110.
1991 Dental Enamel Hypoplasias as Indicators of Nutritional Status. In *Advances in Dental Anthropology*, edited by M. A. Kelly and C. J. Larson, pp. 279–93. Wiley-Liss, New York.

Goodman, Alan H., R. Brooke Thomas, Alan C. Swedlund, and George J. Armelagos
1988 Biocultural Perspective on Stress in Prehistoric, Historical, and Contemporary Population Research. *Yearbook of Physical Anthropology* 31:169–202.

Greene, David L., Dennis P. Van Gerven, and George J. Armelagos
1986 Life and Death in Ancient Populations: Bones of Contention in Paleodemography. *Human Evolution* 1:193–207.

Gumerman, George J., and Emil W. Haury
1979 Prehistory: Hohokam. In *Southwest*, edited by A. Ortiz, pp. 75–90. Handbook of North American Indians, vol. 9, W. C. Sturtevant, general editor. Smithsonian Institution, Washington, D.C.

Hancock, R. G. V., M. D. Bynpoas, and B. Alpert
1987 Are Archaeological Bones Similar to Modern Bones? An INAA Assessment. *Journal of Radioanalytical and Nuclear Chemistry, Articles* 110(1):283–91.

Hare, P. Edward
1980 Organic Geochemistry of Bone and its Relation to the Survival of Bone in the Natural Environment. In *Fossils in the Making*, edited by A. K. Behrensmeyer and A. P. Hill, pp. 208–19. University of Chicago Press, Chicago.

Hatch, James W., and A. A. Geidel
1985 Status-Specific Dietary Variation in Two World Cultures. *Journal of Human Evolution* 14:469–76.

Haury, Emil W.
1974 Before History. In *Indians of Arizona: A Contemporary Perspective*, edited by T. Weaver, pp. 7–25. University of Arizona Press, Tucson.

Hengen, O. P.
1971 Cribra Orbitalia: Pathogenesis and Probable Etiology. *Homo* 22:57–75.

Houk, R.
1992 *Hohokam: Prehistoric Cultures of the Southwest*. Southwest Parks and Monuments Association, Tucson.

Howell, Nancy T.
1982 Village Composition Implied by a Paleodemographic Life Table: The Libben Site. *American Journal of Physical Anthropology* 59:263–69.

Huss-Ashmore, Rebecca, Alan H. Goodman, and George J. Armelagos
1982 Nutritional Inferences from Paleopathology. In *Advances in Archaeological Method and Theory*, vol. 5, edited by M. B. Schiffer, pp. 395–474. Academic Press, New York.

Jones, Debra, and Susan Guise Sheridan
1994 Reconstruction of Hohokam Diet Utilizing Trace Element Variation. In *The Pueblo Grande Project, Volume 6: Bioethnography of a Classic Period Hohokam Population*, edited by D. P. Van Gerven and S. G. Sheridan, pp. 75–85. Soil Systems Publications in Archaeology No. 20. Soil Systems, Phoenix.

Karhu, Sandra L., and Julie Amon
1994 Childhood Stress Recorded in the Enamel Defects of the Hohokam of Pueblo Grande. In *The Pueblo Grande Project, Volume 6: Bioethnography of a Classic Period Hohokam Population*, edited by D. P. Van Gerven and

S. G. Sheridan, pp. 26–45. Soil Systems Publications in Archaeology No. 20. Soil Systems, Phoenix.

Klepinger, Linda L.
1984   Nutritional Assessment from Bone. *Annual Reviews in Anthropology* 13:75–96.

Konigsberg, L. W., and S. R. Frankenberg
1994   Paleodemography: "Not Quite Dead." *Evolutionary Anthropology* 3:92–105.

Kuzawa, Christopher, and Dennis P. Van Gerven
1994   Patterns of Age-Related Bone Loss (osteopenia) at Pueblo Grande. In *The Pueblo Grande Project, Volume 6: Bioethnography of a Classic Period Hohokam Population*, edited by D. P. Van Gerven and S. G. Sheridan, pp. 107–122. Soil Systems Publications in Archaeology No. 20. Soil Systems, Phoenix.

Kyle, J. H.
1986   Effect of Post-Burial Contamination on the Concentrations of Major and Minor Elements in Human Bones and Teeth: The Implications for Paleodietary Research. *Journal of Archaeological Science* 13:403–16.

Lallo, John W., George J. Armelagos, and Robert P. Mensforth
1977   The Role of Diet, Disease, and Physiology in the Origin of Porotic Hyperostosis. *Human Biology* 49:471–83.

Lambert, Joseph B., C. B. Szpunar, and Jane E. Buikstra
1979   Chemical Analysis of Excavated Human Bone from Middle and Late Woodland Sites. *Archaeometry* 21:115–29.

Lambert, Joseph B., S. M. Vlasak, Anne C. Thometz, and Jane E. Buikstra
1982   A Comparative Study of the Chemical Analysis of Ribs and Femurs in Woodland Populations. *American Journal of Physical Anthropology* 59:289–94.

Lambert, Joseph B., Sharon Vlasak Simpson, Jane E. Buikstra, and Douglas Hanson
1983   Electron Microprobe Analysis of Elemental Distribution in Excavated Human Bone. *American Journal of Physical Anthropology* 62:409–23.

Lambert, Joseph B., Sharon Vlasak Simpson, C. B. Szpunar, and Jane E. Buikstra
1984   Copper and Barium as Dietary Discriminants: The Effects of Diagenesis. *Archaeometry* 26:131–38.

Lambert, Joseph B., Sharon Vlasak Simpson, Susan Gorell Weiner, and Jane E. Buikstra
1985   Induced Metal-Ion Exchange in Excavated Human Bone. *Journal of Archaeological Science* 12:85–92.

Larsen, Clark S.
1987   Bioarchaeological Interpretations of Subsistence Economy and Behavior from Human Skeletal Remains. In *Advances in Archaeological Method and Theory*, vol. 10, edited by M. B. Schiffer, pp. 389–93. Academic Press, New York.

Lipe, William D.
1983   The Southwest. In *Ancient North Americans*, edited by J. D. Jennings, pp. 421–94. W. H. Freeman and Company, New York.

Lovejoy, C. Owen, Richard S. Meindel, R. P. Mensforth, and T. J. Barton
1985   Multifactorial Determination of Skeletal Age at Death: A Method and Blind Tests of Its Accuracy. *American Journal of Physical Anthropology* 68:1–14.

Lovejoy, C. Owen, Richard S. Meindel, T. R. Pryzbek, T. S. Barton, K. Heipel, and D. Kotting
1977   Paleodemography of the Libben Site, Ottawa County, Ohio. *Science* 198:291–93.

Martin, Debra L., and George J. Armelagos
1979   Morphometrics of Compact Bone: An Example from Sudanese Nubia. *American Journal of Physical Anthropology* 51:571–77.

Martin, Debra L., Alan H. Goodman, George J. Armelagos, and Ann L. Magennis
1991   *Black Mesa Anasazi Health: Reconstructing Life Patterns from Patterns of Death and Disease.* Southern Illinois University Center for Archaeological Investigation Occasional Paper No. 14. Southern Illinois University, Carbondale.

Martin, Debra L., Ann L. Magennis, and Jerry C. Rose
1987   Cortical Bone Maintenance in an Historic Afro-American Cemetery Sample from Cedar Grove, Arkansas. *American Journal of Physical Anthropology* 74:255–64.

Meindel, Richard S., C. Owen Lovejoy, and R. P. Mensforth
1983   Skeletal Age at Death: Accuracy of Age Determination and Implication for Human Demography. *Human Biology* 55:73–87.

Mensforth, R. P.
1990   Paleodemography of the Carlston Annis (Bt–5) Late Archaic Skeletal Population. *American Journal of Physical Anthropology* 82:81–100.

Mensforth, R. P., and C. Owen Lovejoy
1985   Anatomical, Physiological, and Epidemiological Correlates of the Aging

Process: A Confirmation of Multifactorial Age
Determination in the Libben Skeletal
Population. *American Journal of Physical
Anthropology* 68:87–106.

Mitchell, Douglas R. (editor)
1994   *The Pueblo Grande Project, Volume 7: An
Analysis of Classic Period Mortuary Patterns.*
Soil Systems Publications in Archaeology No.
20. Soil Systems, Phoenix.

Mittler, Diane M., and Susan Guise Sheridan
1992   Sex Determination in Subadults Using
Auricular Surface Morphology: A Forensic
Science Perspective. *Journal of Forensic
Sciences* 37:1064–71.

Mittler, Diane M., and Dennis P. Van Gerven
1994   Porotic Hyperostosis and Diploic Thickening
at Pueblo Grande. In *The Pueblo Grande
Project, Volume 6: Bioethnography of a Classic
Period Hohokam Population,* edited by D. P.
Van Gerven and S. G. Sheridan, pp. 55–73. Soil
Systems Publications in Archaeology No. 20.
Soil Systems, Phoenix.

Moore, K.
1987   *Osteopenia in a Medieval Population from
Sudanese Nubia.* Unpublished Ph.D. dissertation, Department of Anthropology, University
of Colorado, Boulder.

Ortner, Donald, D. W. Von Endt, and M. S. Robinson
1972   The Effect of Temperature on Protein Decay
in Bone: Its Significance in Nitrogen Dating
of Archaeological Specimens. *American
Antiquity* 37:514–20.

Palkovich, Ann M.
1985   Agriculture, Marginal Environments, and
Nutritional Stress in the Prehistoric
Southwest. In *Paleopathology and the Origins
of Agriculture,* edited by M. N. Cohen and
G. J. Armelagos, pp. 425–39. Academic Press,
New York.

Parker, R. B., and H. Toots
1970   Minor Elements in Fossil Bone. *Geological
Society of America Bulletin* 81:925–32.
1980   Trace Elements in Bones as Paleobiological
Indicators. In *Fossils in the Making: Vertebrate
Taphonomy and Paleoecology,* edited by A. K.
Behrensmeyer and A. P. Hill, pp. 197–207.
University of Chicago Press, Chicago.

Pate, D., and K. A. Brown
1985   The Stability of Bone Strontium in the
Geochemical Environment. *Journal of Human
Evolution* 14:483–92.

Price, T. Douglas
1988   Diagenesis of Sr and Other Elements in
Archaeological Bone. Paper presented at
Capetown Conference on Archaeological
Bone Chemistry, June 1988.
1989   Multi-Element Studies of Diagenesis in
Prehistoric Bone. In *The Chemistry of
Prehistoric Human Bone,* edited by T. D. Price,
pp. 126–54. Cambridge University Press,
Cambridge.

Radosevich, S. C.
1993   The Six Deadly Sins of Trace Element
Analysis: A Case of Wishful Thinking in
Science. In *Investigations of Ancient Human
Tissue,* edited by M. K. Sandford, pp. 269–332.
Gordon and Breach Publishers, Pennsylvania.

Reynolds, J.
1962   An Evaluation of Some Roentgenographic
Signs in Sickle Cell Anemia and Its Variants.
Southern Medical Journal 55:1123–28.

Rheingold, J. G.
1983   Dietary Fiber and the Bioavailability of Iron.
In *Nutritional Bioavailability of Iron,* edited by
C. Kies, pp. 143–61. ACS Symposium Series
203. ACS Press, Washington, D.C.

Sandford, Mary Kay, Dennis P. Van Gerven,
    and Robert R. Meglen
1983   Elemental Hair Analysis: New Evidence on
the Etiology of Cribra Orbitalia in Sudanese
Nubia. *Human Biology* 55:831–44.

Schroeder, H. A.
1965   The Biological Trace Elements. *Journal of
Chronic Diseases* 18:217–24.

Schwartz, Jeffrey H.
1996   *Skeleton Keys: An Introduction to Human
Skeletal Morphology, Development, and
Analysis.* Oxford University Press, New York.

Scrimshaw, N.
1964   Ecological Factors in Nutritional Diseases.
American Journal of Nutrition and Infection.
World Health Organization, Geneva.

Sebes, J. I., and L. W. Diggs
1979   Radiographic Changes in the Skull in Sickle
Cell Anemia. *American Journal of
Roentgenology* 132:373–77.

Shaw, J. H., and E. A. Sweeney
1980   Nutrition in Relation to Dental Medicine. In
Modern Nutrition in Health and Disease, 6th
ed., edited by R. S. Goodhart and M. E. Shils,
pp. 852–91. Lea and Febiger, Philadelphia.

Sheridan, Susan Guise
1992   *Minor and Trace Element Distributions in*

Bone: Reconstruction of Diagenetic, Dietary, and Disease Patterns in an Ancient Nubian Population. Unpublished Ph.D. dissertation, Department of Anthropology, University of Colorado, Boulder.

Sheridan, Susan Guise, and Dennis P. Van Gerven
1997   Female Biological Resiliency: Differential Stress Response by Sex in Human Remains from Ancient Nubia. *Human Evolution* 12:241–52.

Shipman, Patricia, Alan Walker, and D. Bichell
1985   *The Human Skeleton.* Harvard University Press, Cambridge.

Sillen, Andrew
1981   Strontium and Diet at Hayonim Cave. *American Journal of Physical Anthropology* 56:131–37.
1989   Diagenesis of the Inorganic Phase of Cortical Bone. In *The Chemistry of Prehistoric Bone,* edited by T. D. Price, pp. 221–29. Cambridge University Press, New York

Sillen, Andrew, and M. A. Kavanagh
1982   Strontium and Paleodietary Research: A Review. *Yearbook of Physical Anthropology* 25:67–90.

Smith, B. Holly
1984   Patterns of Molar Wear in Hunter-Gatherers and Agriculturalists. *American Journal of Physical Anthropology* 63:39–56.

Spielmann, K. A., M. J. Schoeninger, and K. Moore
1990   Plains-Pueblo Interdependence and Human Diet at Pecos Pueblo, New Mexico. *American Antiquity* 55:745–65.

Stodder, A. L. W.
1990   *Paleoepidemiology of Eastern and Western Pueblo Communities in Protohistoric New Mexico.* Unpublished Ph.D. dissertation, Department of Anthropology, University of Colorado, Boulder.

Stuart-Macadam, Patricia
1985   Porotic Hyperostosis: Representative of a Childhood Condition. *American Journal of Physical Anthropology* 74:511–20.

Szuter, C. R.
1991   Hunting by Hohokam Desert Farmers. *Kiva* 56:277–91.

Tanaka, G. I., H. Kawamura, and E. Nomura
1981   Japanese Reference Man II: Distribution of Strontium in the Skeleton and in the Mass of Mineralized Bone. *Health Physics* 40:601–14.

Toots, H., and M. R. Voorhies
1965   Strontium in Fossil Bones and the Reconstruction of Food Chains. *Science* 149:854–55.

Turner, Christy G., II, and Joel D. Irish
1989   Further Assessment of Hohokam Affinity: The Classic Period Population of the Grand Canal and Casa Buena Sites, Phoenix, Arizona. In *Archaeological Investigations at the Grand Canal Ruins: A Classic Period Site in Phoenix, Arizona,* edited by D. R. Mitchell, pp. 775–92. Soil Systems Publications in Archaeology No.12. Soil Systems, Phoenix.

Unicef
1986   *Children of the World.* Population Reference Bureau publication. New York.

Van Gerven, Dennis P., and George J. Armelagos
1983   Farewell to Paleodemography? Rumors of Its Death Have Been Greatly Exaggerated. *Journal of Human Evolution* 12:353–60.

Van Gerven, Dennis P., and Susan Guise Sheridan
1994a   Bone Growth and Cortical Bone Maintenance at Pueblo Grande. In *The Pueblo Grande Project, Volume 6: The Bioethnography of a Classic Period Hohokam Population,* edited by D. P. Van Gerven and S. G. Sheridan, *pp.* 47–54. Soil Systems Publications in Archaeology, No. 20. Soil Systems, Phoenix.

Van Gerven, Dennis P., and Susan Guise Sheridan (editors)
1994b   *The Pueblo Grande Project, Volume 6: The Bioethnography of a Classic Period Hohokam Population.* Soil Systems Publications in Archaeology, No. 20. Soil Systems, Phoenix.

Van Gerven, Dennis P., Susan Guise Sheridan, and William Y. Adams
1995   Health and Nutrition of a Medieval Nubian Population: The Impact of Political and Economic Change. *American Anthropologist* 97:468–80.

Von Endt, D. W., and Donald J. Ortner
1982   Amino Acid Analysis of Bone from a Possible Case of Prehistoric Iron-Deficiency Anemia from the American Southwest. *American Journal of Physical Anthropology* 59:377–85.

Walker, Philip L.
1985   Anemia among Prehistoric Indians of the American Southwest. In *Health and Disease in the Prehistoric Southwest,* edited by C. F. Merbs and R. J. Miller, pp.139–64. Arizona State University Anthropological Research Papers No.34. Arizona State University, Tempe.

Weaver, David S.

1980   Sex Differences in the Ilia of a Known Sex and Age Sample of Fetal and Infant Skeletons. *American Journal of Physical Anthropology* 52:191–95.

Weiss, Kenneth M.

1973   Demographic Models for Anthropology, Part II. *American Antiquity* 38(2).

Wells, Calvin

1964   *Bones, Bodies, and Disease.* Thames and Hudson, London.

White, E. M., and L. A. Hannus

1983   Chemical Weathering of Bone in Archaeological Sites. *American Antiquity* 48:316–22.

Wood, J. W., G. R. Milner, H. C. Harpending, and R. M. Weiss

1992   The Osteological Paradox: Problems of Inferring Prehistoric Health from Skeletal Samples. *Current Anthropology* 33:343–58.

Zaino, E. C.

1968   Elemental Bone Iron in the Anasazi Indians. *American Journal of Physical Anthropology* 29:433–36.

CHAPTER ELEVEN

Unequal Treatment in Life as in Death:
Trauma and Mortuary Behavior at La Plata (A.D. 1000–1300)

Debra L. Martin and Nancy J. Akins

IT IS IRONIC THAT THE ANALYSIS OF DISEASE AND DEATH of past people provides the data that allow us to reconstruct aspects of how a population lived. Death is the end result of an accumulated set of biological, behavioral, and cultural responses to challenges in the social and physical environment. Individuals are constantly adjusting to their environments, and the success of those adjustments is usually reflected in their ability to survive (at the individual level) and to reproduce (at the population level).

Skeletal material is a very distinctive part of the archaeological record because it is the only record of humans as biological entities interacting within a cultural and environmental context. Larsen (1987:340–41) discusses the cumulative nature of skeletal series, suggesting that a record of events reflecting a variety of things such as diet, disease, population size, mobility, physical exercise, and demographic variables are represented in the skeletal material. However, as with other aspects of the archaeological record, the recovery of human remains is hampered by differential preservation, differential archaeological recovery techniques, culturally mediated differences in mortuary behavior, problems with temporal assignment, and a host of other cultural and noncultural circumstances associated with when, where, and how deceased individuals are deposited in the natural environment. Finally, legislation on the limited rights of researchers to recover

human remains without the consent of descendants further inhibits the likelihood of systematic recovery and analysis. This chapter examines the mortuary behavior and patterns of trauma and general health for the La Plata Valley sites at Barker Arroyo and Jackson Lake. These areas were occupied primarily between A.D. 1000–1300 (Pueblo II/Pueblo III). A combined analysis of health profiles and mortuary patterns suggests that although there is much variability, in some places the two realms of life are related. Located near the border of New Mexico and Colorado, the La Plata River Valley was a permanently watered, productive agricultural area in which more than 900 sites have been reported (H. W. Toll 1993). The valley was continuously occupied from A.D. 200 until about A.D. 1300. Large communities were maintained throughout the occupation. This area was lush by local and regional standards, and density of available resources was high. Agricultural potential was likewise very good; there is also ample evidence of hunted and domesticated game in the diet (M. S. Toll 1993). This area is located in the middle of a large and interactive political sphere of influence with Mesa Verde to the north and Chaco Canyon to the south. Trade items and nonutilitarian goods are present. Although indicators of health suggest a robust population, there is also evidence of sustained violence against some individuals (Martin et al. 1995).

Throughout its long history, issues of disease and poor health have played significant roles in Southwestern archaeology. Age and sex are the variables most often reported for Southwest human remains and in this respect are excellent sources of data. Many of the most significant events highlighted by archaeologists from the standpoint of culture history are also demarcated by significant demographic corollaries (Swedlund 1994). Indeed, one of the major questions that plagued the earliest researchers—what happened to the northern Pueblo people—was framed in terms of population processes. Major events in Southwestern prehistory are catalogued or characterized by the demographic manifestations, such as periods of "aggregation," "abandonment," and migration (Nelson et al. 1994:59). Likewise, complexity itself has demographic resonances that imply measures of rate, density, and scale.

Although demography and health are critical factors in the analysis of human remains, the context within which the remains are located can likewise be revealing (Alekshin 1983). Works by Bartel (1982), Binford (1971), Saxe (1970), Beck (1995), and Ucko (1969) make clear the kinds of information that can be gleaned from mortuary analyses. Numerous studies that focus on the mortuary component of Southwest human burials have revealed a great deal about social ranking (Akins 1986; Ravesloot 1988), variability in location and position (Stodder 1986), social organization (Palkovich 1980), treatment of elites (Frisbie 1978), and the relationship between burial location and settlement patterns (Toll and Schlanger 1998.). On the one hand, these and other studies have revealed considerable information about how the ancestral Pueblo people dealt with their dead; on the other hand, even with this intensive focus we actually know very little. Identifying strong burial patterns and practices among the ancient Pueblo people is still quite elusive. Although not random at any given location, burials are found within a number of contexts (middens, room and pitstructure floors, storage pits, extramural pits, and abandoned structures), in a number of positions (flexed, semiflexed, extended, and sprawled) with grave offerings ranging from nothing to one vessel to extensive offerings (that could include turquoise, bead necklaces, multiple ceramic bowls, ladles, jars, pitchers, mugs, birds, and dogs). Orientation of burials may cluster around east-facing, but every other possible compass reading is found as well. Statistically significant relationships among variables such as location, orientation, grave goods, age, and sex have likewise not been forthcoming.

What this variability in mortuary context suggests is that burial customs were not necessarily widely shared among groups living within the same regions or even within the same site. Unlike pottery morphology or design attributes, which can be used to link sites across regions, burial patterns can only be generally characterized for the pre-Contact Pueblo. Although earlier researchers presented grand overviews for shifts in burial customs across temporal units (Pueblo I, II, and III), these are largely no longer relevant (e.g., Frisbie 1978; Morris 1939). For example, although a preference for flexed or semiflexed primary interments is demonstrated in Pueblo I graves, the location of these varies widely. There does seem to be a preference for placing ceramics with these primary interments, although burials with no associated artifacts are quite common. Analysis of the mortuary context for the La Plata Valley burials does not necessarily reveal any strong patterns or trends across sites. The patterning of burial practices does suggest that it is this rich and complicated variability that is interesting and important to document rather than simply assigning burials to one of several large and ambiguous categories (i.e., location, orientation, position, presence/absence of grave good). Stodder (1986, 1987, 1990) and Toll and Schlanger (1998) advocate a more precise and in-depth analysis of burials within sites and between contiguous sites, and focusing more on the relationship of the mortuary features to settlement patterns, organization of subsistence, and ritual activities and demographic variables such as family size, community size, and population density. Although it is not within the scope of this project to undertake an exhaustive study of the La Plata burial configurations, we review the mortuary context here to provide a framework and data for such analyses in the future.

MORTUARY PATTERNING OF THE LA PLATA BURIALS

The single best source of information for the burial context comes from the original field forms and notes which relate in extensive detail the context, condition, deposition, and associations of each burial. Photographs, drawings, and maps likewise are available from the original excavation field forms. For our purposes, we collected a subset of information from these and incorporated it into the skeletal remains database. Briefly, location was recorded as midden, pitstructure, storage pit, room, or "other." Data on strata were categorized by stratigraphic association. For midden burials, it was noted if the remains were in shallow pits or if they were placed deeper into sterile soil. For structures, it was recorded whether the burials were in the upper, middle, or lower fill. Position was recorded as semiflexed, flexed, extended, disturbed, or "other." Based on an analysis of burials within sites, they were divided into categories that distinguished single from multiple burials, primary from secondary burials, and articulated from disturbed remains. Finally, associated artifacts were subjectively placed into categories of none, small, moderate, and extensive offerings.

As a whole the burials from the La Plata Valley repre-

sent the full range of variability in location and amount of grave goods (tables 11.1–11.3), and position (tables 11.4–11.6). In the statistical analysis of a variety of factors (age, sex, date of site, location, position, goods) no significant associations could be found. Although this may be a function of small sample size, an alternative explanation is that the cultural rules for how individuals are to be interred are complex and responsive to a variety of factors.

A great majority of the burials from the La Plata Valley sample are single, articulated, primary interments (approximately 90%). Although some of these burials

TABLE 11.1 Subadult Burials by Age, Location, and Grave Goods

Site No./Feature	Date A.D.	Age[2]	Location	Goods[3]
37593 B3[1]	1100–1300	Fetus	Room; subfloor in pot	None
37603 B2.2	1200–1300	Fetus	With B2.1 pitstructure; upper fill	?
37592 B[1]	1050–1250	.6	Pitstructure; fill	Small
37593 B1[1]	1075–1125	.8	Extramural storage pit	Small
37605 B1	1075–1125	1.5	Room; lower fill	None
65030 B14	1000–1075	1.5	Pitstructure; lower fill	None
65029 B1[1]	1075–1125	1.5	Room; subfloor	Small
65030 B1	1200–1300	2	Room; subfloor	Moderate
37592 B1[1]	1100–1300	2	Pitstructure; upper fill	None
37599 B8.2	1000–1075	2.5	Pitstructure; fill	?
37599 B3	1000–1075	3	Pitstructure; upper fill	Small
37601 B9	1000–1075	3	Pitstructure; fill	Small
65030 B3	1200–1300	3	Room; subfloor	None
65030 B4	1125–1300	3	Extramural pit	None
65030 B17	1000–1075	3	Pitstructure; vent shaft	None
37592 B0.1[1]	1050–1250	4	Extramural storage pit	None
37594 B1[1]	1000–1100	4	Pitstructure; lower fill	Small
37600 B2	1075–1300	4	Extramural pit	None
37592 B2[1]	1100–1300	4.5	Room; pit in floor	Moderate
37593 B4[1]	1075–1125	6	Pitstructure upper fill	?
37605 B4	1075–1125	6	Extramural pit	Small
37605 B3	600–750	8	Pitstructure; upper fill	Moderate
37601 B8	1125–1280	9	Pitstructure; tunnel fill	Small
37601 B11	1125–1180	9	Extramural storage pit	Moderate
37599 B6	1000–1075	10	Pitstructure; fill	Small
65030 B13	1000–1075	11	Pitstructure; lower fill	?
65030 B7	1200–1300	11	Pitstructure; roof fall	None
37595 B2[1]	1000–1075	15	Pitstructure; upper fill	None
37592 B6[1]	1075–1150	15	Room; subfloor	Moderate

[1] Jackson Lake Sites.
[2] The age is the midpoint of the assigned age range.
[3] Small = one associated artifact, moderate = two to three associated artifacts, and extensive is more than three.

TABLE 11.2   Male Burials by Age, Location, and Grave Goods

Site No./Feature	Date A.D.	Age[2]	Location	Goods[3]
37601 B12	1000–1075	22	?	?
65030 B12	1000–1075	22	Pitstructure; lower fill	None
37599 B9	1000–1075	25	Pitstructure; floor pit	Small
37599 B5	1000–1075	25	Pitstructure; fill	None
37601 B6	1000–1075	28	Extramural storage pit	? Small
37601 B1	1125–1280	30	Pitstructure; tunnel	Moderate
37599 B10	1000–1075	32	Pitstructure; upper fill	? Small
37601 B5	1125–1180	35	Pitstructure; upper fill	?
37601 B7	1000–1070	42	Pitstructure; lower fill	Small
37599 B4	1000–1075	45	Extramural pit	Moderate
37603 B1	1200–1300	45	Extramural storage pit	Moderate
37598 B1[1]	1000–1075	45	Extramural pit	None
65030 B15	1000–1075	48	Pitstructure; lower fill	None
37593 B3[1]	1100–1150	48	Extramural storage pit	Extensive
37600 B4	1075–1300	50	Extramural pit	None
37600 B3	1100–1300	50	Pitstructure; upper fill	Small

[1] Jackson Lake Sites.
[2] The age is the midpoint of the assigned age range.
[3] Small = one associated artifact, moderate = two to three associated artifacts, and extensive is more than three.

TABLE 11.3   Female Burials by Age, Location, and Grave Goods

Site No./Feature	Date A.D.	Age[2]	Location	Goods[3]
37592 B5[1]	1050–1250	?	Room; subfloor?	?
37600 B0.1	1000–1300	?	?	?
37601 B3	1125–1180	?	Extramural pit	Moderate
65030 B10	1000–1300	?	Extramural storage pit	Moderate
37601 B2	1000–1075	19	Pitstructure; upper fill	Small
65030 B8	1200–1300	20	Pitstructure; roof fall	None
65030 B16	1000–1075	22	Pitstructure; lower fill	None
65030 B2	1000–1125	22	Extramural pit	Moderate
65030 B5	1200–1300	22	Room; fill	Extensive
37599 B7	1000–1075	25	Pitstructure; fill	Moderate
37601 B4	1125–1180	25	Pitstructure; upper fill	None
37595 B1[1]	1000–1075	25	Pitstructure; upper fill	Moderate
37603 B2.1	1200–1300	30	Pitstructure; upper fill	Small
65030 B9	1200–1300	33	Pitstructure; roof fall	None
37593 B2[1]	1000–1075	35	Extramural storage pit	Moderate
37601 B10	1125–1180	38	?	?
65030 B6	1200–1300	38	Pitstructure; roof fall	None
37600 B1	1000–1150	45	Extramural pit	Small +
37592 B71	1050–1250	50	Extramural pit	Moderate

[1] Jackson Lake Sites.
[2] The age is the midpoint of the assigned age range.
[3] Small = one associated artifact, moderate = two to three associated artifacts, and extensive is more than three.

TABLE 11.4   Subadult Burial Position

Site No./ Feature	Leg Position[2]	Arm Position[2]	Axial Skeleton	Face	Interment[3]
37592 B3[1]	Unknown	Unknown	R side	Unknown	Inside a pot
37603 B2.2	Unknown	Unknown	Unknown	Unknown	Unknown
37592 B4[1]	Unknown	Unknown	Unknown	L side	Disturbed by backhoe; cranium and upper body only
37593 B1[1]	Unknown	Extended along body	Unknown	Unknown	Deliberate
37605 B1	L flexed; R unknown	L unknown; R missing	R side?	R side	Deliberate
65030 B14	Unknown	L unknown; R flexed	L side	L side	Deliberate/ disturbed by backhoe
65029 B1[1]	Flexed; Knees tightly flexed	L unknown; R extended along side?	L side	Up, slightly to the right	Deliberate
65030 B1	Upper flexed	Unknown	Unknown	Unknown	Deliberate/disturbed
37592 B1[1]	Tightly flexed	L unknown; R behind body	Back	Up	Deliberate
37599 B8.2	Unknown	Unknown	Unknown	Unknown	Disarticulated
37599 B3	Unknown	Unknown	Back	Up	Disturbed by water-line trench
37601 B9	Flexed; to left	L along side; R flexed, hand on pelvis	Back	Up	Deliberate
65030 B3	Unknown	Unknown	Chest	Down	Deliberate
65030 B4	Unknown	L extended along side; R missing	R side	R side	Deliberate
65030 B17	Unknown	Unknown	Back	Up	Deliberate
37592 B0.11	Unknown	Unknown	Unknown	Unknown	Disarticulated
37594 B11	Unknown	L unknown, R flexed across chest	Back?	Up	Deliberate
37600 B2	Flexed	Straight along sides	Back	L side	Deliberate
37592 B2[1]	Flexed	L forearm over abdomen; R along body	L side	L side	Deliberate
37593 B4[1]	Unknown	Unknown	Unknown	Unknown	Unknown; found in backhoe back dirt
37605 B4	Unknown	L missing; R extended	Unknown	Unknown	Deliberate/disturbed by utility line
37605 B3	Semiflexed with knees up	Crossed over pelvis	Back	R side	Deliberate
37601 B8	Tightly flexed	Flexed; hands between knees	L side	L side	Deliberate
37601 B11	Tightly flexed and to right	L behind back, Hand on pelvis; R along side with hand on chest	Chest	Thrown back and to the left	Deliberate
37599 B6	Flexed	L flexed with hand to chin; R flexed behind back	Chest	R side	Deliberate

Continued on next page

TABLE 11.4 *Continued*

Site No./ Feature	Leg Position[2]	Arm Position[2]	Axial Skeleton	Face	Interment[3]
65030 B13	Almost extended	Unknown	R side	Unknown	Sprawled/disturbed by carnivores
65030 B7	Extended	Extended out and bent up at elbows	Back	Back	Sprawled
37595 B2[1]	Unknown	Unknown	Unknown	Unknown	Disturbed by carnivores
37592 B6[1]	Tightly flexed	Unknown	Back	Up	Deliberate

[1] Jackson Lake

[2] Flexed means the angle between the axis of the trunk and the femur, the femur and tibia, and/or the humerus and radius/ulna is between 0–90°. Semiflexed is when the angle between these elements are between 90–180°. Extended is when the angle is 180°. For the shoulder, extended is 90° out from the trunk.

[3] Interment refers to whether the burial appears to have been carefully and deliberately placed in a grave. This is distinguished, when possible, from individuals who were merely tossed into an available feature.

were disturbed at the time of excavation (n = 3), the disturbance is largely due to diagenetic and natural causes. Multiple articulated primary interments account for the other 10% of the collection, and these burials are found primarily at site 65030 in one pitstructure (discussed later). These frequencies are quite different from those reported by Stodder (1987) for the Dolores Archaeological Project burials. She found that 51% of the burials were single primary interment, while the other burials were multiple primary and secondary graves. Akins (1986) noted that the majority of the burials from the Chaco small sites were single primary interments. For Kayenta region burial collections, both Ryan (1977) and Martin and colleagues (1991) likewise report that the majority of the burials encountered were single primary interments.

For the La Plata Valley burials that could be positively assigned to a specific location within the site (n = 57), over half (55.7%) were located in pitstructures (table 11.7). The others were located in rooms (14.7%) or extramural pits (29.5%). In looking for location in terms of adults and subadults, there are similar patterns of distribution, although adult males were never encountered in rooms. On the other hand, about one-quarter of the subadults were found in rooms. Across age and sex categories, pitstructure burials accounted for the most significant proportion.

In looking for more subtle variations, females buried in pits were sometimes in the upper fill (50%) and sometimes in the lower. Of the nine females in pitstructures, four were located in the lower fill, one was in the middle,

and four were in the upper. The two females associated with rooms were below the floor. For males, both found in pits were in the upper fill. For the nine males located in pitstructures, three were in the lower, one was in the middle, and three were in the upper layers of fill; two others were in features (pits). There were five males in extramural pits. This general pattern of variability describes the subadults as well.

Of special note is the recovery of two fetuses. The younger one (4–6 lunar months) was placed in a large corrugated jar and placed below the floor of a room. The other one (approximately 8–9 lunar months) was commingled with an adult female in the upper fill of a pitstructure.

The most striking features of this assemblage are the location of burials in domestic locales and the placement of the dead in what appear to be largely abandoned structures. Placement of individuals within the fill of pitstructures, for example, ranges from the bottom (above the floor) and continues throughout the fill suggesting reuse of the abandoned structures for interment over and over through time. Only 12.2% (7) of the individuals were interred in currently occupied sites (presumably the subfloor room burials and a majority of the extramural burial pits).

The preference for using postabandonment structures and features at La Plata Valley is very similar to the pattern found by Stodder (1987) for early Pueblo (Pueblo I) Dolores area burials. Over 70% of the burials recovered were in the fill of structures, although more Dolores buri-

TABLE 11.5 Male Burial Position

Site No./ Feature	Leg Position[2]	Arm Position[2]	Axial Skeleton	Face	Interment[3]
37601 B12	Unknown	Unknown	Unknown	Unknown	Disturbed by backhoe
65030 B12	L flexed; Upper R semiflexed	Unknown	L side	Unknown	Disturbed by carnivores and backhoe
37599 B9	Extended, R bent at knee	Extended, hands at pelvis	Back	R side	Deliberate
37599 B5	L semiflexed; R flexed	L upper along side, hand at chin; R upper along side, lower missing	L side	L side	Deliberate
37601 B6	Hips barely flexed; knees tightly flexed	Along sides and folded over chest	R side	R side	Deliberate
37601 B1	Flexed	L along side and hand between knees; R along side under torso	R side	Unknown	Deliberate
37599 B10	Unknown	Unknown	Back	L side	Deliberate/disturbed by backhoe
37601 B5	Unknown	Unknown	Unknown	Unknown	Disturbed by backhoe
37601 B7	Extended at hips, knees tightly flexed	Along sides and crossed on pelvis	Chest	L side	Deliberate
37599 B4	Flexed	L across pelvis; R long side with hand at chin	R side	Up and on the right side	Deliberate
37603 B1	Loosely flexed at hips; knees tightly flexed	Flexed under body	Down	Down	Deliberate
37598 B1[1]	Partially extended	L across chest; R extended outward	Back	Down	Tossed into a pit
65030 B15	Semiflexed to the left	L extended under body, R extended in front of head	Upper on back; lower to the left	L	Unprepared
37593 B3[1]	Tightly flexed	Tucked against stomach	Down	Down	Deliberate
37600 B4	Tightly flexed	Flexed	L side	L side	Deliberate
37600 B3	Tightly flexed to left	Crossed over pelvis	Back	Back	Deliberate

[1] Jackson Lake

[2] Flexed means the angle between the axis of the trunk and the femur, the femur and tibia, and/or the humerus and radius/ulna is between 0–90°. Semiflexed is when the angle between these elements are between 90–180°. Extended is when the angle is 180°. For the shoulder, extended is 90° out from the trunk.

[3] Interment refers to whether the burial appears to have been carefully and deliberately placed in a grave. This is distinguished, when possible, from individuals who were merely tossed into an available feature.

als were located directly in middens than at La Plata. In a review by Stodder (1987) of burial locations for northern Pueblos from similar time periods as Dolores (Pueblo I-II, Mancos, Badger House, Piedra, and Alkalai Ridge), it was noted that these burials were largely from midden deposits.

A great majority of the burials were found in flexed or semiflexed position (77%) (table 11.8), although there is great variability in leg, arm, axial skeleton, and face positioning (tables 11.4–11.6). The pattern is similar for adults of both sexes and for adults and children. Only one male was intentionally placed in an extended position. The rest

TABLE 11.6 Female Burial Position

Site No./ Feature	Leg Position[2]	Arm Position[2]	Axial Skeleton	Face	Interment[3]
37601 B0.1	Unknown	Unknown	Unknown	Unknown	Unknown
37601 B3	Unknown	Unknown	Unknown	R side	Unknown
65030 B10	Knees flexed to left	L unknown; R upper along torso	Unknown	Up	Deliberate/disturbed by breakage
37601 B2	Tightly flexed to left	Upper along sides, lower L under chin, R across chest	Back	L side	Deliberate
65030 B8	Extended	L extended out; R extended and bent up at elbows	Back	L side and down	Sprawled
37592 B5[1]	Unknown	Unknown	Unknown	Unknown	Lower legs only; rest removed by water line
65030 B16	L semiflexed; R flexed	L along side and under pelvis; R extended out and bent up at elbow	Back	Up	Deliberate? but unprepared
65030 B2	Flexed; knees tightly flexed	Extended in front of torso	L side	L side	Deliberate
65030 B5	Upper extended; knees tightly flexed under upper	L folded over chest; R unknown	Back	Disturbed	Deliberate/disturbed by mechanical equipment
37599 B7	Flexed	Flexed at chest	R side	Down and right	Deliberate
37601 B4	L missing; R upper semiflexed, flexed at knee	L extended out and up; R along side	Back	L side	Deliberate
37595 B1[1]	Tightly flexed	L semiflexed over chest; R flexed over chest	Back	Up	Deliberate
37603 B2.1	Semiflexed at hips, flexed at knees, to right	L semiflexed along chest; R disturbed	Back	Up?	Deliberate/disturbed by mechanical intrusion
65030 B9	L extended; R slightly flexed	L extended out and bent up; R extended out add semiflexed up	Back	Back with chin up	Sprawled
37593 B2[1]	L semiflexed?	L across pelvis?; R extended?	Back?	L side	Deliberate/disturbed by backhoe
37601 B10	Unknown	Unknown	Unknown	Unknown	Disturbed by backhoe
65030 B6	Upper at right angle, knees tightly flexed	Along sides and between legs	Down	Down	Deliberate
37600 B1	Unknown	Unknown	Unknown	R side	Probably deliberate/ disturbed by backhoe
37592 B7[1]	Upper extended; knees tightly flexed	L across neck; R extend along side	Back	Up but twisted	Unusual position

[1] Jackson Lake

[2] Flexed means the angle between the axis of the trunk and the femur, the femur and tibia, and/or the humerus and radius/ulna is between 0–90°. Semiflexed is when the angle between these elements are between 90–180°. Extended is when the angle is 180°. For the shoulder, extended is 90° out from the trunk.

[3] Interment refers to whether the burial appears to have been carefully and deliberately placed in a grave. This is distinguished, when possible, from individuals who were merely tossed into an available feature.

TABLE 11.7 Burial Location

	Pitstructure	Roomblock	Extramural Pit
Female (17)	52.9% (9)	11.8% (2)	35.3% (6)
Male (15)	60.0% (9)	—	40.0% (6)
Subadults (29)	57.7% (16)	24.1% (7)	20.7% (6)
Total (61)	55.7% (34)	14.7% (9)	29.5% (19)

Note: Sample size is in parentheses.

TABLE 11.8 Burial Position

	Flexed/Semiflexed	Extended	Other
Female (14)	71.4% (10)	—	28.5% (4)
Male (15)	73.3% (11)	6.6% (1)	20.0% (3)
Subadults (19)	84.2% (16)	—	10.5% (3)
Total (48)	77.0% (37)	4.2% (1)	18.7% (10)

Note: Sample size is in parentheses.

of the individuals (noted as "other" in table 11.8) not found in semiflexed, flexed, or extended positions can be described as having postures that seem indiscriminate and haphazard. In some cases, these burials were described in the La Plata field notes as "sprawled," "flung," or "thrown." It should be noted that some of the individuals categorized as semiflexed also demonstrate a more inexact positioning; sometimes arms or body parts cross over each other in a haphazard manner. For example, in the case of one female, the field notes state that it was as if the body had been pushed into a pit and ended up in a semiflexed but disarranged position.

Thus, deliberate placement of bodies in flexed or semiflexed positions was practiced on the majority of individuals, but for about a fifth of the population, the body was disposed of in ways that disregarded orderly placement of limbs relative to the torso. This contrasts with the observations of Morris (1939) who did not encounter these kinds of burials (to the extent that his notations on human remains can be deduced) at La Plata Valley sites (especially Site 41). Examination of the photographs which accompany his text suggest that the flexed burials were all very orderly in placement. However, Stodder (1987:25) notes that of the extended burials in the Dolores sample, some were found in positions which seemed "rather sprawled." In comparing the burials excavated from Dolores, there are some remark-

able similarities in the frequency of these more haphazardly placed burials.

A comparison of positions with Mesa Verde (table 11.9) and Chaco Canyon (table 11.10) burials is enlightening in several regards. Although semiflexed and flexed burials dominate, there are instances of extended burials, especially at Chaco Canyon. For the Mesa Verde burials, in some instances, the semiflexed burials were reminiscent of the more haphazard or "pushed" attitude that some of the La Plata burials demonstrated, although it was difficult to cull this information in a systematic way from the site reports. It was particularly difficult to estimate frequencies for burial locations from the site reports for Mesa Verde, but for Chaco Canyon, there are clear differences when compared to the La Plata Valley graves. Middens and rooms account for the great majority of burial locations at Chaco Canyon, and this may be because of the more intensive use of structures. The midden burials in Chaco are not located in the huge "trash mounds" associated with the great-house sites but rather are in the middens associated with the small sites. Also, most burials in the great houses are located in rooms (Akins 1986).

Burials at La Plata with associated artifacts account for a little over half (56.8%) of the total. Of the burials that could be positively identified as having grave offerings among adult males, the frequency was 64.3% and for

TABLE 11.9   Mesa Verde Burials (A.D. 900–1300)

	Mug House Adobe Cave	Big Juniper House	Badger House	Long House	Total
Number of Burials	**46**	**23**	**33**	**39**	**141**
Age Range					
Adult	39.1%	52.1%	63.6%	53.8%	51.0%
Subadult (under 15)	60.8%	47.8%	36.3%	46.1%	48.9%
Position					
Flexed	30.4%	21.7%	18.1%	56.4%	33.3%
Semiflexed	26.0%	39.1%	36.3%	5.1%	24.8%
Extended	6.5%	4.3%	—	—	2.8%
Unknown	36.9%	34.7%	45.4%	38.4%	39.0%
Burials with					
Grave Goods	39.1%	69.5%	78.7%	53.8%	57.4%

Sources: Cattanach (1980), Hayes and Lancaster (1975), Rohn (1971), and Swannack (1969).

TABLE 11.10   Chaco Canyon Burials

Ceramic Period:	Early Red Mesa/ Red Mesa (A.D. 900–1050)	Gallup (A.D. 1030–1150)	McElmo (A.D. 1100–1175)	Mesa Verde (A.D. 1175–1300)
Number of Burials	**48**	**66**	**41**	**11**
Age Range				
Adult	47.9%	54.5%	56.0%	45.4%
Subadult (under 15)	18.7%	34.8%	43.9%	54.5%
Unknown	33.3%	10.6%	—	—
Location				
Room	25.0%	51.5%	73.1%	100%
Midden	75.0%	43.9%	12.1%	—
Misc.	—	4.5%	14.6%	—
Position				
Flexed	10.4%	39.3%	21.9%	9.1%
Semiflexed	50.0%	40.9%	36.5%	36.3%
Extended	18.7%	18.1%	14.6%	9.1%
Unknown	20.8%	1.5%	26.8%	45.4%

Source: Adapted from Akins (1986).

females, 68.7%. Over half of the subadults (56.0%) demonstrated associated grave goods. This is significantly higher than for the Dolores sample where Stodder (1987) found slightly more than one-third to have been buried with grave goods. In examining the distribution of grave goods (small, moderate, and extensive), there is no apparent pattern between sexes, across ages, or through time (tables 11.1–11.3). The most common offerings include ceramic bowls and a few jars. Only a few burials had ladles or pitchers. One burial had a bone awl, and a few burials had ground stone or worked sherds. The majority of the burials with grave goods had a small (n = 1) number of offerings (50.0%), over a third (44.1.0%) had moderate (n = 2 to 3) offerings, and 5.9% have extensive (more than 3) offerings. However, the La Plata Valley individuals with extensive offerings do not compare in any way with the quantity and quality of offerings reported for some Pueblo II-III northern Pueblo burials. For example, Stodder (1987) reports an individual with 36 ceramic vessels, numerous manos, bone tools, and a bear skull. Morris (1939) describes burials from Site 41 with mugs, bowls, jars, and bone and shell artifacts. Akins's (1986) description of Pueblo Bonito burials also are much more extensive than anything discovered in the La Plata Valley.

The three individuals with extensive (by La Plata Valley standards) grave offerings are a nine year old (37601 B11), a 22-year-old female (65030 B5), and a 48-year-old male (37593 B3). The child was placed in a partially filled bell-shaped cist, tightly flexed on the stomach with the knees to the right. Three pots were found with the child. Also in the pit, but not necessarily associated, were a turkey and a dog. The adult female was buried beneath the floor of a room with an elaborate bone bead necklace, ground stone, several bowls, and small pieces of turquoise, and she was possibly wrapped in a shroud. The male, flexed and in a storage pit, had several vessels, a ladle and bowl, and a red-tailed hawk and was placed in the pit with matting. These burials come from three different sites, with dates ranging from A.D. 1100–1300.

Summary of Mortuary Patterning

The La Plata Highway Project is among only a handful of projects in the Southwest that has integrated the human remains and the mortuary component into the ongoing research strategy. Examples of the inclusion of mortuary behavior along with paleopathological and paleodemographic analyses for Pueblo skeletal populations include those by Akins (1986), Stodder (1987), and Palkovich (1980). An analysis focused only on the La Plata remains is hampered by the small sample size, but it can serve to contribute to the growing database on mortuary variability and stands ready to be used by others in more comprehensive and inclusive studies in the future.

Toll and Schlanger (1998) have provided a careful and illuminating analysis of the mortuary component of the burials at La Plata. This important study demonstrates that the burials are not randomly distributed across features in the landscape, rather there appear to be preferred strategies for the disposal of the dead. She finds three unique characteristics of the mortuary behavior in the La Plata Valley (as compared with pre-Contact burials from other parts of North America) that include the lack of a

formal burial ground, the great variability in the number of burials at any given site, and the frequent use of "places for the living" as a resting place for the dead. At La Plata, burials are found with the greatest frequency in pitstructure fill contexts. Extramural pits, floors, subfloor venues, and surface room fill are other places where burials have been located.

Most interesting of the findings by Toll and Schlanger is the occurrence of bench burials in previously occupied pitstructures. A suggestion is made that some graves contain the remains of former inhabitants of abandoned sites. For example, four of the eleven burials recovered from site LA 37601 show distinctive genetic anomalies of the spine. These include one adult male with an extra thoracic vertebrae, two adult males each with an extra lumbar vertebra, and one subadult with a first sacral vertebra that demonstrates lumbar features. This co-occurrence of genetic anomalies suggests that it is possible that family members were buried at a location which had some meaning for them. This line of inquiry demonstrates the need for archaeologists to work closely with skeletal biologists in blending the analyses. Lane and Sublett (1972) have demonstrated that skeletal material can be used to confirm hypotheses about ethnicity, endogamy, and residence patterns. Future collaborative and interdisciplinary studies need to be initiated for the La Plata Valley region.

At La Plata, the frequency of bench burials and the presence of disarticulated human skeletal elements that cannot be explained by natural depositional events suggests that the management and treatment of the dead by the La Plata communities went well beyond simple interment. Because so few studies have included the type of careful analysis afforded by Toll and Schlanger, there are only a handful of comparable studies.

Stodder (1986) has provided a similarly insightful study of the Pueblo I Dolores mortuary program, and there are interesting parallels to be made that highlight how little is known regarding what "normal" pre-Contact burial patterns are. The Dolores Archaeological Project recovered 45 discrete burials that were located in the postoccupational fill of habitation and storage structures, under floors of pitstructures and habitations areas, and in middens. As with the La Plata remains, Stodder found no patterning or association with respect to age or sex for location, position, or amount of grave goods.

The occurrence of several individuals in what has been described as "sprawled" positions on the fill of abandoned pitstructures at La Plata is not unique, but it has also not been intensively described by others working with burial populations except for Stodder's (1986) report on the earlier Dolores sample (Pueblo I).

OSTEOLOGICAL EVIDENCE OF TRAUMA

Tracking trauma and violence in the osteological record is fairly straightforward (Merbs 1989). Applied force leaves a distinctive and permanent record on bone when it is utilized with enough power to cause tissue damage. Evidence of recovery from trauma is likewise among the more unambiguous types of bone changes that can be easily documented. Injuries to the head leave particularly characteristic lesions that last for many, many years after the original injury has long healed, thus providing a record of nonlethal blows to the head (Walker 1989). Bhootra (1985:567) states that "no injury of the head is too trivial to be ignored or so serious as to be despaired of," and for all deaths that result from violence, one-fourth are attributed to head injuries in contemporary society. As background (taken from Gurdjian 1973:94–98), depression fractures begin with a traumatic event, such as a blow to the head, that ruptures blood vessels in the bone marrow and periosteum. There is formation of a hematoma within six to eight hours. This gradually is replaced by young connective tissue, and it transforms into a fibrous callous. Through remodeling, this fibrous callous is gradually replaced with new bone. Depression fractures are produced by a force applied to just one side of the bone. The outer cortex of bone is clearly depressed inward while the underlying diploe space becomes compressed. There are three characteristics of depression fractures: (1) usually fine cracks radiate from the depressed areas; (2) within the depressed area, the inner table of bone is beveled at the edges; and (3) the surrounding areas of the depression are raised as they rebound from the pressure build up. With healing, these all but disappear, but there is usually a diagnostic depression for long periods after the trauma. The depression fracture stays depressed long after healing because of bone necrosis. Traumatic interruption of blood supply will result in the death of bone cells and a sloughing off of dead tissue.

For individuals who survive the initial effect of a blow to the head, one consequence of the process is that not enough oxygen may get to the brain (called hypoxia). Hypoxia further increases swelling and edema which in turn cause increased intracranial pressure. This can lead to

brain herniation. In general, however, moderate increases in intracranial pressure can be survived, but there may be long-lasting neurological problems stemming from the healing process of the original injury. For example, children who survive head injuries are more likely to become hyperactive and have learning disabilities. Injuries to the back of the head are particularly problematic because they knock the brain forward against the skull, which can do damage to the frontal lobe (Curless 1992:164).

Head injuries can produce neurological side effects such as "amnesia, vertigo, epilepsy, poor concentration, reduced rate of information processing, fatigue, headache, irritability, emotional instability, attacks of emotional instability, and antisocial conduct" (Walker 1989:322). These symptoms can reveal themselves months or years after the original trauma. Injury to the left frontal lobe of the brain can cause personality changes (such as loss of inhibition) or hallucination (Allen et al. 1985:31).

The methods for assessment and analysis of trauma on cranial and postcranial remains followed the recommendations of Merbs (1989), Ortner and Putschar (1981), and Walker (1989). The La Plata (n = 65) burial collections were both analyzed by Martin and colleagues (Martin et al. 1995). The remains were treated to systematic data collection for age, sex, pathologies, metrics, and discrete traits using the Paleopathology Standards as a guide (Rose et al. 1991).

Data collection included the following: pathological lesions were scored as osteoclastic/resorptive, osteoblastic/proliferative, or trauma-related lesions. If trauma was present, it was further analyzed as to type, location, extent, and level of remodeling (healing). Cranial depression fractures were measured for width, height, and depth. All fractures were x-rayed, and differential diagnosis was aided by consultation with Dr. Gregory Gordon and Dr. Don Chrisman, both practicing physicians at the time.

The age at death data for the La Plata population demonstrate two clusters of individuals dying at early ages (table 11.11). The first is during the years newborn to age three where there is a cluster of 15 infants. This is not so unusual for preindustrial populations, but it does signal problems in both maternal and infant health. The second cluster of deaths occurs for females aged 19–25, with seven individuals in that category compared with only four males. A closer look at these young adult females revealed an association with traumatic injuries.

Evidence for traumatic violence from the La Plata burial series includes healed fractures or traumatic injuries that are in the remodeling (healing) phase (therefore, injuries that were nonlethal). The cranial wounds at La Plata fit the description of depression fractures caused by blows to the head (e.g., Courville 1948; Merbs 1989; Stewart and Quade 1969; Walker 1989). For the individuals who could be analyzed for cranial and postcranial healed traumatic injuries (n = 51), there were no unambiguous perimortem bone breaks or fractures; therefore, fractures and traumatic injury discussed here occurred sometime during the lifetimes of the individuals (tables 11.12–11.13). Young children were generally free of fractures; only one 15 year old (37592 B6) had a healed compression fracture on the left parietal.

A site-by-site description of individuals with cranial and/or postcranial pathology related to trauma clearly shows different patterns between adult males and females (table 11.12). The ages assigned represent the midpoint age based on the age range assigned using a number of aging techniques (Bass 1995; White 1991). For males, there are three cases of cranial trauma: One 25 year old has a healed compression fracture of the right parietal (37599 B5), another 25 year old has a healed fracture at the corner of the left eye (37599 B9), and a 35 year old has a healed depression fracture on the left parietal (37601 B5). Male postcranial fractures include a healed Colle's fracture of the right radius and ulna (the type one gets when breaking a fall), a healed fractured right thumb, and an individual with several healed rib and vertebrae fractures. All of these postcranial traumas are on males who are aged over 45 years and indicate traumas easily explained by occasional accidents or occupational hazards. These three postcranial fractures did not co-occur with the cranial traumas.

Six females (out of 14) demonstrate healed cranial trauma (largely in the form of depression fractures), and the ages of these women range from 22 to 38. However, the inventory of healed nonlethal cranial wounds for the females is longer and more extensive, with three of the six cases involving multiple head wounds. The youngest female (age 20) has a healed broken nose (65030 B8). Another young female (age 28) with a cranial trauma demonstrates two depression fractures, one on the forehead and one on the back of the head (65030 B15). A 25 year old has multiple depression fractures about the front and side of her head (37601 B4) (figure 11.1). A 33 year old has a large unreunited but healed series of fractures at the top of her head (65030 B9) (figure 11.2). Of the two 38-year-old females, one has a healed fracture above her right eye (37601 B10), and one has a depression fracture at the back of the head (65030 B6) (figure 11.3).

In addition to this, six females demonstrate postcranial trauma. However, two features of lower body trauma are distinctly different from the male pattern: (1) in four out of six cases, the cranial and postcranial fractures co-occur, and (2) the postcranial fractures in the females occur in younger age categories, ranging from 20 to 38. The youngest female (age 20) has fractures in the atlas and axis of the neck vertebrae (she also had a broken nose).

A 25 year old (37601 B4) has several fractures (right shoulder, left humerus, upper neck) along with multiple depression fractures about the head. This female also had a severe case of osteomyelitis that affected numerous bones. Parts of the sternum are thickened with osteophytic

TABLE 11.11 Summary by Age and Sex

Site No.	0–3	4–8	9–18	19–25 ♀	19–25 ♂	26–35 ♀	26–35 ♂	36–45 ♀	36–45 ♂	46+ ♀	46+ ♂	Adult ♀	Adult ?	All	♀	♂	Sub.
LA 37592	3	2	1	—	—	—	—	—	—	1	—	1	—	8	2	—	6
LA 37593	1	1	—	—	—	1	—	1	—	—	1	—	—	4	1	1	2
LA 37594	—	1	—	—	—	—	—	—	—	—	—	—	—	1	—	—	1
LA 37595	—	—	1	1	—	—	—	—	—	—	—	—	—	2	1	—	1
LA 37598	—	—	—	—	—	—	—	—	—	—	1	—	—	1	—	1	—
LA 37599	2	—	1	1	2	—	—	—	2	—	—	—	2	10	1	4	3
LA 37600	—	1	—	—	—	—	—	—	—	1	2	1	1	6	2	2	1
LA 37601	1	—	2	2	1	—	3	1	1	—	—	1	—	12	4	5	3
LA 37603	1	—	—	—	—	1	—	—	1	—	—	—	—	3	1	1	1
LA 37605	1	2	—	—	—	—	—	—	—	—	—	—	—	3	—	—	3
LA 65029	1	—	—	—	—	—	—	—	—	—	—	—	—	1	—	—	1
LA 65030	5	—	2	4	1	1	—	1	—	—	1	1	—	16	7	2	7
Totals	15	7	7	8	4	3	3	2	4	2	5	4	3	67	19	16	29

reactive bone covering all surfaces. Some parts of the bone surface appear smooth and rounded, and these areas were likely caused by lytic lesions and subsequent sclerotic processes (Ortner and Putschar 1981:111). The scapulae, clavicles, and distal portion of one humerus are likewise massively remodeled and affected by the same process. Differential diagnosis relying primarily on x-ray examination suggests osteomyelitis, although the original cause of this massive infection confined to the shoulder and chest area can only be speculated upon. The right scapula near the spine and the sixth and seventh ribs show roughened depressed areas that look like healed fractures. There appears also to be localized, trauma-induced osteophytes on the third through fifth cervical vertebrae. It is possible that this woman was struck with an object hard enough to cause not only cranial fracturing, but also lacerated wounds on the shoulders and chest area as well.

Other postcranial traumas on the females include a 33-year-old that demonstrates fractures of the left hip as well as on the top of her head. The oldest female (age 38) showed healed fractures on the left hip and also had a depression fracture at the back of her head. The two cases of a solo lower body fracture are in a 30-year-old female who may have died during childbirth because a term-fetus was found commingled. She had a fracture of the right distal radius. The other female of unknown age had a fractured tibia.

The frequencies of healed trauma for adults at La Plata reveal that females have a three-fold increase in the frequency of cranial trauma over males (14.2% versus 42.8%),

TABLE 11.12 Trauma

Site No./ Feature	Age/Sex	Cranial	Postcranial
37592 B6	15	L Parietal, 7 x 12 mm depression fracture	—
37593 B3	48 M	—	R Rib 6 and L Rib 9, healed fractures; vertebrae thoracic 8, 9, osteophytes and wedging
37594 B4	45 M	—	R Metacarpal 1, healed fracture
37599 B5	25 M	R parietal, 30 x 30 mm depression fracture (partly unreunited)	—
37599 B9	25 M	L frontal orbit, 6 x 9 mm depression fracture	—
37600 B4	50 M	—	R radius and ulna distal ends, remodeled, misshapen lesions—healed fractures
37601 B4	25 F	L parietal and center on frontal above orbits, 6+ well-rounded depression fractures of various sizes	R scapula, roughened depression near spine; R ribs 6, 7, healed fractures, remodeled w/depression; L humerus, large pits and remodeling near lesser tubercle, healed fracture; C3–5, trauma induced osteophytes
37601 B5	35 M	L parietal near occipital, 20 x 15 mm depression fracture	—
37601 B10	38 F	R frontal above eye, 20 x 15 mm depression fracture	—
37603 B2.1	30 F	—	R radius, distal healed fracture
65030 B6	38 F	Occipital, 24 x 24 mm depression fracture	L hip acetabulum and related area, osteophytes and raised area
65030 B8	20 F	R and L nasals, healed broken nose	Vertebrae cervical 1, 2, healed fracture
65030 B9	33 F	At bregma, 57 x 77 mm area with large bump, sutures unreunited	L pelvis, fracture at pubic plate
65030 B16	28 F	R frontal, 17 x 17 mm depression fracture; occipital, 7 x 7 mm depression fracture	—
37592 B5	? F	—	R fibula fracture

TABLE 11.13   Frequencies of Healed Trauma

	Children	Males	Females
Cranial	1/21 (4.7%)	2/14 (14.2%)	6/14 (42.8%)
Postcranial	0/19 (0.0%)	3/16 (18.7%)	6/14 (42.8%)

and a two-fold increase in postcranial trauma (18.7% versus 42.8%). Adult frequencies greatly outnumber those for subadults who have an overall rate of 4.7% for cranial trauma and virtually no cases of postcranial trauma.

In reviewing other factors associated with health for adult males and females at La Plata, females have more cases of infection (46.1%) than males (13.3%), and some of these may be related to sequelae from the injury that produced the fractures (table 11.14). In addition, females demonstrated higher frequencies of childhood growth disruption (for four out of six teeth, females had more hypoplastic lines). Females with cranial trauma have

FIGURE 11.2   Female Age 33 with Large Unreunited and Completed Healed Series of Fractures at the Top of the Head (LA 65030 B9)

more enamel defects than females without. For example, at Barker Arroyo site LA 65030, four females have cranial trauma and co-occurring severe or multiple hypoplastic defects, whereas the other two females from this site show no trauma and have few defects.

Other characteristics of the females with cranial trauma are that these women as a group generally have more frequent involvement with anemia and systemic infection. A final observation regarding women with cranial trauma is that several exhibit more left/right asymmetry of 2–6 mm in long bone proportions (three individuals in particular are asymmetrical, LA 65030 B6, B8, and B9) and more pronounced cases of postcranial ossified ligaments, osteophytes at joint surfaces (unrelated to general osteoarthritis or degenerative joint disease) and localized periosteal reactions (enthesopathies). Whether these observations are the result of occupational stress (Kennedy 1989) or the sequelae of injuries that caused unusual and differential biomechanical problems is not clear.

An apparent association emerges when the mortuary contexts of the individuals with cranial trauma are

FIGURE 11.1   Female Age 25 with Multiple Depression Fractures on the Frontal Bone (LA 65030 B15)

FIGURE 11.3   Female Age 38 with a Depression Fracture on the Occipital Bone at the Back of the Head (LA 65030 B6)

examined. The majority of the burials from La Plata are flexed or semiflexed and placed within abandoned structures or in storage pits. Often burials contain associated objects, usually ceramic vessels or ground stone (as example, figure 11.4a). Every female at La Plata with cranial trauma had a mortuary context that did not follow this pattern. All were found in positions that were loosely flexed, prostrate, or sprawled. Particularly at two sites, both from Barker Arroyo (LA 37601 and LA 65030), the mortuary context of females with cranial trauma reveals that, unlike their age-matched counterparts without signs of trauma, they were generally haphazardly placed in abandoned pitstructures, and there were no associated grave goods.

At Barker Arroyo site LA 65030, three individuals found in the lower fill of Pitstructure 1 appear to have all died at approximately the same time and were interred together. These include two adult women aged at 20 and 33 and an 11-year-old child. All are in a haphazard position (as if thrown from a higher elevation) (figure 11.4b-d). Cause of death could not be ascertained for any of these individuals. Also in Pitstructure 1, located in the middle fill on top of the roof fall, another female aged at 38 was placed facing downward in a semiflexed position with no grave offerings (figure 11.5a). In the lower fill of Pitstructure 8, a 22-year-old female was placed in semiflexed position with

no grave offerings (figure 11.5b). At another site, LA 37601, a 25-year-old female with cranial and postcranial trauma was located in a similar position with no grave goods (figure 11.5c). Of the three males with cranial trauma, at least one 25 year old from site LA 37599 was placed in Pitstructure 2 in a similar fashion with no grave goods (figure 11.5d). Unfortunately, the mortuary context of the other two males with cranial trauma is unknown.

To summarize, the association of healed cranial trauma and mortuary context, out of a total sample size of 14 adult females with crania, five show trauma and were buried with no grave goods in either sprawled or semiflexed positions (one female with cranial trauma could not be assigned to a mortuary condition); six females had no trauma and were in a flexed or semiflexed positions with associated grave goods; one female had no cranial trauma, a semiflexed burial but no grave goods; and one female with no cranial trauma had an unknown mortuary context.

For the 14 males that could be assessed for cranial trauma, six had no cranial trauma and were flexed burials with grave goods; five had no cranial trauma but also no grave goods (with a variety of positions ranging from extended to flexed); and of the three males with cranial trauma, one had grave goods, and two did not although all were in a semiflexed position. There is definitely more variability in the relationship between cranial trauma and burial treatment for the males, with more males in general having no grave goods.

The variation in overall size and dimensions of the depressions suggest that any number of implements could have been used to cause these fractures. The location of two out of three of the male cranial fractures is on the parietals (one on the left and one on the right, both toward the back). For females, the lesions are largely located around the front of the head or on the far back (occipital) portion of the head. It is difficult to verify exactly what type of implement was used in each case of

TABLE 11.14   Differences by Sex for Stature and Pathology

	Male	Female
Anemia	4/12 (33.3%)	4/11 (36.4%)
Infection	2/15 (13.3%)	6/13 (46.1%)
Stature	161.4	152.2

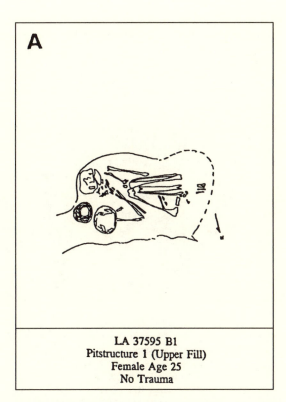

LA 37595 B1
Pitstructure 1 (Upper Fill)
Female Age 25
No Trauma

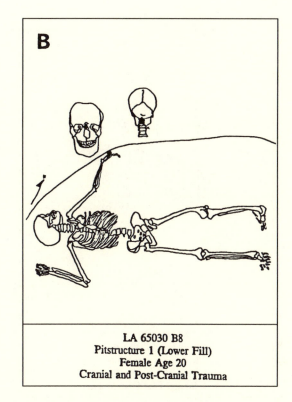

LA 65030 B8
Pitstructure 1 (Lower Fill)
Female Age 20
Cranial and Post-Cranial Trauma

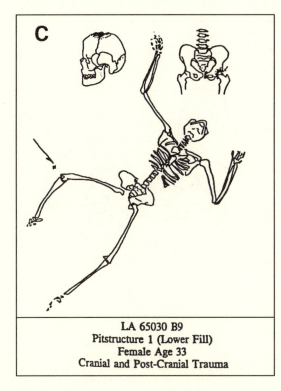

LA 65030 B9
Pitstructure 1 (Lower Fill)
Female Age 33
Cranial and Post-Cranial Trauma

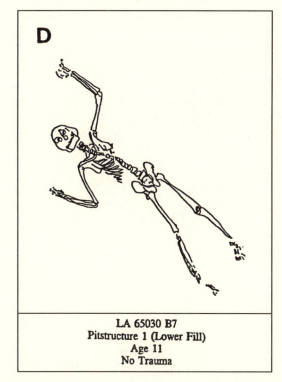

LA 65030 B7
Pitstructure 1 (Lower Fill)
Age 11
No Trauma

FIGURE 11.4.   Drawings from Field Sketches Demonstrating the In Situ Position of Burials (A) in a Flexed Position
with Grave Goods and (B, C, and D) with Both Healed Lesions (see inset drawings) and Haphazard
Burial Positions

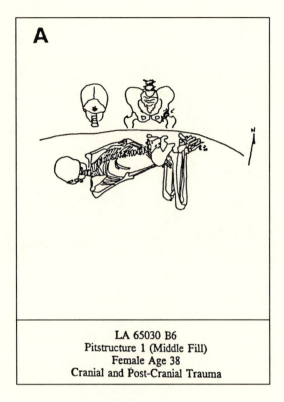

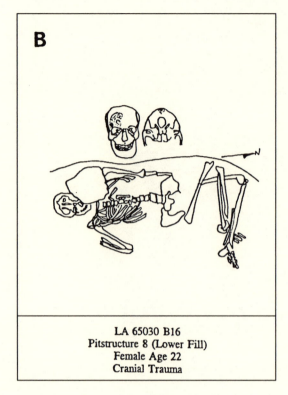

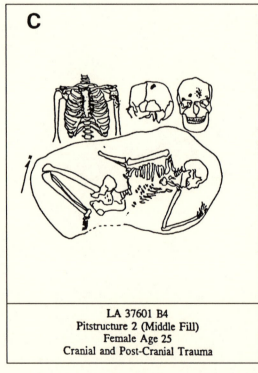

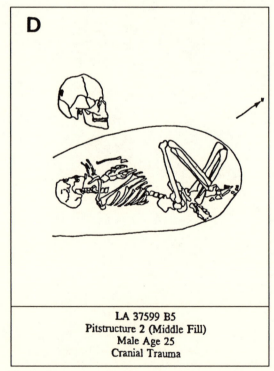

FIGURE 11.5 Drawings from Field Sketches Demonstrating the In Situ Position of Burials with Both Healed Lesions (see inset drawings) and Haphazard Burial Positions (A-D)

cranial trauma at La Plata, but modern forensic information suggests that fractures of the head can be made with any number of blunt or sharp implements (Petty 1980). In their review of artifacts associated with warfare and hand combat, Wilcox and Haas (1994:223–24) find little evidence for the manufacture of objects solely to be used as weapons. The strongest evidence that they could garner was of two bipointed axes found with a male burial at Aztec Ruin, and wooden sword-like implements found at Chaco Canyon.

While it is easy to envision a stone axe, hammer stone, core, chopper, or projectile point causing damage, it is equally likely that bone, antler, and wood objects could be used as well. For example, in a forensic case involving cranial and postcranial wounds similar to those at La Plata, the injuries were caused when being struck repeatedly with a common wooden yard broom (Bhootra 1985) not unlike the size and shape of a Pueblo digging stick (Colton 1960:96). Digging sticks were most likely common in an agricultural community such as that of the Barker Arroyo sites at La Plata, and the use of such objects was primarily within the domain of men (at least in historic Pueblo societies) (Dozier 1970). Colton (1960:98) states that sometimes wooden digging sticks also had a hoe made of hafted stone or with triangular pieces of basalt or sandstone. In addition, a variety of stone tools such as tchamahias and axes were found in the La Plata Valley, and any of these items could be used to cause injury.

LINKAGE BETWEEN TRAUMA, HEALTH, AND MORTUARY TREATMENT

Trauma is absent in children and generally benign in adult males (particularly the postcranial trauma which was all minor and occurred in elderly males). Females carry an unequal burden of traumatic injuries in this group. The location and size of the cranial injuries showed that by overall dimensions and size in area, female injuries covered a larger area, involved more bony elements, often occurred in multiples, and caused internal (endocranial) damage in some cases. Furthermore, the comorbidity factors of cranial and postcranial trauma, infections, and decreased life expectancy (there were very few females represented in the older age categories) suggest truly suboptimal conditions for some adult females. Females with these health problems are more likely to have been in mortuary contexts described as haphazardly thrown or discarded and

with no associated grave offerings. As a group, they were younger when they died than females who had traditionally prepared graves.

An examination of other attributes suggests that they were part of the Pueblo culture to the extent that most of these women have occipital or lambdoidal flattening consistent with the use of cradleboarding during infancy. Only one female with a compression fracture (37601 B10) did not show flattening, but this is not unusual (Morris 1939; Renaud 1927). Cranial metrics and cranial and postcranial discrete traits cannot be used to characterize the subgroups because of small sample size. This is very unfortunate because to understand the physical injury and differential mortuary treatment, it would be important to verify if the women with trauma were genetically related to the group as a whole.

The one physical characteristic that distinguishes at least several of the women with trauma is a pattern of nonpathological lesions and abnormalities associated with occupational stress or habitual use of select muscle groups. For example, both females in Pitstructure 1 from site LA 65030 demonstrate asymmetrical measurements for many of the width proportions of the long bones. Particularly, the humerus, radius and ulna are most affected. Trinkaus and colleagues (1994) examined modern, extant and extinct groups and found that humeral bilateral asymmetry related most often to activity-related functional changes.

Another attribute of some of these women is the findings of isolated osteophytes in places that correspond to muscle insertions. Because as a group these women are generally too young to have the osteoarthritic changes associated with aging, these morphological changes could be related to habitual use of certain muscles which can lead to the build up of bone and changes at the site of the most biomechanical stress. Bridges (1990) examined the osteological correlates of weapon use in two pre-Contact groups from Alabama and showed that the shift from hunting and gathering to agriculture can be correlated with nonpathological changes in morphology relating to different use of tools and weapons. Bridges noted that there were changes in porosity and osteophytic lipping at the shoulder joints and the elbow in particular. She also found bilateral asymmetry in the diameters of the radius and ulna between the groups. Although somewhat subjective at this point, many of the La Plata females within the subgroup do demonstrate osteophytes and asymmetries, and therefore the most distinguishing element of their physical make-up is one that is developmental and relates to occupation or habitual performance of certain activities.

Although the subgroup sample sizes limit a detailed quantitative analysis of occupational stress markers, it is possible to speculate on a division of labor that was both by sex and possibly by "class" as well. Spencer and Jennings (1965), Titiev (1972), and Dozier (1970) summarize sexual division of labor for Pueblo people suggesting that traditionally, women ground corn, prepared food, gathered wood, built and mended houses, made pottery and clothing, gathered wild foods, and made baskets. Men were responsible for farming, occasional hunting, and religious and ceremonial activities. The difficult task of grinding corn into meal belonged to the women, who might spend as many as eight to nine hours a day at the grindstone.

In traditional subsistence societies, with agricultural intensification, there is often a concomitant pressure on women to increase their productivity simultaneously with a decrease in birth spacing (Harris and Ross 1987:49). This places an enormous burden on women to partition their time, energy, and activities between very different and competing tasks: economic labor and bearing and rearing children. Harris and Ross cite summary data (1987:50) on the number of hours that women work daily in agriculturally based villages, and it ranges from 6.7 to 10.8 hours a day (with the high end representing intensive agriculturalists).

It is possible that as the La Plata Valley population increased (through a combination of immigration and increased fertility), several conditions could arise. There would be a need to increase production of food to feed the increasing number of people, and therefore there would be a need for an increased labor pool. As more people moved into the La Plata Valley, it is possible that the more local or "native" populations maintained access and control of the resources. That is, natal groups would have preferred access to food and other resources over nonrelated newcomers. This could effectively establish an underclass of people who were exploited in any number of ways. Reproductive-aged females would be the most advantageous group to exploit because they could aid in domestic tasks and food production, as well as in child rearing. This would not rule out the exploitation of males as well, although they would be less vulnerable to physical injury because of their ability to be more readily mobile (without children) and to fight and use weapons.

Haas and Creamer (1993) and Wilcox and Haas (1994) provide detailed overviews of archaeological data that demonstrate evidence of sustained intervillage conflict (e.g., fortification, palisades, towers, burned structures) that likely increased over time. Although not everyone agrees with these interpretations (e.g., Cameron 1990), defensive architecture and strategic location of sites seems to have been important factors in the building of many Southwest villages.

Another feature of the precolonial Pueblo landscape is the occasional occurrence of human skeletal assemblages that are disarticulated, broken, chopped, sometimes burned, and that often show signs of dismembering. These collections (which include both children and adult males and females) have been variously interpreted to represent cannibalism (Turner 1993; White 1992), witchcraft retribution (Darling 1993), warfare (Wilcox and Haas 1994) or ritualized dismemberment (Ogilvie and Hilton 1993). Whatever the motivation behind presumed violent deaths and perimortem alterations of the victims' bodies, it does suggest some evidence for violent action directed against subgroups that seem to be demographically representative in most cases (i.e., infants, children, young and old men and women).

Collectively, the archaeological data on fortification and strategic location and the osteological data on victims and mass graves suggest that fighting in the form of ambushes, raids, skirmishes, or attacks by a group of aggressors may have been the status quo in many parts of the pre-Contact Southwest. Haas and Creamer (1993) suggest that these patterns of "chronic warfare" pushed previously egalitarian and loosely connected groups into larger, politically centralized units between A.D. 1100–1300.

The litany of injury and trauma on individual skeletal remains has been noted in the literature as well but not always with much specificity and rarely linked to other aspects of local or regional dynamics. On the one hand there are places where virtually no intentional violence is apparent. For example, Miles analyzed 179 burials from Wetherill Mesa (A.D. 1200), and he states that "the relative absence of fractures of major external force indicates that these people lived a rather quiet life without frequent warfare, and that they did not sustain many serious falls from the cliffs and mesas where they lived" (Miles 1975:20). He further states that "there were no depressed skull fractures, and no arrowheads or other foreign bodies imbedded in bone" (Miles 1975:24).

Akins (1986) likewise found little evidence of trauma in the Chaco series that she examined. Exceptions to this include a male (Number 14 from Room 33 at Pueblo

Bonito) who has "two holes and a gash in the frontal bone" suggesting that he died in a confrontation (Akins 1986: 116–17). For skeletal remains from Chaco small sites, Akins notes a few cases of postcranial fractures, and one female (age 30+) who had four depression fractures on the parietal.

On the other hand, some sites have yielded evidence of strife. For the Transwestern Pipeline series (circa A.D. 1200), Hermann (1993) notes that several adult females have postcranial fractures in the fibula, sacrum, radius, and tibia. Several women had multiple healed fractures on their lower body. One female had three depression fractures on the frontal bone (she also had postcranial healed fractures), and one female had a perimortem fracture on the maxilla. At Carter Ranch (circa A.D. 1200) Danforth and colleagues summarize trauma in the following manner: "One-quarter of 24 scorable adults had healed fractures. There are two nasal fractures, one associated with a broken mandible and the other with a broken humerus, two radius fractures, a clavicle fracture and a femur fractures. Four of the six cases can be interpreted as the result of blows" (Danforth et al. 1994:96). Sex of the individuals is not specified.

Stewart and Quade (1969) present one of the more thorough accounts of bone lesions from North American pre-Contact series. They provide information on frontal lesions from Pueblo Bonito and Hawikku (together) and derived a population frequency rate of 9% for males and 5.8% for female in the Southwest. The authors state that most of the lesions they saw from the Pueblo sites are due to trauma (Stewart and Quade 1969:89).

For the Pecos collection, Hooton (1930) presents a detailed inventory of cranial trauma by sex. Out of a total sample size of 581, he found 20 cases of cranial trauma, representing a 3.4% frequency. Of these 20 cases, five (25%) are on females and the rest are on males (75%). The depression fractures are largely located on the frontal bones, although other areas of the crania are implicated as well.

Stodder (1989:187) compiled a frequency chart for a number of archaeological populations from the Greater Southwest (New Mexico, parts of Texas, south-central Colorado). These frequencies range from 2% to 22% with the highest percentages located at the Gallina sites. Regarding the frequency data, Stodder states that "the Gallina sample exhibits the highest reported frequencies of postcranial and cranial trauma is not surprising, as they are most often identified as warlike, with defensive architecture in relatively isolated locations" (Stodder

1989:187). The likewise relatively high rates of cranial injury at San Cristobal (8%) is primarily in the males "suggesting that they were engaged in warfare" (Stodder 1989:187).

Allen and colleagues (1985) analyzed ten cases of scalping at Navakwewtaqa (A.D. 1200–1300) and Grasshopper Ruin (A.D. 1300). Some of the individuals who had been scalped exhibited depression fractures as well. For example, at Navakwewtaqa, there were four males ranging in age from 25 to 40+ who were scalped, and three females ranging in age from 25 to 35. One female has a depression fracture on the left frontal bone, and one female has a ovoid-shaped hole in the left parietal suggesting penetration by a weapon and the probable cause of death. At Grasshopper, two males (ages between 35 and 40+) were scalped and a young female (age 15) exhibited a depression fracture above the left orbit as well. Interestingly, many of these individuals were buried with associated grave goods such as bowls, beads, bone awls, and quartz crystals. The authors suggest that this "indicates that it was members of these two communities themselves who were the victims of the practice [scalping]" (Allen et al. 1985:30). However, the authors go on to state that "skeletal evidence for violence at the two sites is almost non-existent" and that it is "possible that the ten individuals described here were victims of isolated raids" (Allen et al. 1985:30).

This cursory review of some of the pertinent literature on trauma presents a rather complex view for the pre-Contact past. Extreme variability exists in the ways that injurious actions sometimes occurred. Mass slayings, individual dismemberments, burning, possible cannibalism, scalping, intentional injury, and limited hand-to-hand combat do exist in the Southwest archaeological record, and these span the height of occupation (circa A.D. 800–1300). The extent to which these isolated incidences occur and their relationship to other political, economic, and ideological currents is of interest. These cases of violence may represent relatively isolated examples, or they may be indicative of a more large-scale and integrated system of power dynamics, show of force, oppression, coercion, or conflict resolution. It is possible that in order to maintain unanimity and harmony across diverse (economically, linguistically, and ideologically) Pueblo communities, some show of force may have been necessary, but the degree to which this is the case needs much more systematic study.

Although speculative, the pattern of violence against women at La Plata can be at least partially explained by increased population density and increased stratification, at least to the degree that subclasses were created. La Plata communities may have felt it necessary to construct rigid rules about resource allocation, and they may have chosen a strategy that targeted a subgroup within the population. In this case, that may have been reproductive-aged women who migrated into the area. They may have, in a sense, become indentured servants to others who had the power to enforce domination of this subgroup. How they came to be servant/laborers is less clear; it could have been through raiding and abduction of women from other villages, or through migration into the area of women who became part of an underclass.

The picture that emerges is one of an agricultural population that was doing relatively well, given the circumstances of crowded living and subsistence farming. Anemia and infectious disease are expected outcomes of group living and agrarian lifeways. These disease conditions are not pronounced at La Plata. In comparison to nearby groups in the Mesa Verde and Chaco Canyon regions, La Plata individuals seem to be faring quite well, if not better than expected. However, all of this is shadowed by the high frequencies of trauma found in the female subpopulation.

Ironically, archaeologists have written that La Plata was a "bread basket" and a favored place to live (W. H. Toll 1993). La Plata and the surrounding densely settled communities such as those in the Mesa Verde region may have instead chosen a strategy of labor production and distribution that created classes of people and targeted groups. Economic security did not ensure equality for women; women may have been subject to increased violence either as captured or enslaved laborers, or as victims of abuse caught in the struggle for control over labor, production, and resources.

CONCLUSION

Reviewed in this chapter are two different but related kinds of information on the La Plata burial population. Analysis of the mortuary context, critical for the assessment of biases introduced into the burial assemblage by mortuary practices or excavation procedures, demonstrated several things. First, although there are some patterns of interment that hold across sites (single articulated primary burials in semiflexed or flexed position), there was a significant degree of variation in burial location, associated grave

goods, and in age and sex distribution for burials with and without trauma. The mortuary component compares most closely with that of the earlier (Pueblo I) Dolores Archaeological Project burials which also displayed a great deal of variability in interment. La Plata burials are different from contemporaneous Mesa Verde region burials, La Plata sites excavated by Morris (such as Site 41), and Chaco small sites. Toll and Schlanger (1998) suggested that the use and reuse of abandoned domestic features is meaningful and can be used to better understand the motivating factors behind burial patterns and ties to certain places in the landscape.

Secondly, there is a relationship between pathologies present in the population and mortuary treatment. The individuals with the highest morbidity burden in terms of healed traumatic lesions, infections, nutritional anemia, and site-specific osteoarthritis are also those who, at death, were not provided with grave goods or placed in prepared grave pits.

While "spatial segmentation of cemeteries, destructive burial practices, imperfect preservation and incomplete archaeological recovery all serve to bias a skeletal sample" (Buikstra and Mielke 1985:366), through careful consideration of potential biases, we believe that sound interpretations regarding the representativeness of the skeletal population under study can be offered.

The Southwest provides a distinctive setting for combined health and mortuary studies because of the long-term residence by ancestral Pueblo Indians. With thousands of years of habitation in the Southwest, the Pueblo groups offer insight into the mechanisms underlying adaptability and behavioral flexibility in the face of changes over time. The available osteological and archaeological literature on mortuary treatment, diet, nutrition, disease, trauma, and warfare in precolonial times in the Southwest is relatively small, and only recently have larger reviews and synthetic research surfaced which focus on this.

It is difficult at this stage to make any kind of summary statement that accurately situates La Plata Valley burials vis-à-vis burials from other sites in the Southwest. There are questions that could be framed for burials that would shift the focus into different arenas. For example, what similarities exist in overall health status and treatment of the dead? Do intra- or intergroup tensions and strife enter into a group's mortuary practices? Is there a pattern relating cause of death (admittedly difficult to determine) and mortuary behavior? Is status (and therefore differential treatment at death) defined in political, economic, social, or spiritual terms? Can information gleaned from the skeletons be used in inferring ethnicity, endogamy, and residence patterns? These types of questions shift the focus of traditional research into mortuary behavior and could link burials into a broader discussion of biocultural processes underlying adaptability and population dynamics through time and across space.

REFERENCES CITED

Akins, Nancy J.
1986   *A Biocultural Approach to Human Burials from Chaco Canyon, New Mexico*. Reports of the Chaco Center No. 9. National Park Service, Santa Fe.

Alekshin, V. A.
1983   Burial Customs as an Archaeological Source. *Current Anthropology* 24:137–50.

Allen, W. H., C. F. Merbs, and W. H. Birkby
1985   Evidence for Prehistoric Scalping at Nuvakwewtaqa (Chavez Pass) and Grasshopper Ruin, Arizona. In *Health and Disease in the Prehistoric Southwest*, edited by C. F. Merbs and R. J. Miller, pp. 23–42. Anthropological Research Papers No. 34. Arizona State University, Tempe.

Bartel, B.
1982   A Historical Review of Ethnological and Archaeological Analyses of Mortuary Practice. *Journal of Anthropological Archaeology* 1:32–58.

Bass, William M.
1995   *Human Osteology: A Laboratory and Field Manual of the Human Skeleton*. 4th ed. University of Missouri Archaeological Museum Society, Columbia.

Beck, Lane A. (editor)
1995   *Regional Approaches to Mortuary Analysis*. Plenum Press, New York.

Bhootra, B. K.
1985   An Unusual Penetrating Head Wound by a Yard Broom and Its Medicolegal Aspects. *Journal of Forensic Sciences* 30:567–71.

Binford, Lewis R.
1971   Mortuary Practices: Their Study and Their Potential. In *Approaches to the Social Dimensions of Mortuary Practices*, organized and edited by J. A. Brown, pp. 6–29. Memoirs of the Society for American Archaeology, no.

25. Society for American Archaeology, Washington, D.C. (Issued as *American Antiquity* 36(3) Pt. 2, July 1971.)

Bridges, P. S.
1990   Osteological Correlates of Weapon Use. In *A Life in Science: Papers in Honor of J. Lawrence Angel*, edited by J. Buikstra, pp. 87–98. Center for American Archaeology Scientific Papers 6. Washington, D.C.

Buikstra, J. E., and J. H. Mielke
1985   Demography, Diet, and Health. In *Analysis of Prehistoric Diet*, edited by R. I. Gilbert and J. H. Mielke, pp. 359–422. Academic Press, New York.

Cameron, Catherine M.
1990   Pit Structure Abandonment in the Four Corners Region of the American Southwest. *Journal of Field Archaeology* 17:27–37.

Cattanach, G. S.
1980   *Long House, Mesa Verde National Park, Colorado*. Publications in Archaeology 7H, Wetherill Mesa Studies. U.S. Department of the Interior, National Park Service, Washington, D.C.

Colton, Harold S.
1960   *Black Sand, Prehistory in Northern Arizona*. University of New Mexico Press, Albuquerque.

Courville, C. B.
1948   Cranial Injuries among the Indians of North America: A Preliminary Report. *Los Angeles Neurological Society* 13:181–219.

Curless, M. R.
1992   New Thinking on Head Bumps. *Redbook* March:164.

Danforth, M. E., D. C. Cook, and S. G. Knick III
1994   The Human Remains from Carter Ranch Pueblo, Arizona: Health in Isolation. *American Antiquity* 59:88–101.

Darling, J. A.
1993   Mass Inhumation and the Execution of Witches in the North American Southwest. Unpublished preliminary draft. On file, Office of Archaeological Studies, Santa Fe.

Dozier, Edward P.
1970   *The Pueblo Indians of North America*. Holt, Rinehart and Winston, New York.

Frisbie, T. R.
1978   High Status Burials in the Greater Southwest. In *Across the Chichimec Sea*, edited by C. R. Riley and B. C. Hedrick, pp. 202–27. Southern Illinois University Press, Carbondale.

Gurdjian, E. S.
1973   *Head Injury from Antiquity to the Present with Special Reference to Penetrating Head Wounds.* Charles C. Thomas Press, Springfield.

Haas, J., and W. Creamer
1993   *Stress and Warfare among the Kayenta Anasazi of the Thirteenth Century A.D.* Field Museum of Natural History, Chicago.

Harris, M., and E. B. Ross
1987   *Death, Sex, and Fertility: Population Regulation in Preindustrial and Developing Societies.* Columbia University Press, New York.

Hayes, A. C., and J. A. Lancaster
1975   *Badger House Community, Mesa Verde National Park, Colorado.* Publications in Archaeology 7E, Wetherill Mesa Studies. U.S. Department. of the Interior, National Park Service, Washington D.C.

Herrmann, N. P.
1993   Burial Interpretations. In *Across the Colorado Plateau: Anthropological Studies for the Transwestern Pipeline Expansion Project, vol. XVIII: Human Remains and Burial Goods,* edited by N. P. Herrmann, M. D. Ogilvie, C. E. Hilton, and K. L. Brown, pp. 77–95. Office of Contract Archeology and Maxwell Museum of Anthropology, Albuquerque.

Hooton, E. A.
1930   *The Indians of Pecos Pueblo: A Study of Their Skeletal Remains.* Papers of the Southwestern Expedition 4. Yale University Press, New Haven.

Kennedy, K. A. R.
1989   Skeletal Markers of Occupational Stress. In *Reconstruction of Life from the Skeleton,* edited by M. Y. Iscan and K. A. R. Kennedy, pp. 129–60. Alan R. Liss, New York.

Lane, R. A., and A. J. Sublett
1972   Osteology of Social Organization: Residence Pattern. *American Antiquity* 37:186–201.

Larsen, Clark S.
1987   Bioarchaeological Interpretations of Subsistence Economy and Behavior from Human Skeletal Remains. In *Advances in Archaeological Method and Theory,* vol. 10, edited by M. B. Schiffer, pp. 339–445. Academic Press, New York.

Martin, Debra L., Nancy J. Akins, Alan H. Goodman, and Alan C. Swedlund
1995   *Harmony and Discord: Bioarchaeology of the La Plata Valley.* Office of Archaeological Studies, Museum of New Mexico Press, Santa Fe.

Martin, Debra L., Alan H. Goodman, George J. Armelagos, and Ann L. Magennis
1991   *Black Mesa Anasazi Health: Reconstructing Life from Patterns of Death and Disease.* Southern Illinois University Center for Archaeological Investigation Occasional Paper No. 14. Southern Illinois University Press, Carbondale.

Merbs, C. F.
1989   Trauma. In *Reconstruction of Life from the Skeleton,* edited by M. Y. Iscan and K. A. R. Kennedy, pp. 161–99. Alan R. Liss, New York.

Miles, J. S.
1975   *Orthopedic Problems of the Wetherill Mesa Populations.* Publications in Archaeology 7G, Wetherill Mesa Studies. U.S. Department of the Interior, National Park Service, Washington, D.C.

Morris, Earl H.
1939   *Archaeological Studies in the La Plata District.* Carnegie Institution, Washington, D. C.

Nelson, Ben A., Debra L. Martin, Alan C. Swedlund, Paul R. Fish, and George J. Armelagos
1994   Studies in Disruption: Demography and Health in the Prehistoric American Southwest. In *Understanding Complexity in the Prehistoric Southwest,* edited by G. J. Gumerman and M. Gell-Mann, pp. 59–112. Addison-Wesley, Reading.

Ogilvie, M. D., and C. E. Hilton
1993   Analysis of Selected Human Skeletal Material from Sites 423–124 and –131. In *Across the Colorado Plateau: Anthropological Studies for the Transwestern Pipeline Expansion Project,* vol. XVIII: *Human Remains and Burial Goods,* edited by N. P. Herrmann, M. D. Ogilvie, C. E. Hilton, and K. L. Brown, pp. 97–128. Office of Contract Archeology and Maxwell Museum of Anthropology, Albuquerque.

Ortner, D. J., and W. G. J. Putschar
1981   *Identification of Pathological Conditions in Human Skeletal Remains.* Smithsonian Institution, Washington, D.C.

Palkovich, Ann M.
1980   *The Arroyo Hondo Skeletal and Mortuary Remains.* School of American Research Press, Santa Fe.

Petty, C. S.
1980   Death by Trauma: Blunt and Sharp Instruments and Firearms. In *Modern Legal Medicine, Psychiatry, and Forensic Science,*

edited by W. J. Curran, A. C. McGarry, and
C. S. Petty, pp. 100–121. Davis Publishers,
Philadelphia.

Ravesloot, John C.
1988   *Mortuary Practices and Social Differentiation
at Cases Grandes, Chihuahua, Mexico.*
Anthropological Papers No. 49. University of
Arizona Press, Tucson.

Renaud, E. B.
1927   Undeformed Prehistoric Skulls from La Plata,
Colorado, and Canon del Muerto, Arizona.
The University of Colorado Studies 16(1):5–36.

Rohn, A. H.
1971   *Mug House, Wetherill Mesa Excavations, Mesa
Verde National Park, Colorado.* Archaeological
Research Series 7D. U.S. Department of the
Interior, National Park Service, Washington,
D.C.

Rose, J. C., S. C. Anton, A. C. Aufderheide, J. E. Buikstra,
L. Eisenberg, J. B. Gregg, E. E. Hunt, and B. Rothschild
1991   *Paleopathology Association Skeletal Data Base
Recommendations.* Paleopathology
Association Press, Detroit.

Ryan, D. J.
1977   *The Paleopathology and Paleoepidemiology of
the Kayenta Anasazi Indians of Northeastern
Arizona.* Ph.D. dissertation, Department of
Anthropology, Arizona State University,
Tempe.

Saxe, Arthur A.
1970   *Social Dimensions of Mortuary Practices in
a Mesolithic Population from Wadi Halfa,
Sudan.* Unpublished Ph.D. dissertation,
Department of Anthropology, University of
Michigan, Ann Arbor.

Spencer, R. F., and J. D. Jennings
1965   *The Native Americans: Prehistory and
Ethnology.* Harper and Row, New York.

Stewart, T. D., and L. G. Quade
1969   Lesions of the Frontal Bone in American
Indians. *American Journal of Physical
Anthropology* 30:89–110.

Stodder, A. W.
1986   Complexity in Early Anasazi Mortuary
Behavior: Evidence from the Dolores
Archaeological Program. Paper presented at
the 51st Annual Meeting of the Society for
American Archaeology, New Orleans.
1987   The Physical Anthropology and Mortuary
Practice of the Dolores Anasazi: An Early
Pueblo Population in Local and Regional
Perspective. In *Dolores Archaeological Program*

*Supporting Studies: Settlement and
Environment,* edited by K. L. Peterson and
J. D. Orcutt, pp. 339–504. U.S. Bureau of
Reclamation, Engineering and Research
Center, Denver.
1989   Bioarcheological Research in the Basin and
Range Region. In *Human Adaptations and
Cultural Change in the Greater Southwest,* by
A. H. Simmons, A. L. W. Stodder, D. D.
Dykeman, and P. A. Hicks, pp. 167–90.
Arkansas Archeological Survey Research
Series No. 32. Wrightsville.
1990   *Paleoepidemiology of Eastern and Western
Pueblo Communities in Protohistoric New
Mexico.* Unpublished Ph.D. Dissertation,
Department of Anthropology, University of
Colorado, Boulder.

Swannack, J. D., Jr.
1969   *Big Juniper House, Mesa Verde National Park,
Colorado.* Publications in Archaeology 7C.
U. S. Department of the Interior, National
Park Service, Washington D.C.

Swedlund, A. C.
1994   Issues in Demography and Health. In
*Understanding Complexity in the Prehistoric
Southwest,* edited by G. J. Gumerman and M.
Gell-Mann, pp. 39–58. Addison-Wesley,
Reading.

Titiev, Mischa
1972   *The Hopi Indians of Old Oraibi.* University of
Michigan Press, Ann Arbor.

Toll, H. Wolcott
1993   *The Role of the Totah in Regions and Regional
Definitions.* Paper presented at the 5th
Occasional Anasazi Symposium, San Juan
College, Farmington, New Mexico.

Toll, H. Wolcott, and Sarah H. Schlanger
1998   Redefining and Reifying the Landscape: Reuse
of Cultural Locations in the La Plata Valley,
New Mexico. Paper presented at the 63rd
Annual Meeting of the Society for American
Archaeology, Seattle.

Toll, M. S.
1993   *The Archaeobotany of the La Plata Valley in
Totah Perspective.* Paper presented at the 5th
Occasional Anasazi Symposium, San Juan
College, Farmington, New Mexico.

Trinkaus, E., S. E. Churchill, and C. B. Ruff
1994   Postcranial Robusticity in *Homo.* II: Humeral
Bilateral Asymmetry and Bone Plasticity.
American Journal of Physical Anthropology
93:1–34.

Turner, Christy G., II

1993　Cannibalism in Chaco Canyon: The Charnel Pit Excavated in 1926 at Small House Ruin by Frank H. H. Roberts, Jr. *American Journal of Physical Anthropology* 91:421–39.

Ucko, P. J.

1969　Ethnography and Archaeological Interpretation of Funerary Remains. *World Archaeology* 1:262–81.

Walker, Philip L.

1989　Cranial Injuries as Evidence of Violence in Prehistoric Southern California. *American Journal of Physical Anthropology* 80:313–23.

White Tim D.

1991　*Human Osteology*. Academic Press, Orlando.

1992　*Prehistoric Cannibalism at Mancos 5MTUMR-2346*. Princeton University Press, Princeton.

Wilcox, D. R., and J. Haas

1994　The Scream of the Butterfly: Competition and Conflict in the Prehistoric Southwest. In *Themes in Southwest Prehistory*, edited by G. J. Gumerman, pp. 211–38. School of American Research Press, Santa Fe.

CHAPTER TWELVE

Ancient Southwest Mortuary Practices: Perspectives from Outside the Southwest

Lynne Goldstein

READING THE CHAPTERS HAS MADE ME REALIZE JUST how far outside the Southwest I am; somehow, I was unaware of the tenuous grasp I had on the quantity, quality, and range of mortuary data available from the region. In thinking about Southwestern mortuary data or analyses that have been published and widely cited outside the Southwest, what comes to mind are some biological anthropology studies, various scholars' examinations of cannibalism and warfare, and debates about whether or not there were ranked societies in the prehistoric Southwest. In some senses, this volume follows in that general tradition in that its primary focus is on the exploration of past social complexity. It differs from past work in that its database is both rich and extensive. Given the extensive database, however, it is interesting that the mortuary literature, and particularly the literature associated with the development of mortuary theory, has not generally been associated with research in the Southwest. Because much other theory has been based on Southwestern research, the surprise is even greater. In reading these chapters and thinking about the literature, I have decided to focus the majority of my discussion on why this may be the case.

The chapters represent a range of studies, from traditional mortuary analyses to osteological analyses to synthetic chapters on mortuary practices within regions. It is both important and reassuring that so much attention is being paid to mortuary studies in an area in which the data are so rich and the topic not so fully explored. The authors are to be commended for their efforts and for trying to work with the Southwestern mortuary data and a set of theoretical frameworks that were not necessarily designed for such data.

First, I should note that the chapters are not representative of the entire region, and there is a clear and heavy bias toward Hohokam sites. I do not see this as a problem but simply a statement of the range of data available and used by the authors of this volume. Nonetheless, I would guess that the average non-Southwestern archaeologist has little idea of how extensive the data are, not just in terms of number of sites with multiple and extensive mortuary remains but also in terms of number of individuals. Even though there are obvious problems of data quality, bias, and comparability (all of which are generally recognized and addressed by the authors), comparisons between sites and regions are clearly possible. The fact that little formal comparison has been attempted in this volume is interesting but perhaps not surprising given the overall focus of the authors on understanding the nature of the societies within each portion of the region. With the focus on Hohokam sites, an overview of Hohokam society based on these varying perspectives would also have been instructive for those who do not work in the region. I do not think that any of the varying opinions or analyses are inherently right or wrong, and in general, although the authors focus on different sites or on somewhat different aspects of ritual and its meaning, the conclusions are not necessarily contradictory. This comment is made by someone who has nothing invested in Hohokam research, however, and I am certain that I likely missed some of the nuances that result in years of point and counterpoint articles.

As an outsider, it is striking to me how much concern is represented in the chapters on whether or not ancient Southwestern societies were ranked or stratified or not. The general literature in archaeology and in anthropology has moved away from determination of indicators of ranking and away from labeling societies as stratified, but many of the chapters here have included this kind of examination, even when they indicate their plans to do otherwise. I do not necessarily see this as a failing of the articles, however. Rather, I think the problem is that the authors are trying to fit their work into the frameworks previously developed for mortuary analyses, and as many postprocessual and other recent authors have suggested (see Morris 1992), too many of these studies have focused exclusively on status and ranking. When applied to Southwestern societies that don't fit neatly into categories such as "ranked," the models do not work as well. The kinds of analytic problems outlined by McGuire, for example, make this point abundantly clear.

Most scholars agree that societies traditionally labeled as "egalitarian" can also be complex, and solving the question of whether ancient Southwestern societies represent ranked or complex egalitarian groups does not seem to be the most interesting question one can ask of the data. Virtually every chapter that tries to identify ranking demonstrates that there are differences between groups of people within one or more mortuary sites or contexts, but rarely does an author identify many of these subgroups or explain what these differences might actually mean in the society. Certainly there is differentiation present, and the nature of Southwestern societies in the past and today would make this an obvious conclusion, but whether such differentiation is a signal of a stratified society is debatable. Whittlesey and Reid's finding that they could support totally alternative hypotheses is a fascinating one, and one that I think tells us more about the nature of the questions asked and assumptions made than about the nature of the data.

The Southwest should provide an ideal laboratory to move away from questions of ranking and complexity and to move toward a more complex and complete analysis of mortuary ritual. One of the reasons that mortuary analysis in the Southwest may not have been in the forefront of the development of mortuary theory is because the region is considered by many to represent groups of more egalitarian, and therefore less differentiated, societies. With the focus in archaeology in the 1970s and 1980s on determination of social ranking, the Southwest represented a less desirable or at least less simple place to examine such issues. Further, at the time, there was not as much mortuary data available; as Mitchell and Brunson-Hadley note, much of the data discussed in this volume was recovered in the 1980s. Although chapters such as those by McGuire, Mitchell and Brunson-Hadley, Whittlesey and Reid, and Martin and Akins go beyond the old style analysis of social ranking and demonstrate a real appreciation of the role of symbolic and ritual behavior, I think that a focus on social complexity may still be too narrow. Some of the more interesting questions might include how and why people may have employed a particular social structure, why mortuary ritual changed and/or differed over space and through time, and what parts of the entire mortuary ritual can be inferred. As Martin and Akins note, there is a whole set of health and other osteological data that should also be included and linked to these broader questions of social structure and ritual. As an outsider reading the chapters, I am more struck by the variability and *lack* of differentiation in mortuary practices than I am by strong evidence of ranking or stratification; this does not, however, mean that I think there is a lack of complexity.

The Southwestern United States includes an incredibly rich ethnographic database from which to draw, including both historic and modern information. The willingness of at least some tribes (see Ferguson, Dongoske, and Kuwanwisiwma in this volume) to work with archaeologists enhances this fact, and most of the authors in this volume attempt to use ethnographic and historical data to inform their studies. Although the authors have a clear understanding of how important the ethnographic data are, few authors use the ethnographic data in other than a confirmatory manner; they do not use ethnography to develop their argument but tend to look for matches between the ethnographic data and what they see archaeologically. These are the kinds of comparisons that all of us make and perhaps must make, but there is also potential for even more interesting work that might develop theory. One example is the use of oral traditions. It seems to me that the Southwest is an ideal location for ground-breaking work in the application of oral traditions to mortuary analysis (and to archaeology in general); how can such data be applied and what are some of the "rules" and constraints that are needed to employ such data? The Native American Graves Protection and Repatriation Act (NAGPRA) lists oral traditions as one of the categories of data by which cultural affiliations can be determined, but how else might such data inform our studies of mortuary behavior?

As in other areas, the excellent preservation in the region allows examination of some variables that simply are not present or preserved in other archaeological contexts. Authors tend to ignore this fact, in all likelihood because they are used to working in this rich context. I find it interesting that a number of authors are concerned by disturbances of mortuary contexts. There are always questions of data quality, but one of the most interesting things about mortuary practices in this region is the *quantity* of ancient disturbances. Such disturbances are not surprising given disposal in occupation contexts, but such disturbances may be worthy of study on their own and may be beneficial in learning about the nature of mortuary ritual. Why are people disturbing earlier graves? Is there any regularity or patterning in how the graves are disturbed, or in which graves are disturbed?

Mortuary ritual is extremely conservative and represents critical social and symbolic aspects of societies. It is rare that change in such fundamentally important rites comes about solely for environmental or economic reasons. The important discussion in this volume associated with changes in ritual is the shift from cremation to inhumation and the combination of cremation and inhumation. In my opinion, this is an area worthy of more detailed examination and analysis. Why cremation, why not something else? If the shift from cremation to inhumation is the result of economic or environmental factors (e.g., lack of wood, frozen ground), are the mortuary patterns otherwise analogous, as one might expect if this is just a simple shift based on available resources? What other variables are associated with cremation and inhumation? What are the similarities and differences between the mortuary programs?

I do not want my comments to read as though I were disappointed with the chapters—that is not the case at all. I find the chapters to be extremely well considered and thoughtful. However, the one area of analysis I question is the continued reliance and focus on the analysis of grave goods. Certainly a majority of mortuary analyses have grave goods as a major focus, but I think this limits what can be said about mortuary and social behavior. Grave goods are certainly one of the most obvious correlates of mortuary behavior, but they cannot be the exclusive focus of analysis. Several chapters demonstrate the validity of this observation (see Martin and Akins), but other authors note other aspects of mortuary behavior, then turn their analysis solely to the number and kind of grave goods. Once quantified, these numbers have a tendency to take on a life of their own, and scholars forget about other variables that can be equally or more significant. Each society symbolizes in different ways, and one cannot assume that grave goods are the key distinguishing attribute, especially when so many burials have no grave goods at all.

As scholars have criticized processual archaeology for its focus on ranking and status, archaeologists have begun to see that questions of symbolics and ritual are equally important to consider (see Morris 1992 for discussion of critique). The mortuary site or grave generally represents the *end* of the mortuary ritual, and more research is needed on the stages of ritual. Although it might seem difficult to isolate and identify ritual stages, in part such work may be more a question of recognizing that something like burial is the end of a process or series of steps. With such a perspective, the focus can shift away from what ended up in the grave and toward how the grave came to be located where it is. In this volume, McGuire begins to do some of this work with his proposal about the nature of Hohokam cremation, but more systematic efforts are needed.

My own work in mortuary analysis has focused on the importance of the spatial dimension of mortuary sites (see Goldstein 1980, 1995), and with the increasing interest in landscapes and site settings (e.g., Bradley 1993, 1998; Tilley 1994), I had hoped to see new work on the spatial dimensions of mortuary practices in the Southwest. When spatial aspects of mortuary practices are included in analyses, the authors in this volume tend to look only at several variables, such as whether or not someone is buried within or outside a room, within or outside a designated cemetery area, or within a midden. The relative placements within these contexts, within the community, and against the landscape are not explored. Given complex sets of relationships and groupings in modern Southwest societies and the importance of space and how it is used, this seems to be a potentially fruitful area of research. My suggestion would be that more detailed in-site analysis and landscape analysis of mortuary contexts would be productive in the future. Based on the chapters, the spatial placement of graves suggests a very strong link between the nature and structure of habitation sites and ideas about death and social structure.

I must temper any criticism of the "grave goods" approach by acknowledging again that the majority of mortuary studies conducted worldwide have tended to focus on grave goods, so this is certainly not something unique to the authors in this volume. However, perhaps one or two examples of why this is a problem might be instructive. The most obvious example is the situation when the mortuary site includes a group of burials without grave goods—these individuals are then totally omitted from any analysis or are included only as "other." The possibility of understanding the range of behavior is automatically constrained and limited. In my own work, my study of the Moss and Schild cemeteries in Illinois (Goldstein 1980) analyzed the burials two ways: first, looking only at grave associations and second, looking at grave goods and other variables. The approach demonstrated that an analysis using grave goods alone tended to differentiate individuals, but when other variables such as body positioning, spatial placement of items, and relative placement of burials in relation to each other were included, group affiliations and distinctions were highlighted. Including more than grave goods allowed me to identify possible corporate and kin groupings, and these divisions were further informed by adding biological/health data.

A study I conducted more recently of Effigy Mound sites in Wisconsin (Goldstein 1995) posed a number of analytical problems that could not be addressed solely by the examination of associated grave goods for very different reasons: Effigy Mound sites represent groups of mounds, some of which are in the shape of animals, some of which are conical or oval or linear in shape. Some, but not all, of the mounds have burials (although every mound group seems to have at least one burial), and the burials clearly do not represent all of the population. How can one study Effigy Mound mortuary practices in these circumstances? I compared the structure of the burial features that had been excavated, looking for patterns and regularities. Next, I looked at who was buried in the mounds and the form of burials (primary, secondary, etc.). I also examined the location of the burial features within the mounds and the mound groups, and finally, I examined the distribution of the mounds across the landscape. From this work, I posited that Effigy Mounds are placed in very specific kinds

of landscape situations, people are buried in them as part of a group ritual, and the mounds likely represent yearly group gathering and/or dispersal points, as well as possible "maps" of the landscape. The point is that looking at grave goods alone or grave goods and a few other general variables will only provide a portion of the picture and will never allow the researcher to tease apart the entire mortuary ritual or set the ritual in a meaningful context. In circumstances in which there are any burials without grave associations, a "grave goods only" analysis will certainly overlook something. In the case of the Southwest, is there any patterning as to where within a site graves are found? Is this pattern similar across sites? How does the distribution of graves relate to the overall landscape and placement of sites? The answers to such questions may not prove enlightening, but they should be addressed.

It is impossible to discuss mortuary analysis today and not include some mention of repatriation. In fact, one could argue that it is not only impossible, it is unethical, both from the perspective of consideration of native views and from the perspective of whether or not there will be data left to study. Although only the Hopi modern perspective is included in this collection, it is my personal opinion that some of the most interesting and valuable mortuary analysis to be done in the future will be the result of interactions between archaeologists and tribes. As the authors of the Hopi chapter point out, such analysis is not necessarily something that modern Hopi desire, but such work is often undertaken to address a greater or more significant issue. It is also important to note, at least in the case of the Hopi, that they are willing to remain open to the possibility of mortuary analysis, and in fact, the tribe invites archaeologists to consult with the Hopi Preservation Office. Quite obviously these discussions will not always result in the end desired by the archaeologist, but as in the example of cannibalism in this chapter, such discussions will be fruitful and will force archaeology to look at alternative explanations and possibilities. The exploration of mortuary analysis and potential cultural affiliation is one obvious area for constructive collaborative work. There is no question that NAGPRA has changed the complexion of archaeology and especially of mortuary analysis. I believe that archaeologists must work with tribes to bring greater meaning and relevance to their work, and it is entirely reasonable to ask that archaeologists defend and explain the work that they propose to undertake. I also think it is very dangerous to suggest that tribes will or should dictate the future of research, however, but as long as everyone understands that disagreement does not mean disrespect, I think the potential for better explanations and better research is great. Many tribes will not encourage or allow archaeological research on human remains, and this is unfortunate. It does not, however, mean that all such work is impossible. As the implementation of NAGPRA continues, and as tribes and archaeologists develop new working relationships, more possibilities should become available.

The chapters are impressive in substance and in scope, and they have made me think about Southwestern mortuary practices in new and different ways. I now have an appreciation for the variety and scale of practices, as well as for the significant data sets available for study and comparison. I hope that the authors seriously consider addressing some of the questions raised above, as well as other new questions, in their future studies. The simple act of collecting these varied studies and reading about other related data sets should prompt some new and exciting work. The Southwest may be the place that can best ask and answer new questions about the nature and development of complexity and what it may mean.

REFERENCES CITED

Bradley, Richard
1993 *Altering the Earth: The Origins of Monuments in Britain and Continental Europe.* Society of Antiquities of Scotland, Monograph Series No. 8. Edinburgh, Scotland.
1998 *The Significance of Monuments: On the Shaping of Human Experience in Neolithic and Bronze Age Europe.* Routledge, London.

Goldstein, Lynne
1980 *Mississippian Mortuary Practices: A Case Study of Two Cemeteries in the Lower Illinois Valley.* Northwestern University Archaeology Program, Scientific Papers No. 4. Northwestern University, Evanston.
1995 Landscapes and Mortuary Practices: A Case for Regional Perspectives. In *Regional Approaches to Mortuary Analysis,* edited by L. A. Beck, pp. 101–21. Plenum Press, New York.

Morris, Ian
1992 Death-Ritual and Social Structure in Classical Antiquity. Cambridge University Press, Cambridge.

Tilley, Christopher
1994 A Phenomenology of Landscape: Places, Paths, and Monuments. Berg Publishers, Providence.

Epilogue

Judy L. Brunson-Hadley and Douglas R. Mitchell

THE LAST DECADE HAS SEEN RADICAL CHANGES IN THE science and technology of anthropological studies, as well as changes in the rights of Native American tribes to participate in the decision-making process for the repatriation of human remains. Controversies have erupted over the decision-making role that Native Americans should have in the scientific studies of ancient people. Some scientists have claimed that their ability to study the past has been greatly compromised by restrictions tribal groups put on analysis. Some Native Americans have complained that based on their religions, no analyses should be performed. Some people question what will happen to mortuary studies in the future. Controversies abound.

As history has shown over and over, whenever a religious group has tried to dictate the course of scientific studies, important information can be lost, and a variety of controversies develop (see Schuldenrein 1999 for a brief essay on science, religion, and the Native American Graves Protection and Repatriation Act [NAGPRA]). That does not mean, however, that religious beliefs should be ignored. As Ferguson, Dongoske, and Kuwanwisiwma point out in chapter 2, often tribes with religious concerns also have important information to impart to provide a better understanding of the people who lived in the past. The challenge continues to be finding a means where both science and religion can be utilized to contribute important information to understanding the people and cultures who lived before us. Within the United States today, many anthropologists and Native Americans are struggling to come together to try and find a working middle ground to learn about human ancestry.

It is not an easy task for anyone involved in, or concerned about, mortuary studies. Many of the difficult issues are painfully and diligently being addressed by archaeologists, physical anthropologists, and Native Americans; but questions abound. Who should dictate when and how studies should be done? To better understand the past, is there a way to incorporate religious views and concerns into a scientific study of the people found during an archaeological excavation? Are there studies that anthropologists can do that would aid the inquiries, questions, and needs of a modern descended group? Affinity studies are important to some groups and may become an even larger issue as repatriation plans move forward, and multiple claims are occurring. Are there better means for anthropologists to address the concerns of the descendants and learn about the past? Medical studies of the past can help people living today. Is there a better way to present the findings so the lay person can understand their significance? How do we anticipate the needs and questions of the future generations about the past generations? What other studies should anthropologists provide that are of importance to related descendants of today? Trying to address many of these questions, will hopefully help bring currently divergent groups closer together.

Another question to be addressed, is how far back can claims of cultural affinity be made. When does the claim of one group over another stop, and when can the individuals exhumed be recognized as important individuals for the collective history of all people? For many people of all ethnic backgrounds, identifying their ancestors and history are important to them. For others, recognizing a collective ethnic past and the responsibilities of their religion also are important. How can anthropologists better contribute to understanding that history? The issue of how far back a claim of cultural affinity may be made may be addressed in the near future, at least with respect to one time frame. Currently, controversy surrounds the important finding of the Kennewick Man, an approximately 9,000-year-old individual who appears to have important characteristics that may help rewrite the course of history on the peopling of the Americas. Scientists want to study him, and some Native American groups want to rebury him immediately. Other groups also have made claims of cultural affinity. The importance of Kennewick Man to understanding our past cannot be understated. However, the controversy raises one of the persisting issues created by NAGPRA: How far back can any one group be allowed to claim cultural affinity? When does the past belong to everyone, and not to one specific group or groups?

In her foreword to this book, Lippert emphasized that as archaeologists, we need to be better at humanizing the information on the individuals found in burials. We agree. Scientists have a tendency to use abstract terms to not impose their own beliefs on the data. A burial of a man and woman would indeed suggest they were husband and wife. However, other explanations also can be offered, so the question becomes how best to present the empirical evidence in a format that does not prejudice the perception about the people found but also gives them the humanity they fully deserve. Certainly, there are numerous examples where information is available that we, as anthropologists, can provide more humanity in our discussion of the people of the past.

For at least two decades now, anthropologists have talked about presenting information in a format that both laymen and scientists can understand. There have been tremendous advances on this approach, but much more work is needed. Often for large archaeological excavations now, two reports are created; one technical report for the scientist and one with less scientific jargon for the nonscientist. One of our challenges for the future is to work further on the subject, to bring to life the human history

of all groups so everyone can understand and appreciate the people who have lived before us.

With respect to science and religion, there will never be a perfect melding of scientific objectivity and religious beliefs. However, it is the goal of many archaeologists and physical anthropologists to learn about the people who lived in the past, and based in that goal is a respect for the people and a desire to preserve their history and humanity. For many Native Americans, their goal is to respect their past and follow the tenets of their religious beliefs. With those two different overall goals, there is still the mutual respect of the people of the past. With that thought in mind, we need to continue working together to learn what those in the past have to tell us and give them the humanity and respect they deserve.

A primary goal of this book was to gather together studies of prehistoric populations that could inform us about the different lifeways of cultures in the American Southwest. The process of burial includes with it important clues about the lives of the people and the ways in which their societies operated. As Goldstein points out, future mortuary studies will undoubtedly need to increase their scope to include a broader view of the cultural landscape. Perhaps this will become an important area where archaeologists and Native Americans can work together to understand the past. Ethnographic studies are another important and rich source of data that can be shared by archaeologists and contemporary Native Americans. The studies of prehistoric mortuary practices, rituals, and linkages to extinct cultures will continue to be an integral part of archaeological studies in the Southwest.

The future brings with it exciting possibilities. With the increase in scientific technology and medical advancement, our ability to understand the past will be enhanced. By working together—archaeologists, physical anthropologists, and Native Americans—our potential for understanding the past, and bringing its message about the history of specific groups and human history, holds great promise.

REFERENCES CITED

Schuldenrein, Joseph
1999   Charting a Middle Ground in the NAGPRA
          Controversy: Secularism in Context. *Society
          for American Archaeology Bulletin*
          17(4):22–23, 33.

List of Contributors

NANCY J. AKINS, Cultural Resources Specialist, Office of Archaeological Studies, Museum of New Mexico, Santa Fe, New Mexico

JUDY L. BRUNSON-HADLEY, Brunson Cultural Resource Services L. L. C., Mesa, Arizona and Arizona State University, Department of Anthropology, Tempe, Arizona

KURT E. DONGOSKE, Tribal Archaeologist, Cultural Preservation Office, The Hopi Tribe, Kykotsmovi, Arizona

T. J. FERGUSON, Partner, Heritage Resources Management Consultants, Tucson, Arizona

LYNNE GOLDSTEIN, Professor & Chairperson, Department of Anthropology, Michigan State University, East Lansing, Michigan

JOHN W. HOHMANN, Regional Director and Chief Archaeologist, The Louis Berger Group, Inc., Phoenix, Arizona

TODD L. HOWELL, Project Director, Pueblo of Zuni, Cultural Resource Enterprise, Zuni, New Mexico

LEIGH J. KUWANWISIWMA, Director, Cultural Preservation Office, The Hopi Tribe, Kykotsmovi, Arizona

DEBRA L. MARTIN, Professor of Biological Anthropology, Director, U.S. Southwest and Mexico Program, School of Natural Science, Hampshire College, Amherst, Massachusetts

RANDALL H. MCGUIRE, Professor of Anthropology, Binghamton University, Binghamton, New York

DOUGLAS R. MITCHELL, Division Director, SWCA, Inc. Environmental Consultants, Phoenix, Arizona

SUSAN GUISE SHERIDAN, Assistant Professor, Department of Anthropology, University of Notre Dame, Notre Dame, Indiana

Index

Note: Page numbers for figures appear in bold type.